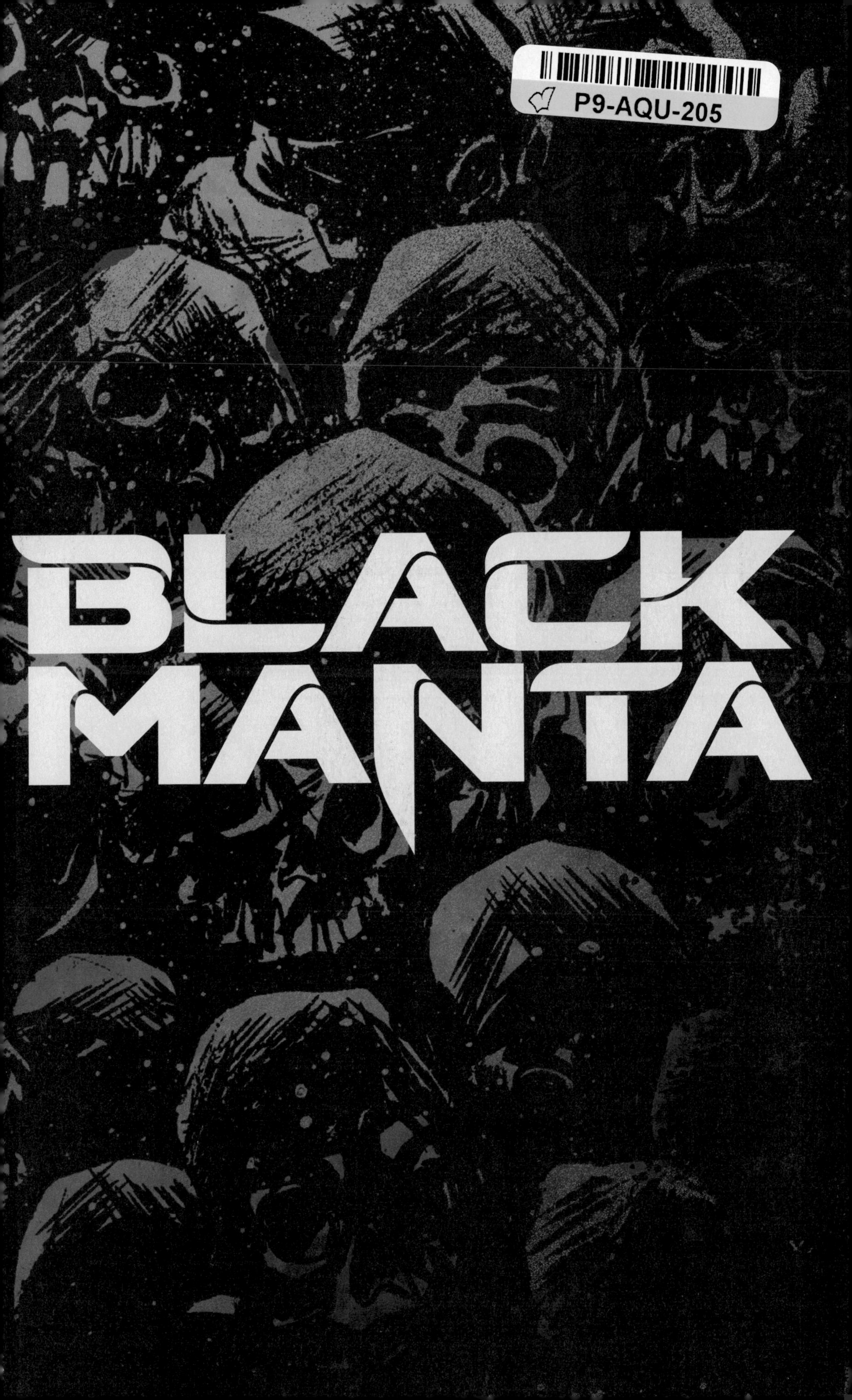
BLACK
MANTA

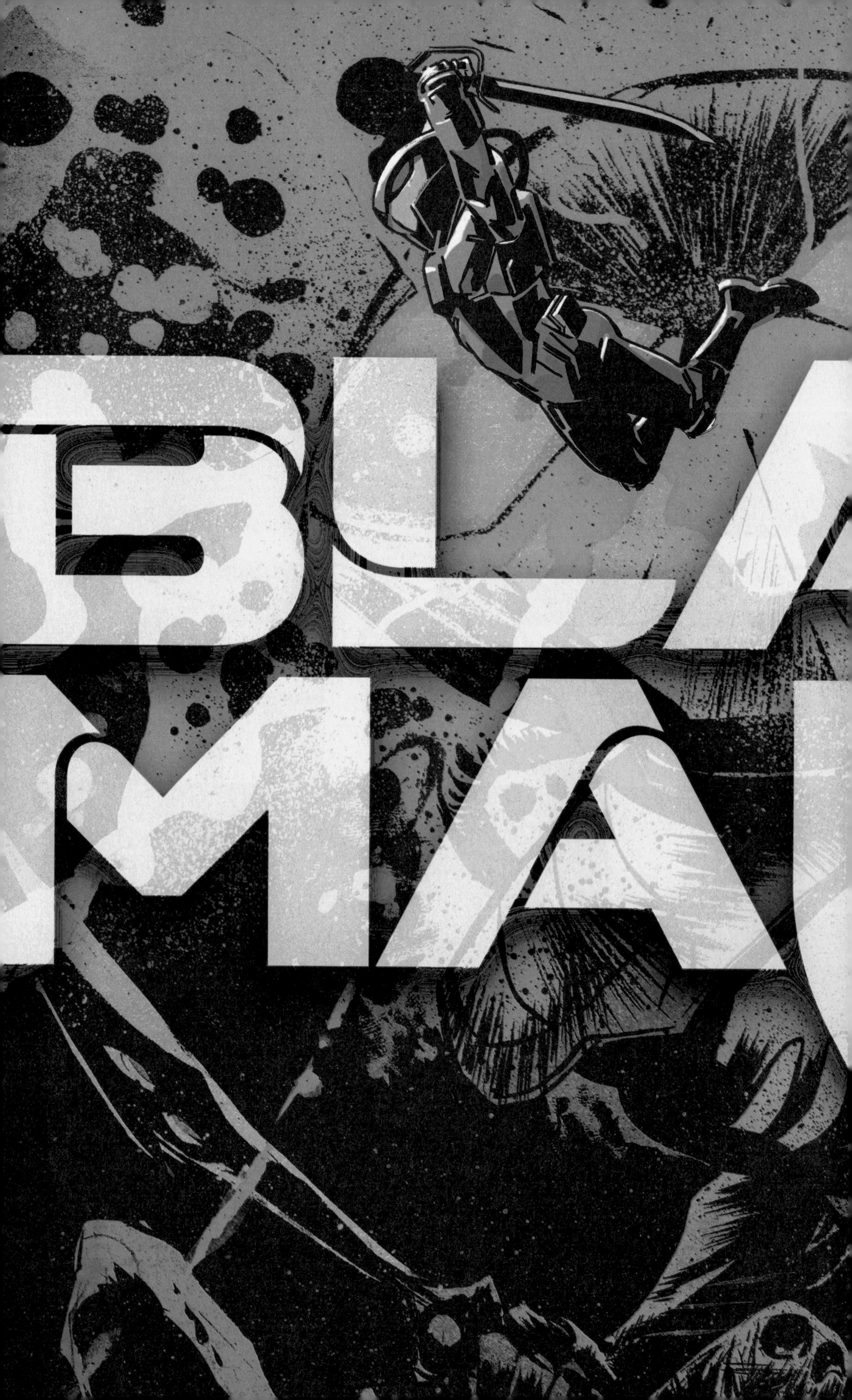

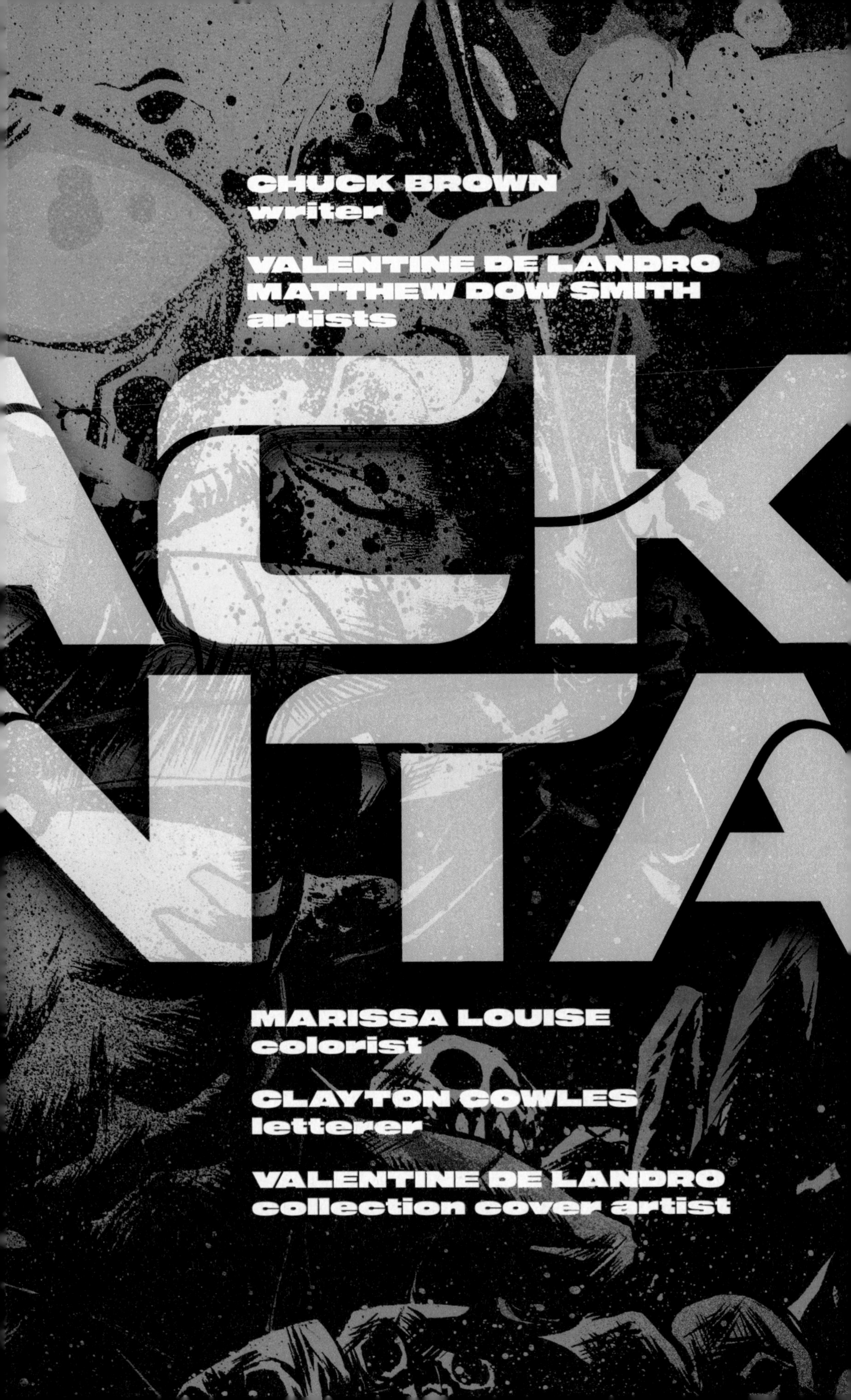

CHUCK BROWN
writer

VALENTINE DE LANDRO
MATTHEW DOW SMITH
artists

MARISSA LOUISE
colorist

CLAYTON COWLES
letterer

VALENTINE DE LANDRO
collection cover artist

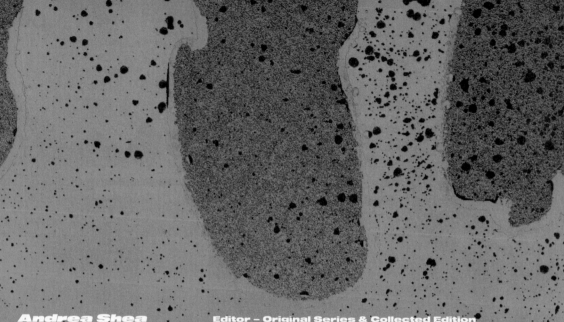

Andrea Shea	Editor – Original Series & Collected Edition
Bixie Mathieu	Assistant Editor – Original Series
Steve Cook	Design Director – Books
Louis Prandi	Publication Design
Erin Vanover	Publication Production
Marie Javins	Editor-in-Chief, DC Comics
Anne DePies	Senior VP – General Manager
Jim Lee	Publisher & Chief Creative Officer
Don Falletti	VP – Manufacturing Operations & Workflow Management
Lawrence Ganem	VP – Talent Services
Alison Gill	Senior VP – Manufacturing & Operations
Jeffrey Kaufman	VP – Editorial Strategy & Programming
Nick J. Napolitano	VP – Manufacturing Administration & Design
Nancy Spears	VP – Revenue

BLACK MANTA

DC Comics, 2900 West Alameda Ave., Burbank, CA 91505. Printed by LSC Communications, Owensville, MO, USA. 6/24/22. First Printing. ISBN: 978-1-77951-713-5

Library of Congress Cataloging-in-Publication Data is available.

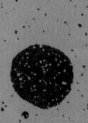

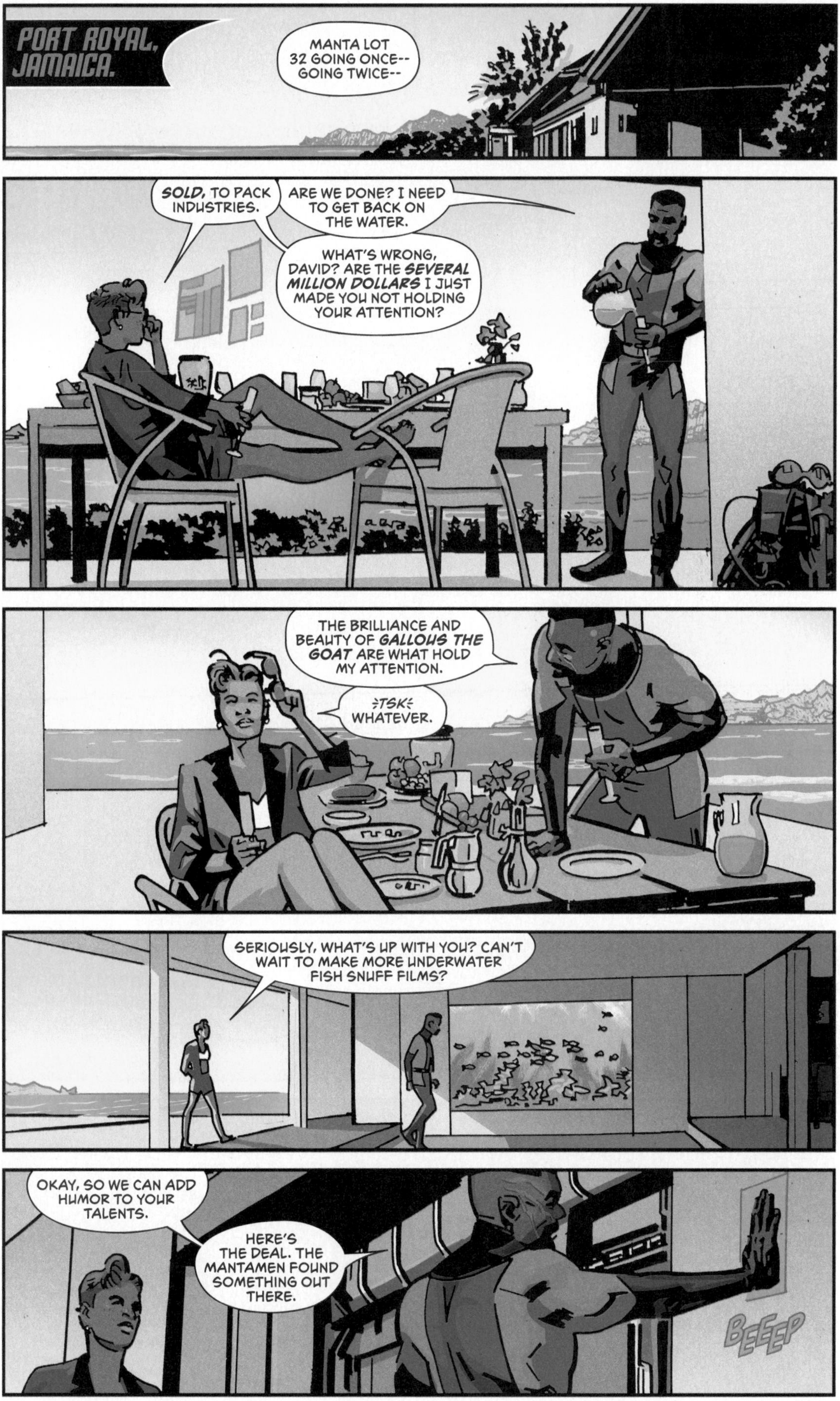
PORT ROYAL, JAMAICA.
MANTA LOT 32 GOING ONCE-- GOING TWICE--
SOLD, TO PACK INDUSTRIES.
ARE WE DONE? I NEED TO GET BACK ON THE WATER.
WHAT'S WRONG, DAVID? ARE THE SEVERAL MILLION DOLLARS I JUST MADE YOU NOT HOLDING YOUR ATTENTION?
THE BRILLIANCE AND BEAUTY OF GALLOUS THE GOAT ARE WHAT HOLD MY ATTENTION.
TSK WHATEVER.
SERIOUSLY, WHAT'S UP WITH YOU? CAN'T WAIT TO MAKE MORE UNDERWATER FISH SNUFF FILMS?
OKAY, SO WE CAN ADD HUMOR TO YOUR TALENTS.
HERE'S THE DEAL. THE MANTAMEN FOUND SOMETHING OUT THERE.
BEEEP

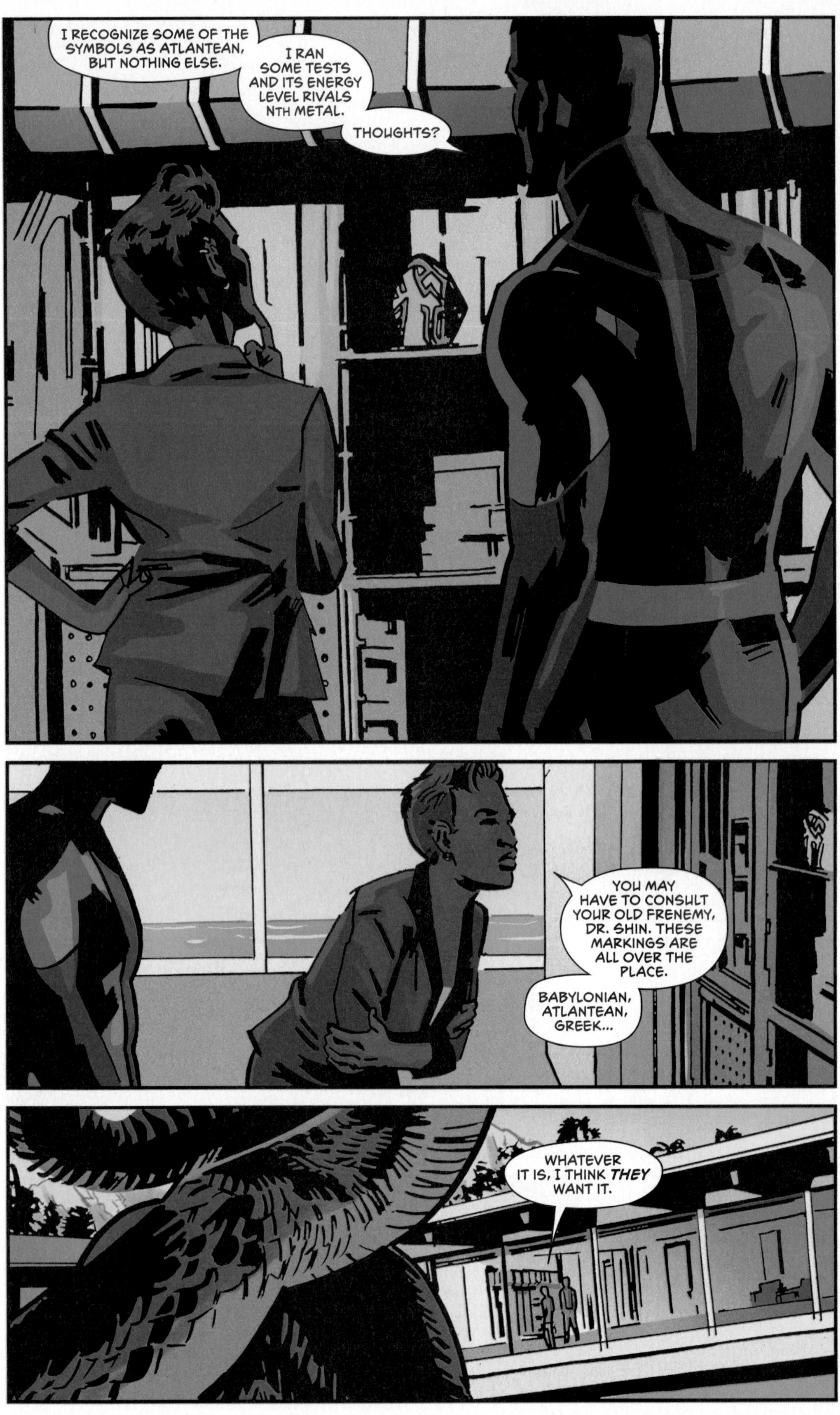
I RECOGNIZE SOME OF THE SYMBOLS AS ATLANTEAN, BUT NOTHING ELSE.
I RAN SOME TESTS AND ITS ENERGY LEVEL RIVALS NTH METAL.
THOUGHTS?
YOU MAY HAVE TO CONSULT YOUR OLD FRENEMY, DR. SHIN. THESE MARKINGS ARE ALL OVER THE PLACE.
BABYLONIAN, ATLANTEAN, GREEK...
WHATEVER IT IS, I THINK *THEY* WANT IT.

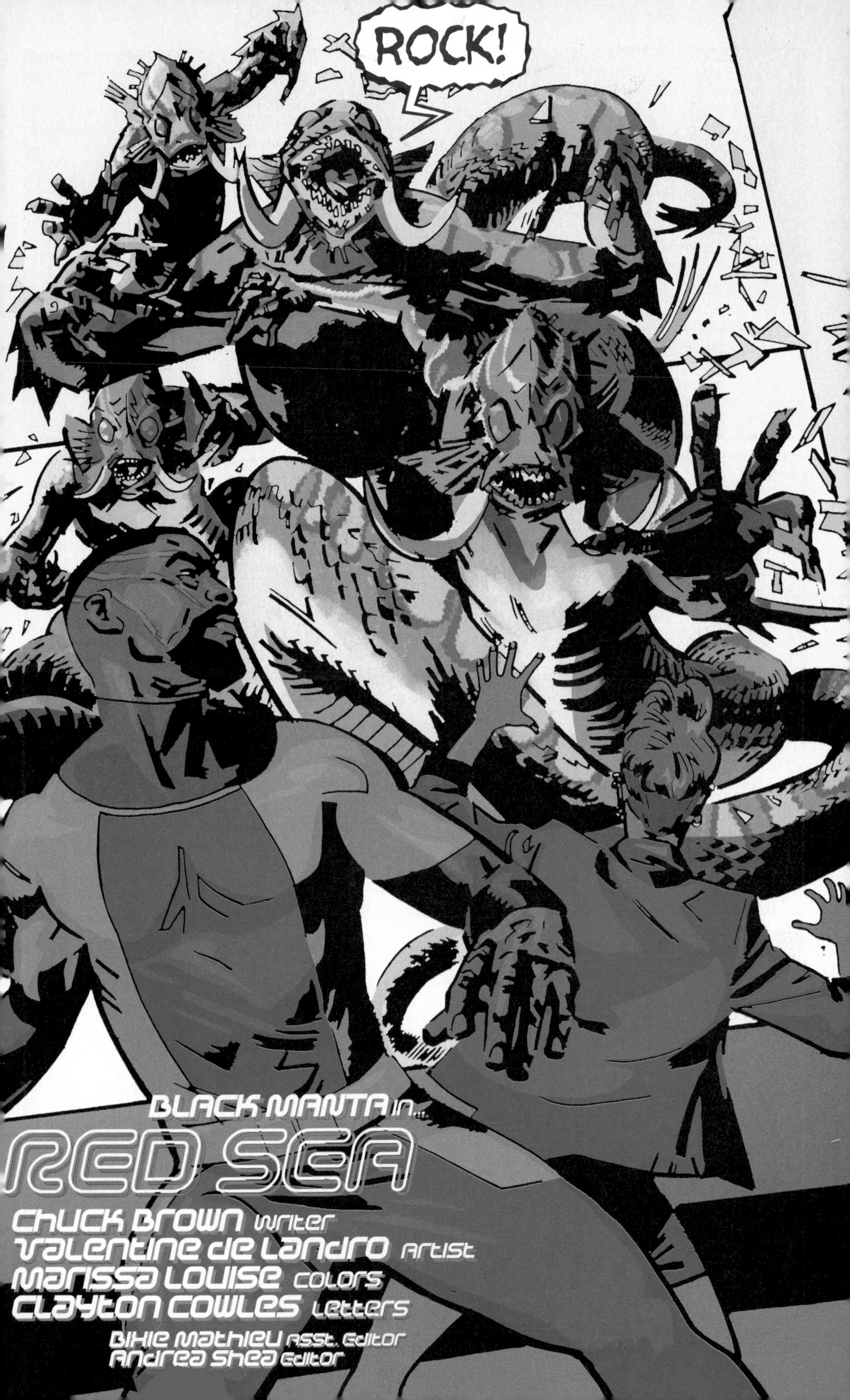
ROCK!
BLACK MANTA in...
RED SEA
CHUCK BROWN writer
VALENTINE DE LANDRO Artist
MARISSA LOUISE colors
CLAYTON COWLES letters
BIXIE MATHIEU Asst. Editor
ANDREA SHEA Editor

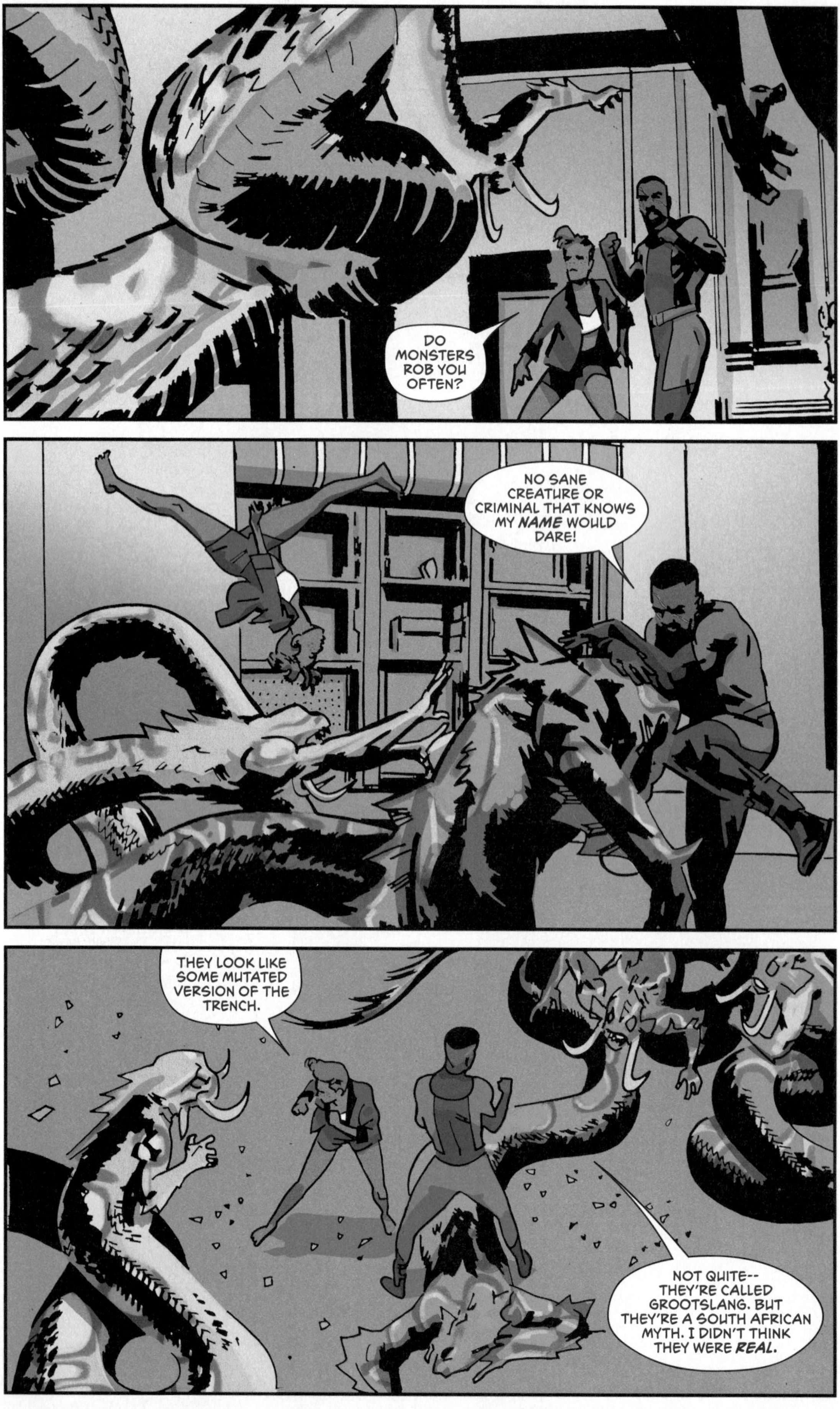
DO MONSTERS ROB YOU OFTEN?
NO SANE CREATURE OR CRIMINAL THAT KNOWS MY *NAME* WOULD DARE!
THEY LOOK LIKE SOME MUTATED VERSION OF THE TRENCH.
NOT QUITE-- THEY'RE CALLED GROOTSLANG. BUT THEY'RE A SOUTH AFRICAN MYTH. I DIDN'T THINK THEY WERE *REAL.*

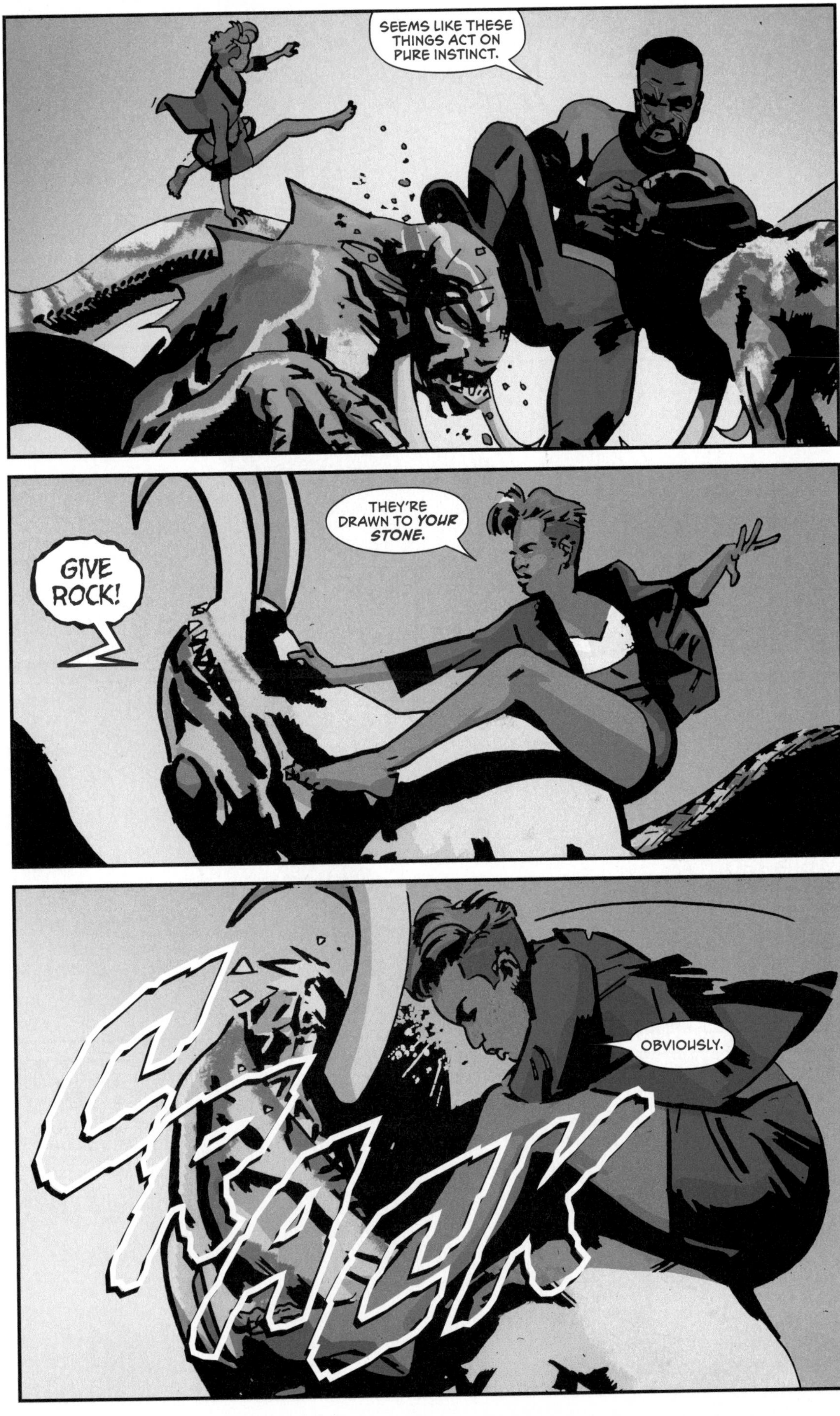
SEEMS LIKE THESE THINGS ACT ON PURE INSTINCT.
GIVE ROCK!
THEY'RE DRAWN TO *YOUR STONE.*
CRACK
OBVIOUSLY.

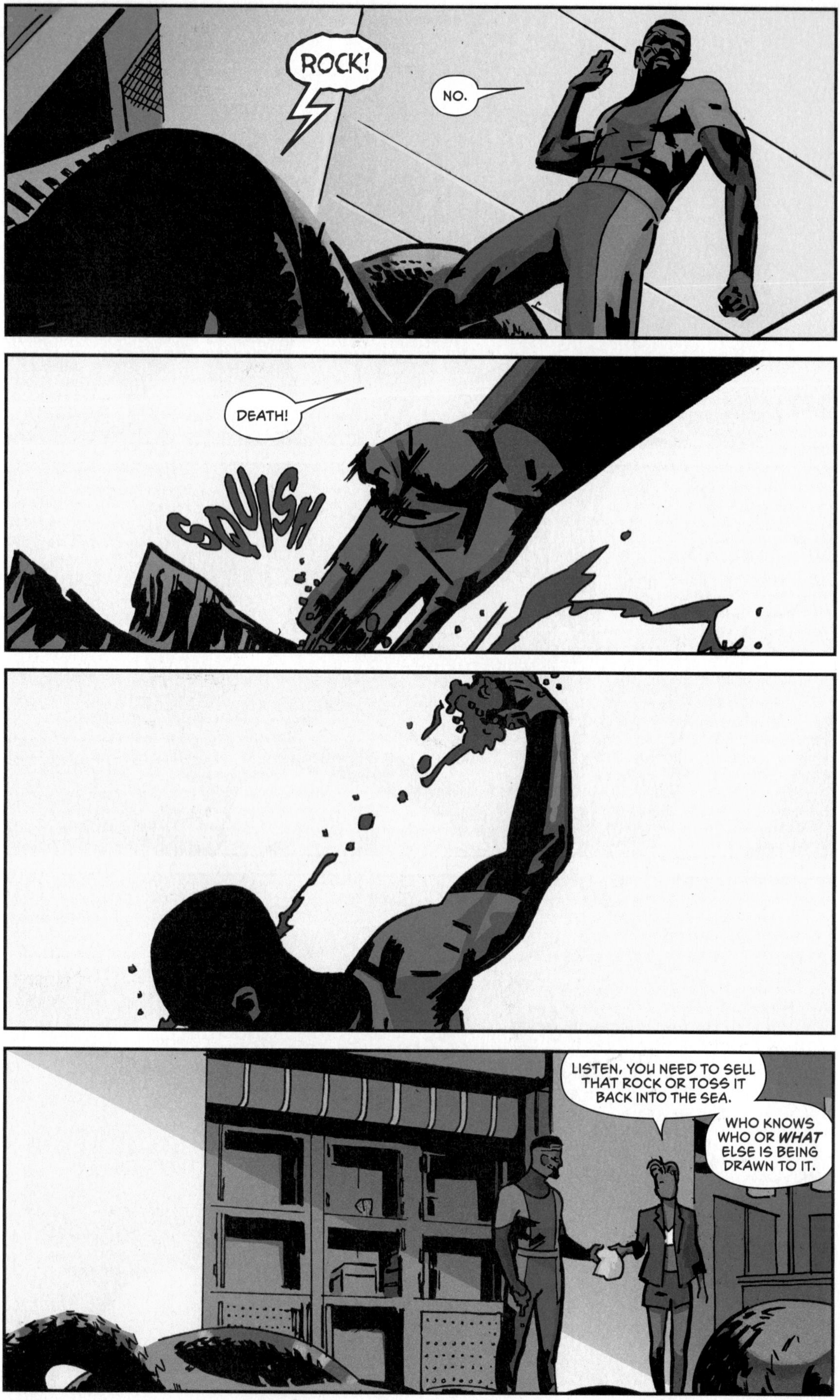
ROCK!
NO.
DEATH!
SQUISH
LISTEN, YOU NEED TO SELL THAT ROCK OR TOSS IT BACK INTO THE SEA.
WHO KNOWS WHO OR *WHAT* ELSE IS BEING DRAWN TO IT.

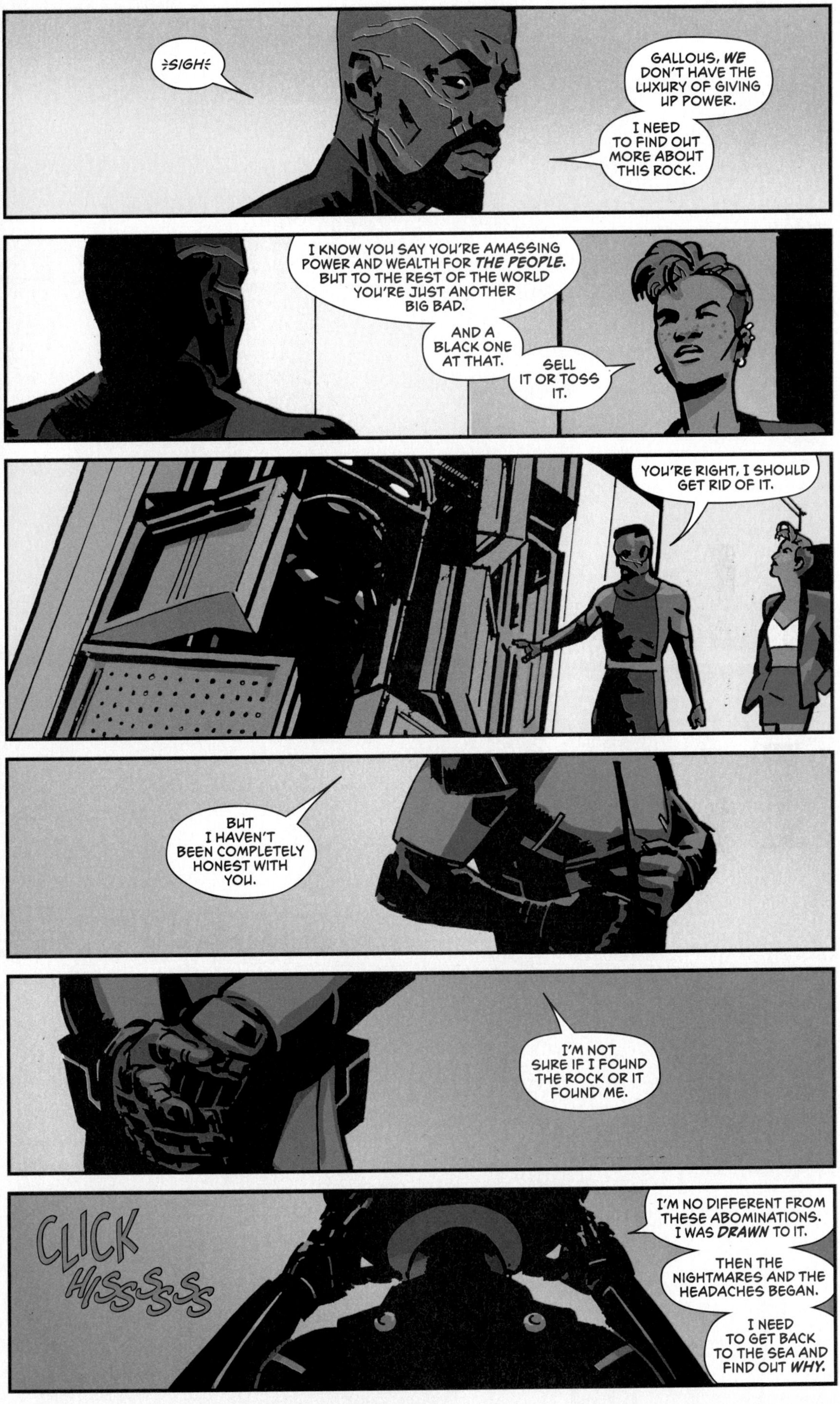

⸗SIGH⸗
GALLOUS, WE DON'T HAVE THE LUXURY OF GIVING UP POWER.
I NEED TO FIND OUT MORE ABOUT THIS ROCK.
I KNOW YOU SAY YOU'RE AMASSING POWER AND WEALTH FOR THE PEOPLE. BUT TO THE REST OF THE WORLD YOU'RE JUST ANOTHER BIG BAD.
AND A BLACK ONE AT THAT.
SELL IT OR TOSS IT.
YOU'RE RIGHT, I SHOULD GET RID OF IT.
BUT I HAVEN'T BEEN COMPLETELY HONEST WITH YOU.
I'M NOT SURE IF I FOUND THE ROCK OR IT FOUND ME.
CLICK
HISSSSSS
I'M NO DIFFERENT FROM THESE ABOMINATIONS. I WAS DRAWN TO IT.
THEN THE NIGHTMARES AND THE HEADACHES BEGAN.
I NEED TO GET BACK TO THE SEA AND FIND OUT WHY.

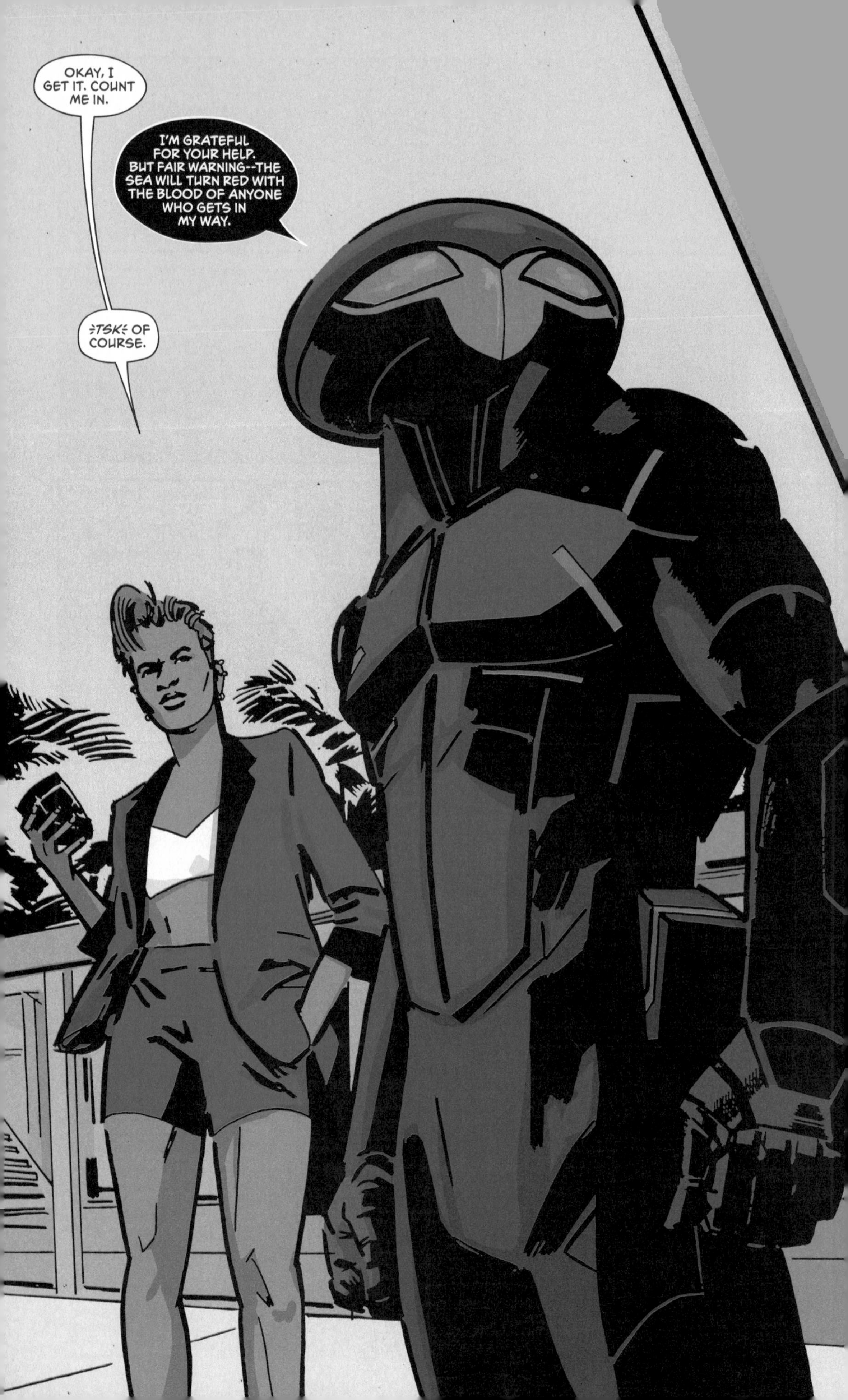
OKAY, I GET IT. COUNT ME IN.
I'M GRATEFUL FOR YOUR HELP. BUT FAIR WARNING--THE SEA WILL TURN RED WITH THE BLOOD OF ANYONE WHO GETS IN MY WAY.
TSK OF COURSE.

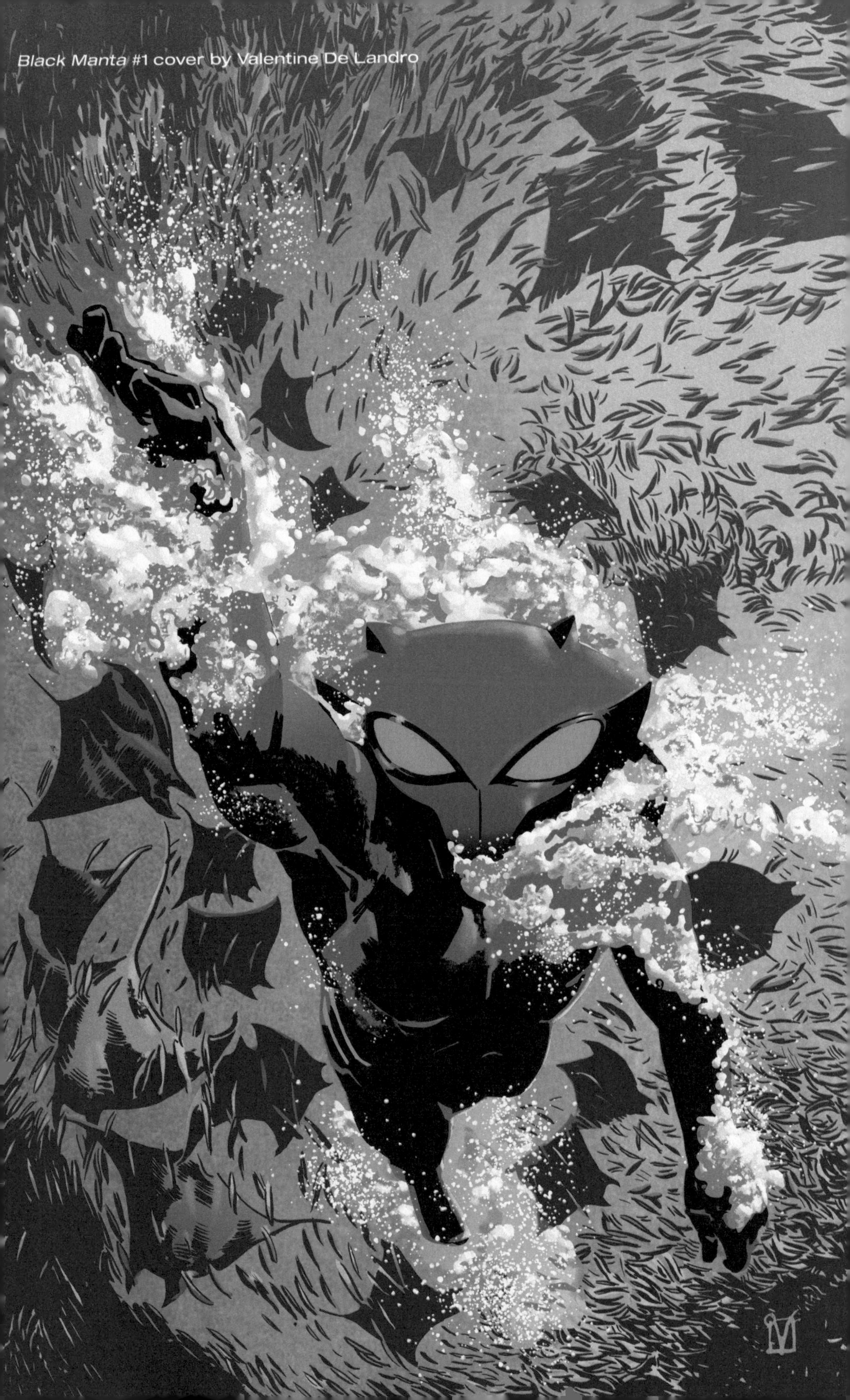

Black Manta #1 cover by Valentine De Landro

Black Manta #1 variant cover by Sanford Greene

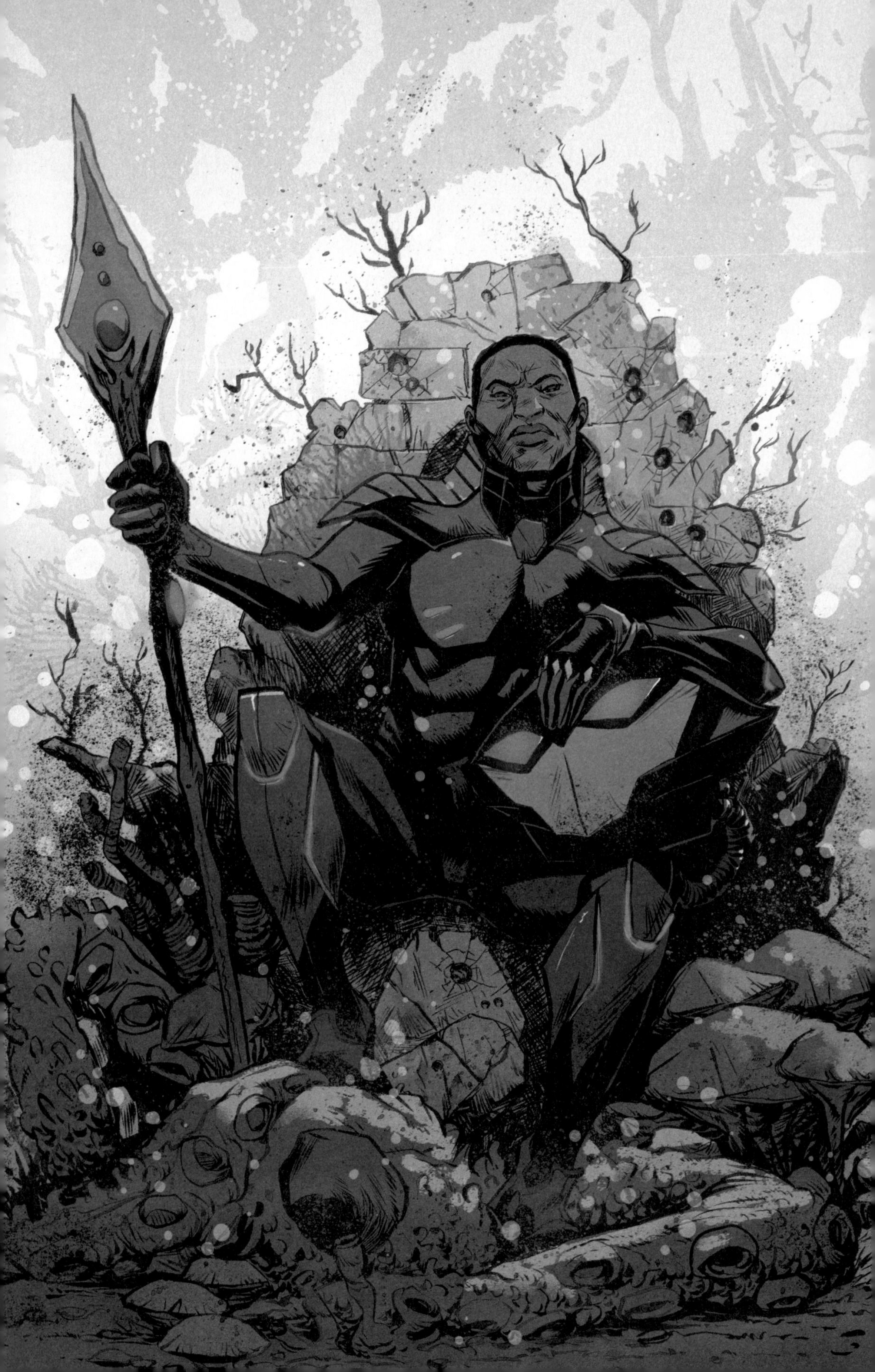

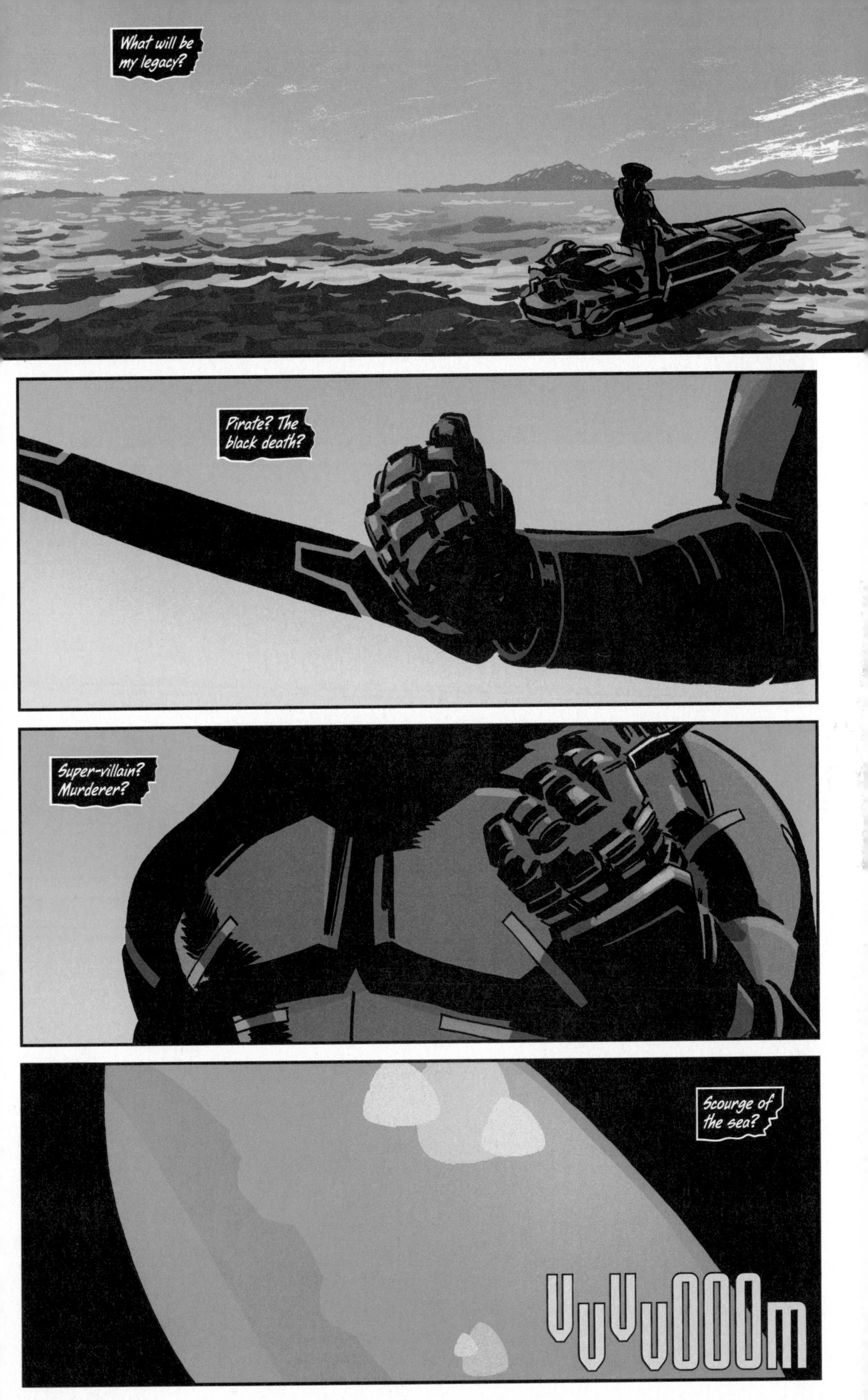
What will be my legacy?
Pirate? The black death?
Super-villain? Murderer?
Scourge of the sea?
VVVVOOOm

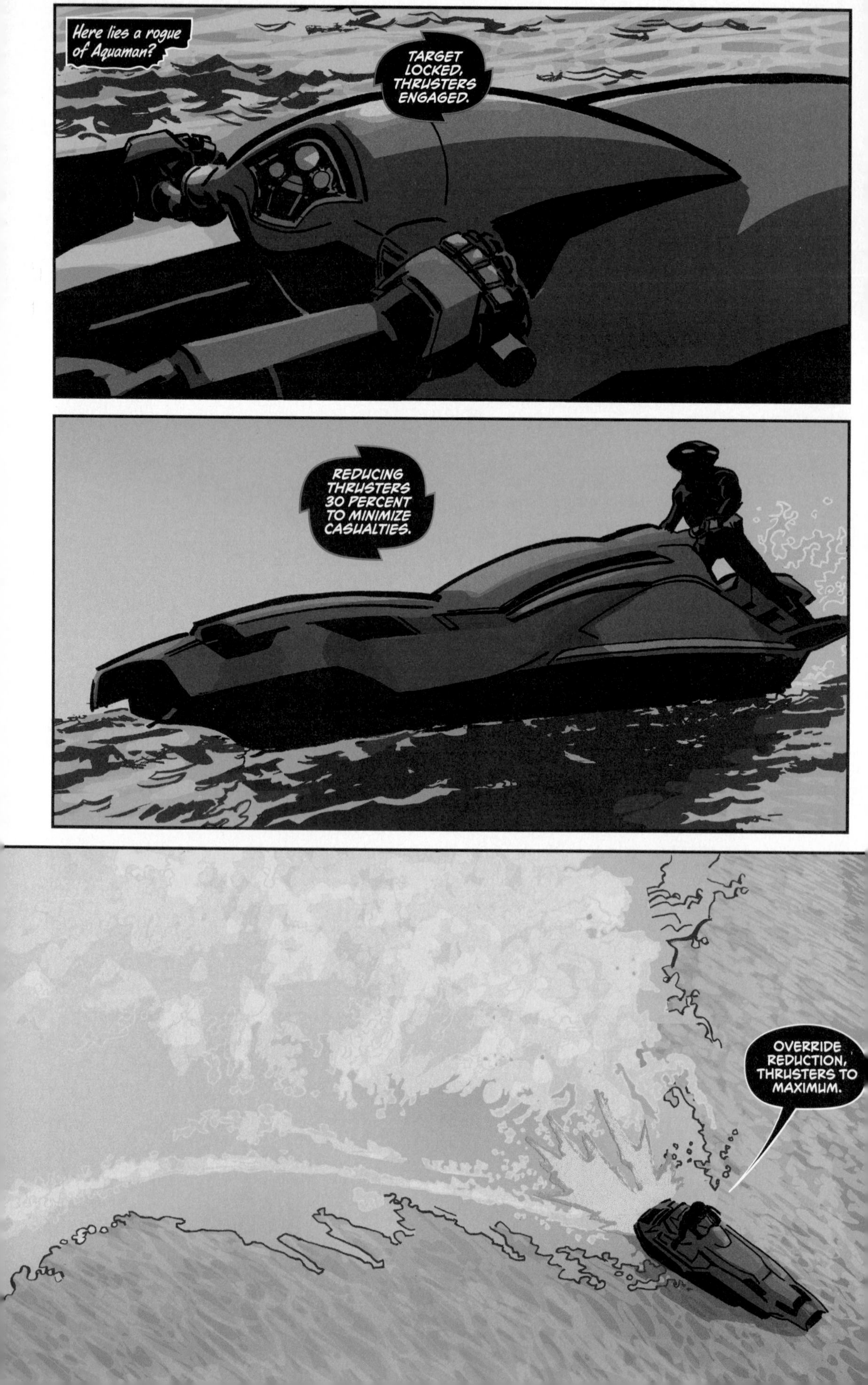
Here lies a rogue of Aquaman?
TARGET LOCKED, THRUSTERS ENGAGED.
REDUCING THRUSTERS 30 PERCENT TO MINIMIZE CASUALTIES.
OVERRIDE REDUCTION, THRUSTERS TO MAXIMUM.

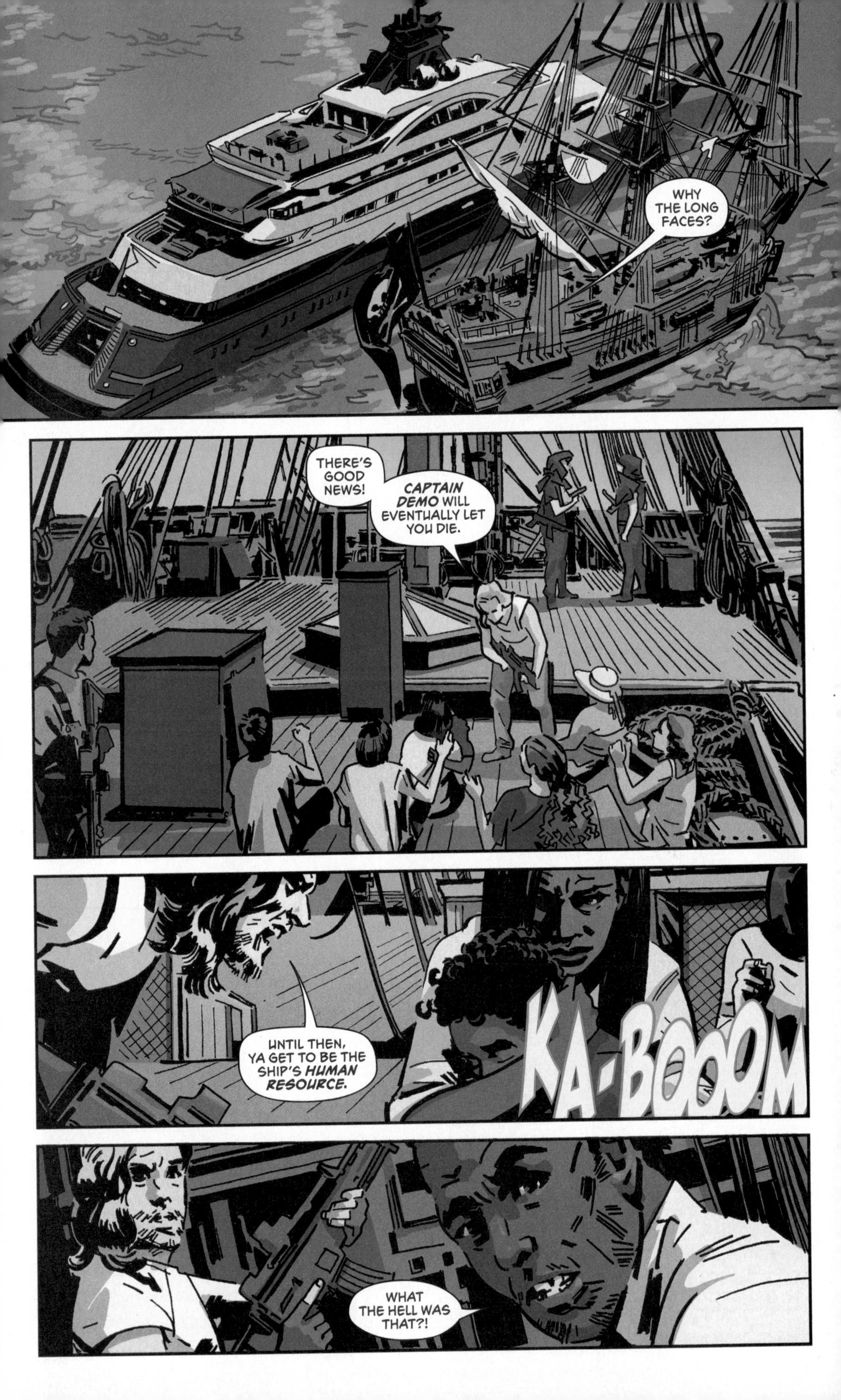
WHY THE LONG FACES?
THERE'S GOOD NEWS!
CAPTAIN DEMO WILL EVENTUALLY LET YOU DIE.
UNTIL THEN, YA GET TO BE THE SHIP'S *HUMAN RESOURCE*.
KA-BOOOM
WHAT THE HELL WAS THAT?!

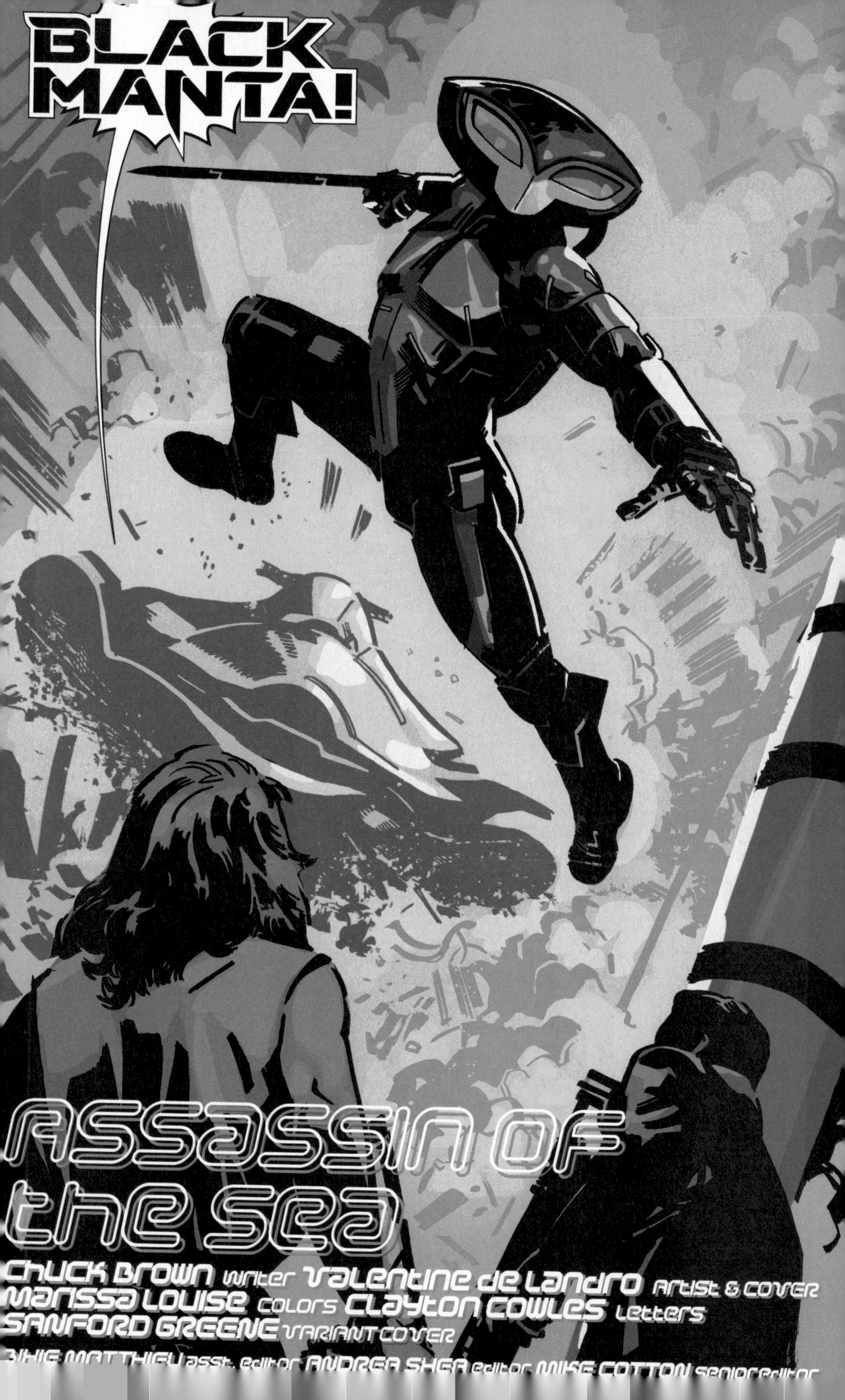
BLACK MANTA!
ASSASSIN OF THE SEA
CHUCK BROWN writer VALENTINE DE LANDRO artist & cover
MARISSA LOUISE colors CLAYTON COWLES letters
SANFORD GREENE variant cover
BIXIE MATTHIEU asst. editor ANDREA SHEA editor MIKE COTTON senior editor

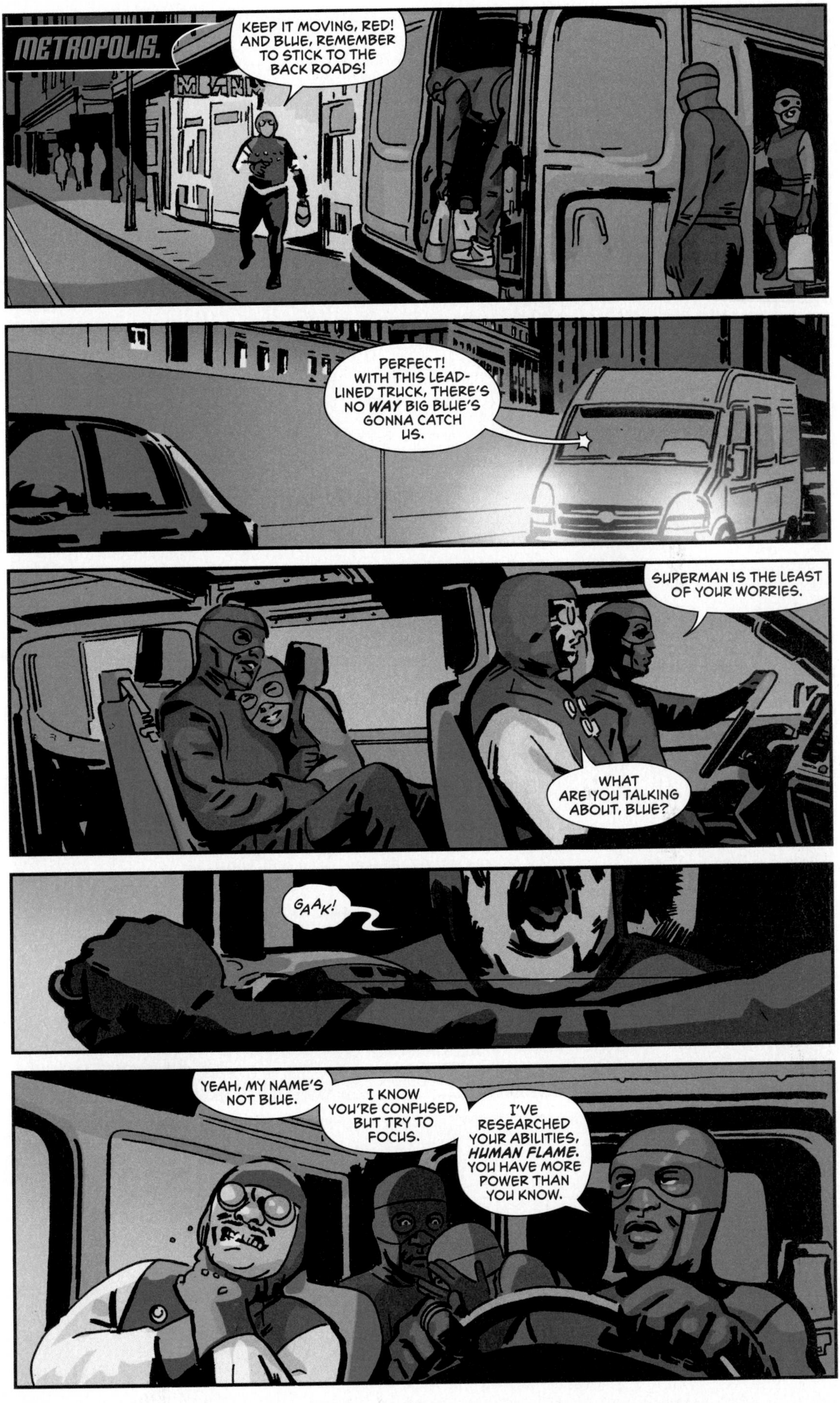
METROPOLIS.
KEEP IT MOVING, RED! AND BLUE, REMEMBER TO STICK TO THE BACK ROADS!
PERFECT! WITH THIS LEAD-LINED TRUCK, THERE'S NO WAY BIG BLUE'S GONNA CATCH US.
SUPERMAN IS THE LEAST OF YOUR WORRIES.
WHAT ARE YOU TALKING ABOUT, BLUE?
GAAK!
YEAH, MY NAME'S NOT BLUE.
I KNOW YOU'RE CONFUSED, BUT TRY TO FOCUS.
I'VE RESEARCHED YOUR ABILITIES, HUMAN FLAME. YOU HAVE MORE POWER THAN YOU KNOW.

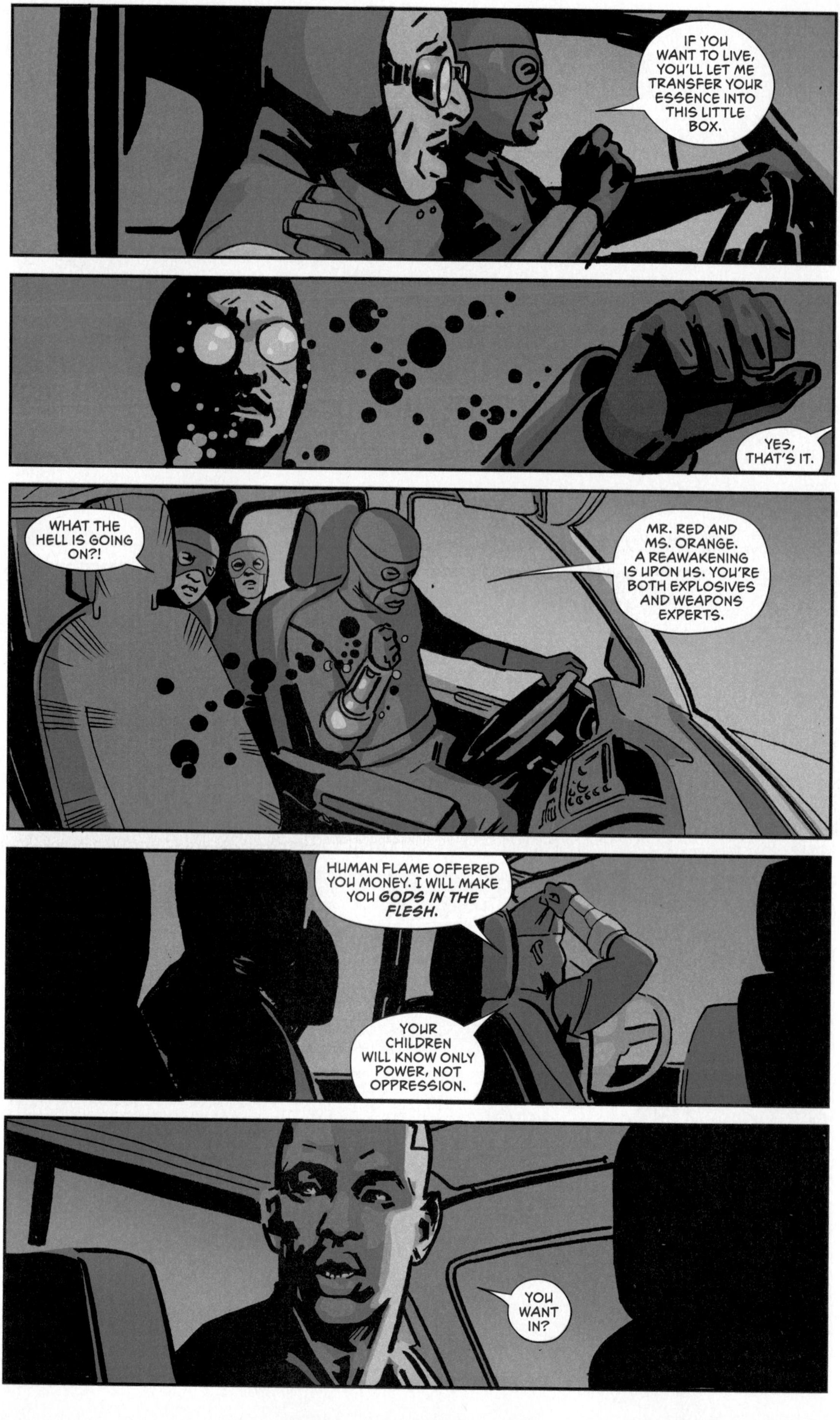
IF YOU WANT TO LIVE, YOU'LL LET ME TRANSFER YOUR ESSENCE INTO THIS LITTLE BOX.
YES, THAT'S IT.
WHAT THE HELL IS GOING ON?!
MR. RED AND MS. ORANGE. A REAWAKENING IS UPON US. YOU'RE BOTH EXPLOSIVES AND WEAPONS EXPERTS.
HUMAN FLAME OFFERED YOU MONEY. I WILL MAKE YOU ***GODS IN THE FLESH.***
YOUR CHILDREN WILL KNOW ONLY POWER, NOT OPPRESSION.
YOU WANT IN?

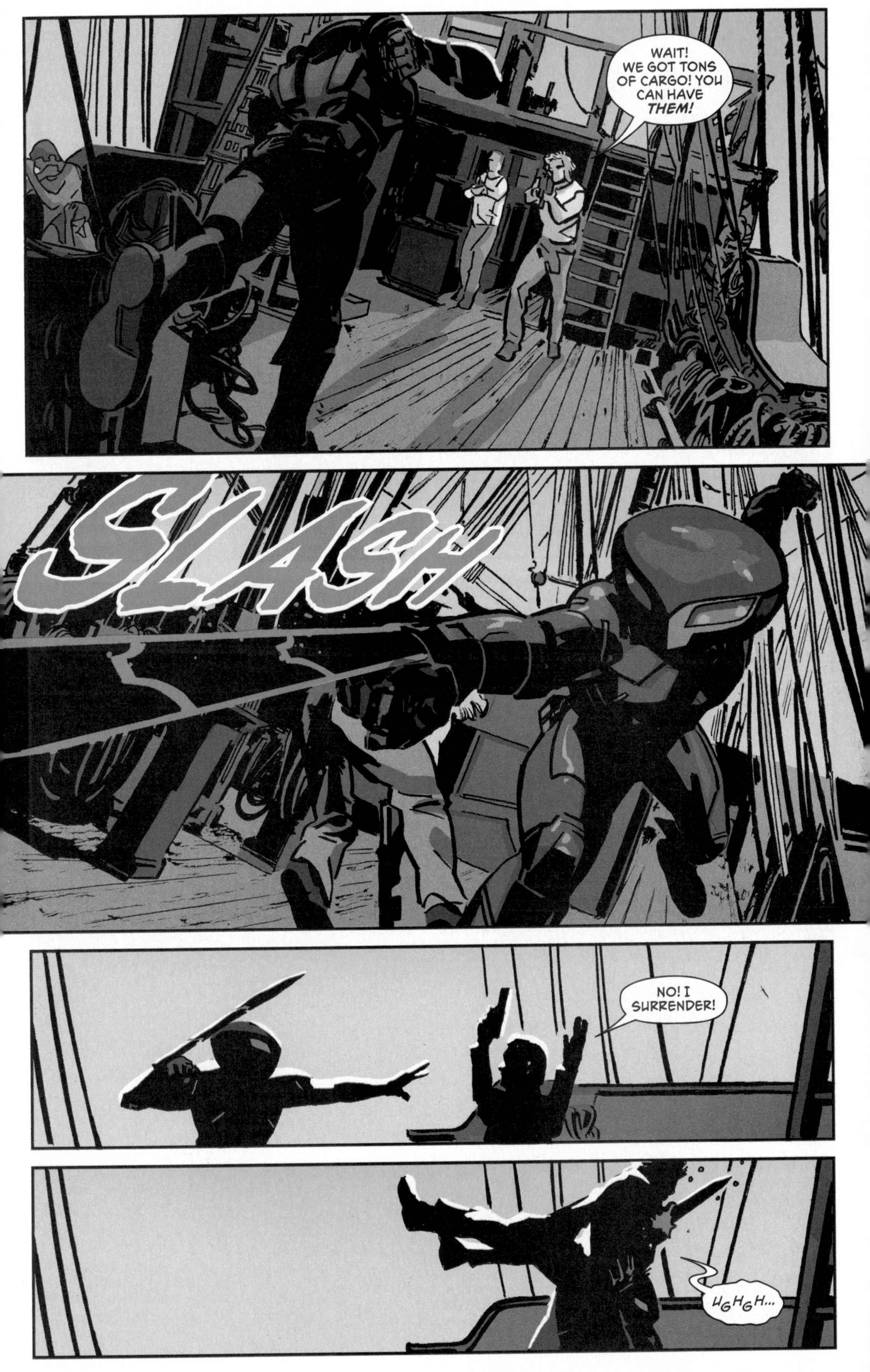
WAIT! WE GOT TONS OF CARGO! YOU CAN HAVE *THEM!*
SLASH
NO! I SURRENDER!
UGHGH...

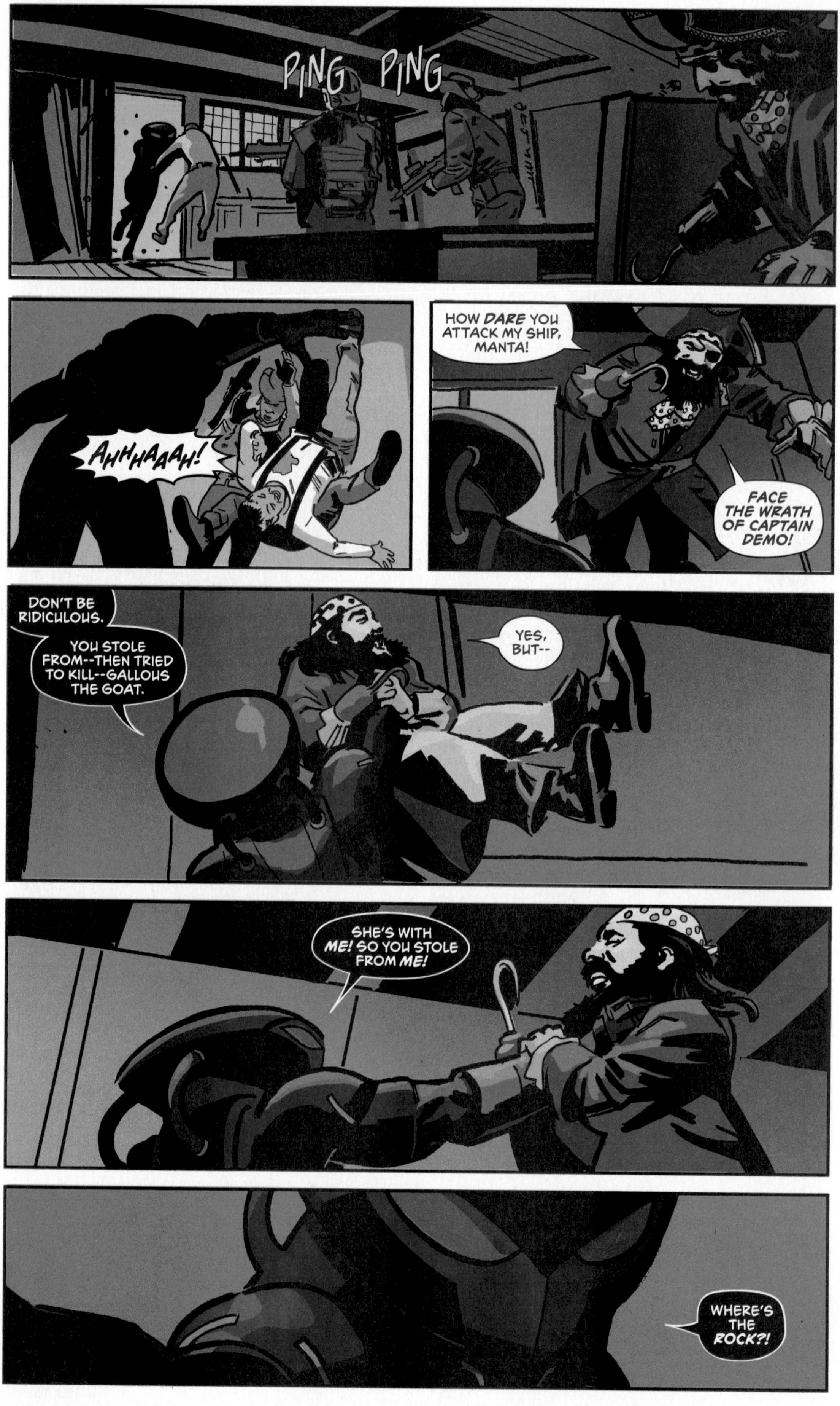
PING PING
AHHHAAAH!
HOW DARE YOU ATTACK MY SHIP, MANTA!
FACE THE WRATH OF CAPTAIN DEMO!
DON'T BE RIDICULOUS.
YOU STOLE FROM--THEN TRIED TO KILL--GALLOUS THE GOAT.
YES, BUT--
SHE'S WITH ME! SO YOU STOLE FROM ME!
WHERE'S THE ROCK?!

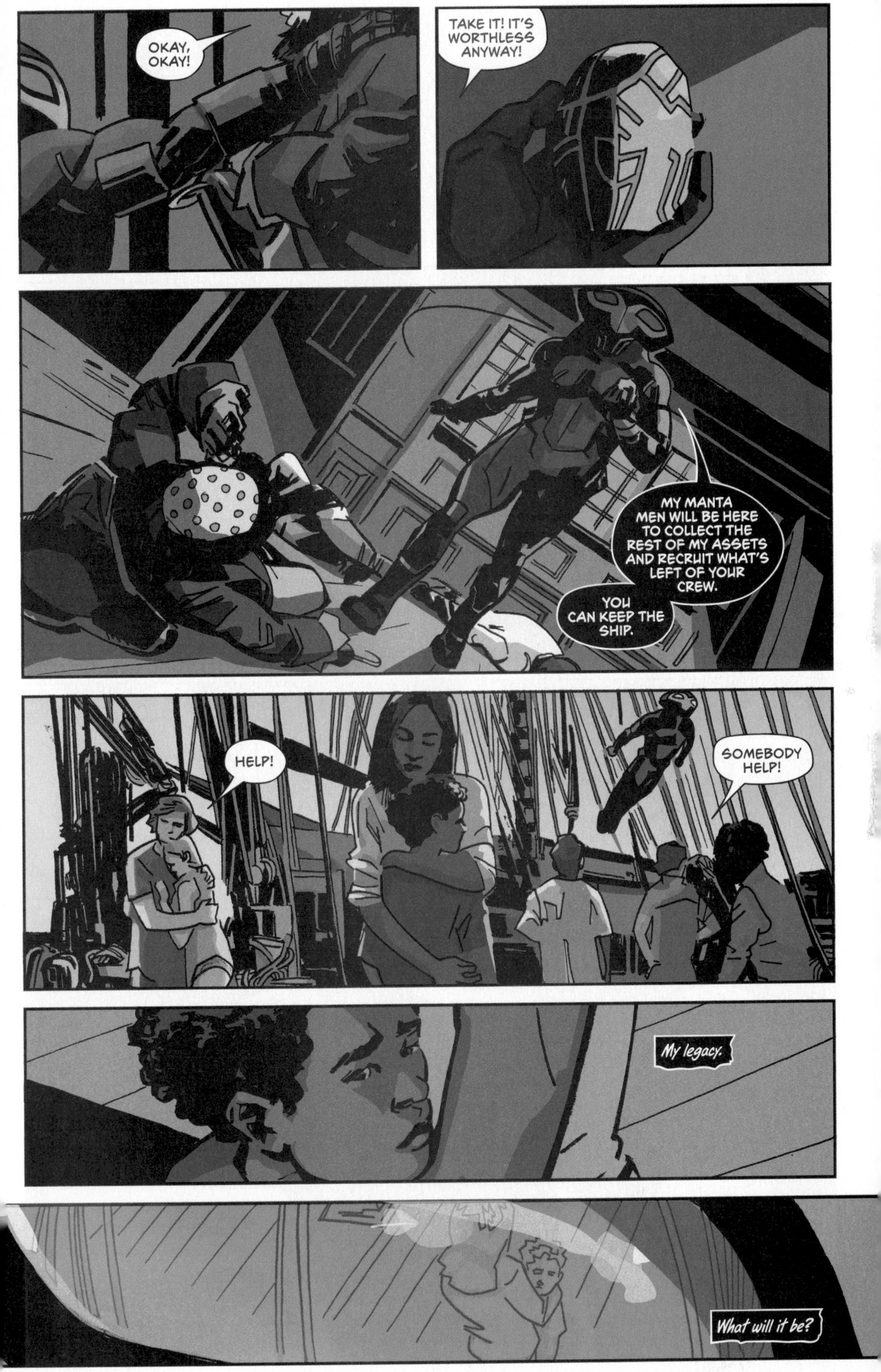
OKAY, OKAY!
TAKE IT! IT'S WORTHLESS ANYWAY!
MY MANTA MEN WILL BE HERE TO COLLECT THE REST OF MY ASSETS AND RECRUIT WHAT'S LEFT OF YOUR CREW.
YOU CAN KEEP THE SHIP.
HELP!
SOMEBODY HELP!
My legacy.
What will it be?

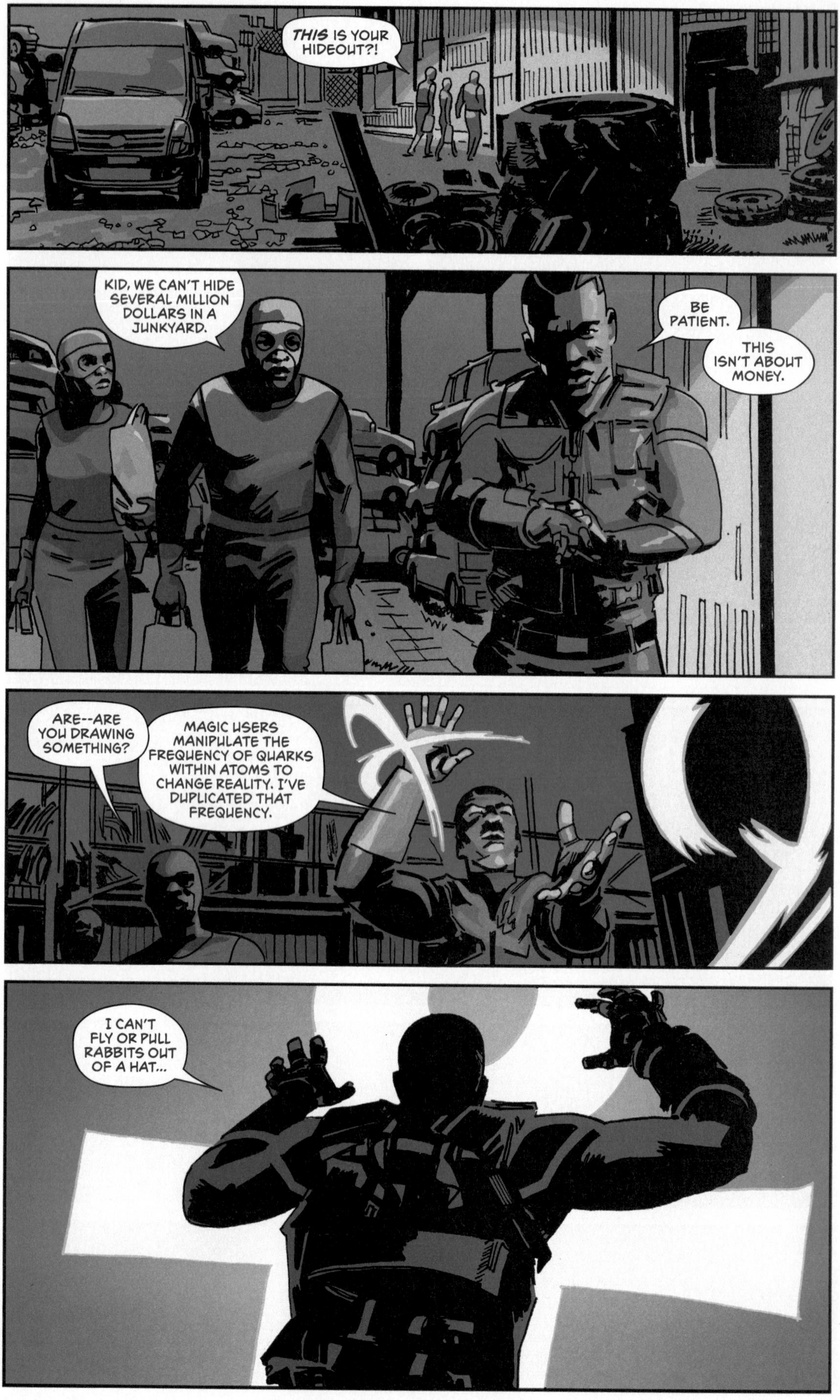

THIS IS YOUR HIDEOUT?!
KID, WE CAN'T HIDE SEVERAL MILLION DOLLARS IN A JUNKYARD.
BE PATIENT.
THIS ISN'T ABOUT MONEY.
ARE--ARE YOU DRAWING SOMETHING?
MAGIC USERS MANIPULATE THE FREQUENCY OF QUARKS WITHIN ATOMS TO CHANGE REALITY. I'VE DUPLICATED THAT FREQUENCY.
I CAN'T FLY OR PULL RABBITS OUT OF A HAT...

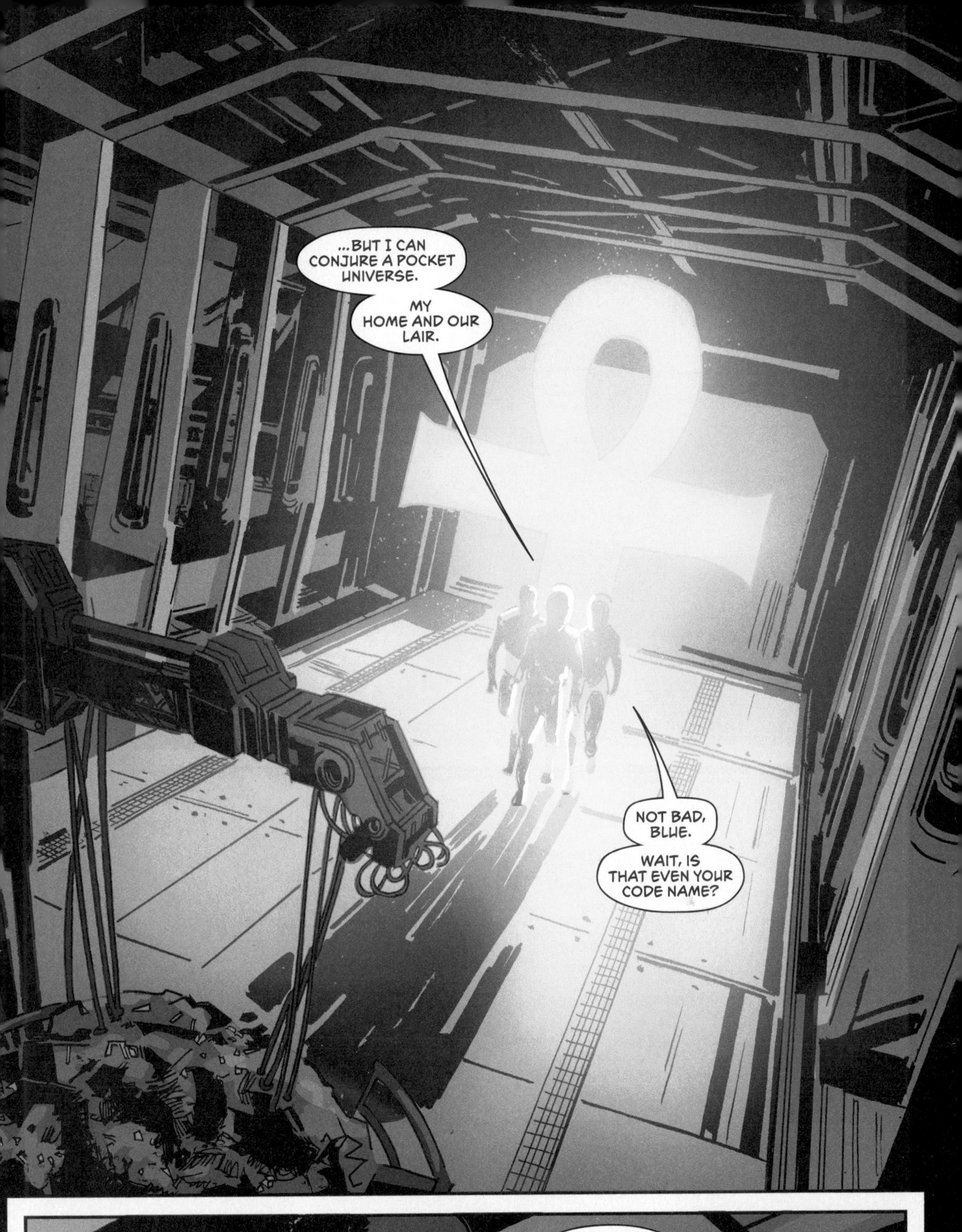
...BUT I CAN CONJURE A POCKET UNIVERSE.
MY HOME AND OUR LAIR.
NOT BAD, BLUE.
WAIT, IS THAT EVEN YOUR CODE NAME?

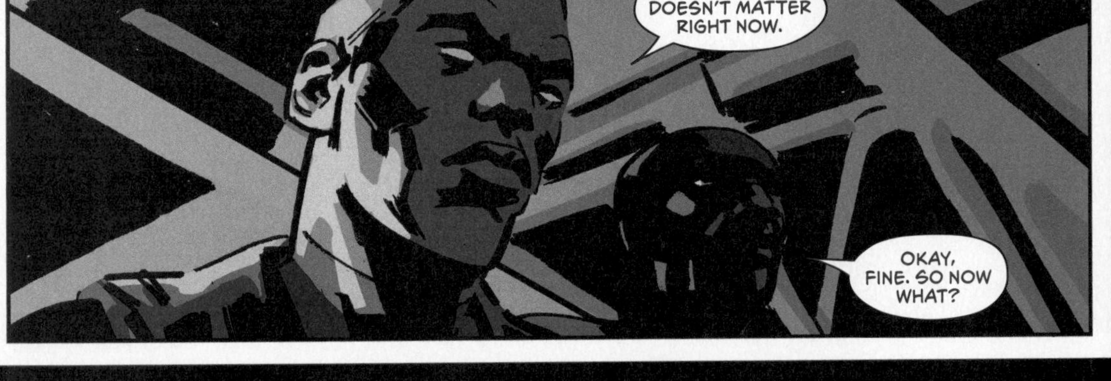
MY NAME DOESN'T MATTER RIGHT NOW.
OKAY, FINE. SO NOW WHAT?

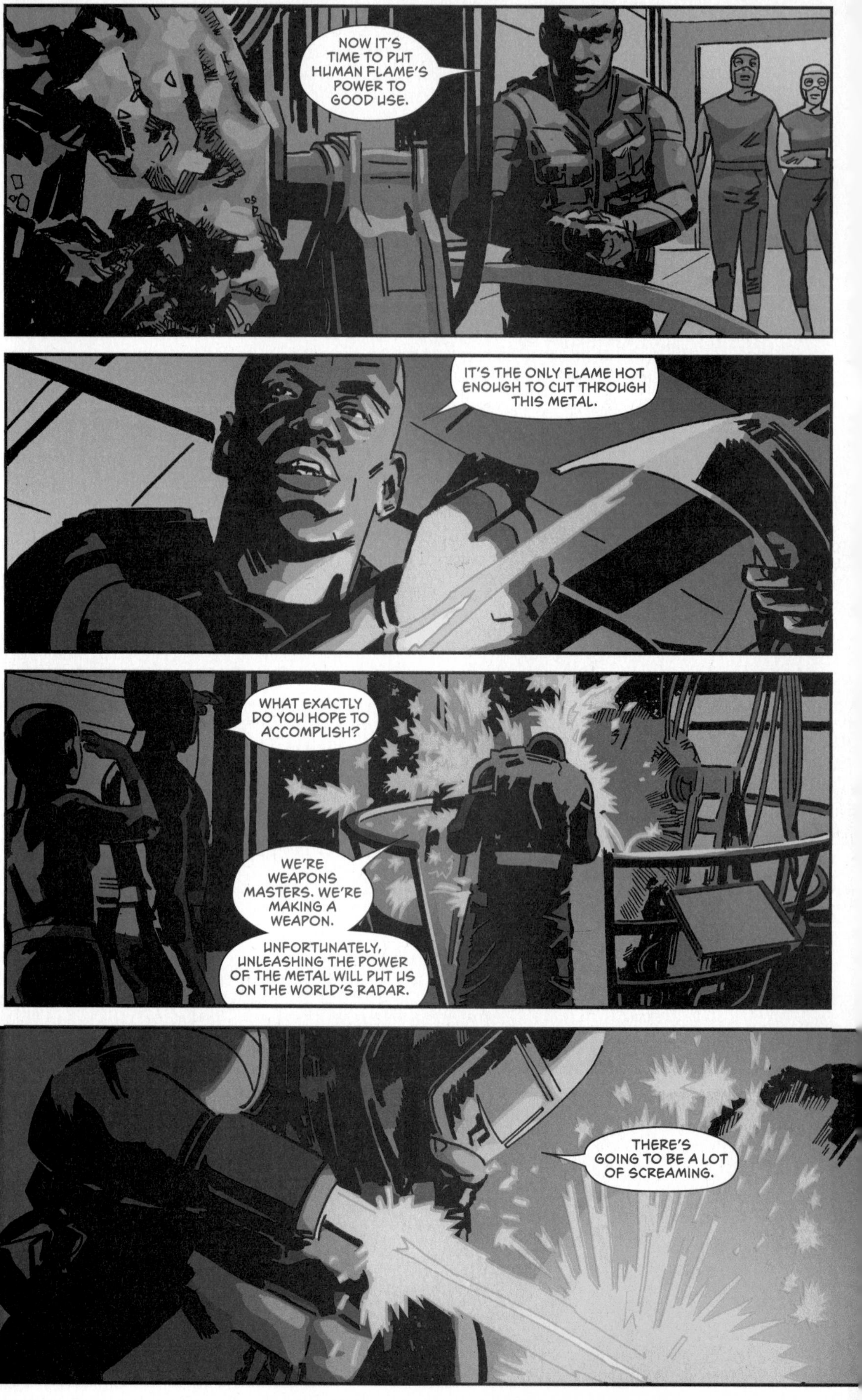
NOW IT'S TIME TO PUT HUMAN FLAME'S POWER TO GOOD USE.
IT'S THE ONLY FLAME HOT ENOUGH TO CUT THROUGH THIS METAL.
WHAT EXACTLY DO YOU HOPE TO ACCOMPLISH?
WE'RE WEAPONS MASTERS. WE'RE MAKING A WEAPON.
UNFORTUNATELY, UNLEASHING THE POWER OF THE METAL WILL PUT US ON THE WORLD'S RADAR.
THERE'S GOING TO BE A LOT OF SCREAMING.

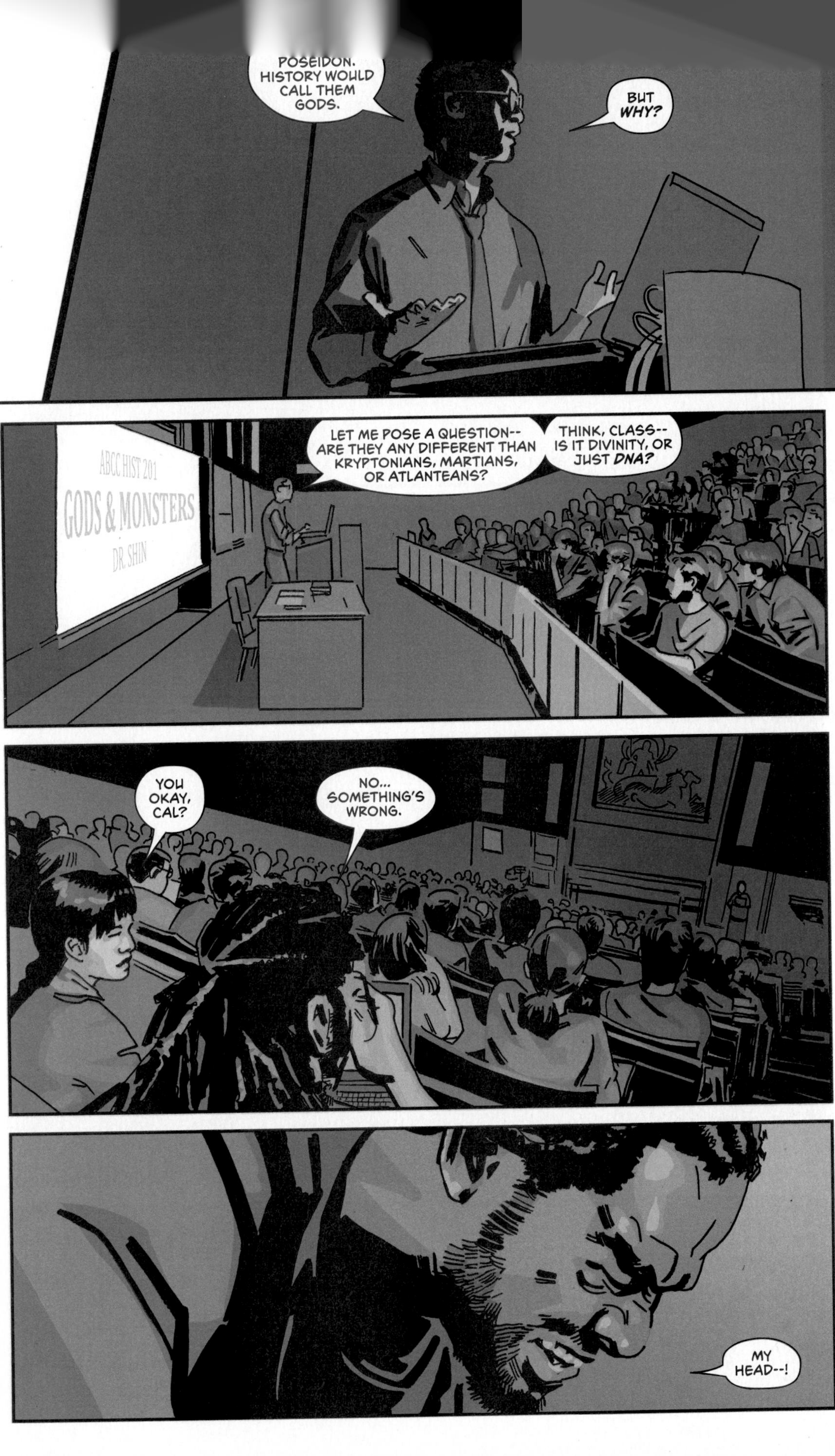
POSEIDON. HISTORY WOULD CALL THEM GODS.
BUT WHY?
ABCC HIST 201
GODS & MONSTERS
DR. SHIN
LET ME POSE A QUESTION-- ARE THEY ANY DIFFERENT THAN KRYPTONIANS, MARTIANS, OR ATLANTEANS?
THINK, CLASS-- IS IT DIVINITY, OR JUST DNA?
YOU OKAY, CAL?
NO... SOMETHING'S WRONG.
MY HEAD--!

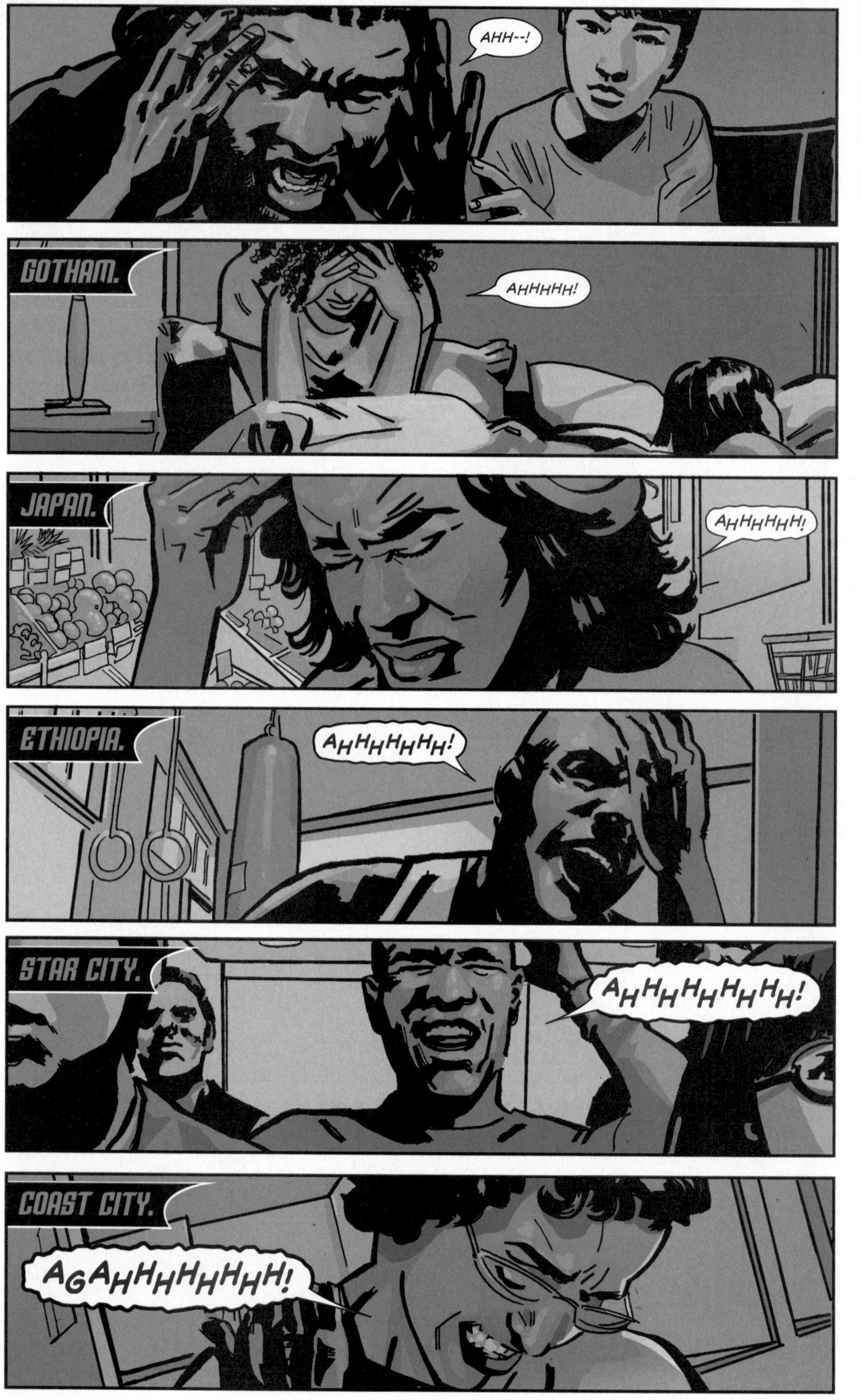
AHH--!
GOTHAM.
AHHHHH!
JAPAN.
AHHHHHH!
ETHIOPIA.
AHHHHHHH!
STAR CITY.
AHHHHHHHHH!
COAST CITY.
AGAHHHHHHHH!

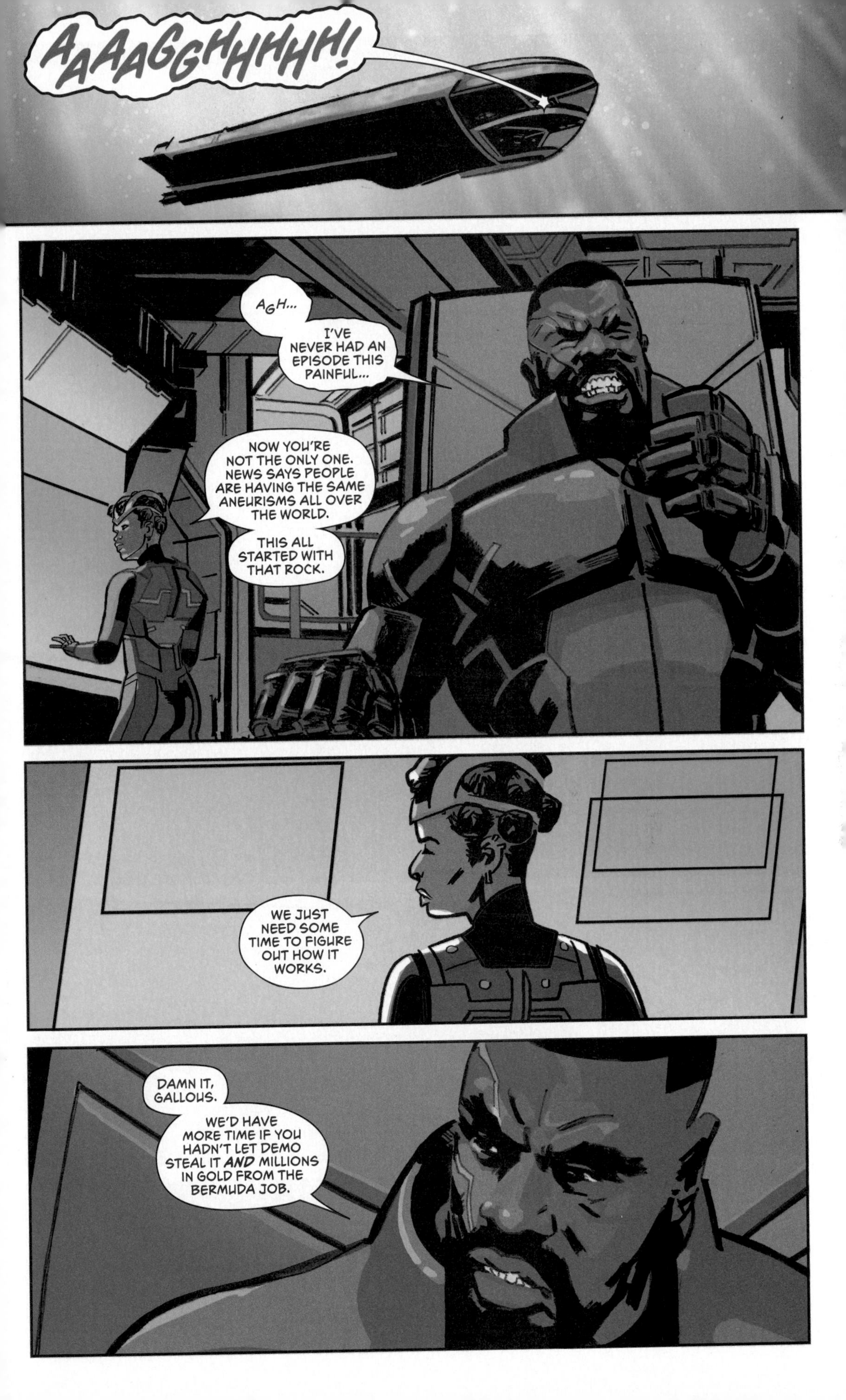
AAAAGGHHHHHH!
AGH...
I'VE NEVER HAD AN EPISODE THIS PAINFUL...
NOW YOU'RE NOT THE ONLY ONE. NEWS SAYS PEOPLE ARE HAVING THE SAME ANEURISMS ALL OVER THE WORLD.
THIS ALL STARTED WITH THAT ROCK.
WE JUST NEED SOME TIME TO FIGURE OUT HOW IT WORKS.
DAMN IT, GALLOUS.
WE'D HAVE MORE TIME IF YOU HADN'T LET DEMO STEAL IT AND MILLIONS IN GOLD FROM THE BERMUDA JOB.

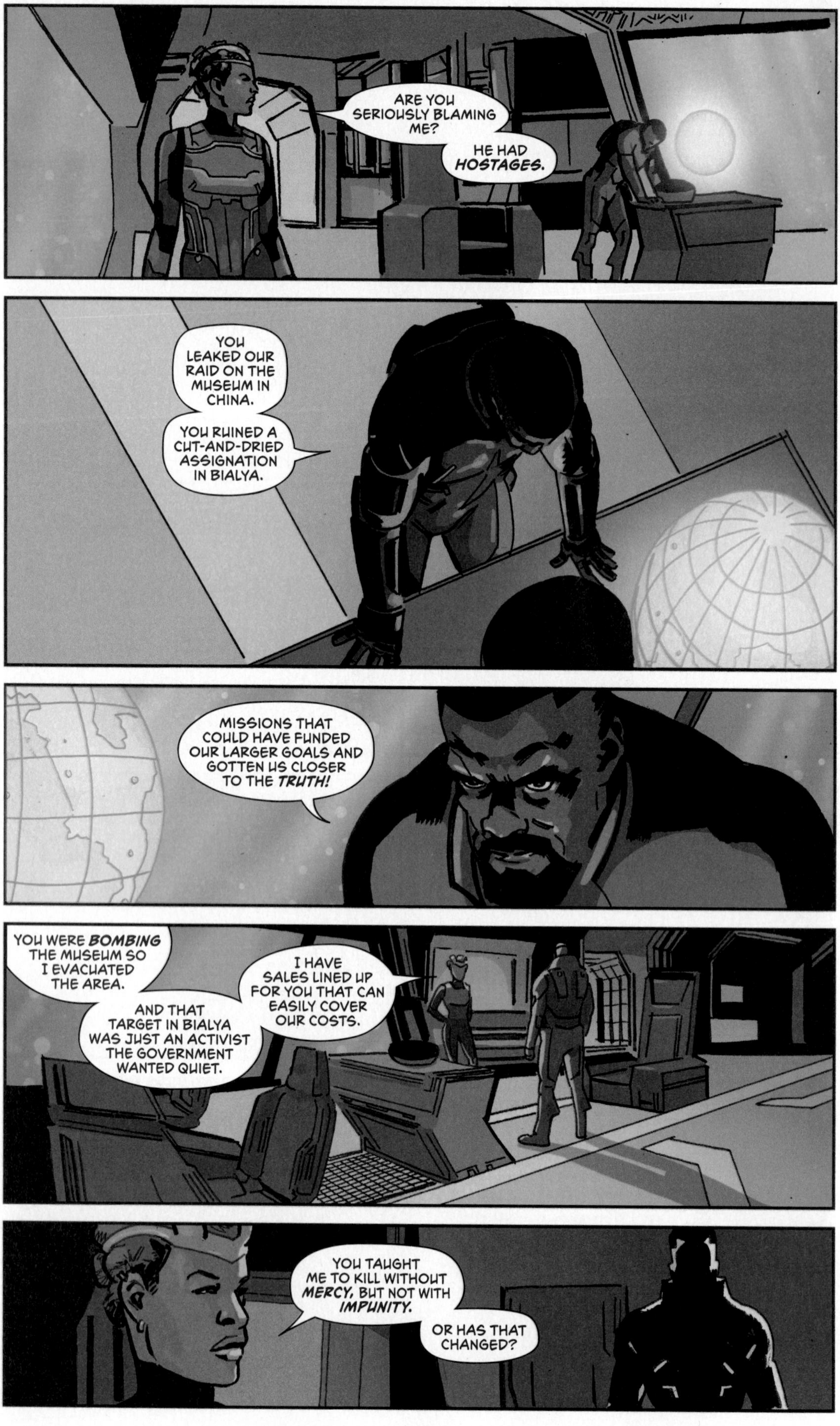

ARE YOU SERIOUSLY BLAMING ME?
HE HAD *HOSTAGES.*
YOU LEAKED OUR RAID ON THE MUSEUM IN CHINA.
YOU RUINED A CUT-AND-DRIED ASSIGNATION IN BIALYA.
MISSIONS THAT COULD HAVE FUNDED OUR LARGER GOALS AND GOTTEN US CLOSER TO THE *TRUTH!*
YOU WERE *BOMBING* THE MUSEUM SO I EVACUATED THE AREA.
AND THAT TARGET IN BIALYA WAS JUST AN ACTIVIST THE GOVERNMENT WANTED QUIET.
I HAVE SALES LINED UP FOR YOU THAT CAN EASILY COVER OUR COSTS.
YOU TAUGHT ME TO KILL WITHOUT *MERCY,* BUT NOT WITH *IMPUNITY.*
OR HAS THAT CHANGED?

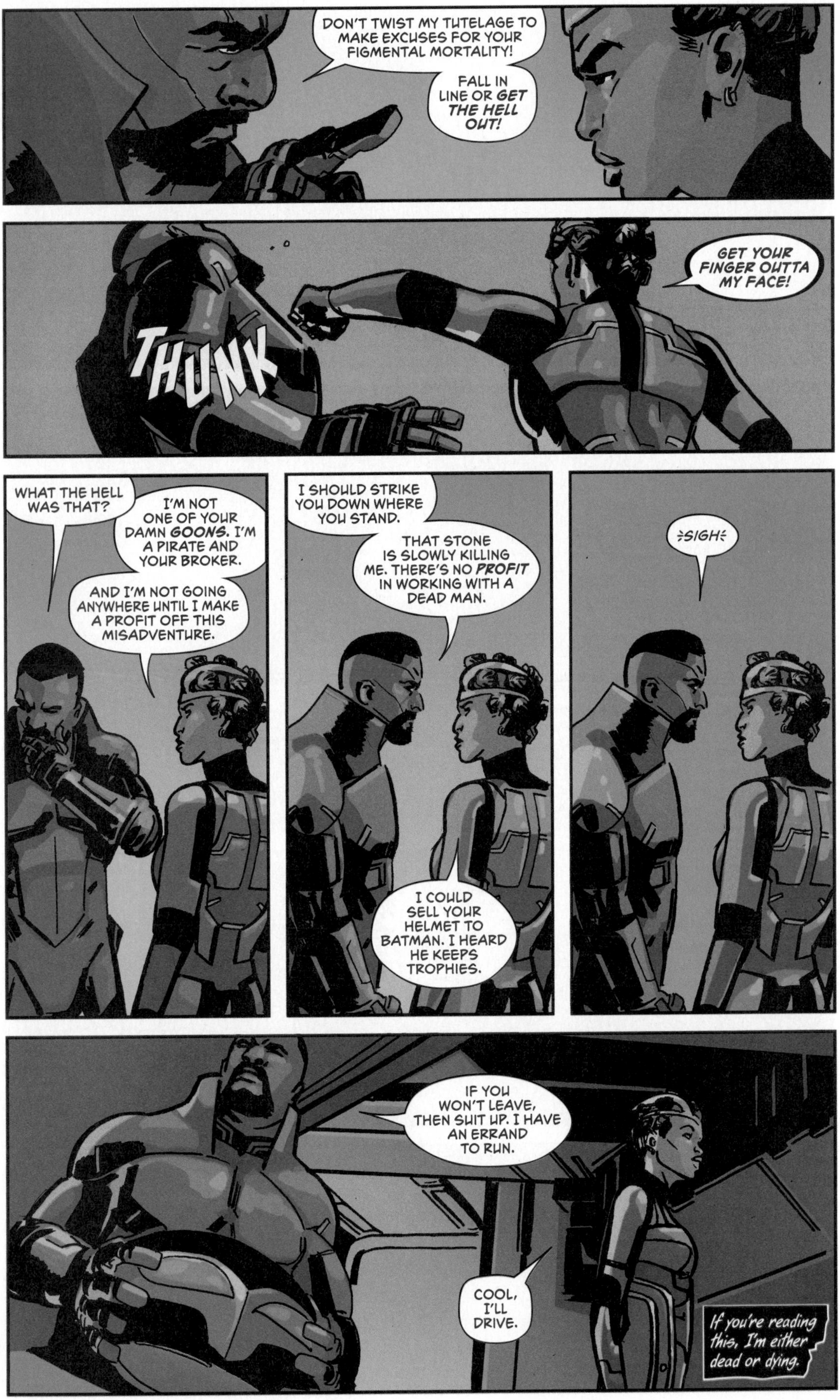
DON'T TWIST MY TUTELAGE TO MAKE EXCUSES FOR YOUR FIGMENTAL MORTALITY!
FALL IN LINE OR *GET THE HELL OUT!*
GET YOUR FINGER OUTTA MY FACE!
THUNK
WHAT THE HELL WAS THAT?
I'M NOT ONE OF YOUR DAMN *GOONS.* I'M A PIRATE AND YOUR BROKER.
AND I'M NOT GOING ANYWHERE UNTIL I MAKE A PROFIT OFF THIS MISADVENTURE.
I SHOULD STRIKE YOU DOWN WHERE YOU STAND.
THAT STONE IS SLOWLY KILLING ME. THERE'S NO *PROFIT* IN WORKING WITH A DEAD MAN.
I COULD SELL YOUR HELMET TO BATMAN. I HEARD HE KEEPS TROPHIES.
SIGH
IF YOU WON'T LEAVE, THEN SUIT UP. I HAVE AN ERRAND TO RUN.
COOL, I'LL DRIVE.
If you're reading this, I'm either dead or dying.

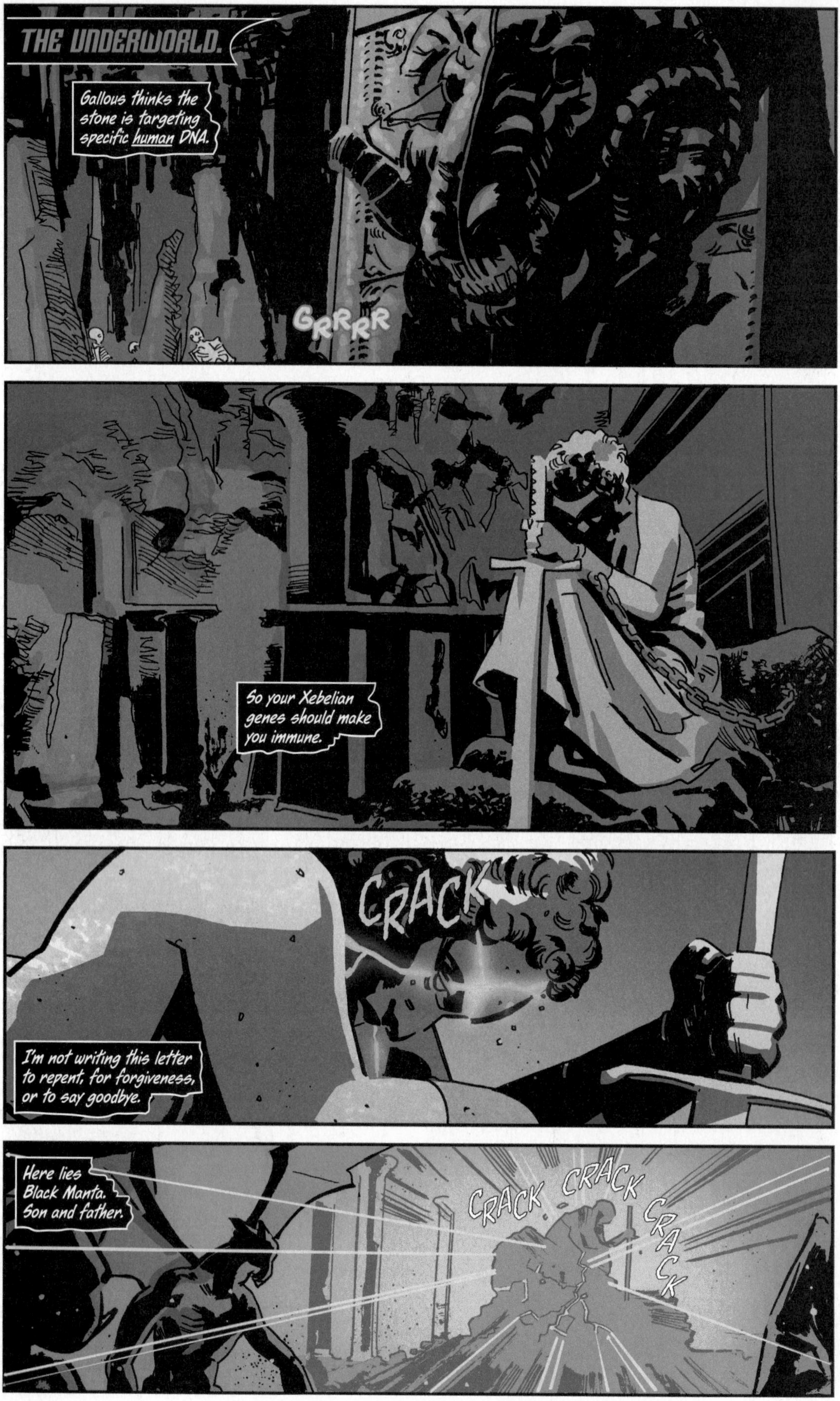

THE UNDERWORLD.
Gallous thinks the stone is targeting specific human DNA.
GRRRR
So your Xebelian genes should make you immune.
CRACK
I'm not writing this letter to repent, for forgiveness, or to say goodbye.
Here lies Black Manta. Son and father.
CRACK CRACK CRACK

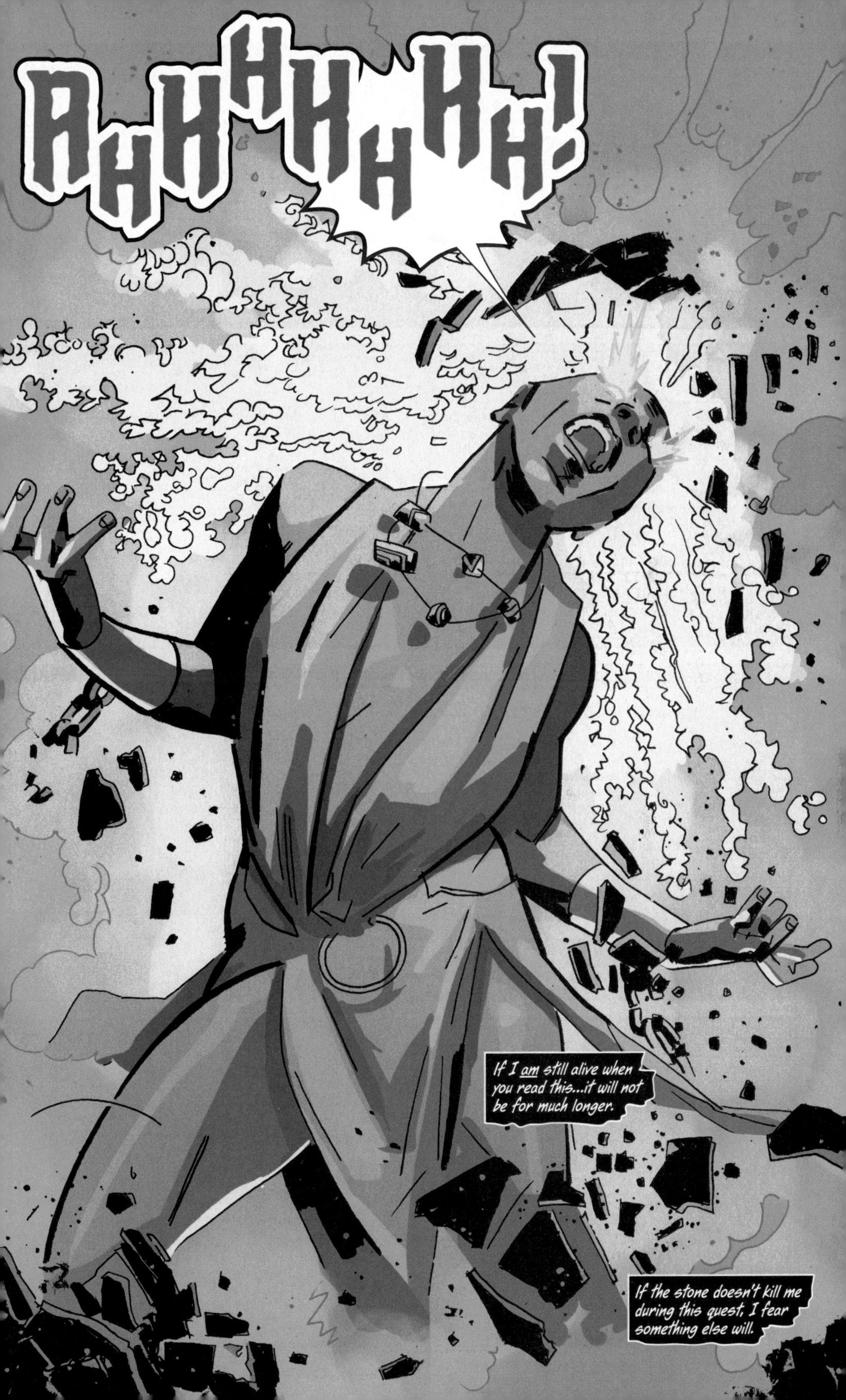
AHHHHHHHH!
If I am still alive when you read this...it will not be for much longer.
If the stone doesn't kill me during this quest, I fear something else will.

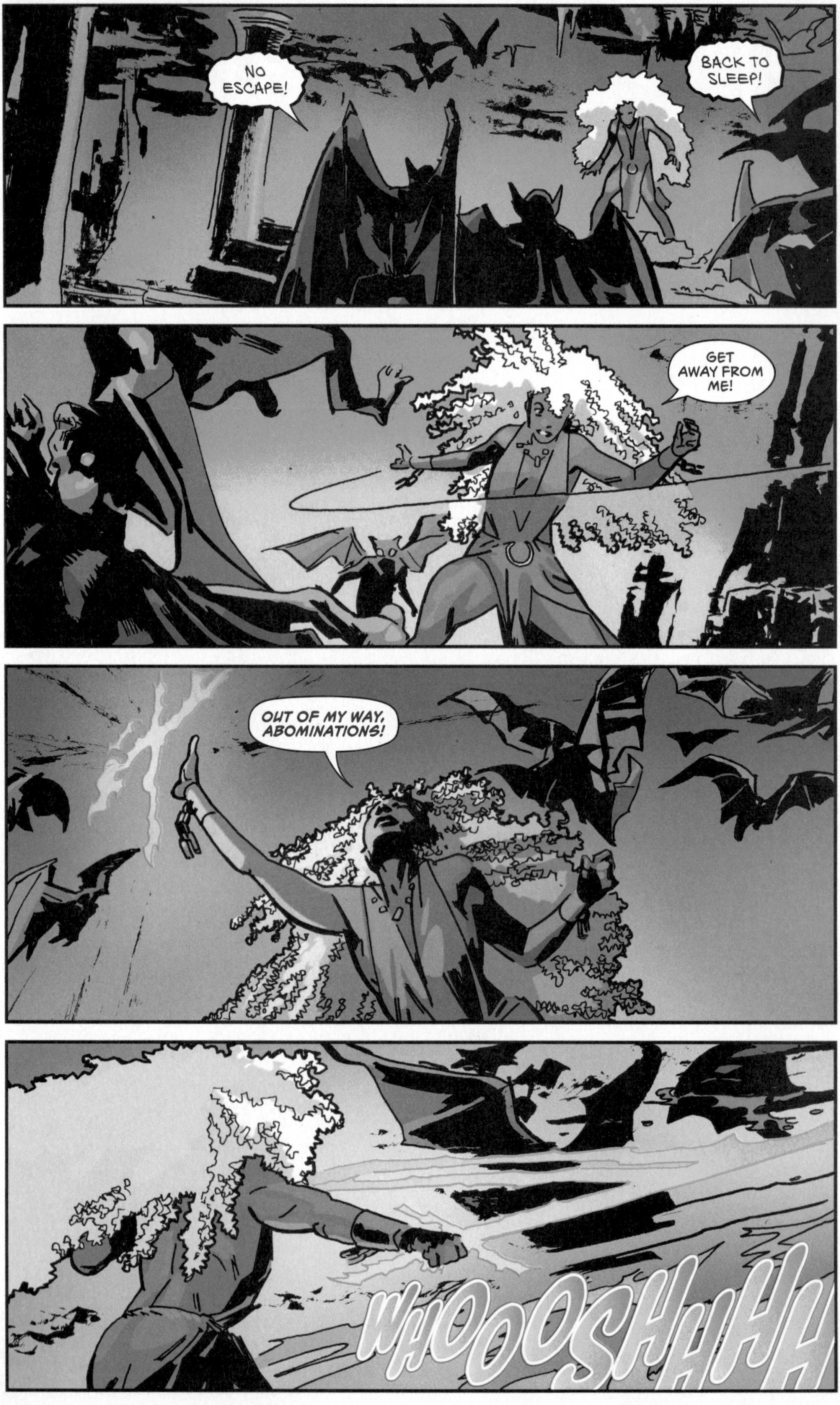
NO ESCAPE!
BACK TO SLEEP!
GET AWAY FROM ME!
OUT OF MY WAY, ABOMINATIONS!
WHOOOSHHHH

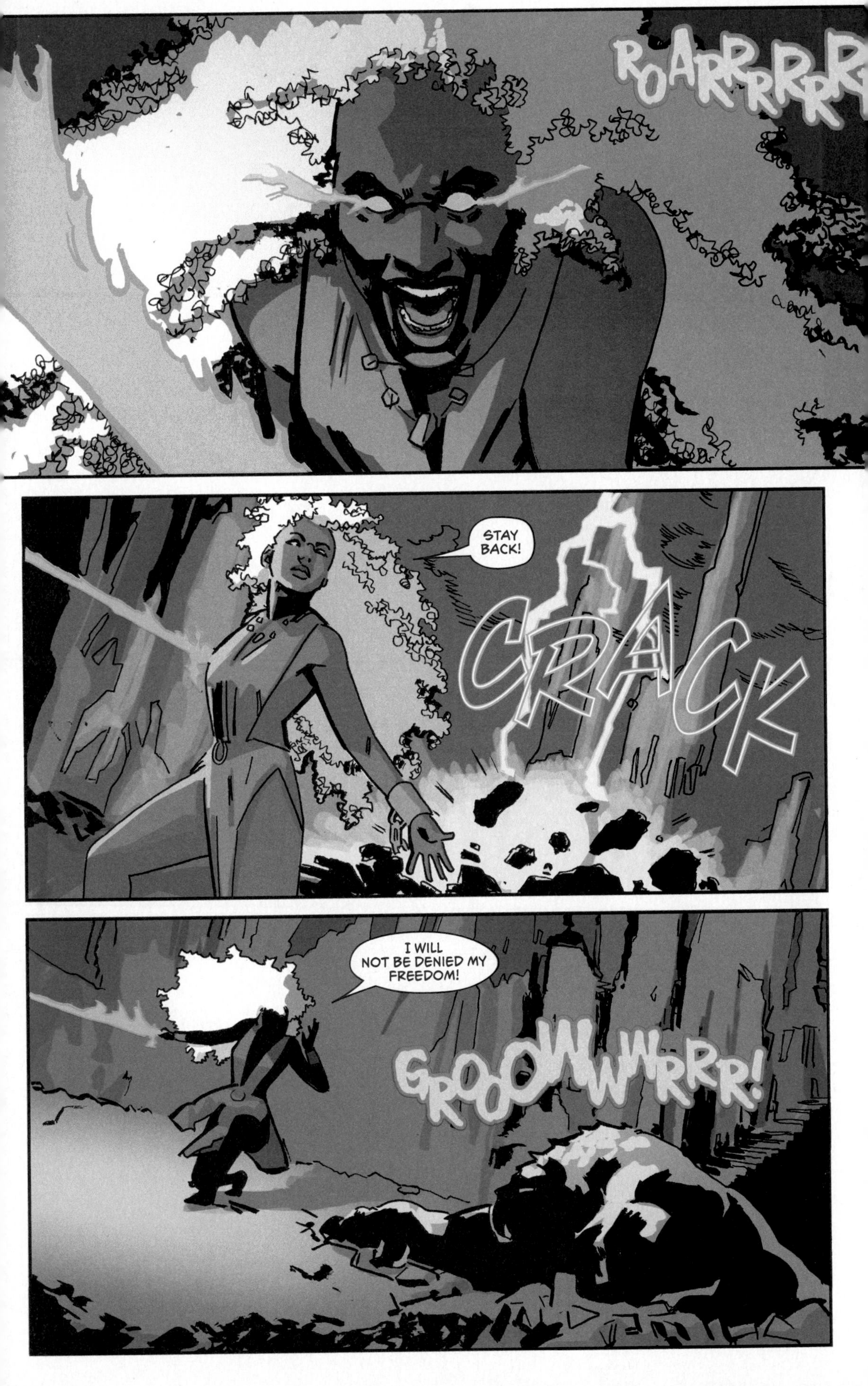
ROARRRRR
STAY BACK!
CRACK
I WILL NOT BE DENIED MY FREEDOM!
GROOOWWRRR!

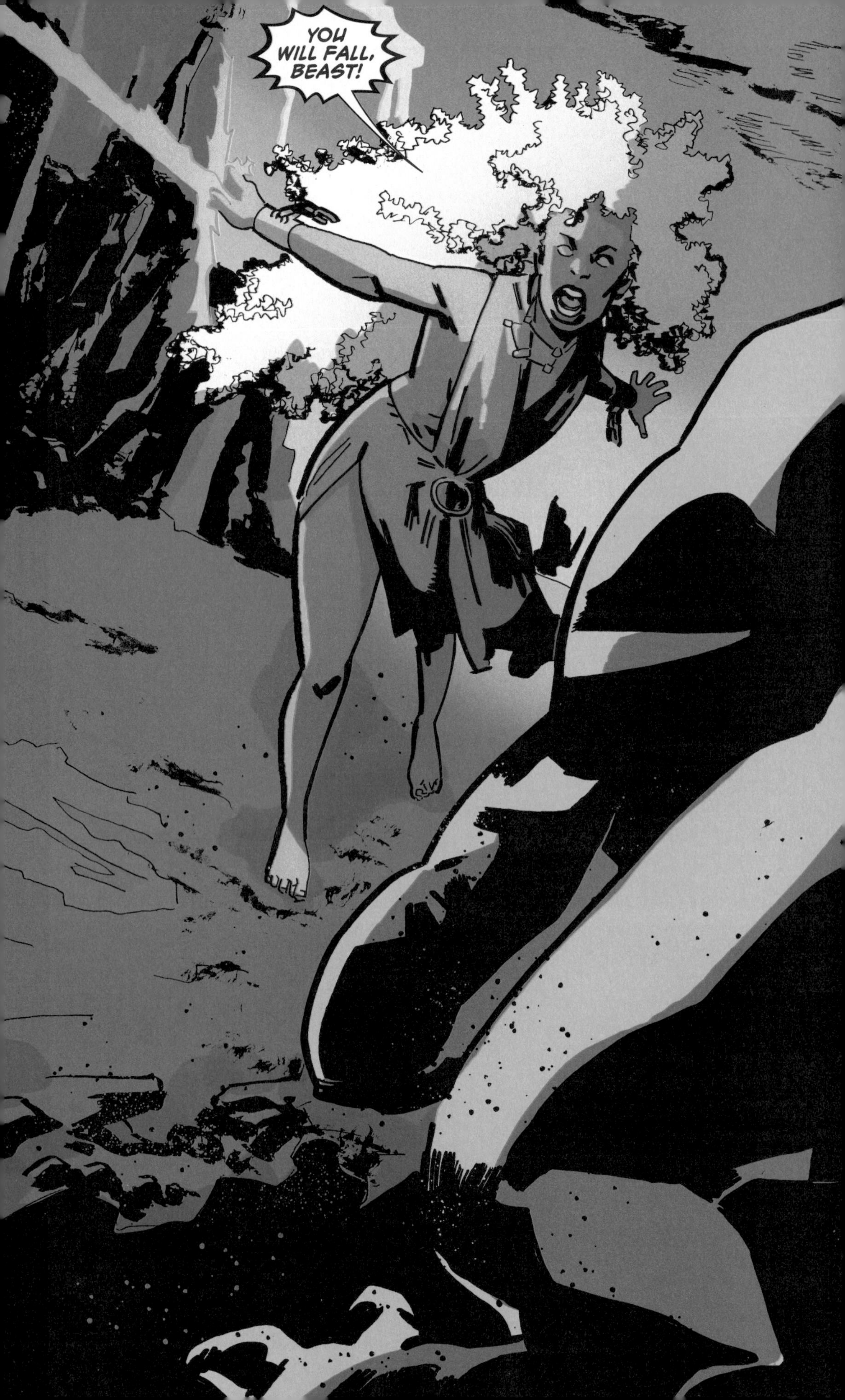
YOU WILL FALL, BEAST!

Black Manta #2 cover by Valentine De Landro and Marissa Louise

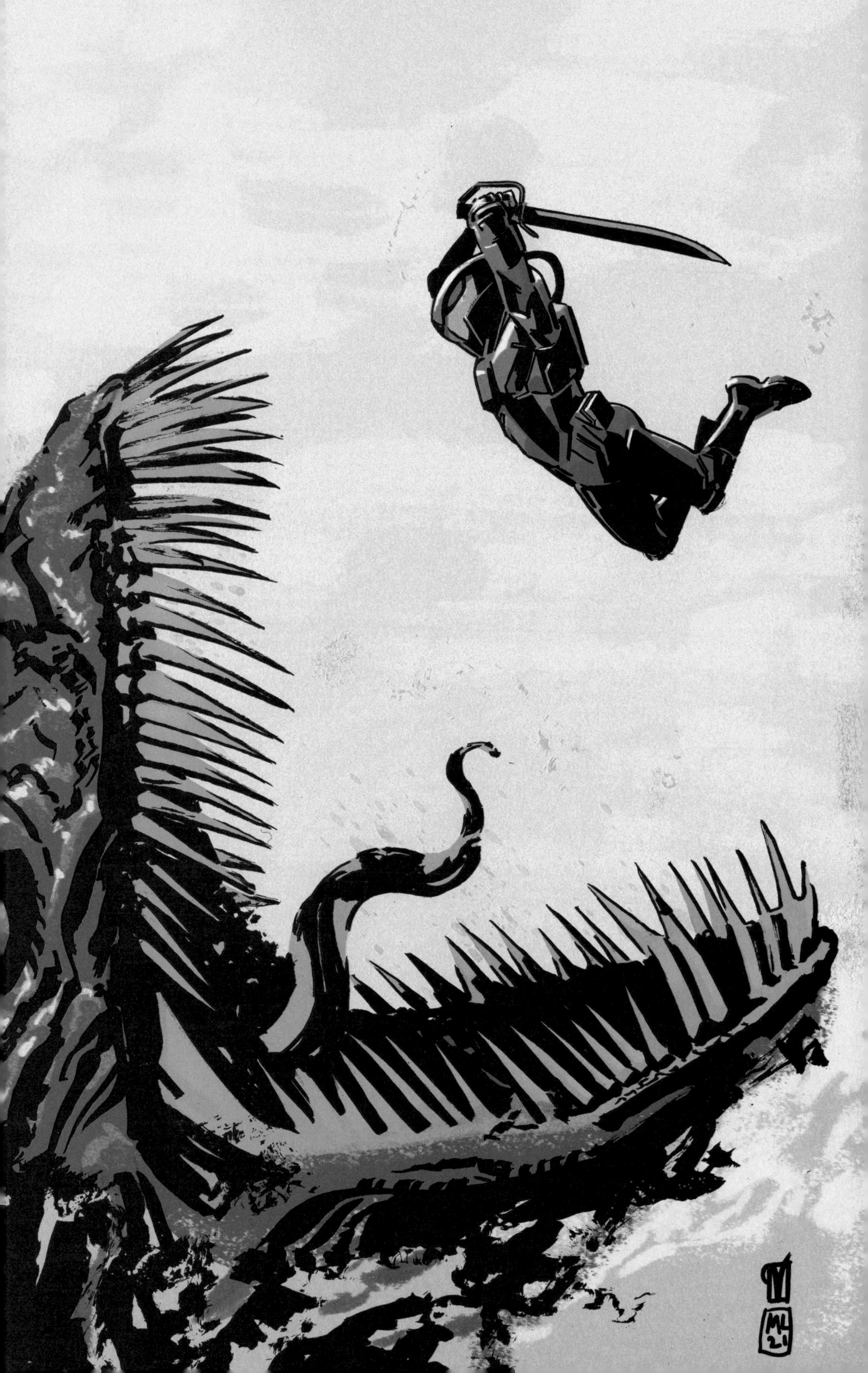

Black Manta #2 variant cover by Sanford Greene

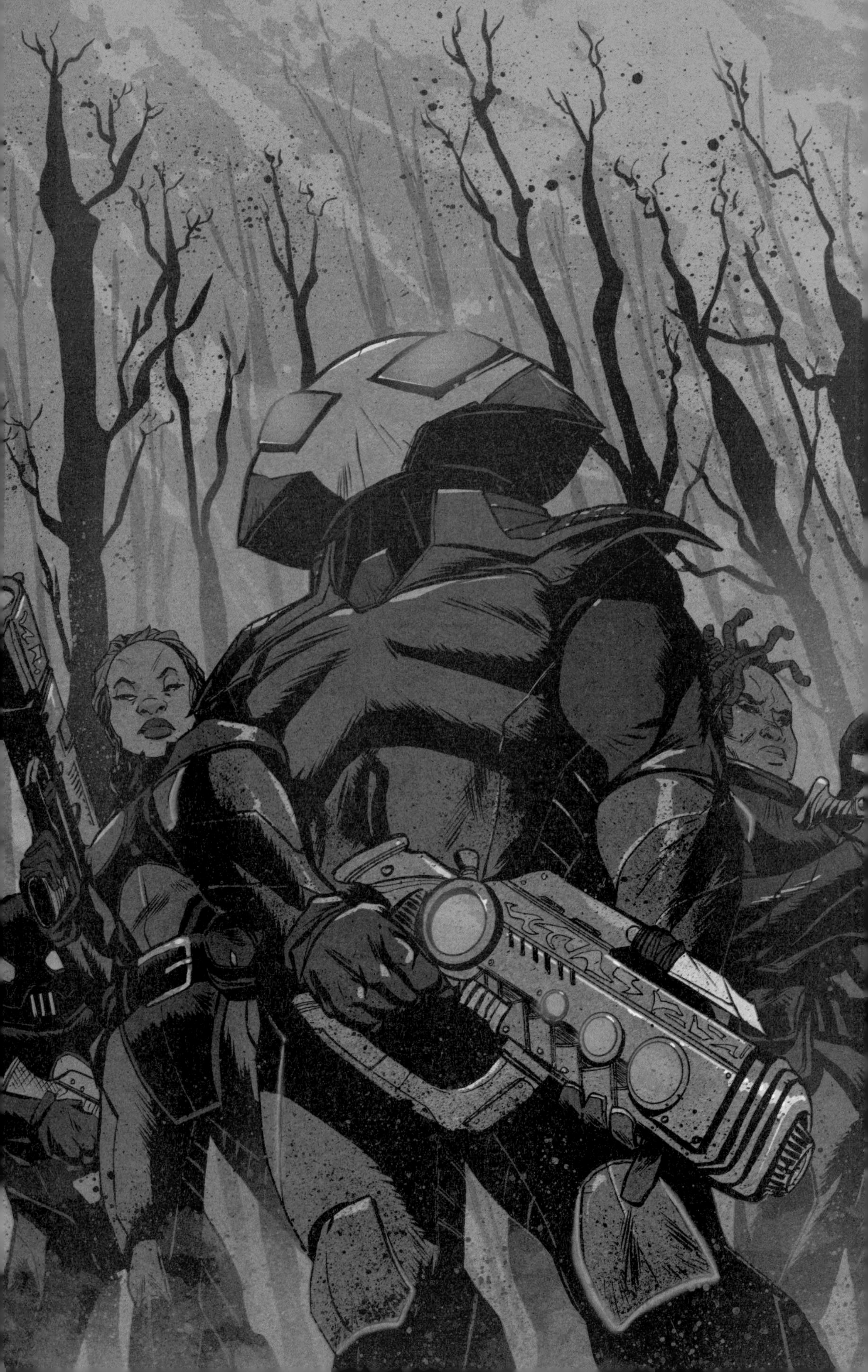

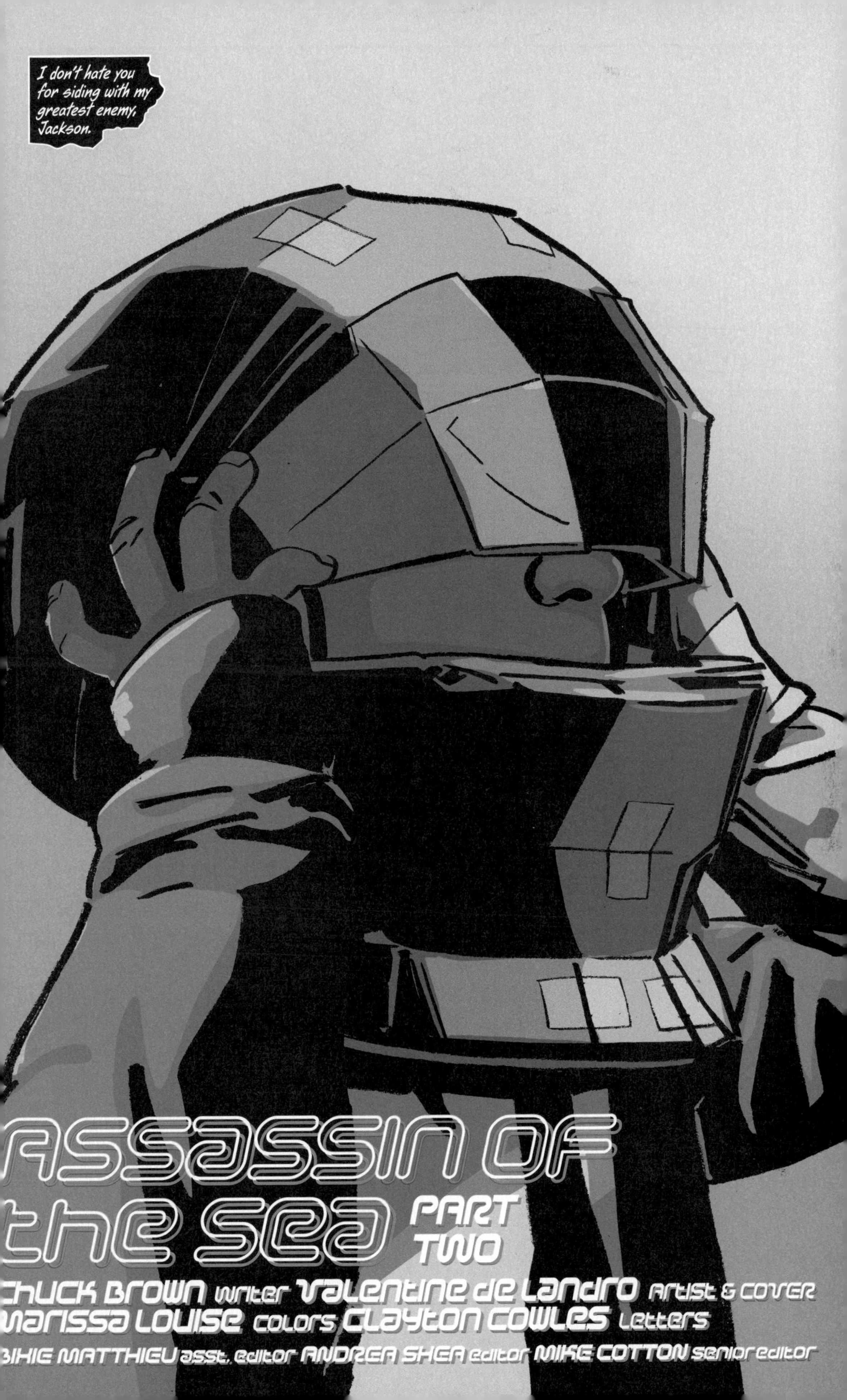

I don't hate you for siding with my greatest enemy, Jackson.
ASSASSIN OF THE SEA PART TWO
CHUCK BROWN writer VALENTINE DE LANDRO artist & cover
MARISSA LOUISE colors CLAYTON COWLES letters
BIXIE MATTHIEU asst. editor ANDREA SHEA editor MIKE COTTON senior editor

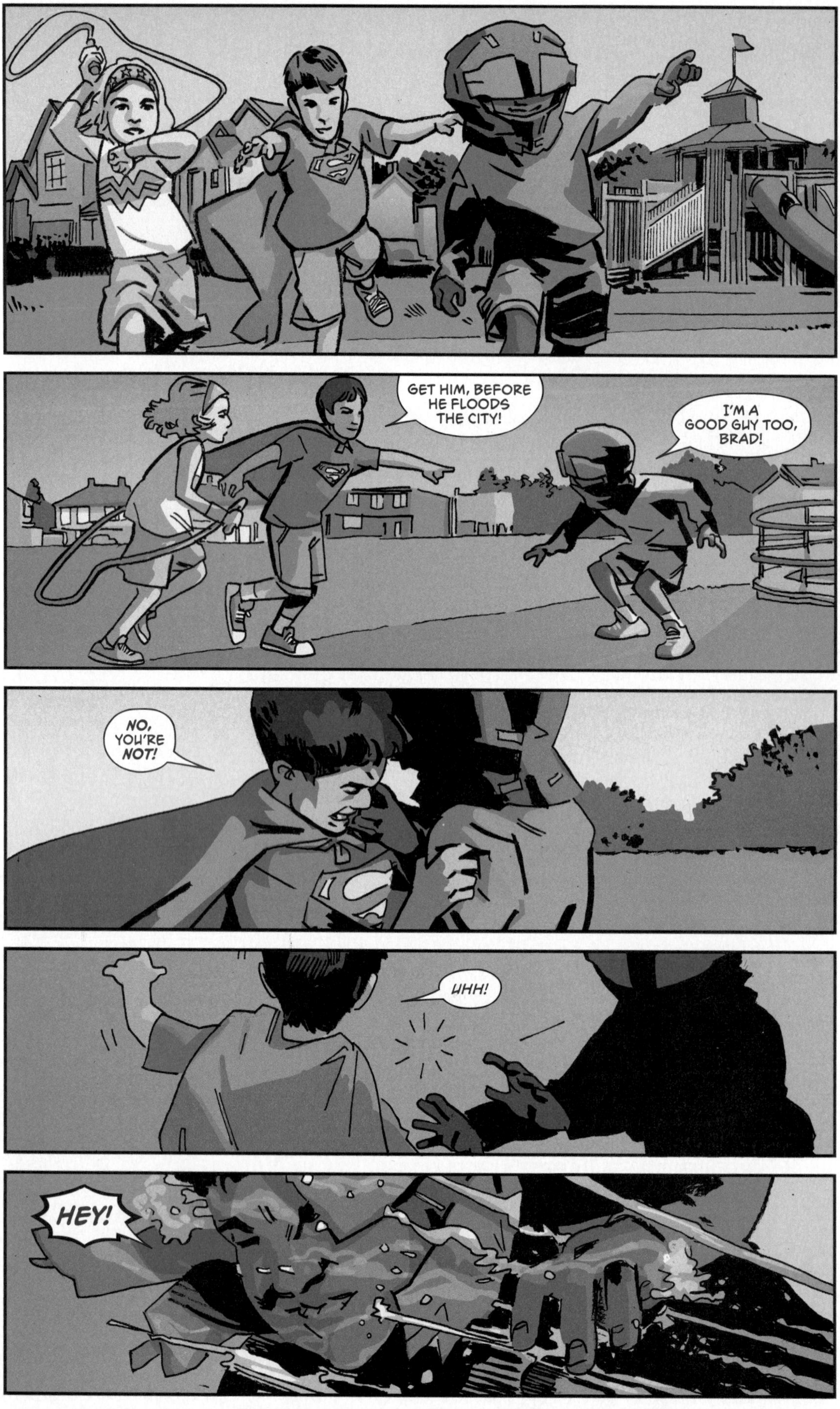
GET HIM, BEFORE HE FLOODS THE CITY!
I'M A GOOD GUY TOO, BRAD!
NO, YOU'RE NOT!
UHH!
HEY!

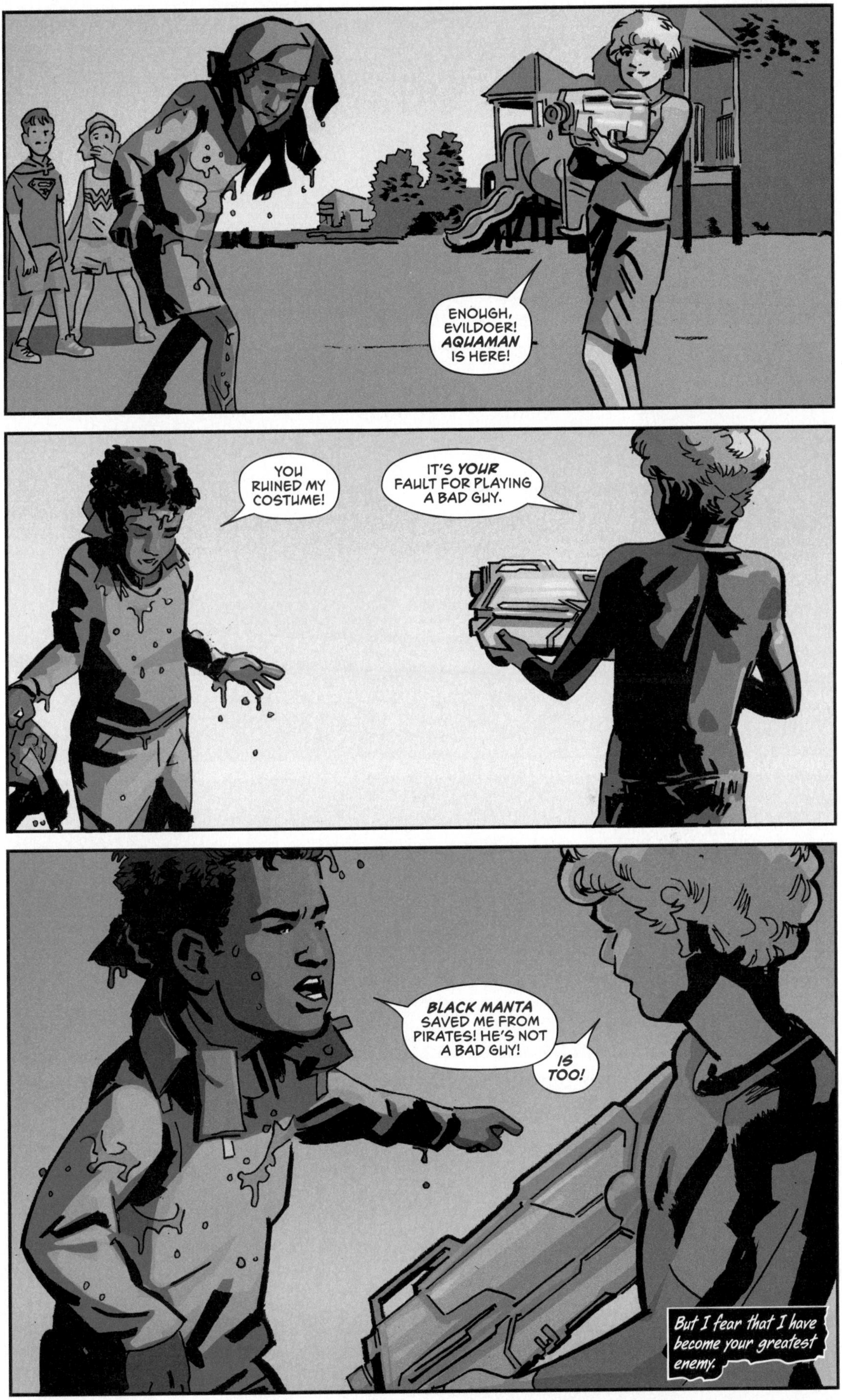
ENOUGH, EVILDOER! AQUAMAN IS HERE!
YOU RUINED MY COSTUME!
IT'S YOUR FAULT FOR PLAYING A BAD GUY.
BLACK MANTA SAVED ME FROM PIRATES! HE'S NOT A BAD GUY!
IS TOO!
But I fear that I have become your greatest enemy.

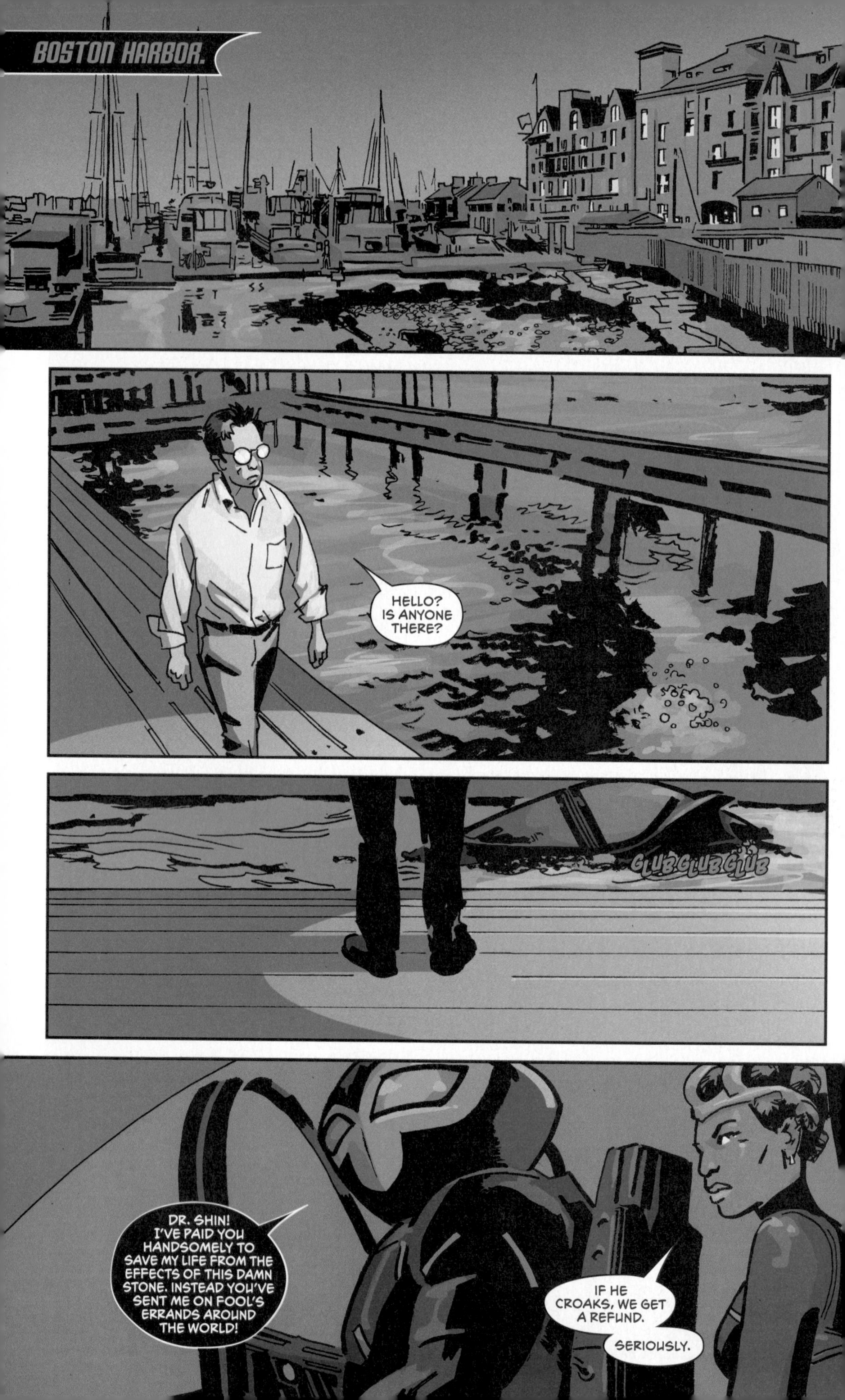
BOSTON HARBOR.
HELLO? IS ANYONE THERE?
GLUB GLUB GLUB
DR. SHIN! I'VE PAID YOU HANDSOMELY TO SAVE MY LIFE FROM THE EFFECTS OF THIS DAMN STONE. INSTEAD YOU'VE SENT ME ON FOOL'S ERRANDS AROUND THE WORLD!
IF HE CROAKS, WE GET A REFUND.
SERIOUSLY.

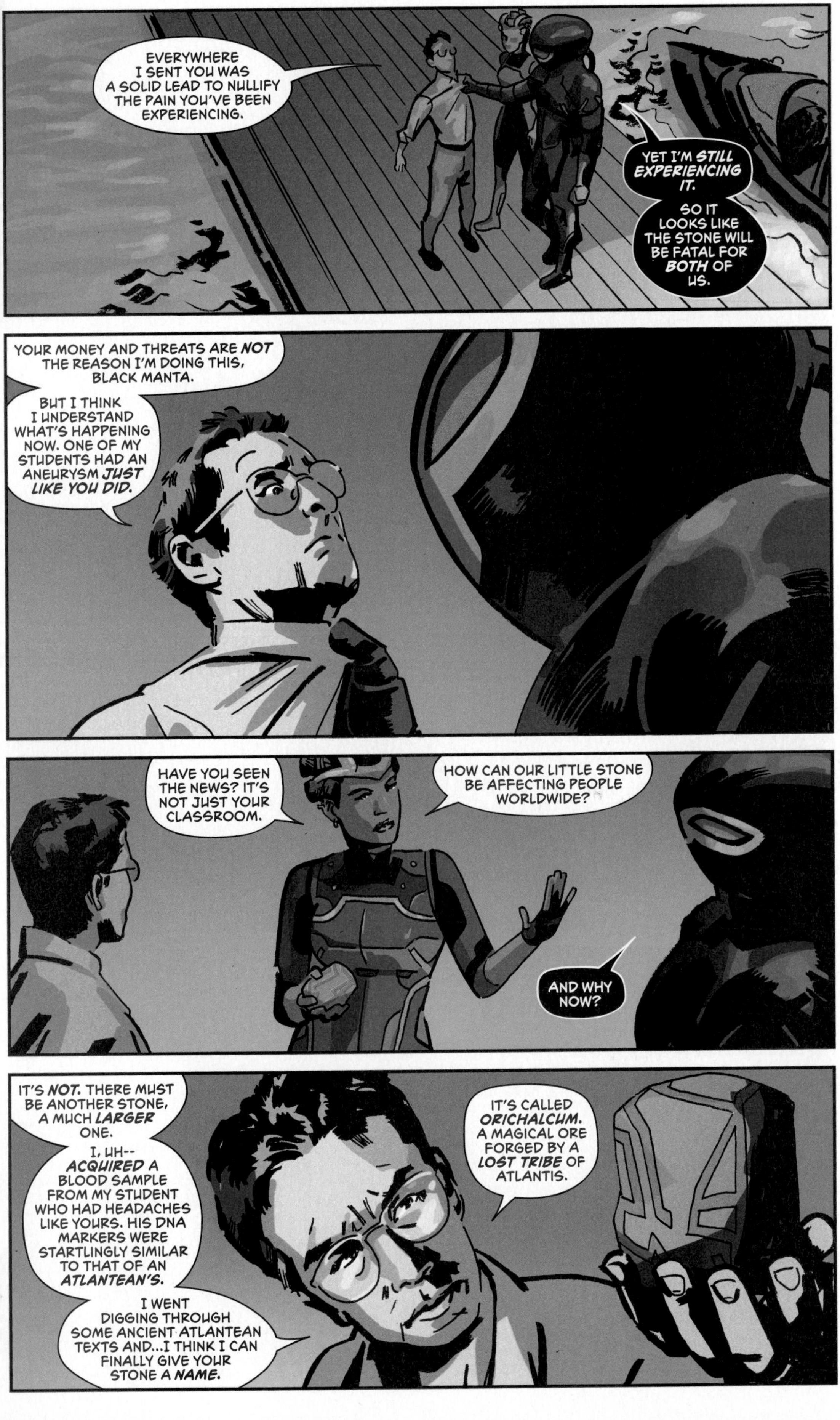

EVERYWHERE I SENT YOU WAS A SOLID LEAD TO NULLIFY THE PAIN YOU'VE BEEN EXPERIENCING.
YET I'M STILL EXPERIENCING IT.
SO IT LOOKS LIKE THE STONE WILL BE FATAL FOR BOTH OF US.
YOUR MONEY AND THREATS ARE NOT THE REASON I'M DOING THIS, BLACK MANTA.
BUT I THINK I UNDERSTAND WHAT'S HAPPENING NOW. ONE OF MY STUDENTS HAD AN ANEURYSM JUST LIKE YOU DID.
HAVE YOU SEEN THE NEWS? IT'S NOT JUST YOUR CLASSROOM.
HOW CAN OUR LITTLE STONE BE AFFECTING PEOPLE WORLDWIDE?
AND WHY NOW?
IT'S NOT. THERE MUST BE ANOTHER STONE, A MUCH LARGER ONE.
I, UH-- ACQUIRED A BLOOD SAMPLE FROM MY STUDENT WHO HAD HEADACHES LIKE YOURS. HIS DNA MARKERS WERE STARTLINGLY SIMILAR TO THAT OF AN ATLANTEAN'S.
I WENT DIGGING THROUGH SOME ANCIENT ATLANTEAN TEXTS AND...I THINK I CAN FINALLY GIVE YOUR STONE A NAME.
IT'S CALLED ORICHALCUM. A MAGICAL ORE FORGED BY A LOST TRIBE OF ATLANTIS.

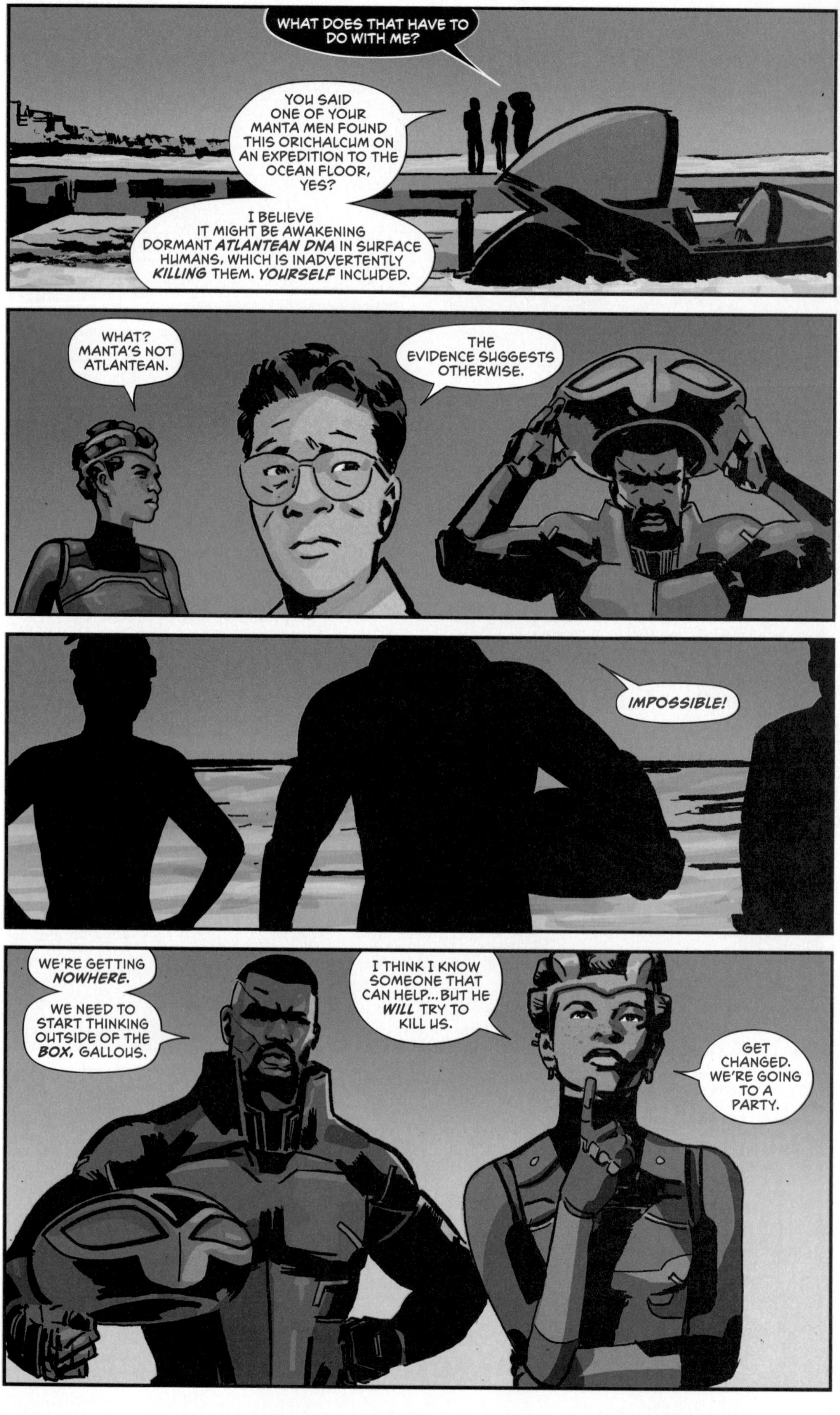
WHAT DOES THAT HAVE TO DO WITH ME?
YOU SAID ONE OF YOUR MANTA MEN FOUND THIS ORICHALCUM ON AN EXPEDITION TO THE OCEAN FLOOR, YES?
I BELIEVE IT MIGHT BE AWAKENING DORMANT ATLANTEAN DNA IN SURFACE HUMANS, WHICH IS INADVERTENTLY KILLING THEM. YOURSELF INCLUDED.
WHAT? MANTA'S NOT ATLANTEAN.
THE EVIDENCE SUGGESTS OTHERWISE.
IMPOSSIBLE!
WE'RE GETTING NOWHERE.
WE NEED TO START THINKING OUTSIDE OF THE BOX, GALLOUS.
I THINK I KNOW SOMEONE THAT CAN HELP...BUT HE WILL TRY TO KILL US.
GET CHANGED. WE'RE GOING TO A PARTY.

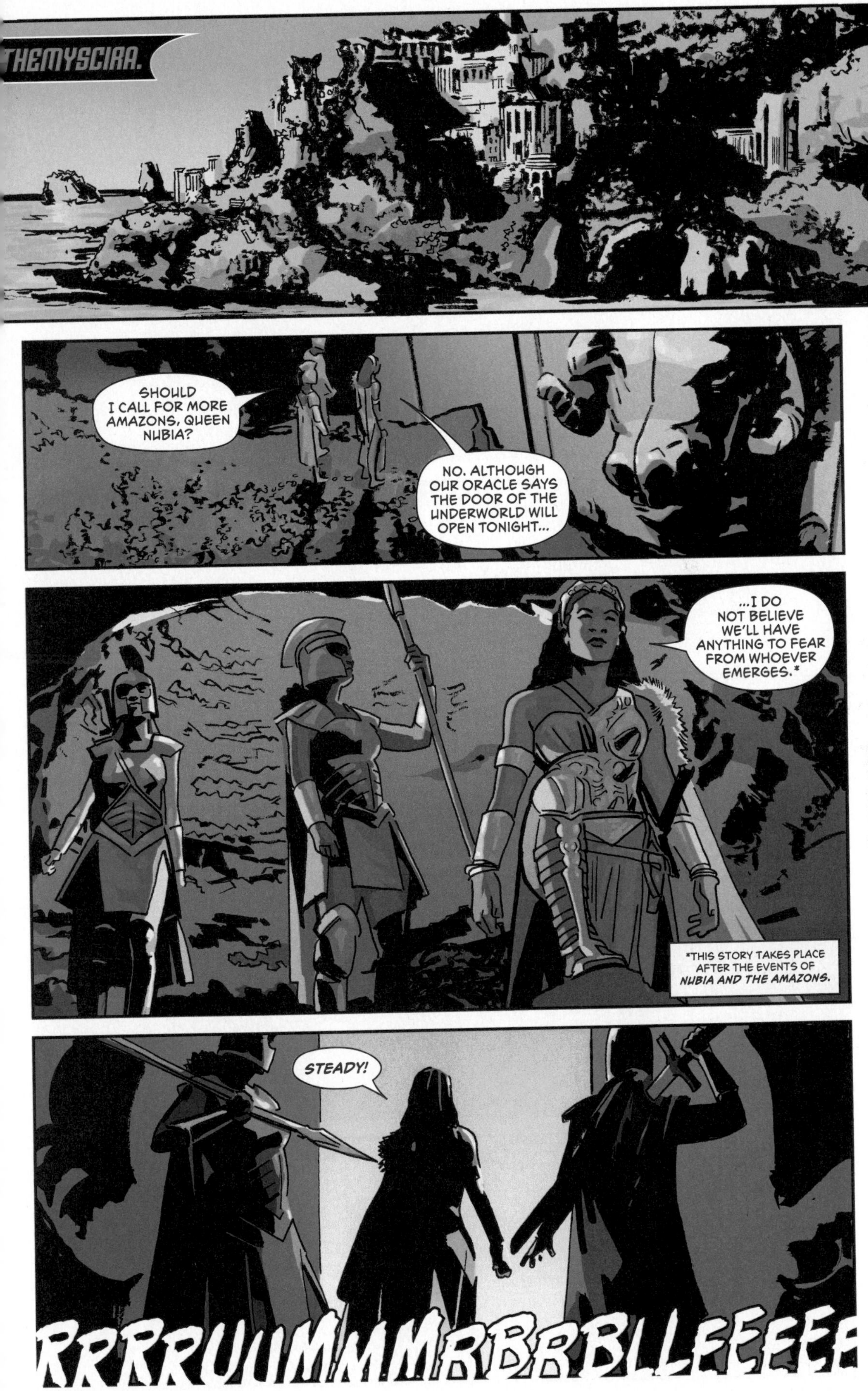
THEMYSCIRA.
SHOULD I CALL FOR MORE AMAZONS, QUEEN NUBIA?
NO. ALTHOUGH OUR ORACLE SAYS THE DOOR OF THE UNDERWORLD WILL OPEN TONIGHT...
...I DO NOT BELIEVE WE'LL HAVE ANYTHING TO FEAR FROM WHOEVER EMERGES.*
*THIS STORY TAKES PLACE AFTER THE EVENTS OF NUBIA AND THE AMAZONS.
STEADY!
RRRRUUMMMRBBRBLLEEEEE

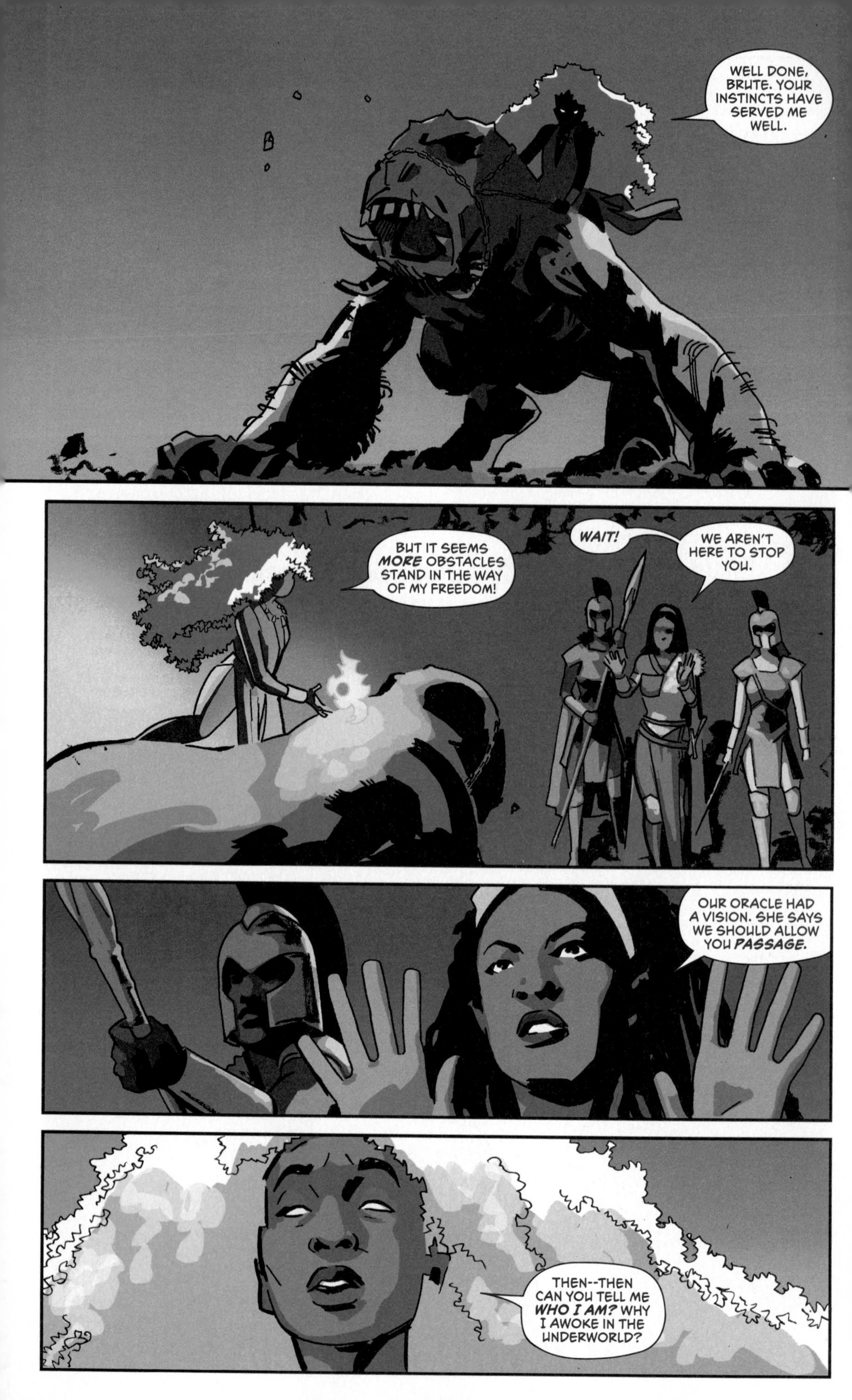
WELL DONE, BRUTE. YOUR INSTINCTS HAVE SERVED ME WELL.
BUT IT SEEMS MORE OBSTACLES STAND IN THE WAY OF MY FREEDOM!
WAIT!
WE AREN'T HERE TO STOP YOU.
OUR ORACLE HAD A VISION. SHE SAYS WE SHOULD ALLOW YOU PASSAGE.
THEN--THEN CAN YOU TELL ME WHO I AM? WHY I AWOKE IN THE UNDERWORLD?

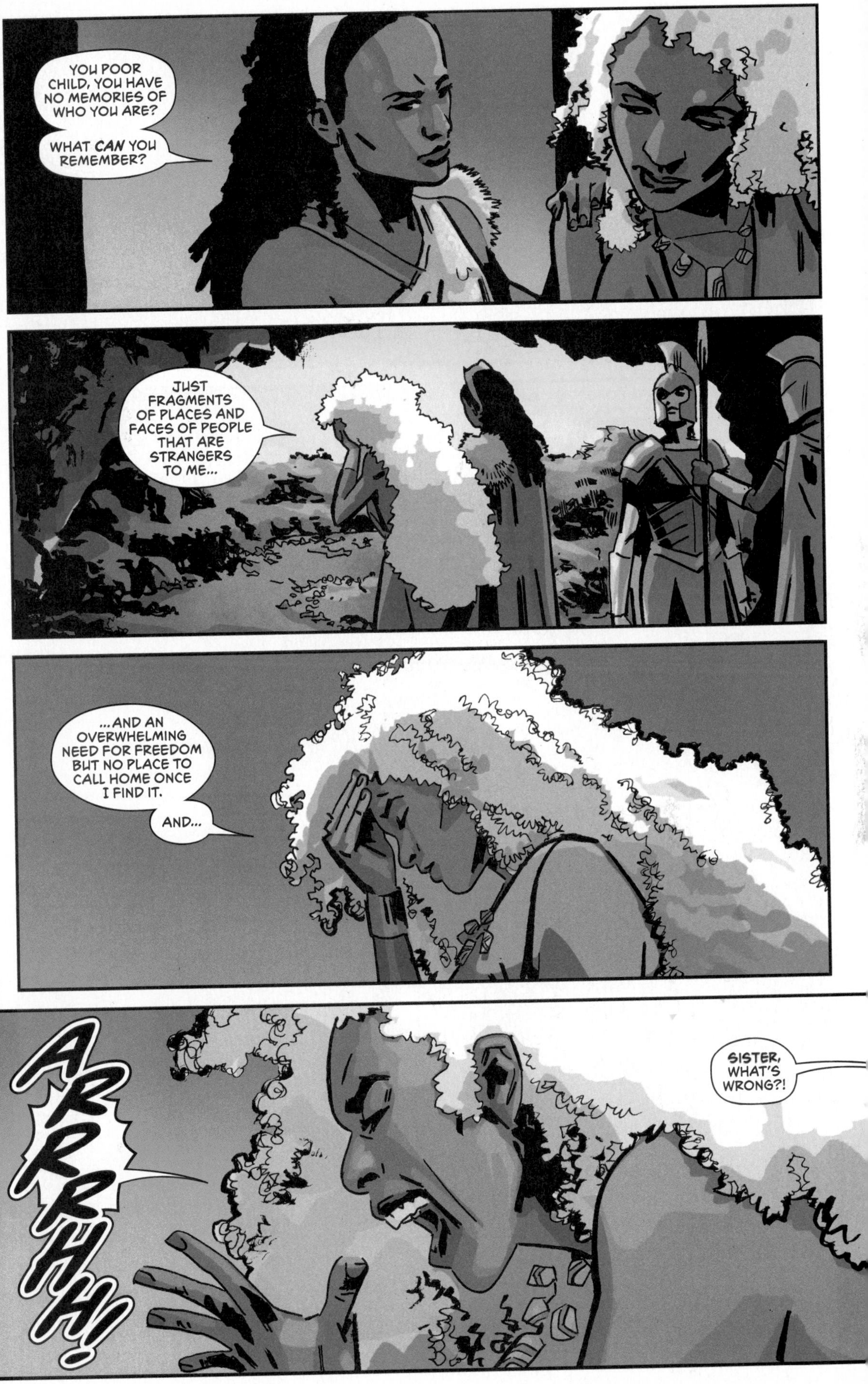

YOU POOR CHILD, YOU HAVE NO MEMORIES OF WHO YOU ARE?
WHAT CAN YOU REMEMBER?
JUST FRAGMENTS OF PLACES AND FACES OF PEOPLE THAT ARE STRANGERS TO ME...
...AND AN OVERWHELMING NEED FOR FREEDOM BUT NO PLACE TO CALL HOME ONCE I FIND IT.
AND...
ARRRHH!
SISTER, WHAT'S WRONG?!

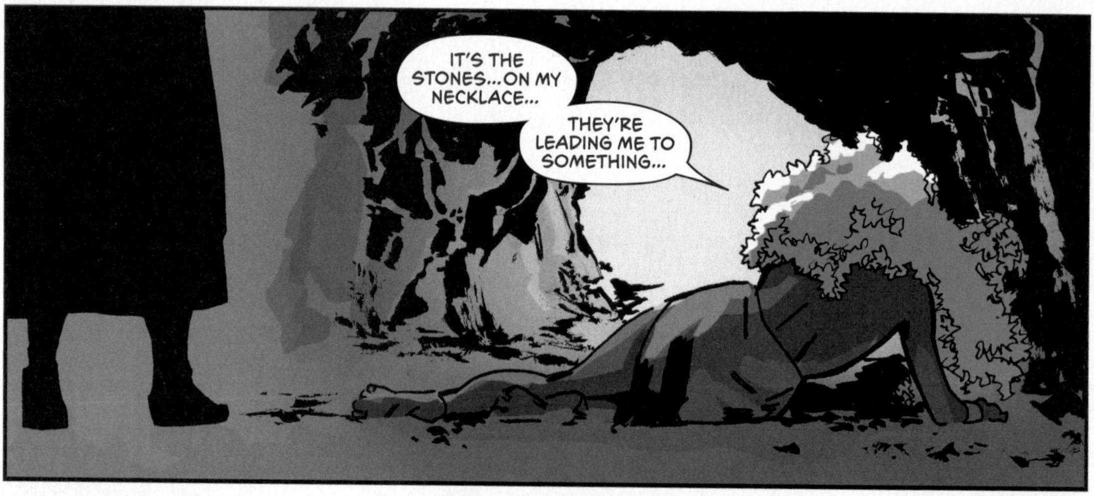
IT'S THE STONES...ON MY NECKLACE...
THEY'RE LEADING ME TO SOMETHING...
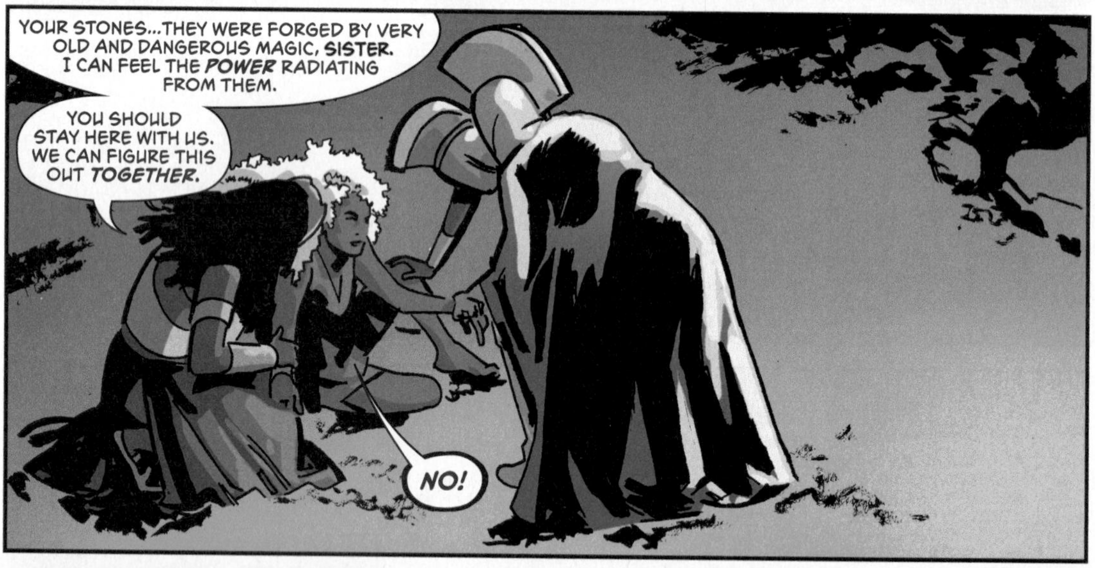
YOUR STONES...THEY WERE FORGED BY VERY OLD AND DANGEROUS MAGIC, SISTER. I CAN FEEL THE POWER RADIATING FROM THEM.
YOU SHOULD STAY HERE WITH US. WE CAN FIGURE THIS OUT TOGETHER.
NO!
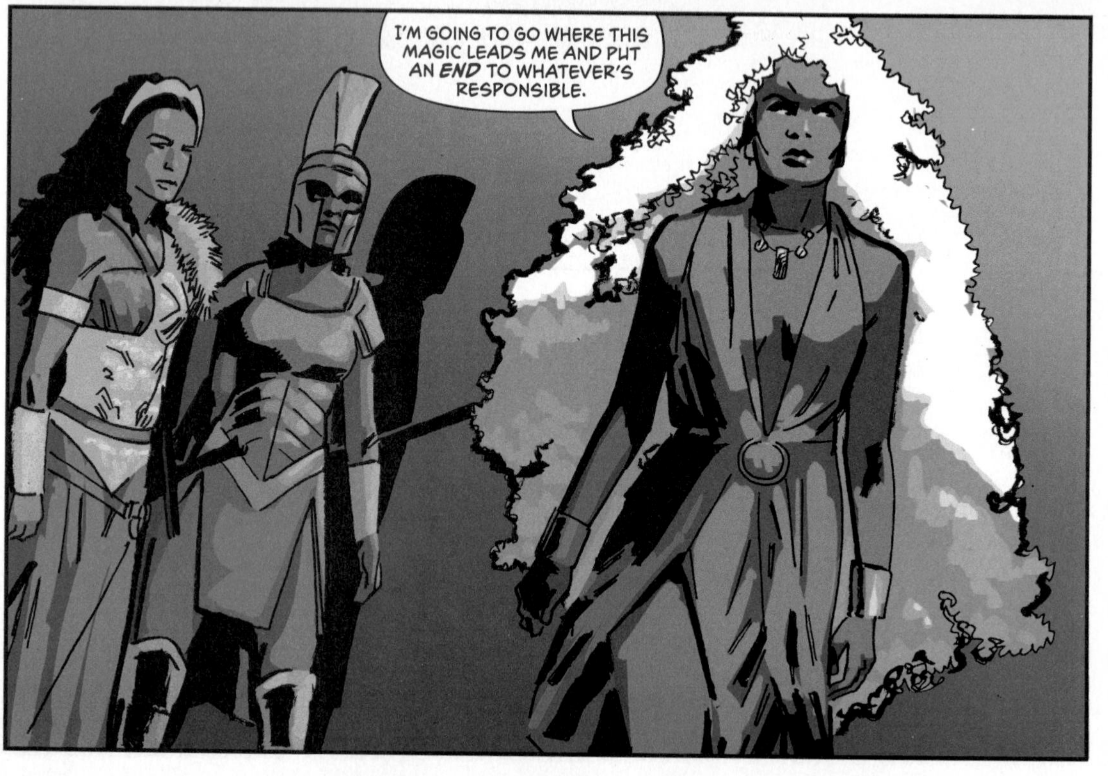
I'M GOING TO GO WHERE THIS MAGIC LEADS ME AND PUT AN END TO WHATEVER'S RESPONSIBLE.

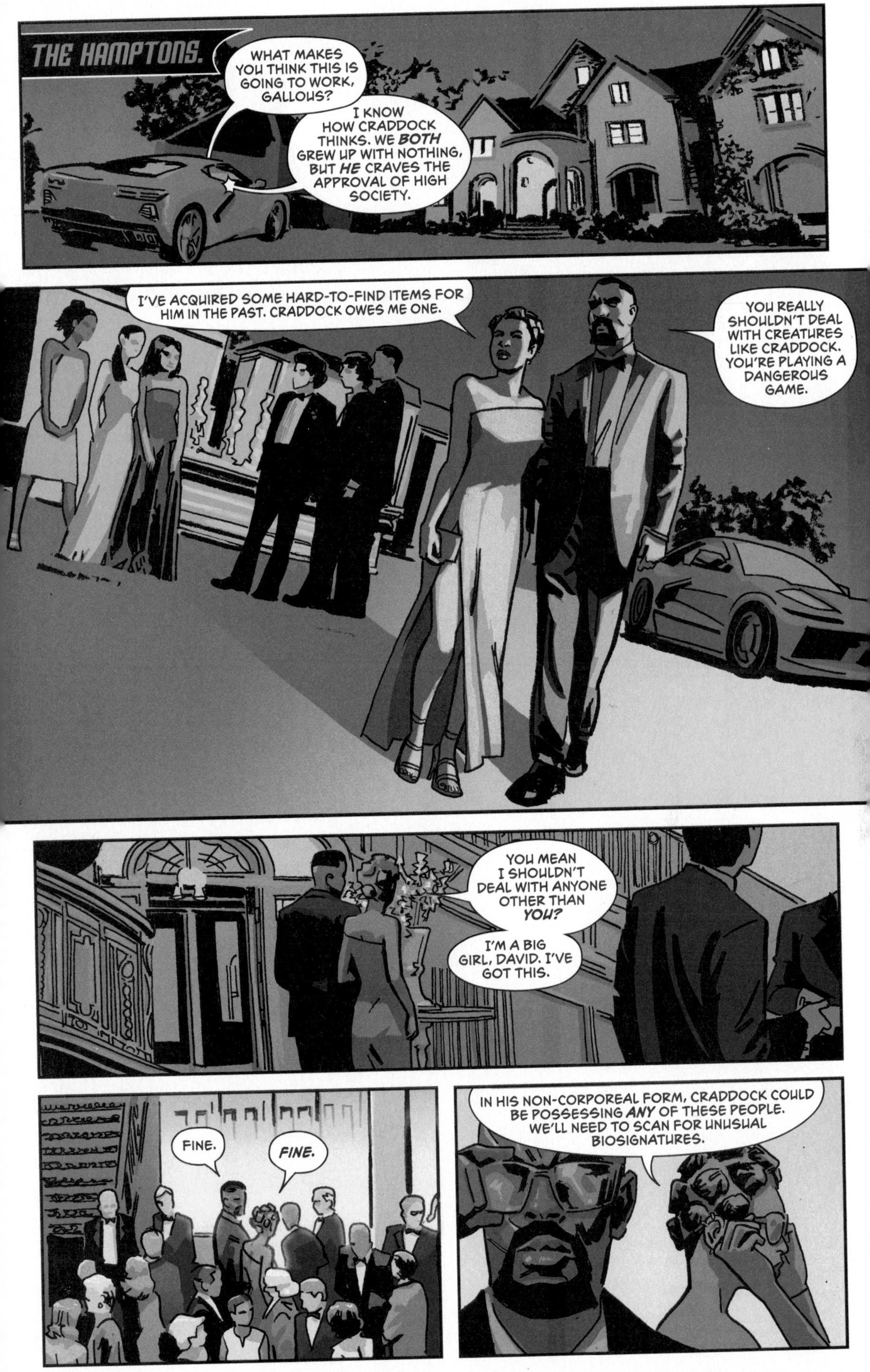
THE HAMPTONS.
WHAT MAKES YOU THINK THIS IS GOING TO WORK, GALLOWS?
I KNOW HOW CRADDOCK THINKS. WE BOTH GREW UP WITH NOTHING, BUT HE CRAVES THE APPROVAL OF HIGH SOCIETY.
I'VE ACQUIRED SOME HARD-TO-FIND ITEMS FOR HIM IN THE PAST. CRADDOCK OWES ME ONE.
YOU REALLY SHOULDN'T DEAL WITH CREATURES LIKE CRADDOCK. YOU'RE PLAYING A DANGEROUS GAME.
YOU MEAN I SHOULDN'T DEAL WITH ANYONE OTHER THAN YOU?
I'M A BIG GIRL, DAVID. I'VE GOT THIS.
FINE.
FINE.
IN HIS NON-CORPOREAL FORM, CRADDOCK COULD BE POSSESSING ANY OF THESE PEOPLE. WE'LL NEED TO SCAN FOR UNUSUAL BIOSIGNATURES.

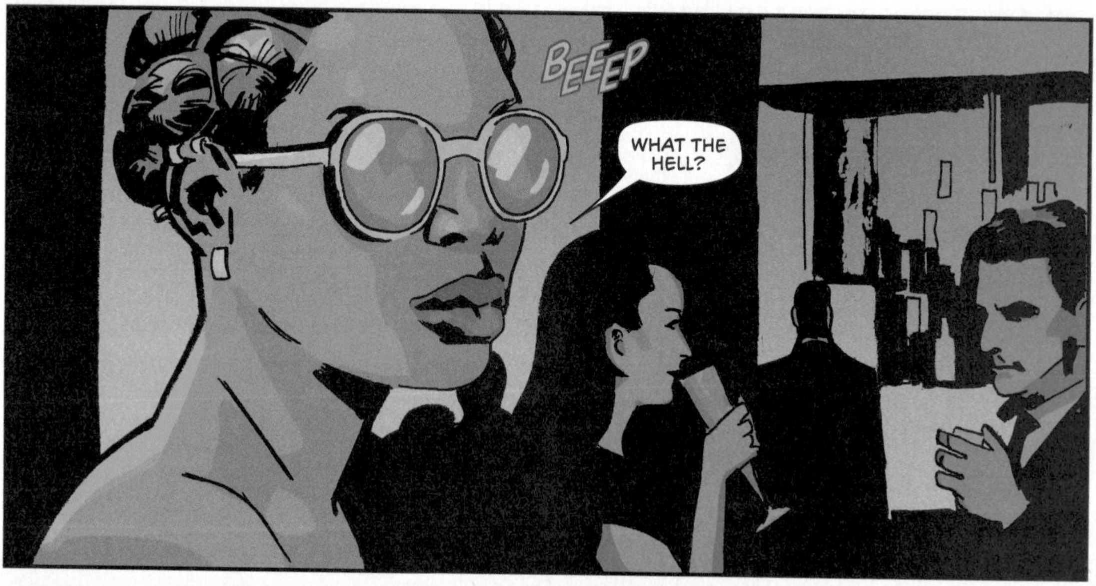
BEEEEP
WHAT THE HELL?

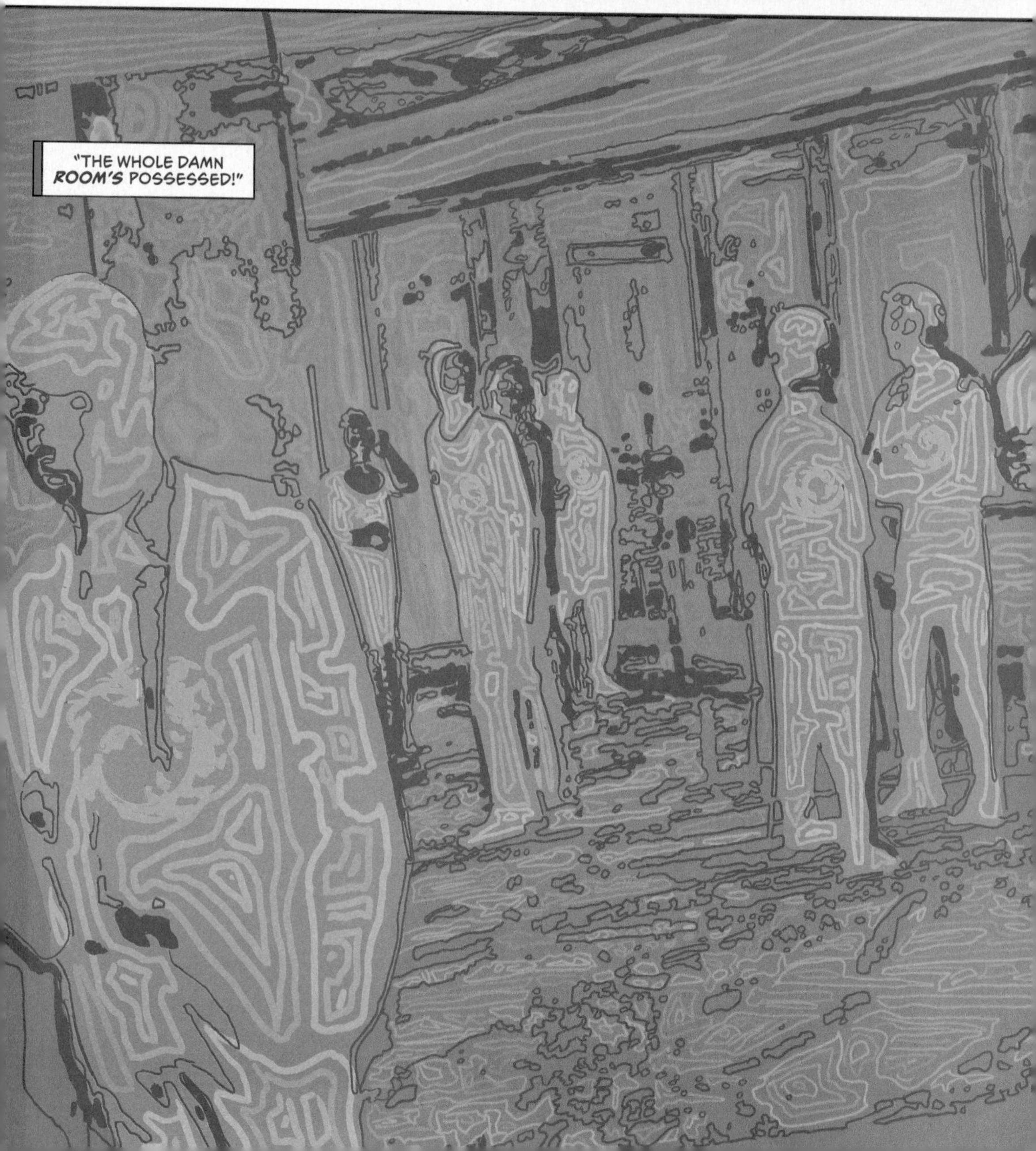
"THE WHOLE DAMN ROOM'S POSSESSED!"

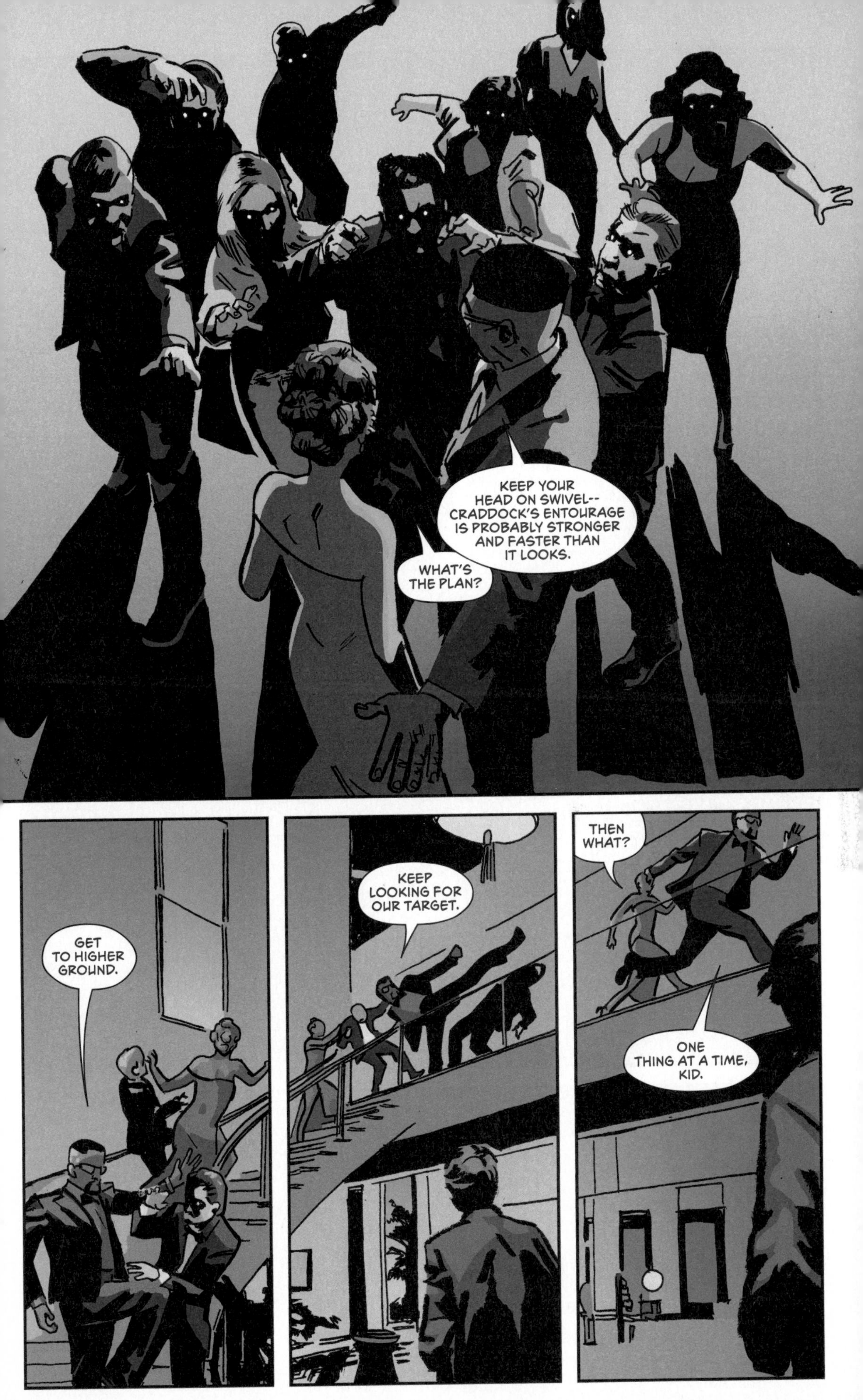
WHAT'S THE PLAN?
KEEP YOUR HEAD ON SWIVEL-- CRADDOCK'S ENTOURAGE IS PROBABLY STRONGER AND FASTER THAN IT LOOKS.
GET TO HIGHER GROUND.
KEEP LOOKING FOR OUR TARGET.
THEN WHAT?
ONE THING AT A TIME, KID.

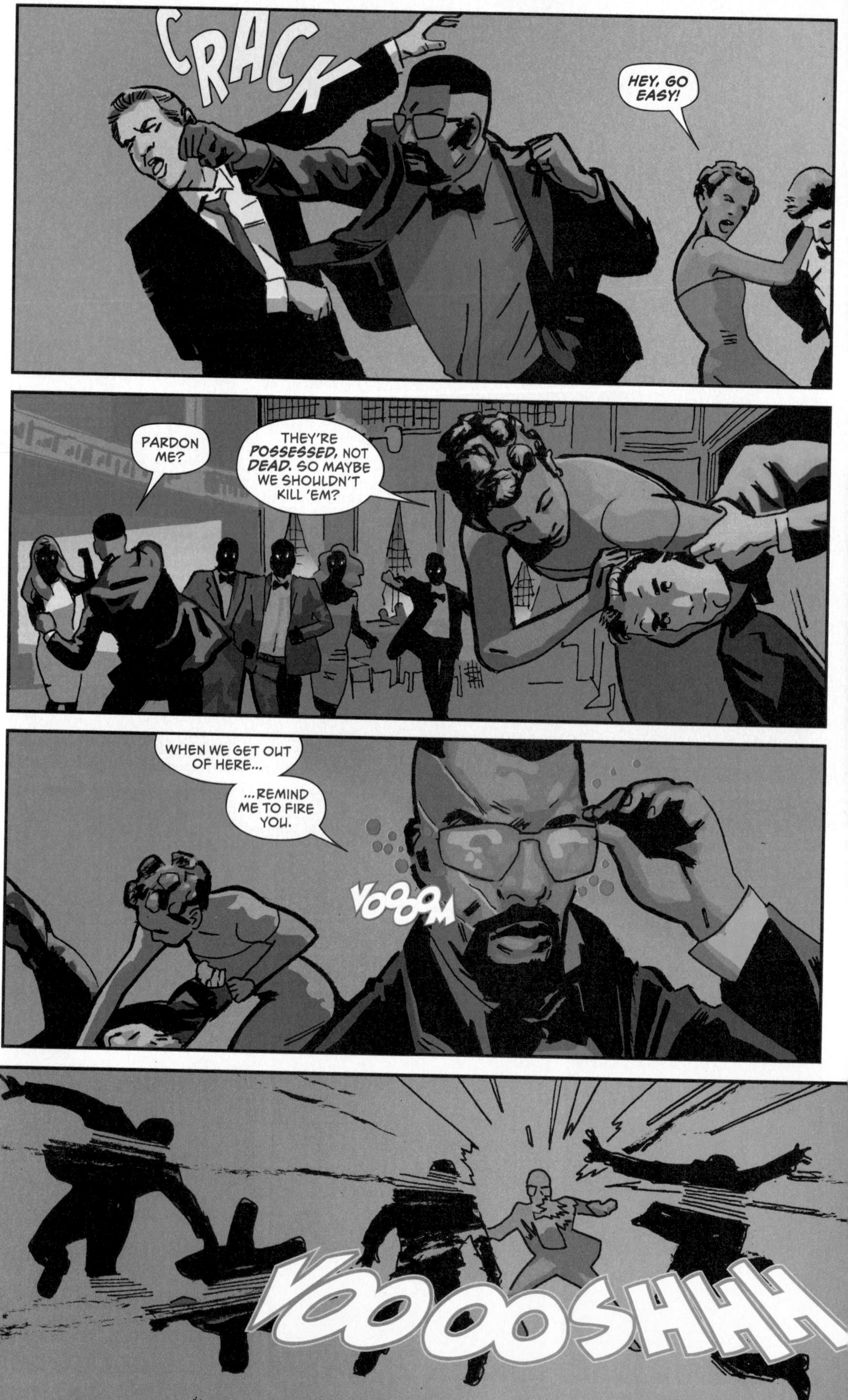
CRACK
HEY, GO EASY!
PARDON ME?
THEY'RE *POSSESSED*, NOT *DEAD*. SO MAYBE WE SHOULDN'T KILL 'EM?
WHEN WE GET OUT OF HERE...
...REMIND ME TO FIRE YOU.
VOOOOM
VOOOOSHHH

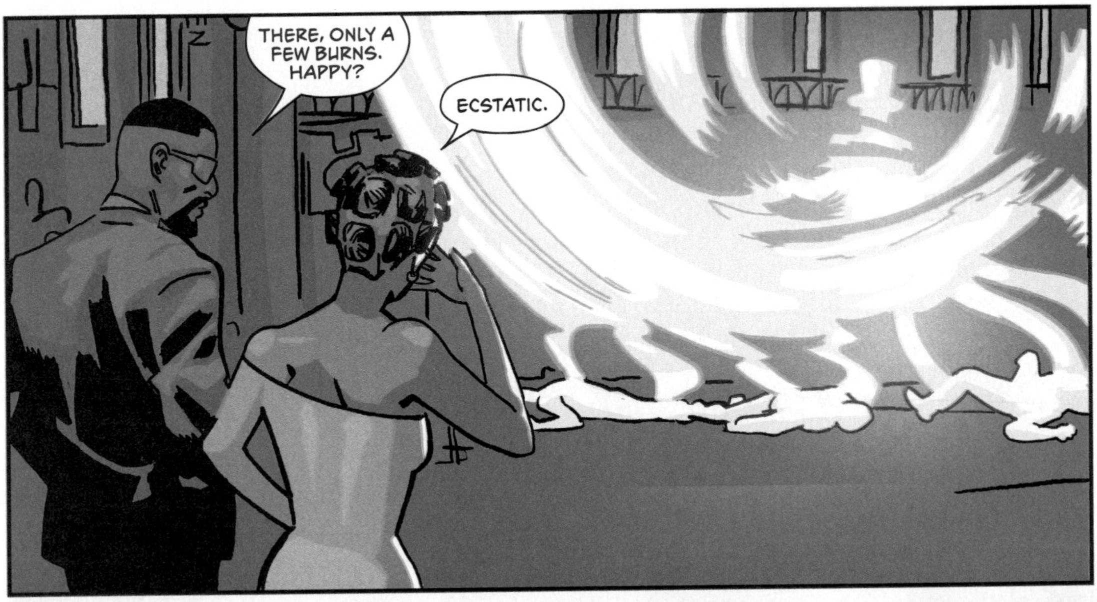
THERE, ONLY A FEW BURNS. HAPPY?
ECSTATIC.

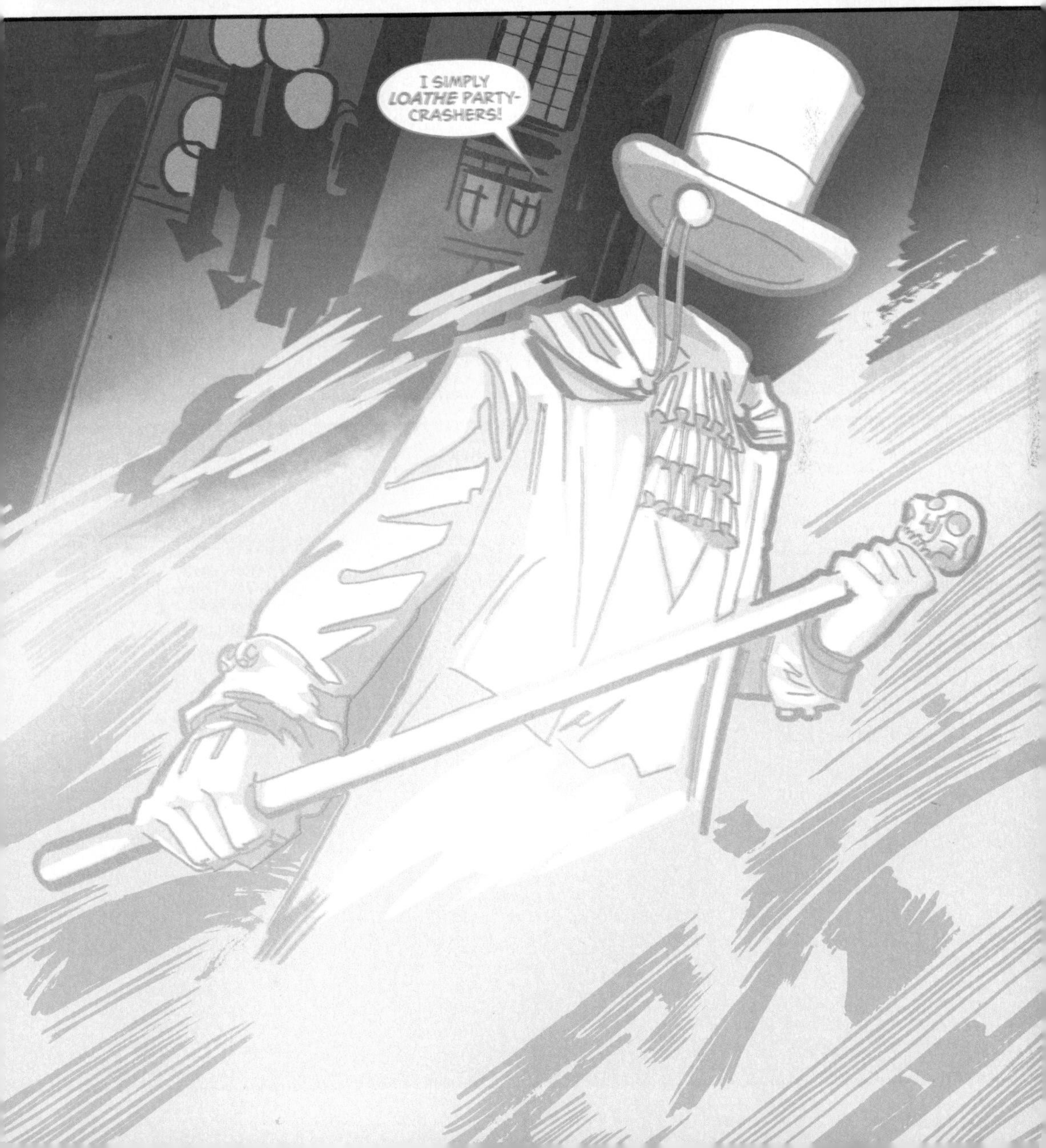
I SIMPLY LOATHE PARTY-CRASHERS!

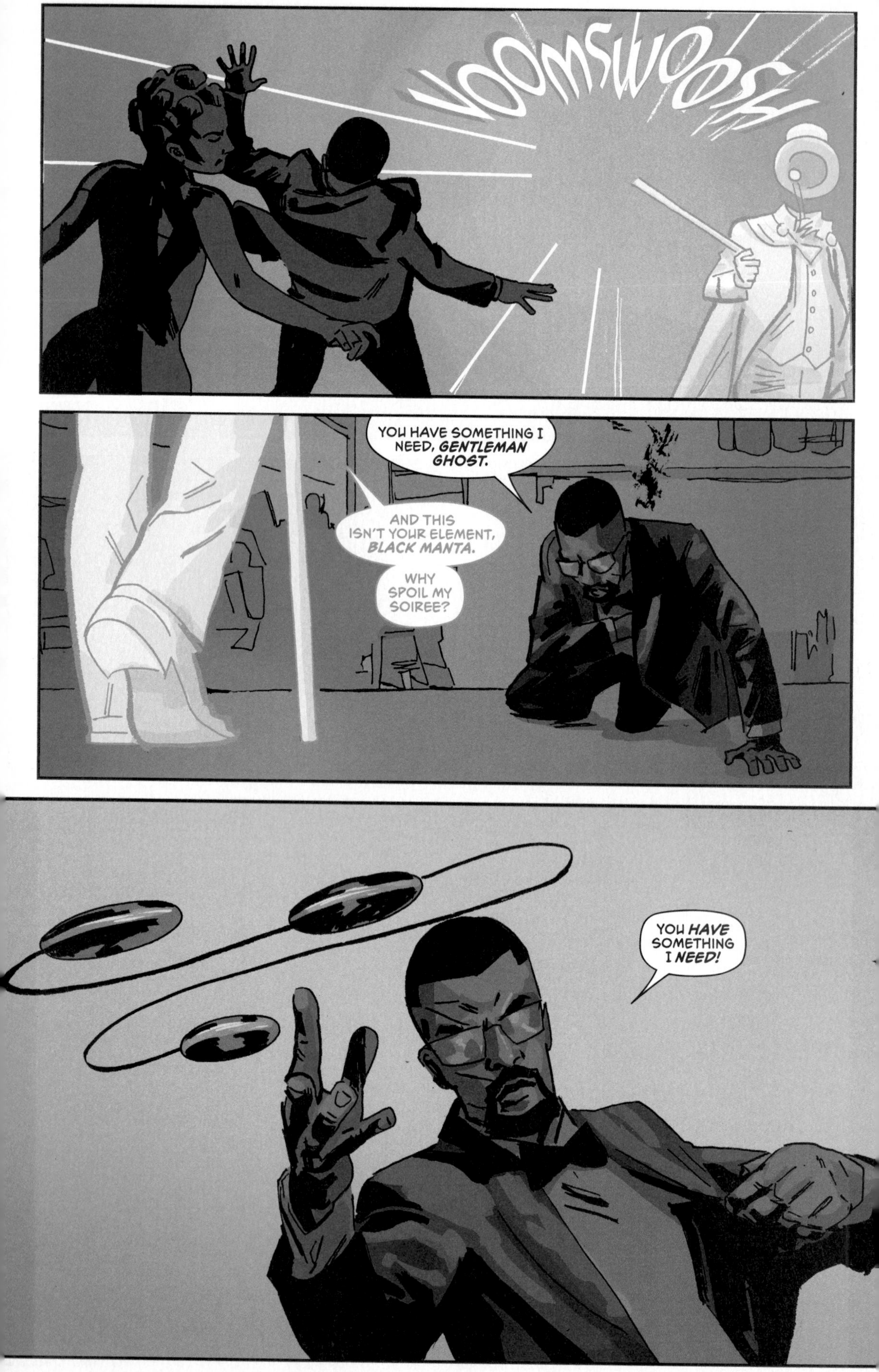
VOOMSWOOSH
YOU HAVE SOMETHING I NEED, GENTLEMAN GHOST.
AND THIS ISN'T YOUR ELEMENT, BLACK MANTA.
WHY SPOIL MY SOIREE?
YOU HAVE SOMETHING I NEED!

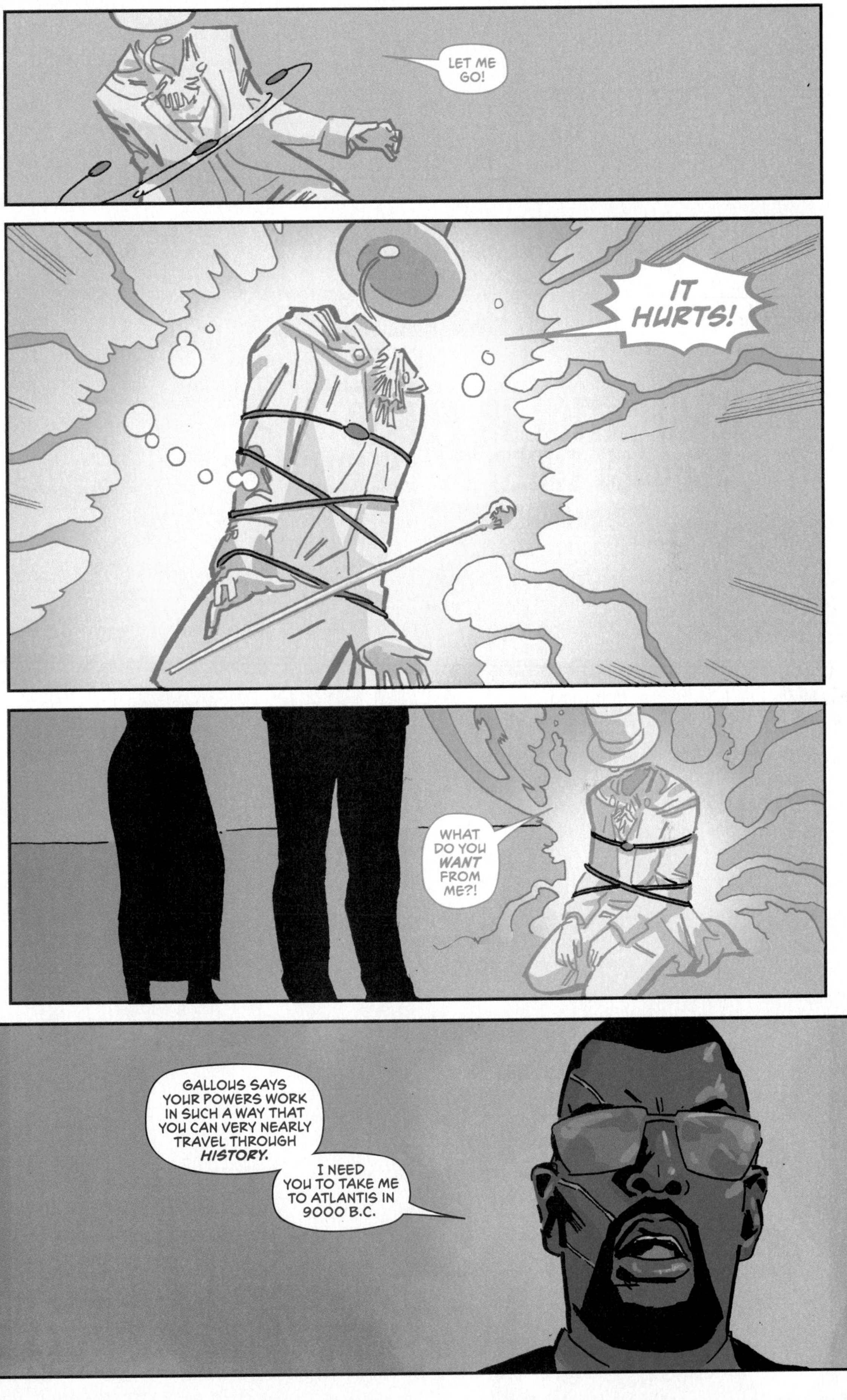
LET ME GO!
IT HURTS!
WHAT DO YOU *WANT* FROM ME?!
GALLOWS SAYS YOUR POWERS WORK IN SUCH A WAY THAT YOU CAN VERY NEARLY TRAVEL THROUGH ***HISTORY.***
I NEED YOU TO TAKE ME TO ATLANTIS IN 9000 B.C.

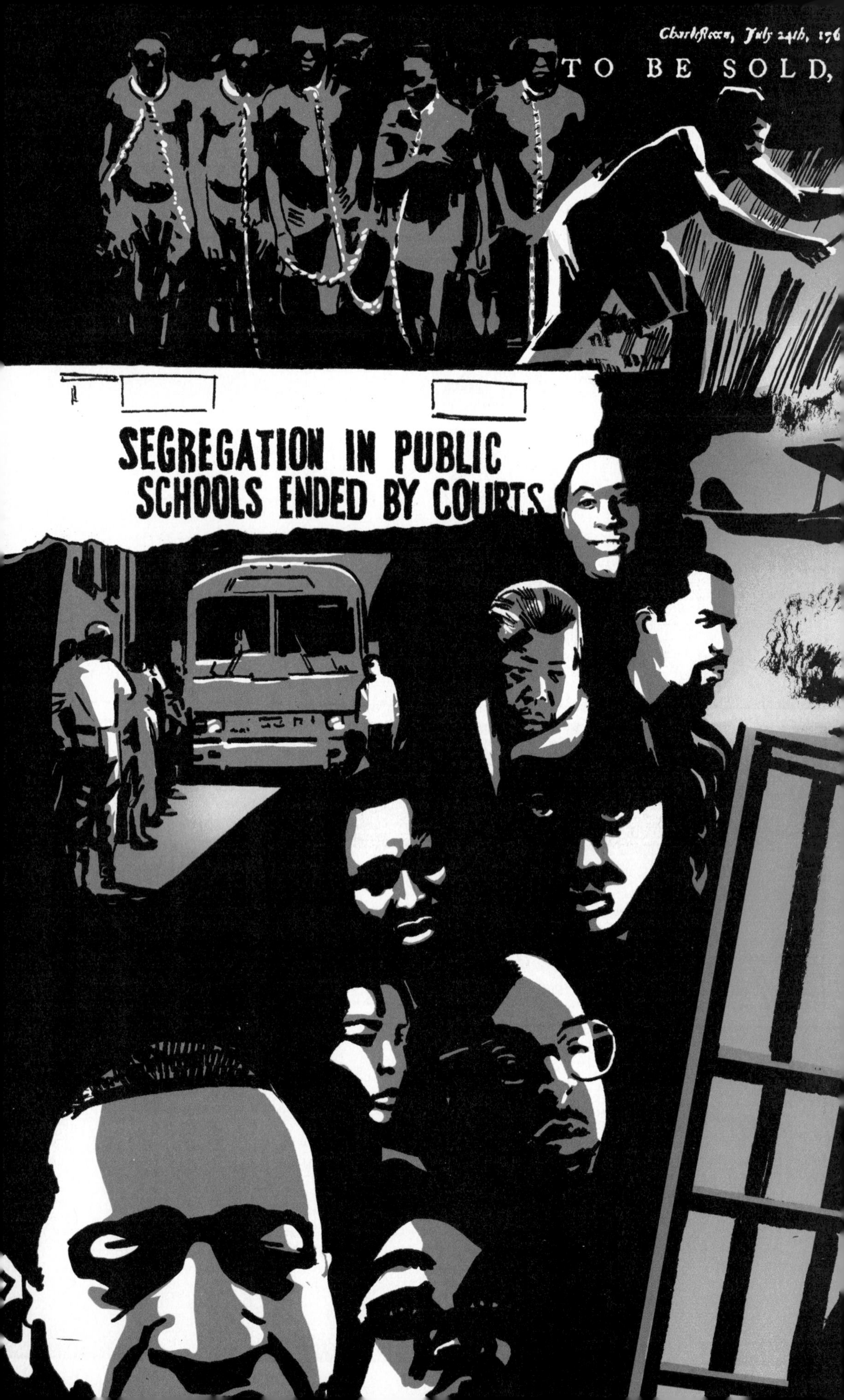
Charlestown, July 24th, 176
TO BE SOLD,
SEGREGATION IN PUBLIC SCHOOLS ENDED BY COURTS

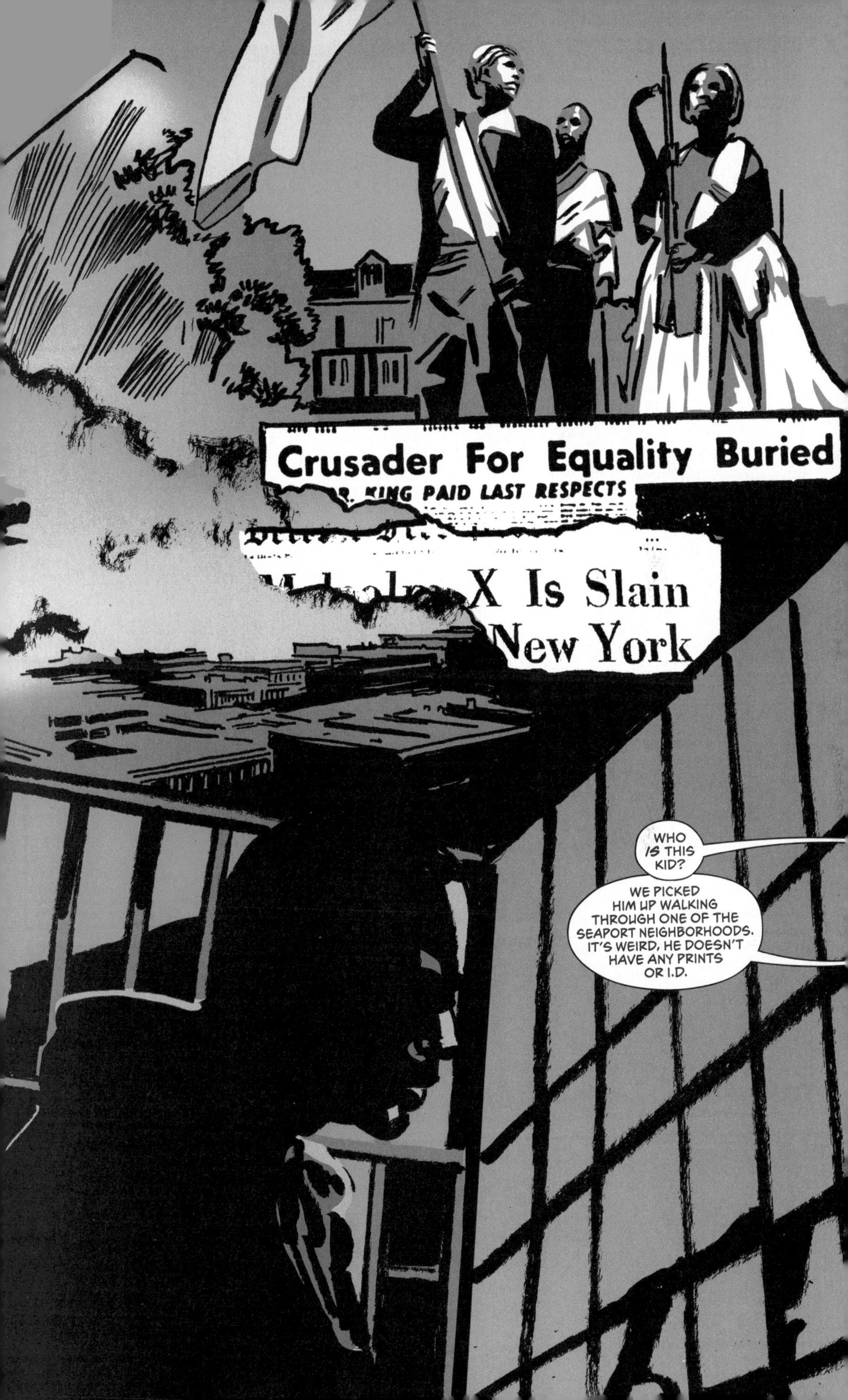
Crusader For Equality Buried
KING PAID LAST RESPECTS
X Is Slain
New York
WHO *IS* THIS KID?
WE PICKED HIM UP WALKING THROUGH ONE OF THE SEAPORT NEIGHBORHOODS. IT'S WEIRD, HE DOESN'T HAVE ANY PRINTS OR I.D.

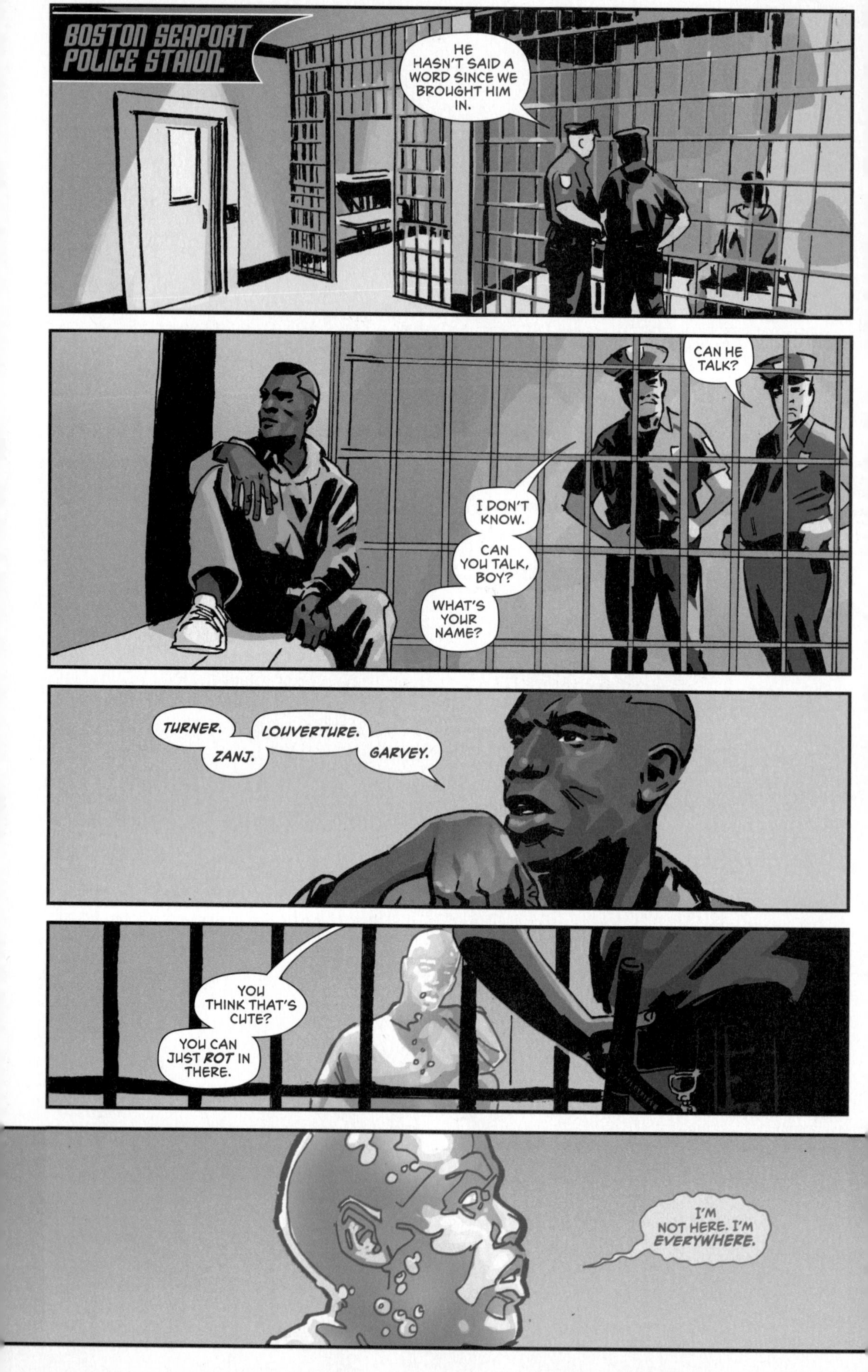
BOSTON SEAPORT POLICE STAION.
HE HASN'T SAID A WORD SINCE WE BROUGHT HIM IN.
CAN HE TALK?
I DON'T KNOW.
CAN YOU TALK, BOY?
WHAT'S YOUR NAME?
TURNER.
ZANJ.
LOUVERTURE.
GARVEY.
YOU THINK THAT'S CUTE?
YOU CAN JUST ROT IN THERE.
I'M NOT HERE. I'M EVERYWHERE.

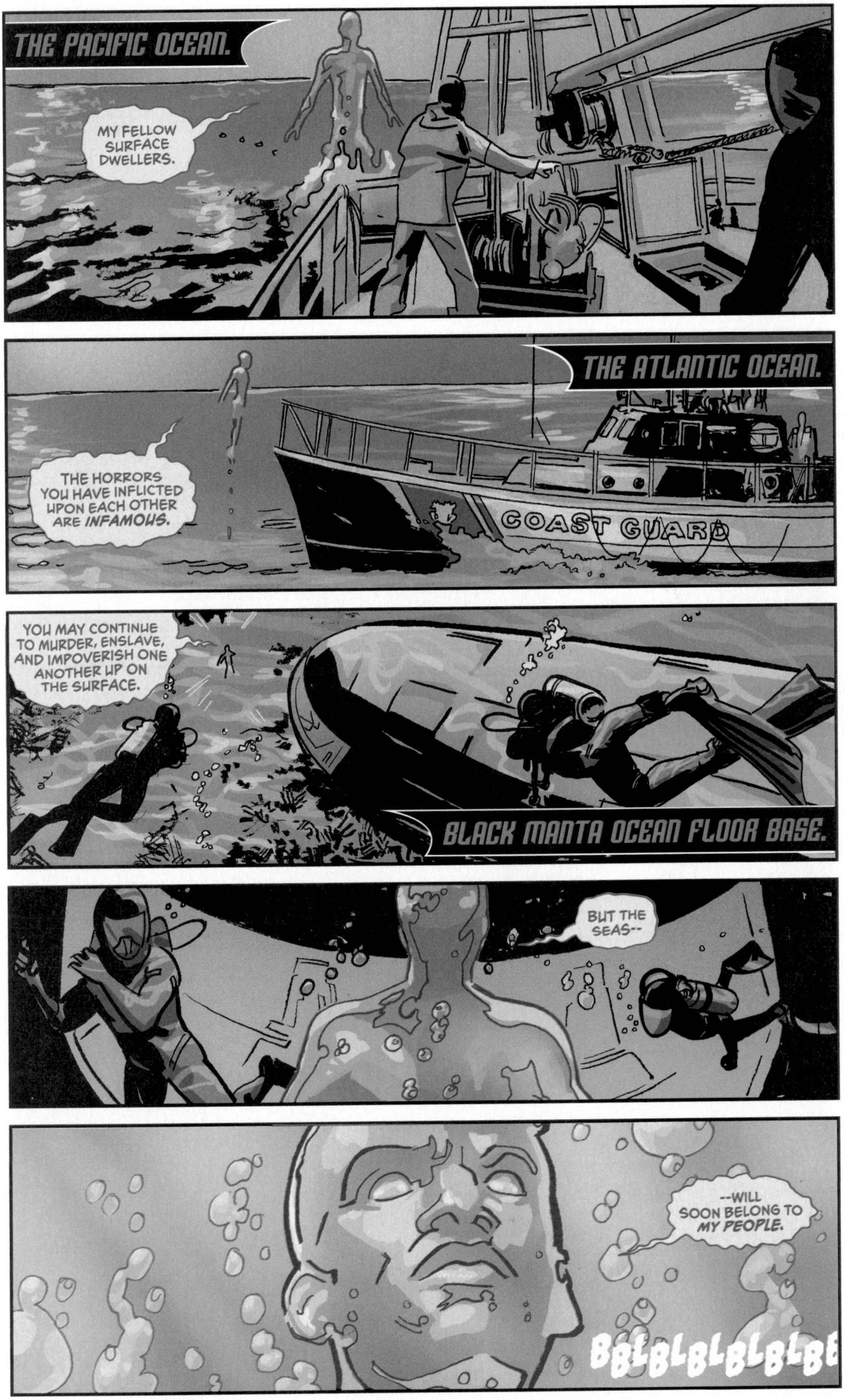
THE PACIFIC OCEAN.
MY FELLOW SURFACE DWELLERS.
THE ATLANTIC OCEAN.
THE HORRORS YOU HAVE INFLICTED UPON EACH OTHER ARE *INFAMOUS*.
COAST GUARD
YOU MAY CONTINUE TO MURDER, ENSLAVE, AND IMPOVERISH ONE ANOTHER UP ON THE SURFACE.
BLACK MANTA OCEAN FLOOR BASE.
BUT THE SEAS--
--WILL SOON BELONG TO *MY PEOPLE*.
BBLBLBLBLBLBLB

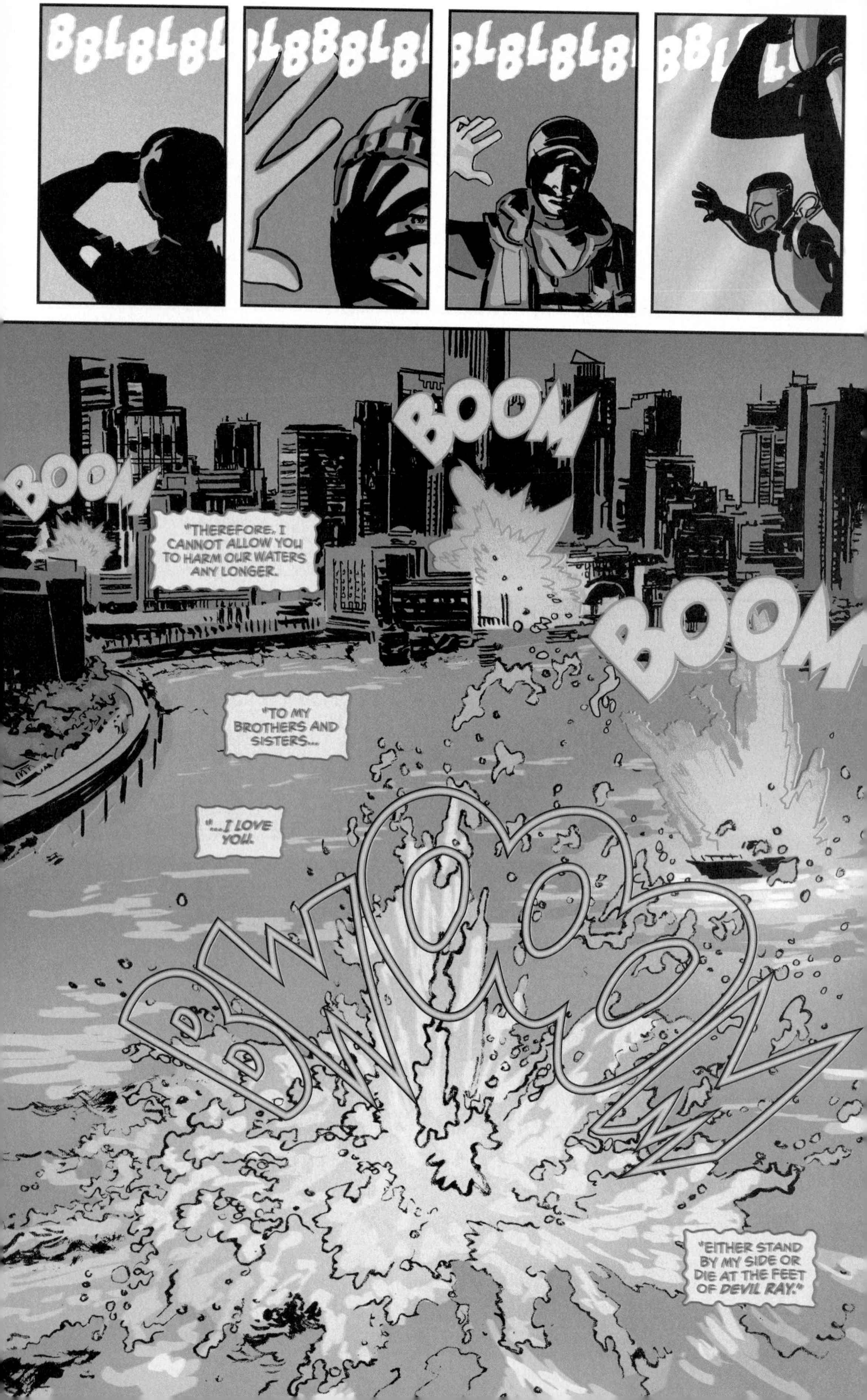
BBLBLBL
BLBBBLB
BLBLBLB
BBL
BOOM
BOOM
"THEREFORE, I CANNOT ALLOW YOU TO HARM OUR WATERS ANY LONGER.
BOOM
"TO MY BROTHERS AND SISTERS...
"...I LOVE YOU.
BWOOOM
"EITHER STAND BY MY SIDE OR DIE AT THE FEET OF *DEVIL RAY*."

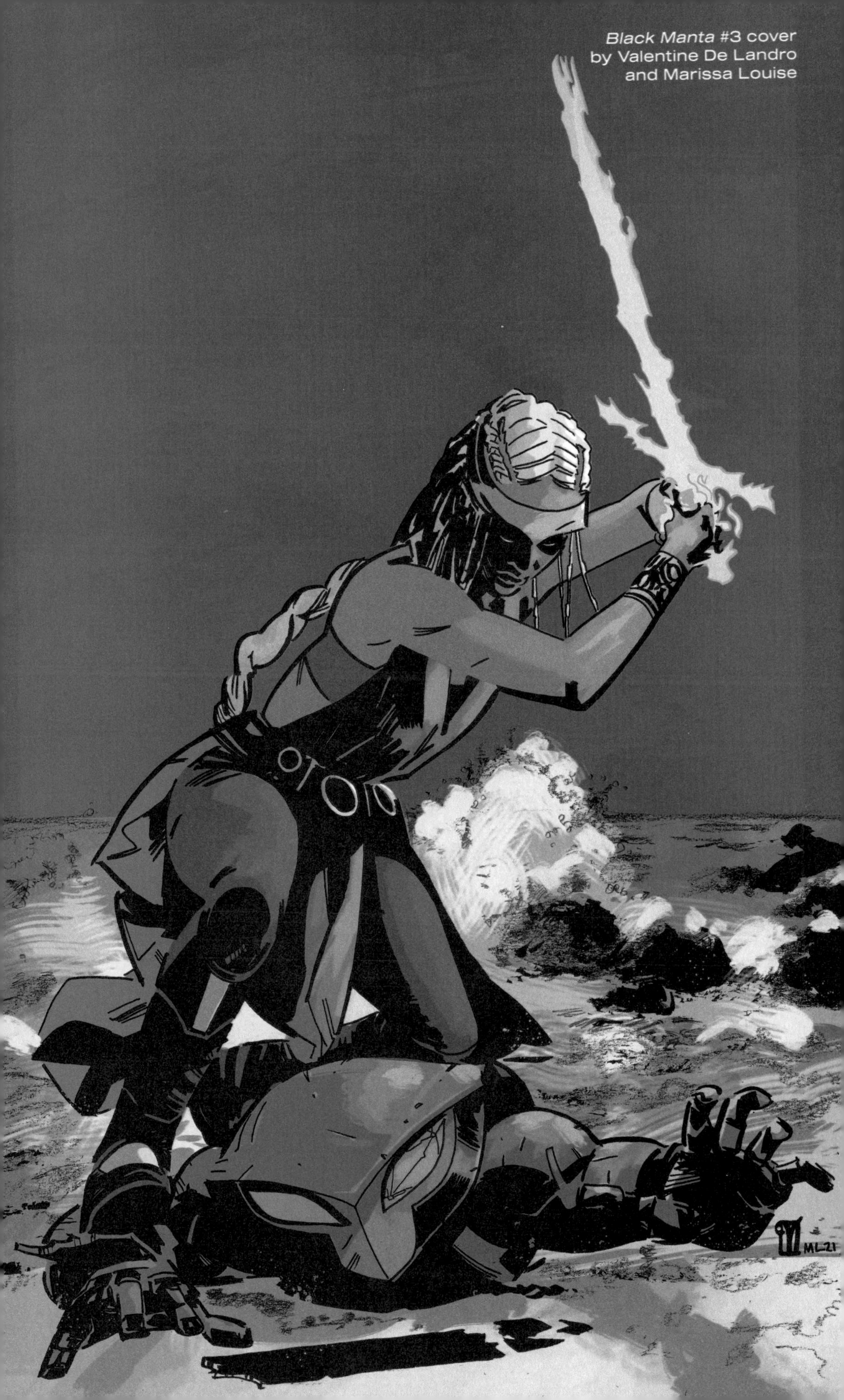

Black Manta #3 cover
by Valentine De Landro
and Marissa Louise

Black Manta #3 variant cover by Sanford Greene

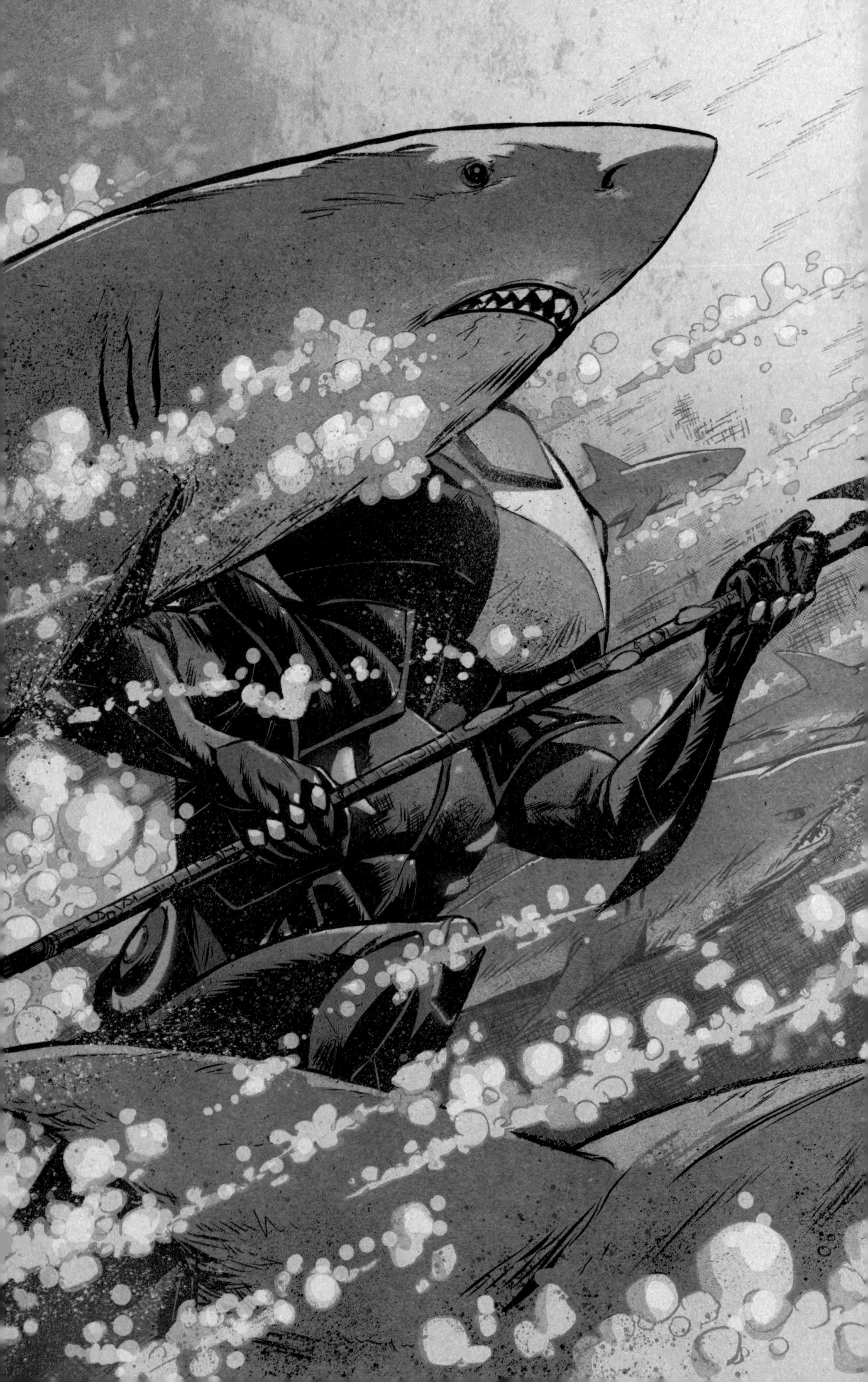

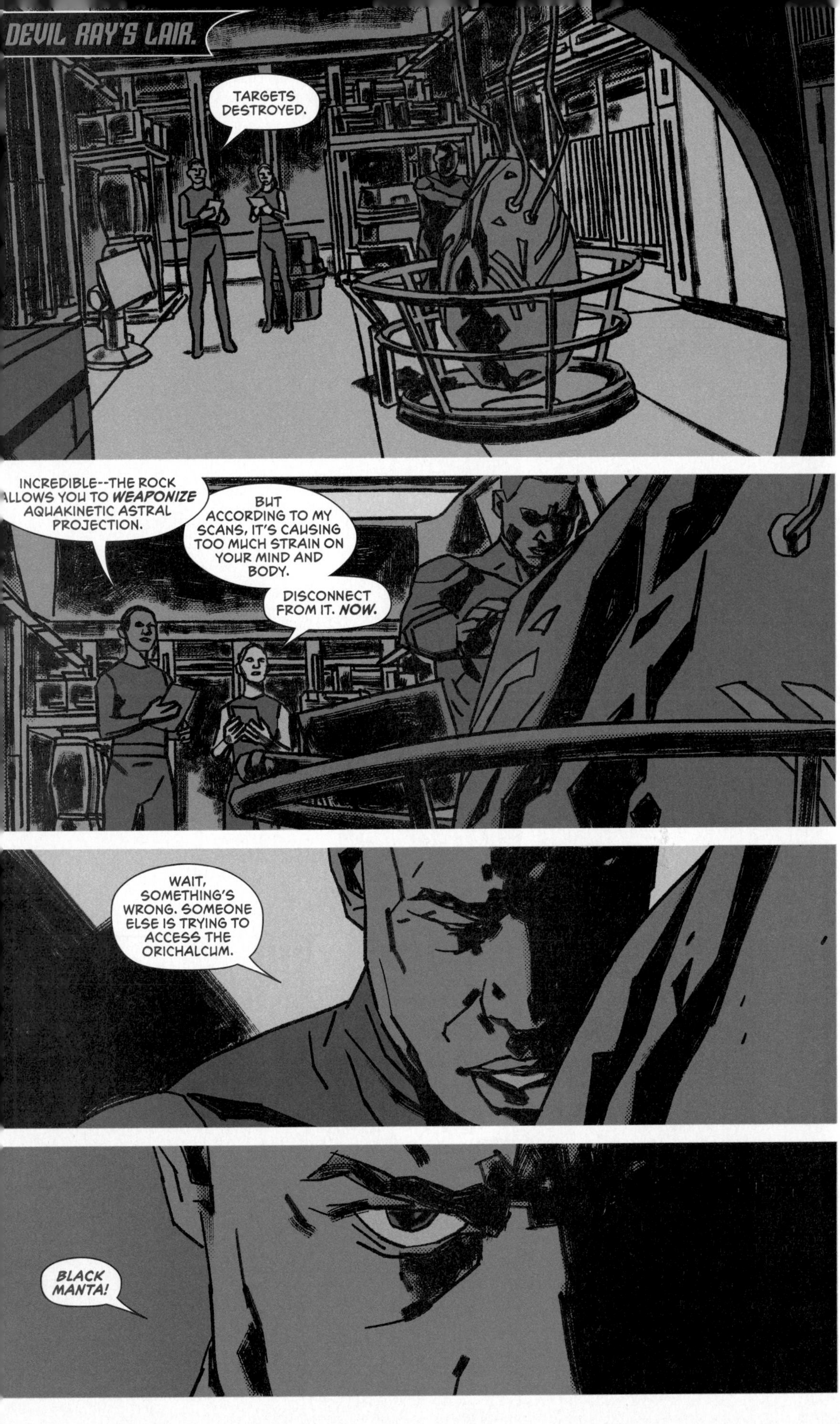
DEVIL RAY'S LAIR.
TARGETS DESTROYED.
INCREDIBLE--THE ROCK ALLOWS YOU TO *WEAPONIZE* AQUAKINETIC ASTRAL PROJECTION.
BUT ACCORDING TO MY SCANS, IT'S CAUSING TOO MUCH STRAIN ON YOUR MIND AND BODY.
DISCONNECT FROM IT. *NOW.*
WAIT, SOMETHING'S WRONG. SOMEONE ELSE IS TRYING TO ACCESS THE ORICHALCUM.
BLACK MANTA!

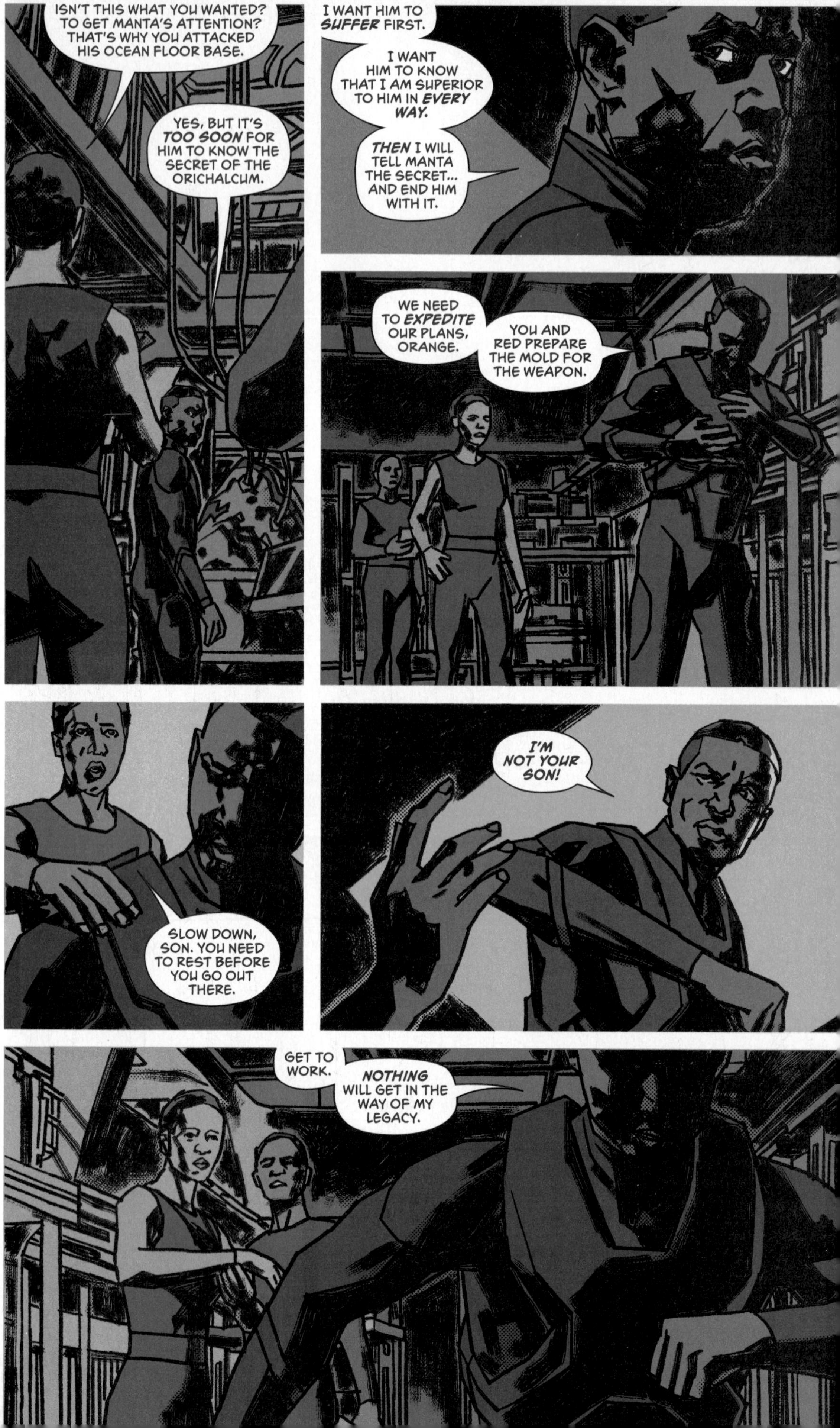
ISN'T THIS WHAT YOU WANTED? TO GET MANTA'S ATTENTION? THAT'S WHY YOU ATTACKED HIS OCEAN FLOOR BASE.
YES, BUT IT'S *TOO SOON* FOR HIM TO KNOW THE SECRET OF THE ORICHALCUM.
I WANT HIM TO *SUFFER* FIRST.
I WANT HIM TO KNOW THAT I AM SUPERIOR TO HIM IN *EVERY WAY.*
THEN I WILL TELL MANTA THE SECRET... AND END HIM WITH IT.
WE NEED TO *EXPEDITE* OUR PLANS, ORANGE.
YOU AND RED PREPARE THE MOLD FOR THE WEAPON.
SLOW DOWN, SON. YOU NEED TO REST BEFORE YOU GO OUT THERE.
I'M NOT YOUR SON!
GET TO WORK.
NOTHING WILL GET IN THE WAY OF MY LEGACY.

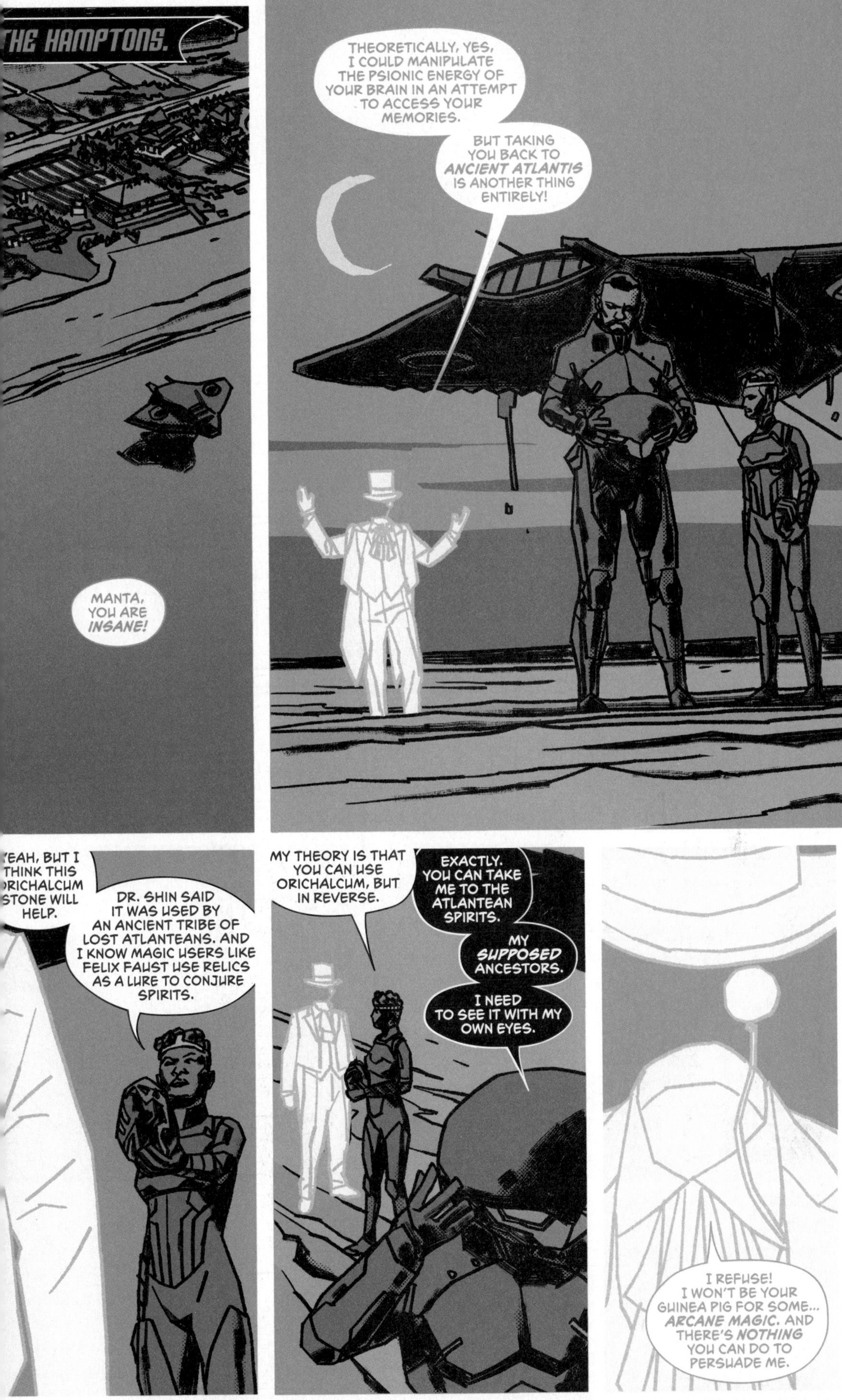
THE HAMPTONS.
THEORETICALLY, YES, I COULD MANIPULATE THE PSIONIC ENERGY OF YOUR BRAIN IN AN ATTEMPT TO ACCESS YOUR MEMORIES.
BUT TAKING YOU BACK TO *ANCIENT ATLANTIS* IS ANOTHER THING ENTIRELY!
MANTA, YOU ARE *INSANE!*
YEAH, BUT I THINK THIS ORICHALCUM STONE WILL HELP.
DR. SHIN SAID IT WAS USED BY AN ANCIENT TRIBE OF LOST ATLANTEANS. AND I KNOW MAGIC USERS LIKE FELIX FAUST USE RELICS AS A LURE TO CONJURE SPIRITS.
MY THEORY IS THAT YOU CAN USE ORICHALCUM, BUT IN REVERSE.
EXACTLY. YOU CAN TAKE ME TO THE ATLANTEAN SPIRITS.
MY *SUPPOSED* ANCESTORS.
I NEED TO SEE IT WITH MY OWN EYES.
I REFUSE! I WON'T BE YOUR GUINEA PIG FOR SOME... *ARCANE MAGIC.* AND THERE'S *NOTHING* YOU CAN DO TO PERSUADE ME.

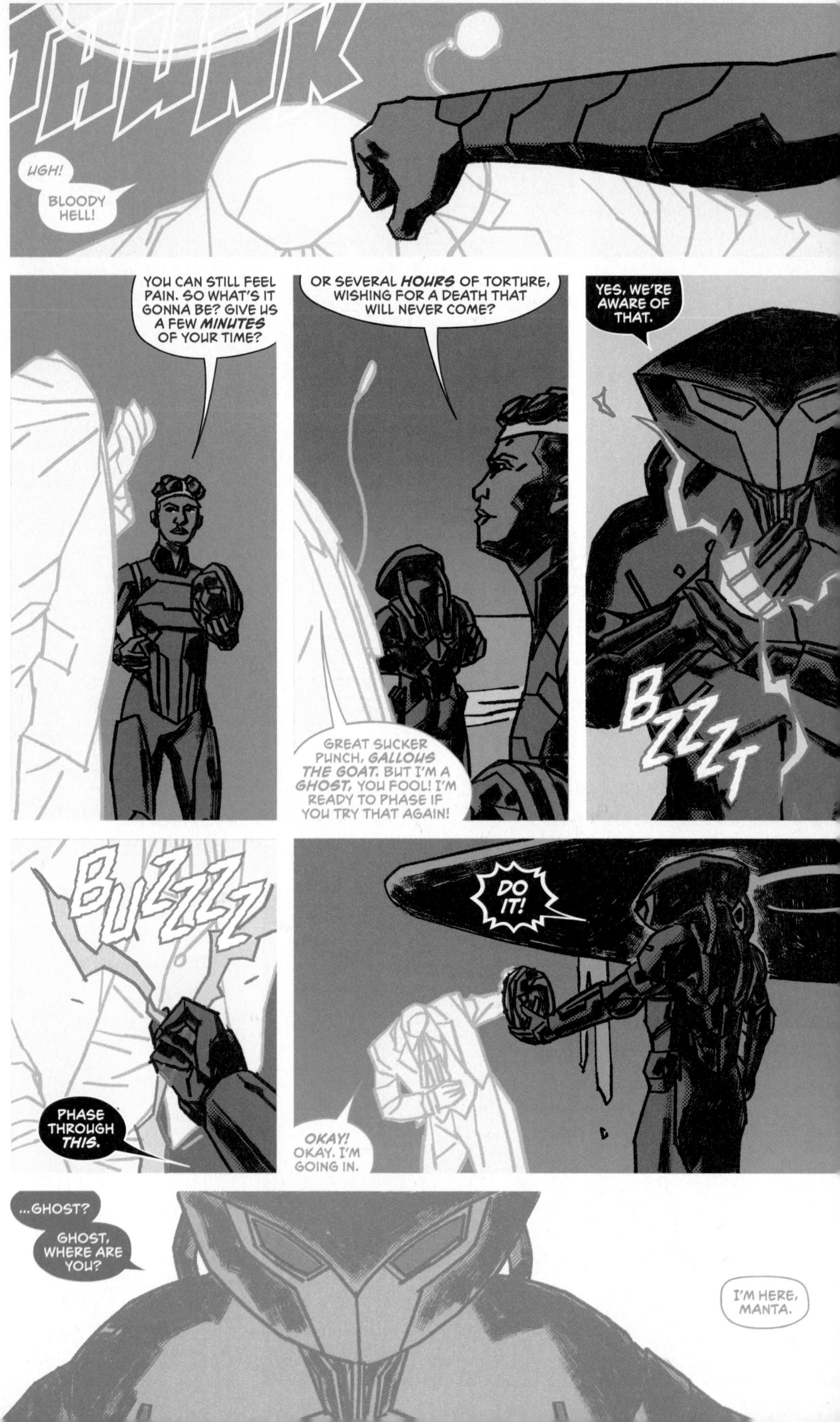
THUNK
UGH!
BLOODY HELL!
YOU CAN STILL FEEL PAIN. SO WHAT'S IT GONNA BE? GIVE US A FEW MINUTES OF YOUR TIME?
OR SEVERAL HOURS OF TORTURE, WISHING FOR A DEATH THAT WILL NEVER COME?
GREAT SUCKER PUNCH, GALLOUS THE GOAT. BUT I'M A GHOST, YOU FOOL! I'M READY TO PHASE IF YOU TRY THAT AGAIN!
YES, WE'RE AWARE OF THAT.
BZZZT
BUZZZZ
PHASE THROUGH THIS.
DO IT!
OKAY! OKAY. I'M GOING IN.
...GHOST?
GHOST, WHERE ARE YOU?
I'M HERE, MANTA.

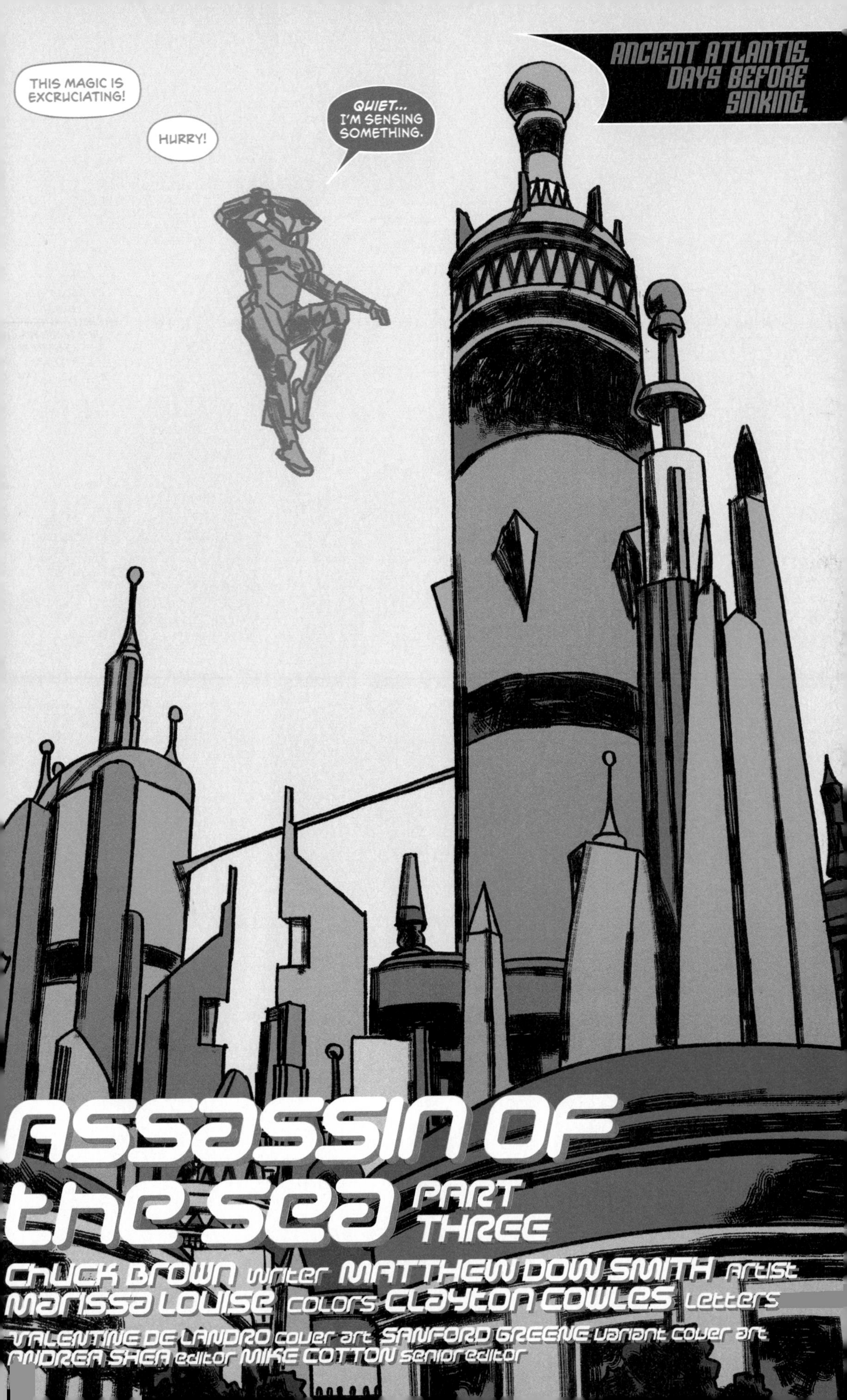
ANCIENT ATLANTIS. DAYS BEFORE SINKING.
THIS MAGIC IS EXCRUCIATING!
HURRY!
QUIET... I'M SENSING SOMETHING.
ASSASSIN OF THE SEA PART THREE
CHUCK BROWN writer MATTHEW DOW SMITH artist
MARISSA LOUISE colors CLAYTON COWLES letters
VALENTINE DE LANDRO cover art SANFORD GREENE variant cover art
ANDREA SHEA editor MIKE COTTON senior editor

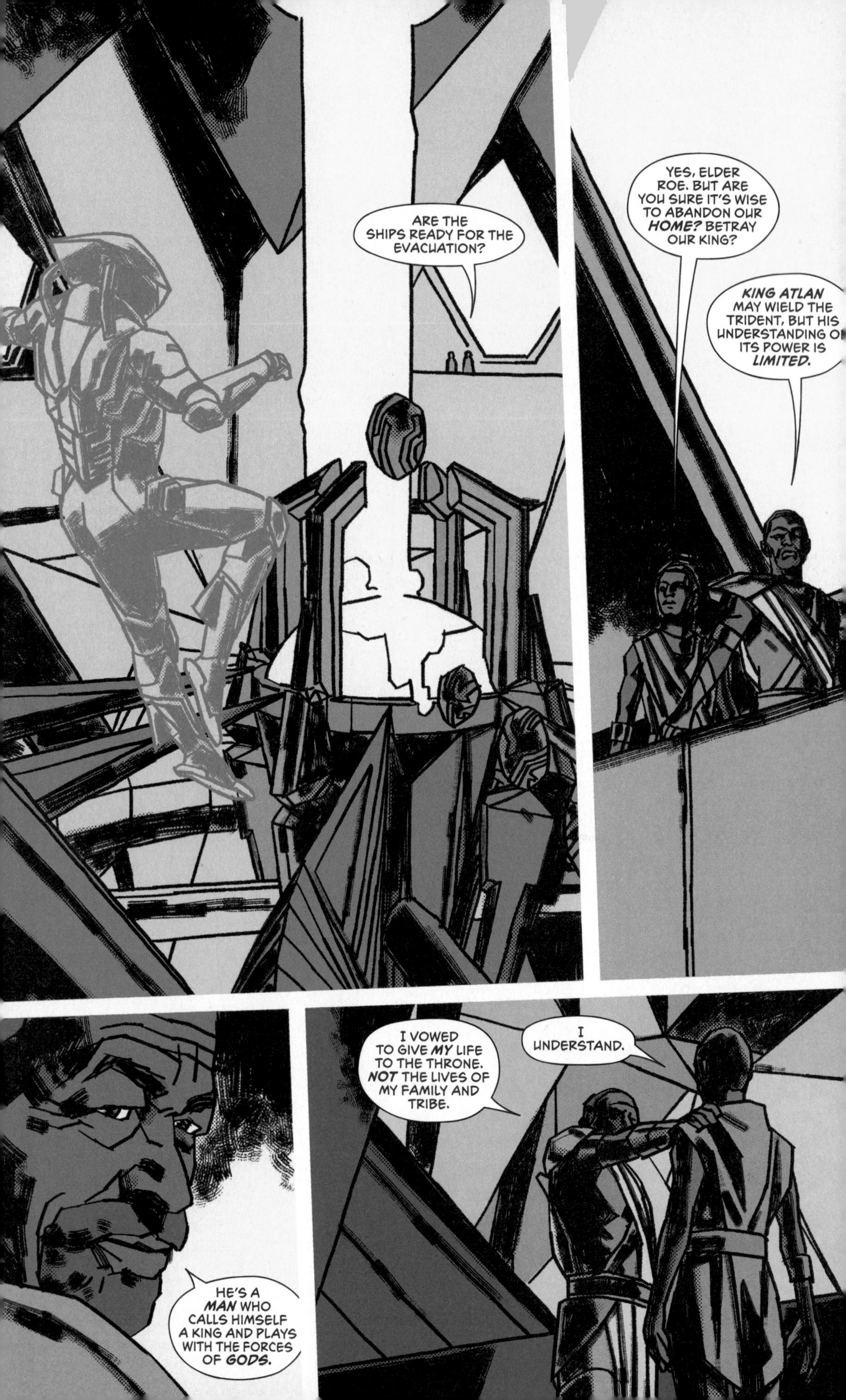
ARE THE SHIPS READY FOR THE EVACUATION?
YES, ELDER ROE. BUT ARE YOU SURE IT'S WISE TO ABANDON OUR HOME? BETRAY OUR KING?
KING ATLAN MAY WIELD THE TRIDENT, BUT HIS UNDERSTANDING OF ITS POWER IS LIMITED.
HE'S A MAN WHO CALLS HIMSELF A KING AND PLAYS WITH THE FORCES OF GODS.
I VOWED TO GIVE MY LIFE TO THE THRONE. NOT THE LIVES OF MY FAMILY AND TRIBE.
I UNDERSTAND.

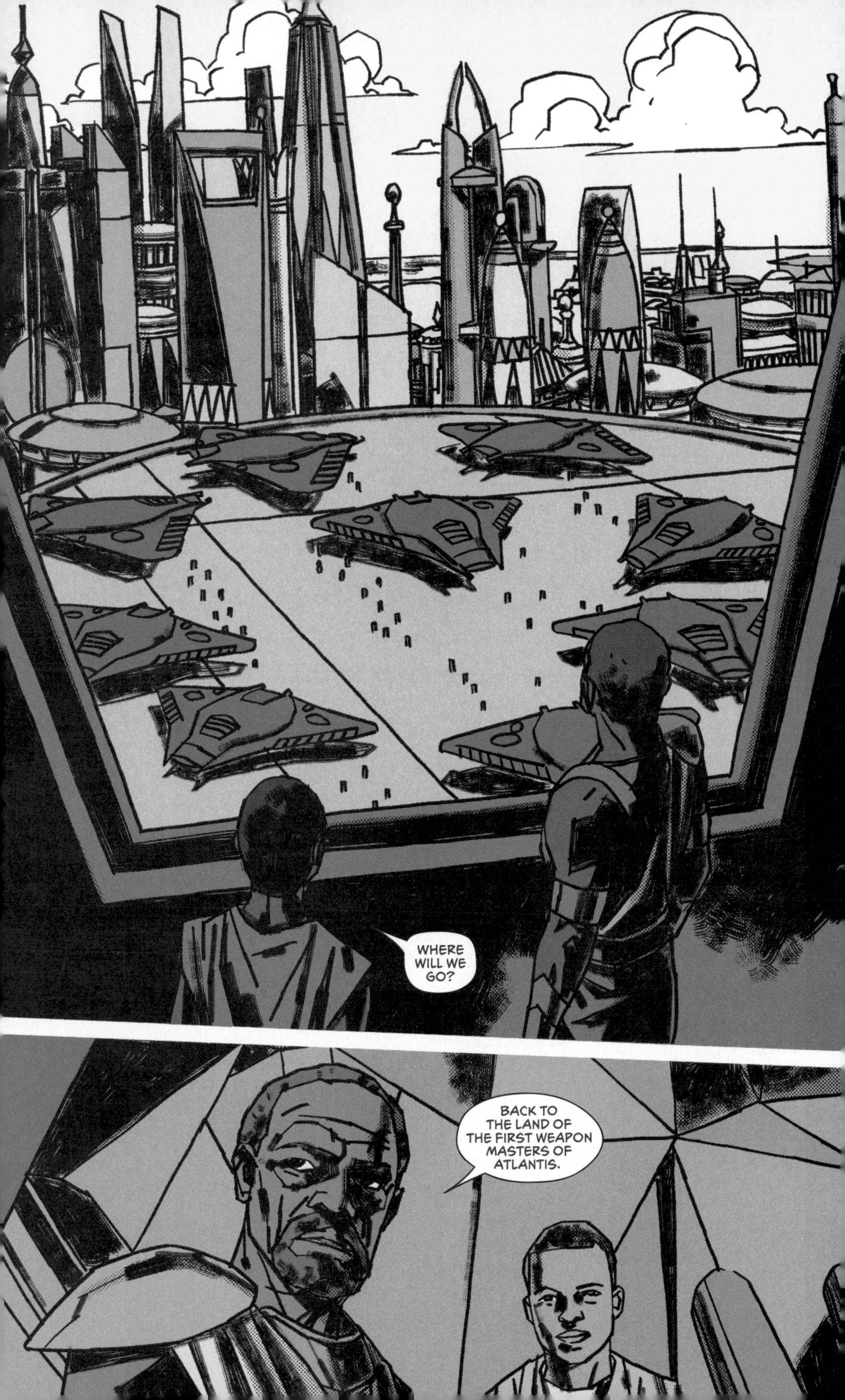
WHERE WILL WE GO?
BACK TO THE LAND OF THE FIRST WEAPON MASTERS OF ATLANTIS.

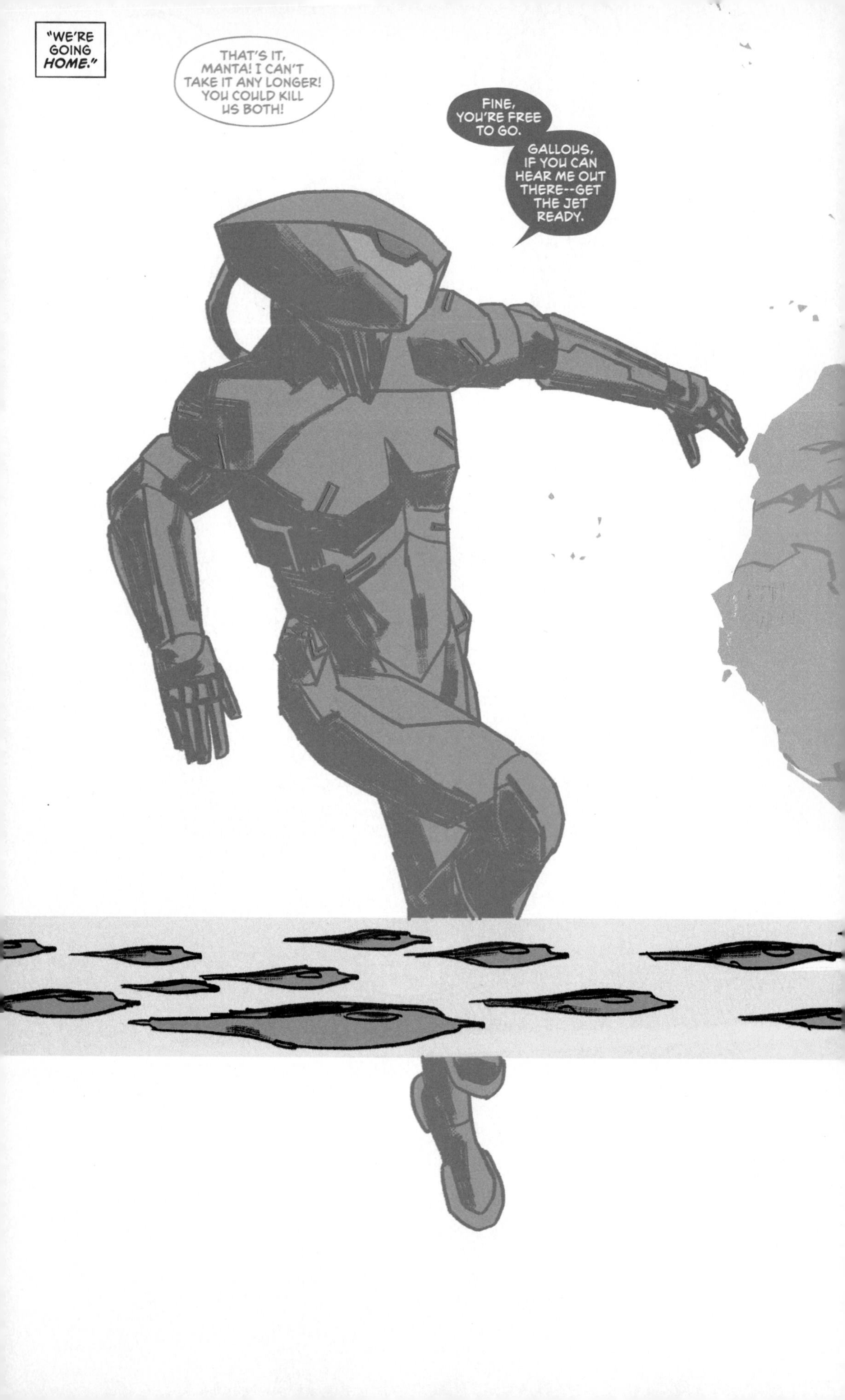

"WE'RE GOING HOME."
THAT'S IT, MANTA! I CAN'T TAKE IT ANY LONGER! YOU COULD KILL US BOTH!
FINE, YOU'RE FREE TO GO.
GALLOUS, IF YOU CAN HEAR ME OUT THERE--GET THE JET READY.

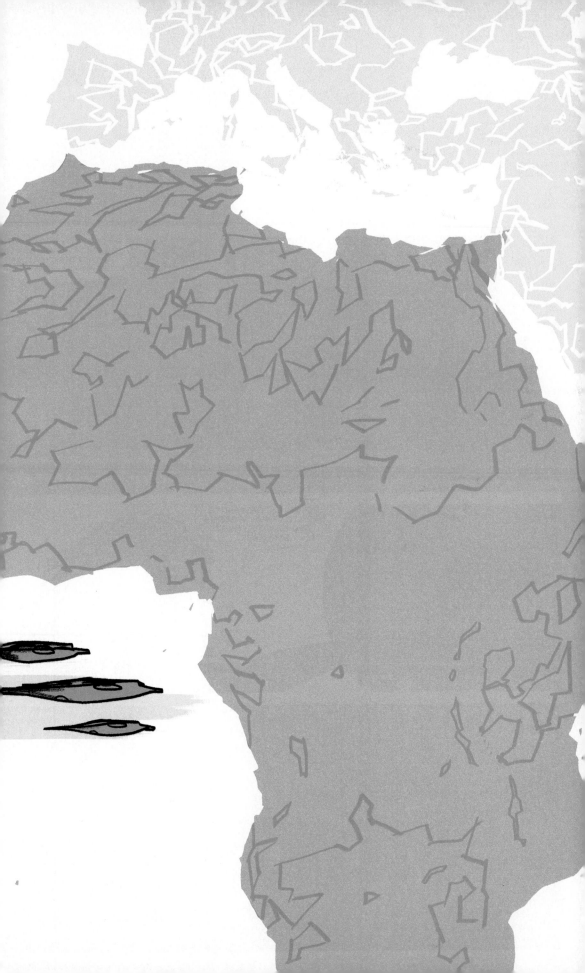

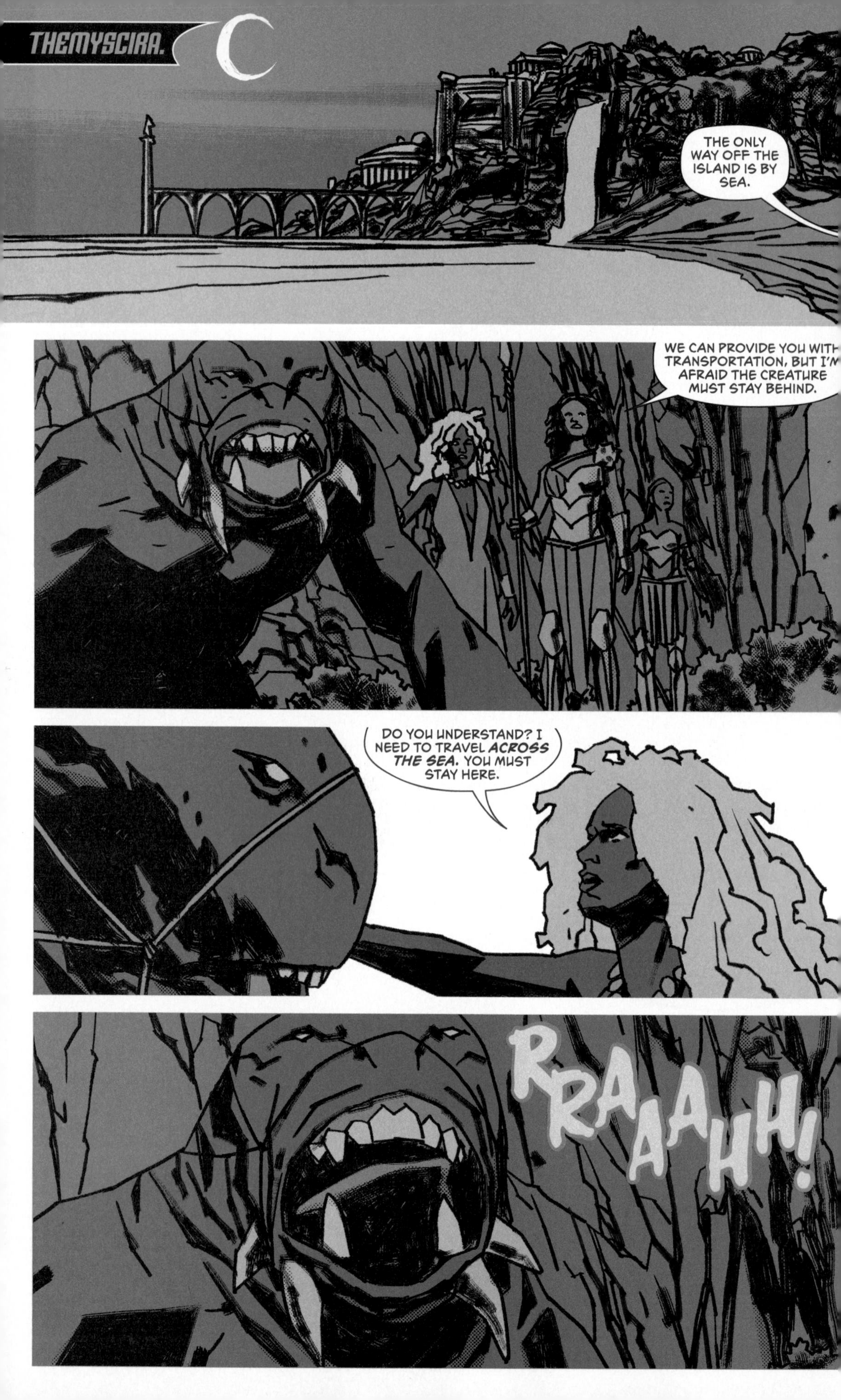
THEMYSCIRA.
THE ONLY WAY OFF THE ISLAND IS BY SEA.
WE CAN PROVIDE YOU WITH TRANSPORTATION, BUT I'M AFRAID THE CREATURE MUST STAY BEHIND.
DO YOU UNDERSTAND? I NEED TO TRAVEL ACROSS THE SEA. YOU MUST STAY HERE.
RRAAAHH!

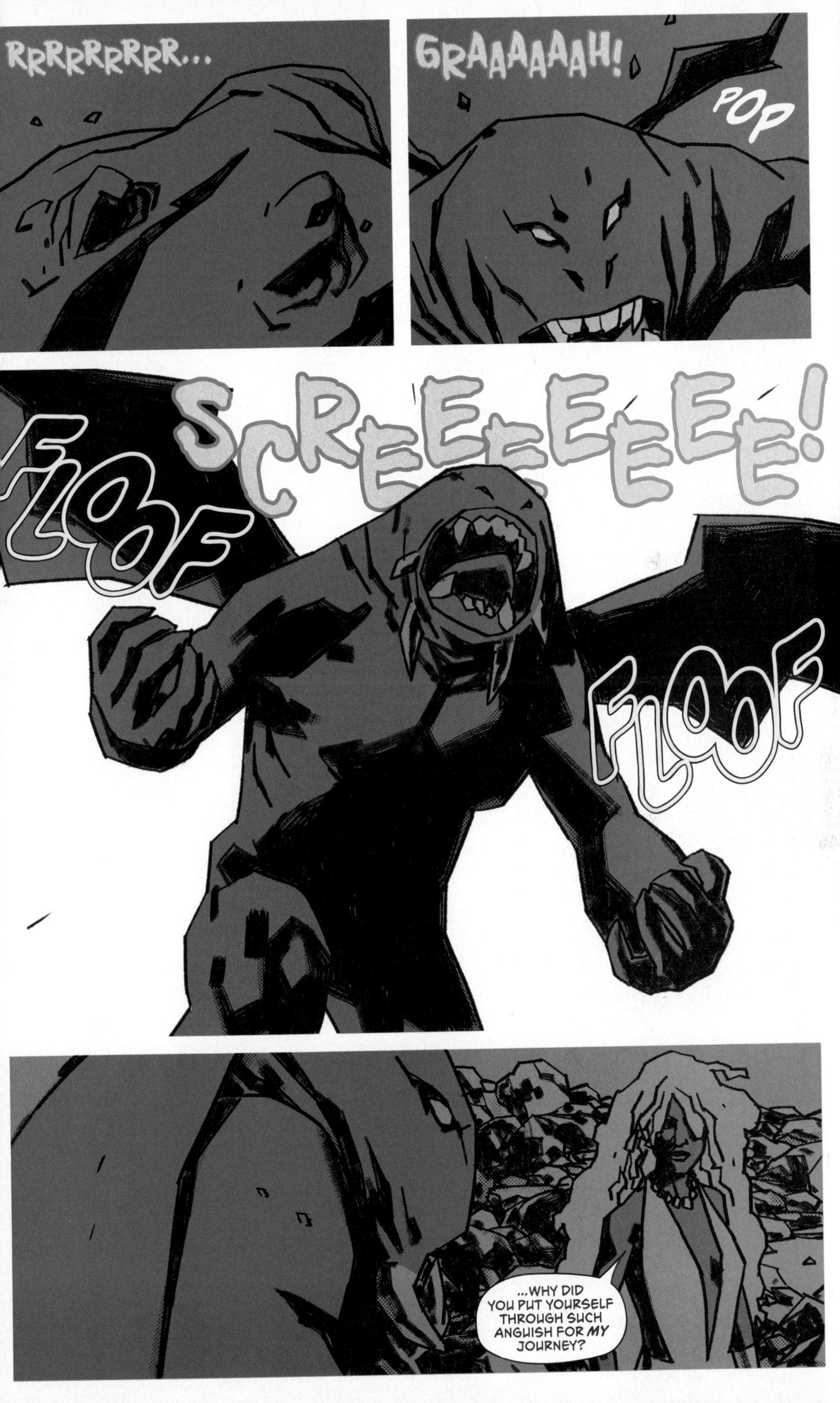
RRRRRRRRR...
GRAAAAAAH!
POP
SCREEEEEEE!
FLOOF
FLOOF
...WHY DID YOU PUT YOURSELF THROUGH SUCH ANGUISH FOR MY JOURNEY?

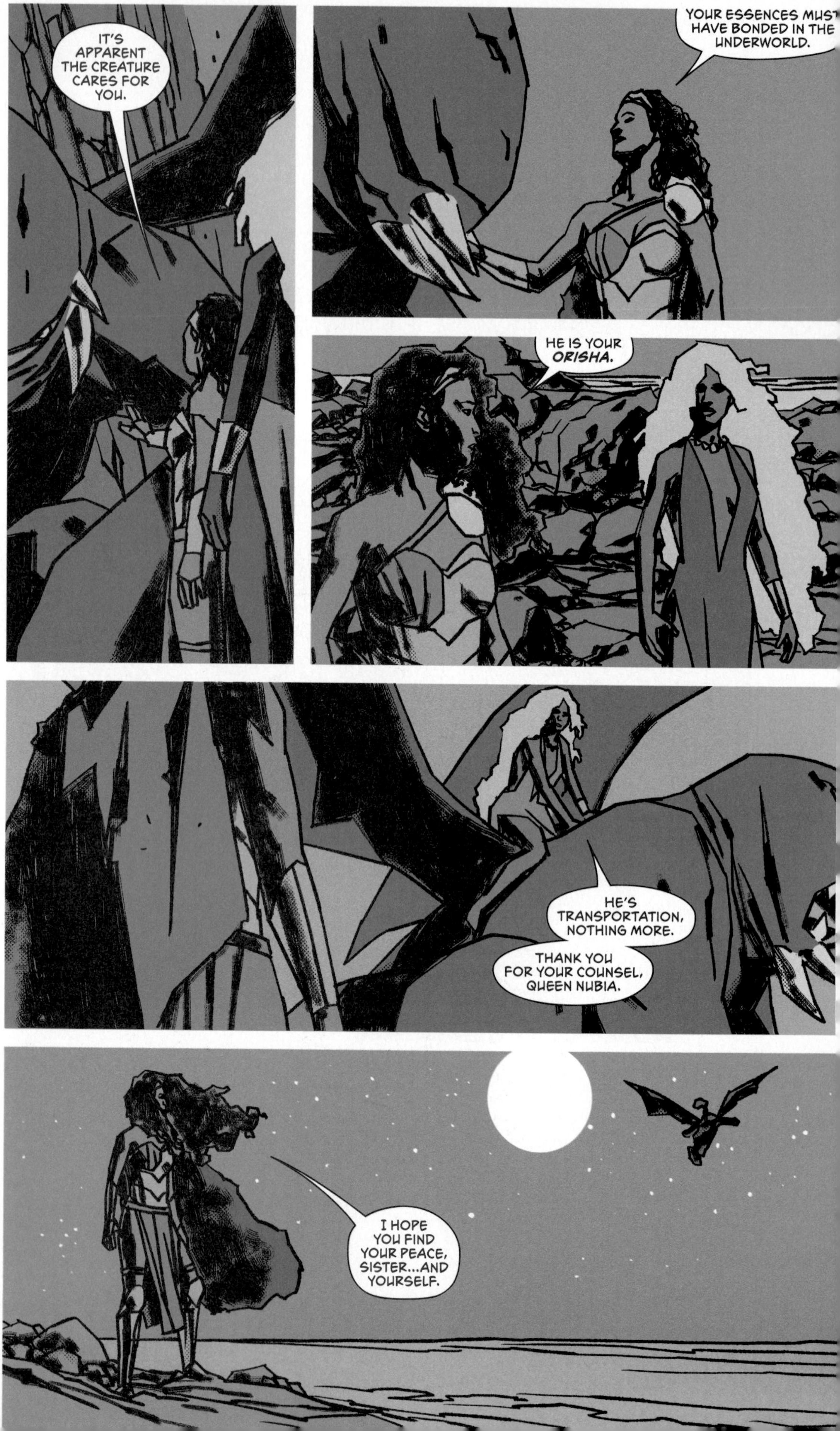
IT'S APPARENT THE CREATURE CARES FOR YOU.
YOUR ESSENCES MUST HAVE BONDED IN THE UNDERWORLD.
HE IS YOUR *ORISHA.*
HE'S TRANSPORTATION, NOTHING MORE.
THANK YOU FOR YOUR COUNSEL, QUEEN NUBIA.
I HOPE YOU FIND YOUR PEACE, SISTER...AND YOURSELF.

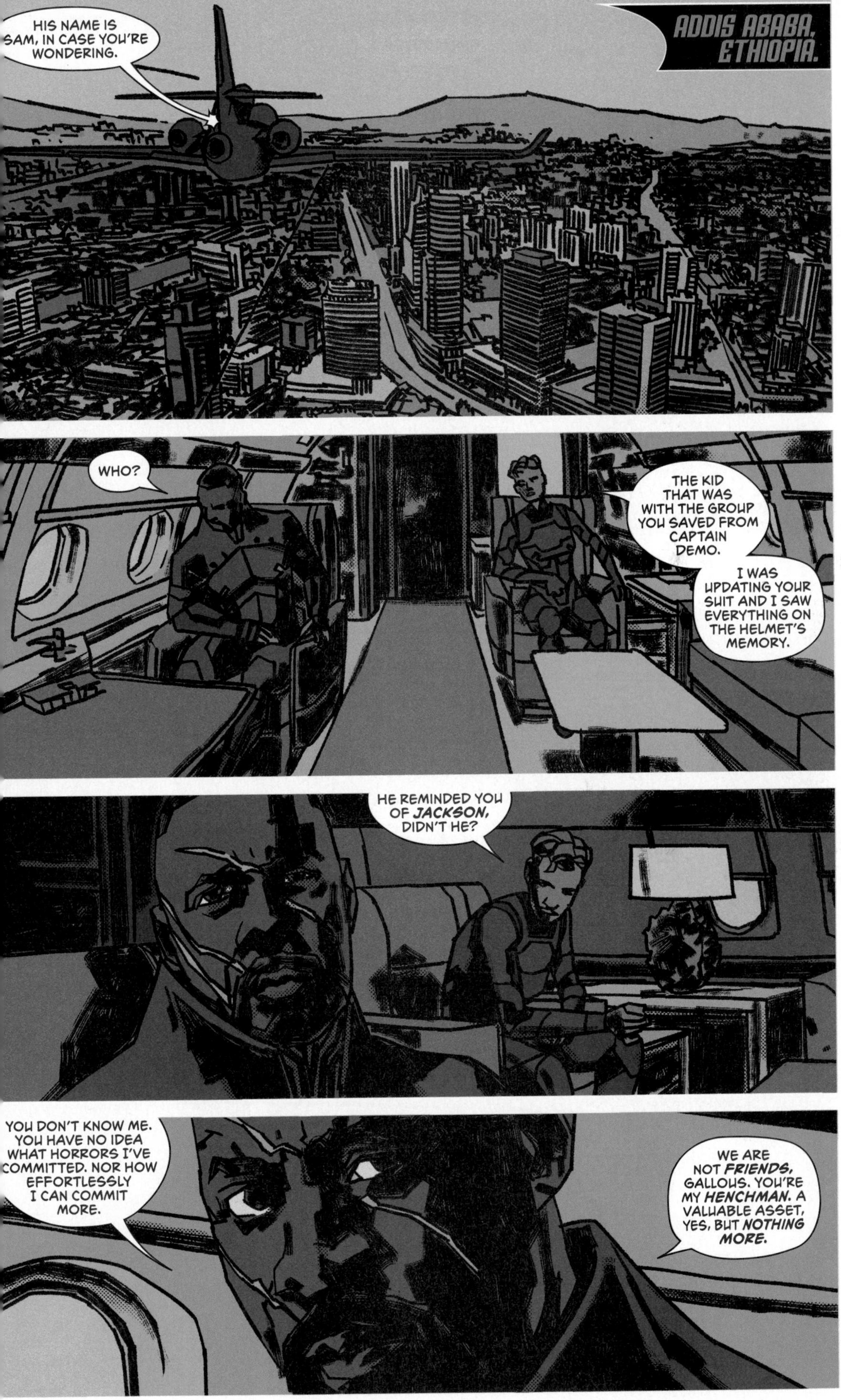

ADDIS ABABA, ETHIOPIA.
HIS NAME IS SAM, IN CASE YOU'RE WONDERING.
WHO?
THE KID THAT WAS WITH THE GROUP YOU SAVED FROM CAPTAIN DEMO.
I WAS UPDATING YOUR SUIT AND I SAW EVERYTHING ON THE HELMET'S MEMORY.
HE REMINDED YOU OF *JACKSON,* DIDN'T HE?
YOU DON'T KNOW ME. YOU HAVE NO IDEA WHAT HORRORS I'VE COMMITTED. NOR HOW EFFORTLESSLY I CAN COMMIT MORE.
WE ARE NOT *FRIENDS,* GALLOUS. YOU'RE MY *HENCHMAN.* A VALUABLE ASSET, YES, BUT *NOTHING MORE.*

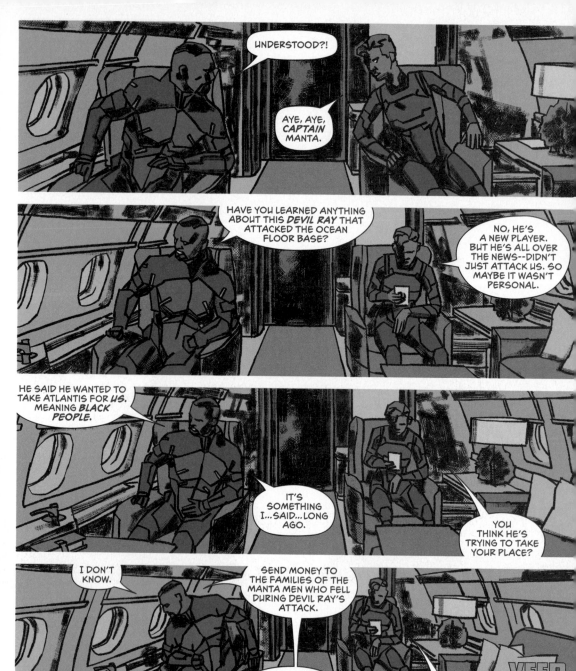

UNDERSTOOD?!

AYE, AYE, *CAPTAIN* MANTA.

HAVE YOU LEARNED ANYTHING ABOUT THIS *DEVIL RAY* THAT ATTACKED THE OCEAN FLOOR BASE?

NO, HE'S A NEW PLAYER. BUT HE'S ALL OVER THE NEWS--DIDN'T JUST ATTACK US. SO MAYBE IT WASN'T PERSONAL.

HE SAID HE WANTED TO TAKE ATLANTIS FOR *US.* MEANING *BLACK PEOPLE.*

IT'S SOMETHING I...SAID...LONG AGO.

YOU THINK HE'S TRYING TO TAKE YOUR PLACE?

I DON'T KNOW.

SEND MONEY TO THE FAMILIES OF THE MANTA MEN WHO FELL DURING DEVIL RAY'S ATTACK.

GET THE ABLE-BODIED SURVIVORS STARTED ON SALVAGE AND REPAIRS.

DONE.

VEEP
VEEP
VEEP

MR. HYDE! BOGIE APPROACHING FROM THE EAST-- PREPARE FOR IMPACT!

WHAT--?!

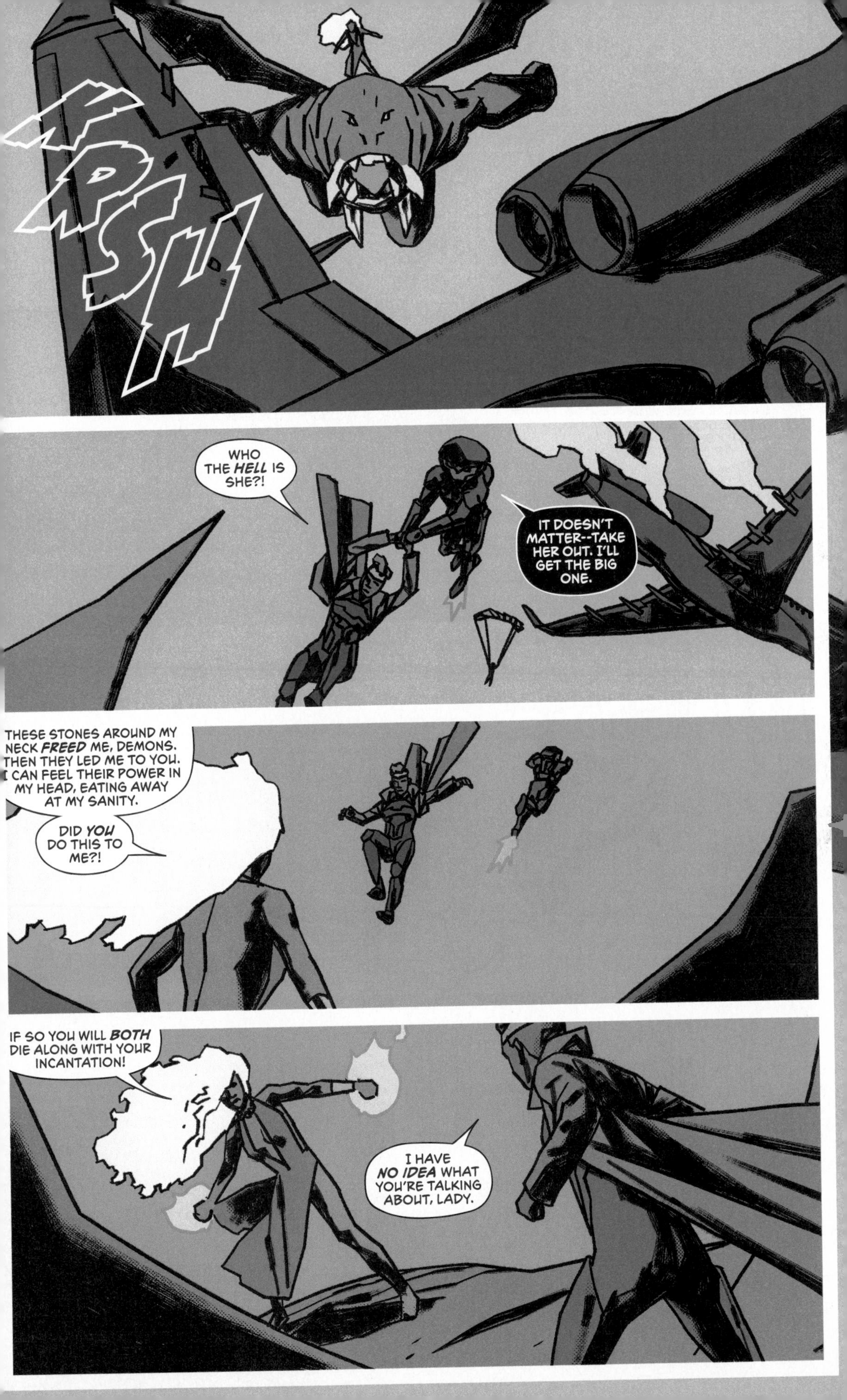

FPSH
WHO THE HELL IS SHE?!
IT DOESN'T MATTER--TAKE HER OUT. I'LL GET THE BIG ONE.
THESE STONES AROUND MY NECK FREED ME, DEMONS. THEN THEY LED ME TO YOU. I CAN FEEL THEIR POWER IN MY HEAD, EATING AWAY AT MY SANITY.
DID YOU DO THIS TO ME?!
IF SO YOU WILL BOTH DIE ALONG WITH YOUR INCANTATION!
I HAVE NO IDEA WHAT YOU'RE TALKING ABOUT, LADY.

WHY WON'T YOU BURN, SORCERESS? WHAT MAGIC DO YOU WIELD?!

IT'S NOT MAGIC. MY JACKET IS KEVLAR MIXED WITH SOME SOUVENIRS STOLEN FROM ATLANTIS.

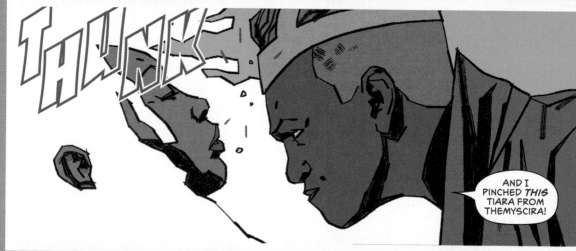

THUNK

AND I PINCHED *THIS* TIARA FROM THEMYSCIRA!

GRRRAAAAAH!

THAT'S IT...

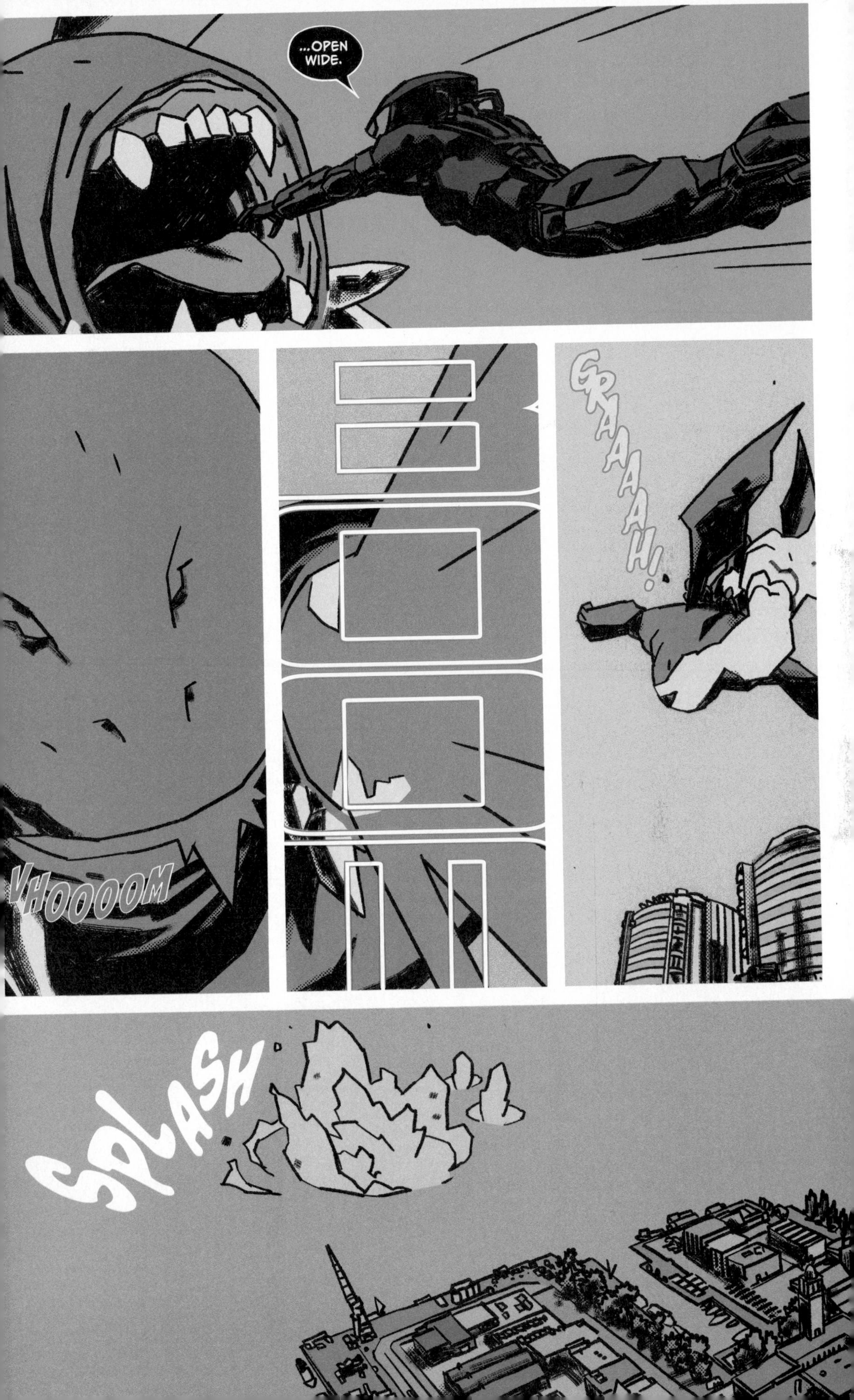

...OPEN WIDE.
VHOOOOM
GRAAAAAH!
SPLASH

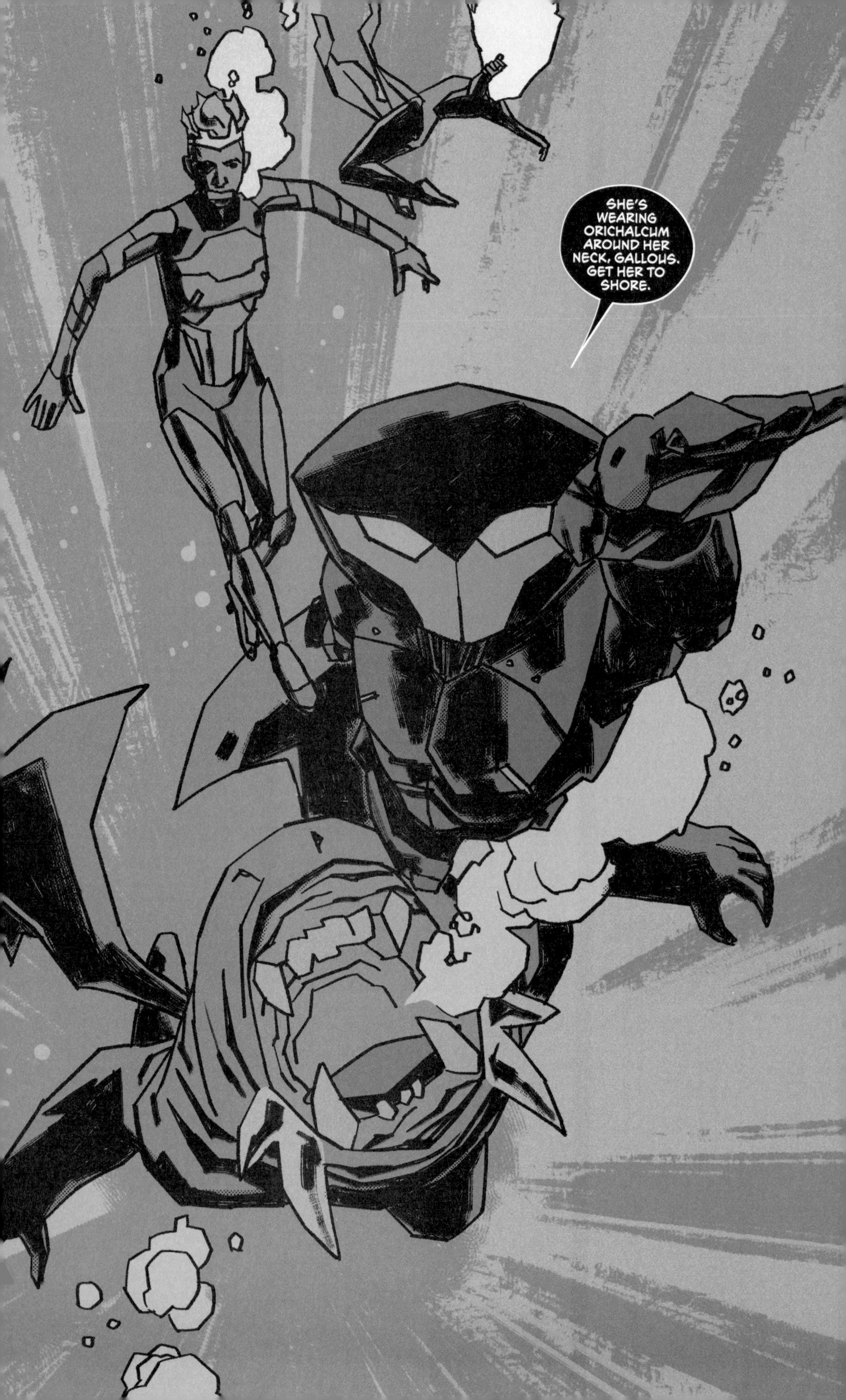
SHE'S WEARING ORICHALCUM AROUND HER NECK, GALLOUS. GET HER TO SHORE.

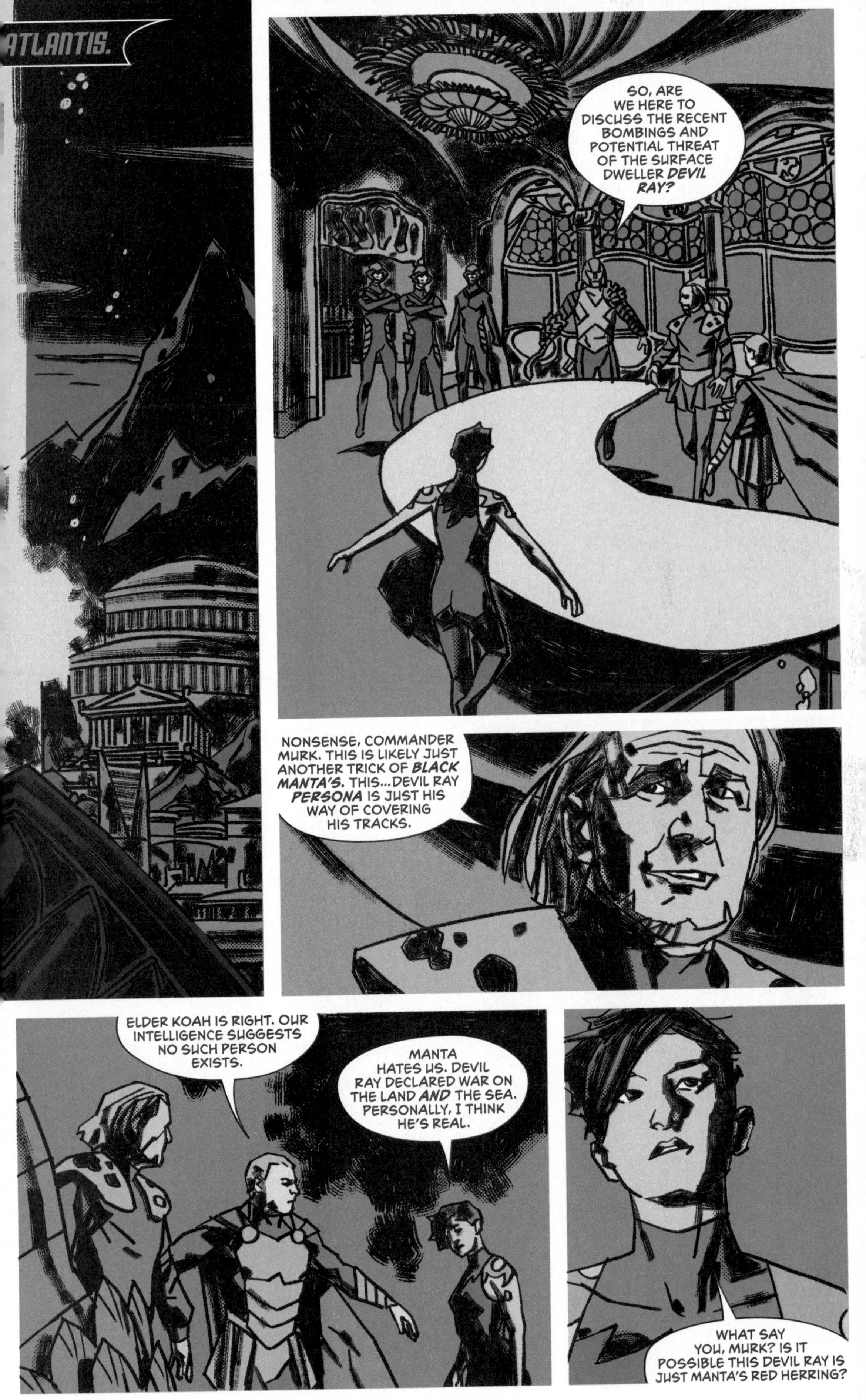

ATLANTIS.
SO, ARE WE HERE TO DISCUSS THE RECENT BOMBINGS AND POTENTIAL THREAT OF THE SURFACE DWELLER *DEVIL RAY?*
NONSENSE, COMMANDER MURK. THIS IS LIKELY JUST ANOTHER TRICK OF *BLACK MANTA'S*. THIS...DEVIL RAY *PERSONA* IS JUST HIS WAY OF COVERING HIS TRACKS.
ELDER KOAH IS RIGHT. OUR INTELLIGENCE SUGGESTS NO SUCH PERSON EXISTS.
MANTA HATES US. DEVIL RAY DECLARED WAR ON THE LAND *AND* THE SEA. PERSONALLY, I THINK HE'S REAL.
WHAT SAY YOU, MURK? IS IT POSSIBLE THIS DEVIL RAY IS JUST MANTA'S RED HERRING?

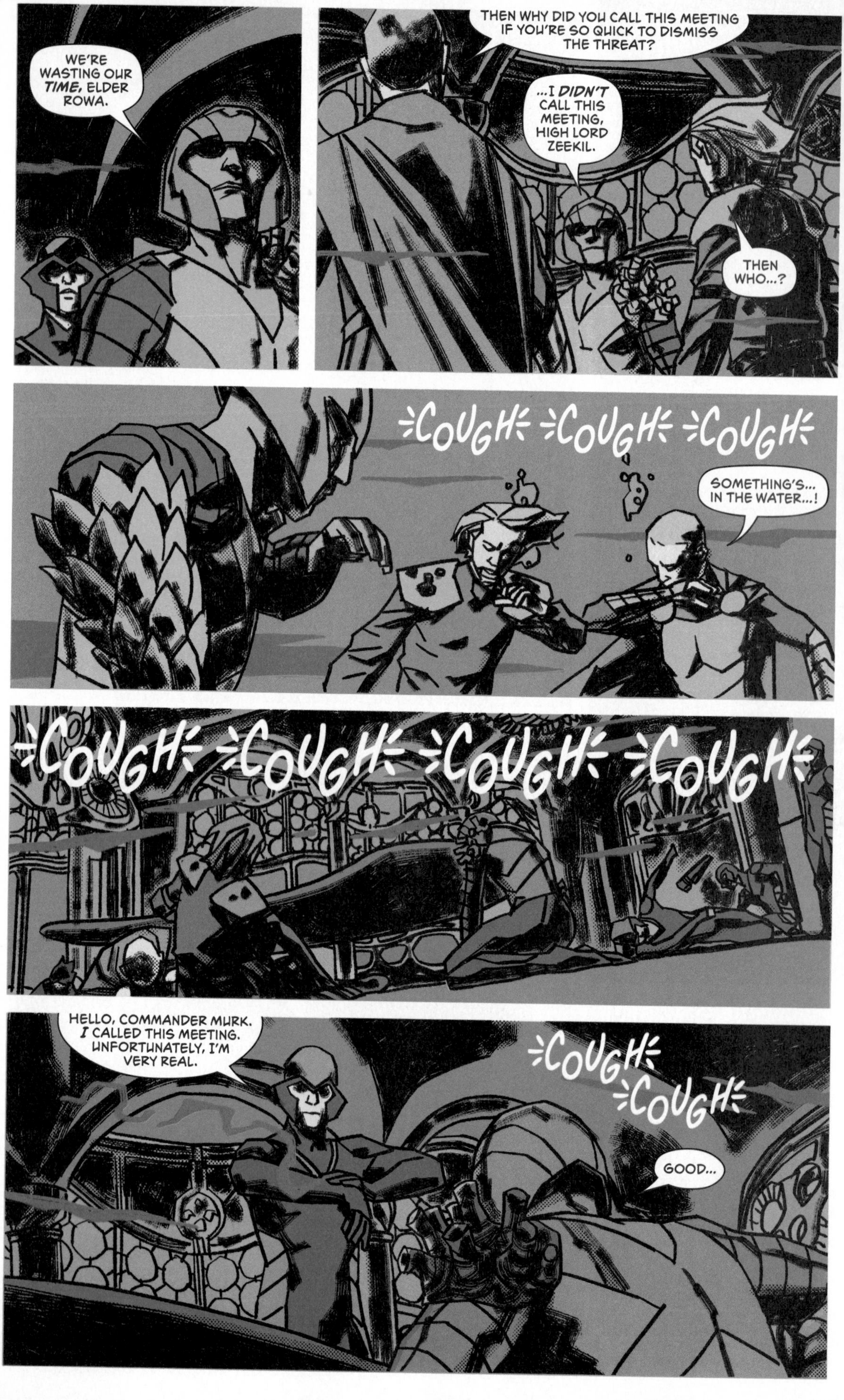
WE'RE WASTING OUR *TIME,* ELDER ROWA.
THEN WHY DID YOU CALL THIS MEETING IF YOU'RE SO QUICK TO DISMISS THE THREAT?
...I *DIDN'T* CALL THIS MEETING, HIGH LORD ZEEKIL.
THEN WHO...?
COUGH COUGH COUGH
SOMETHING'S... IN THE WATER...!
COUGH COUGH COUGH COUGH
HELLO, COMMANDER MURK. *I* CALLED THIS MEETING. UNFORTUNATELY, I'M VERY REAL.
COUGH COUGH
GOOD...

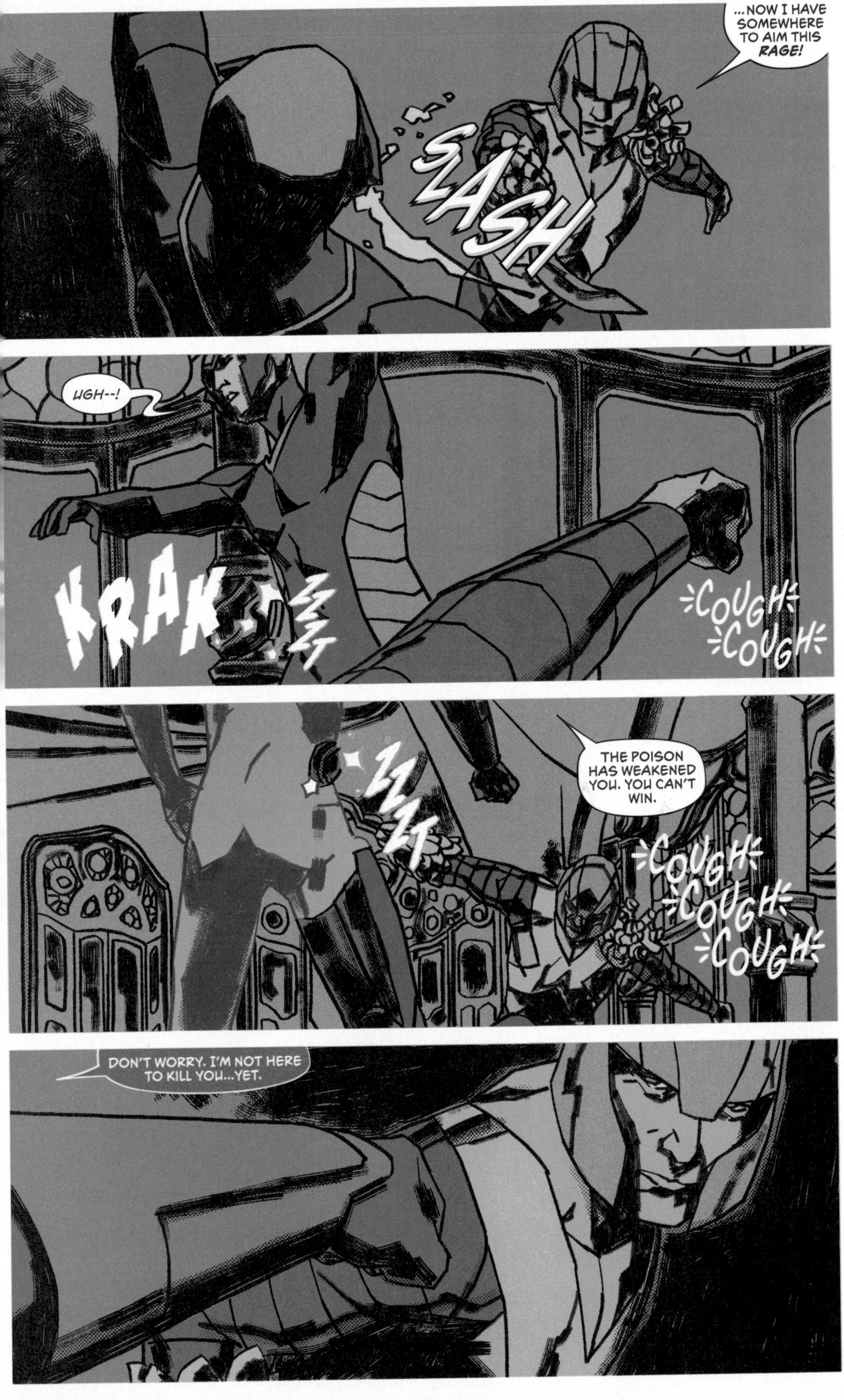
...NOW I HAVE SOMEWHERE TO AIM THIS *RAGE!*
SLASH
UGH--!
KRAK
ZZZZT
COUGH COUGH
ZZZZT
THE POISON HAS WEAKENED YOU. YOU CAN'T WIN.
COUGH COUGH COUGH
DON'T WORRY. I'M NOT HERE TO KILL YOU...YET.

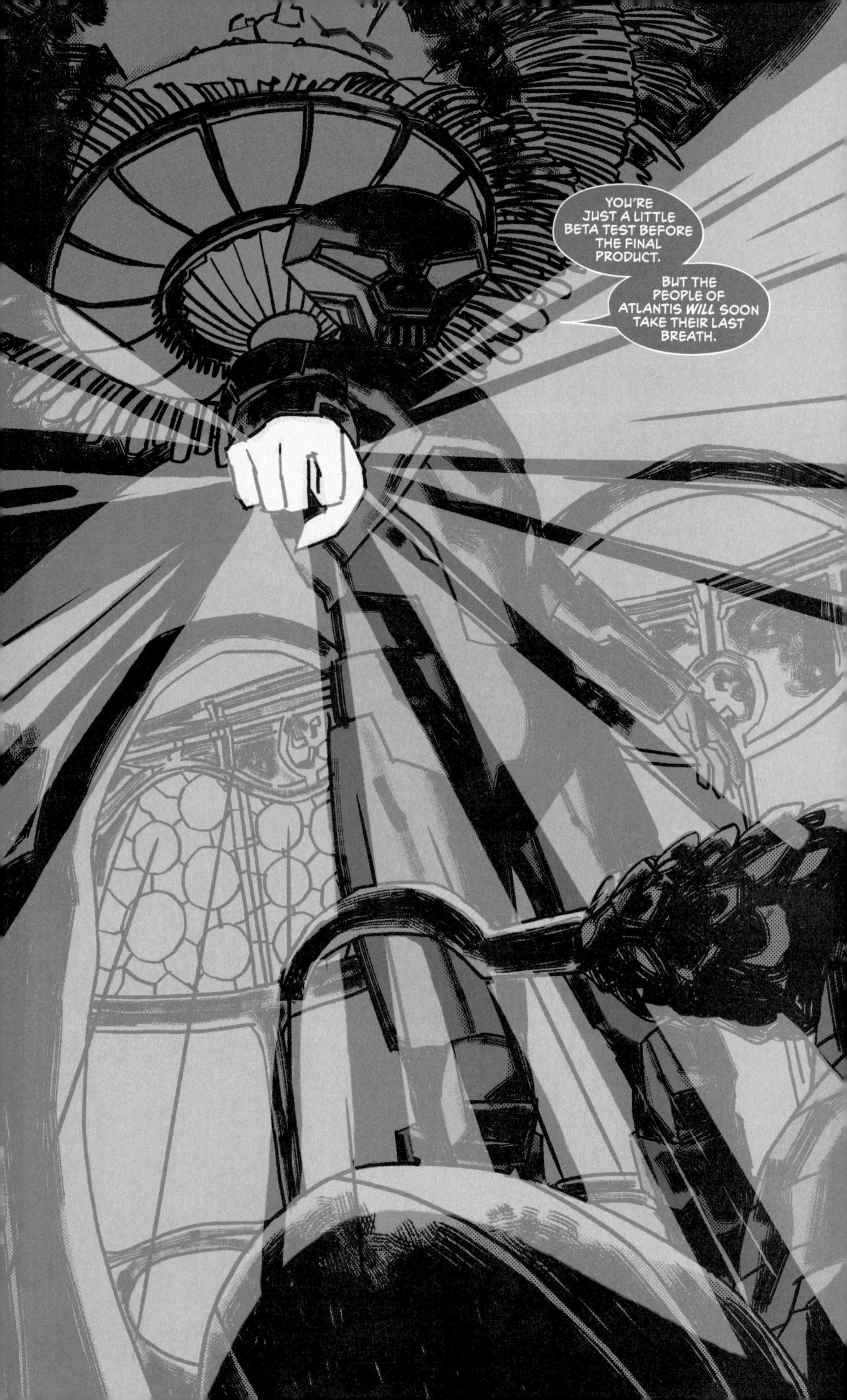
YOU'RE JUST A LITTLE BETA TEST BEFORE THE FINAL PRODUCT.
BUT THE PEOPLE OF ATLANTIS WILL SOON TAKE THEIR LAST BREATH.

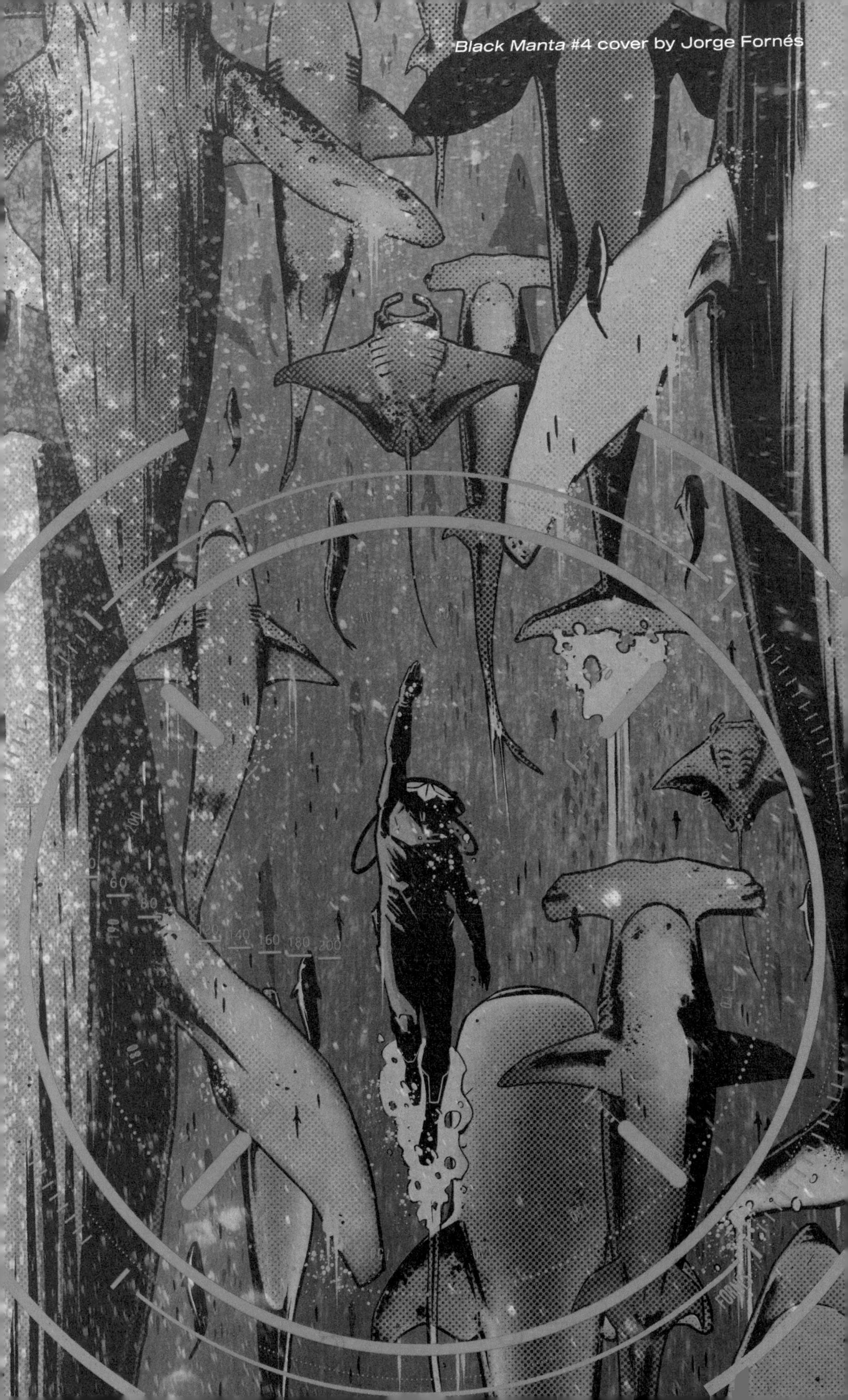
60
80
120 140 160 180 200

Black Manta #4 cover by Jorge Fornés

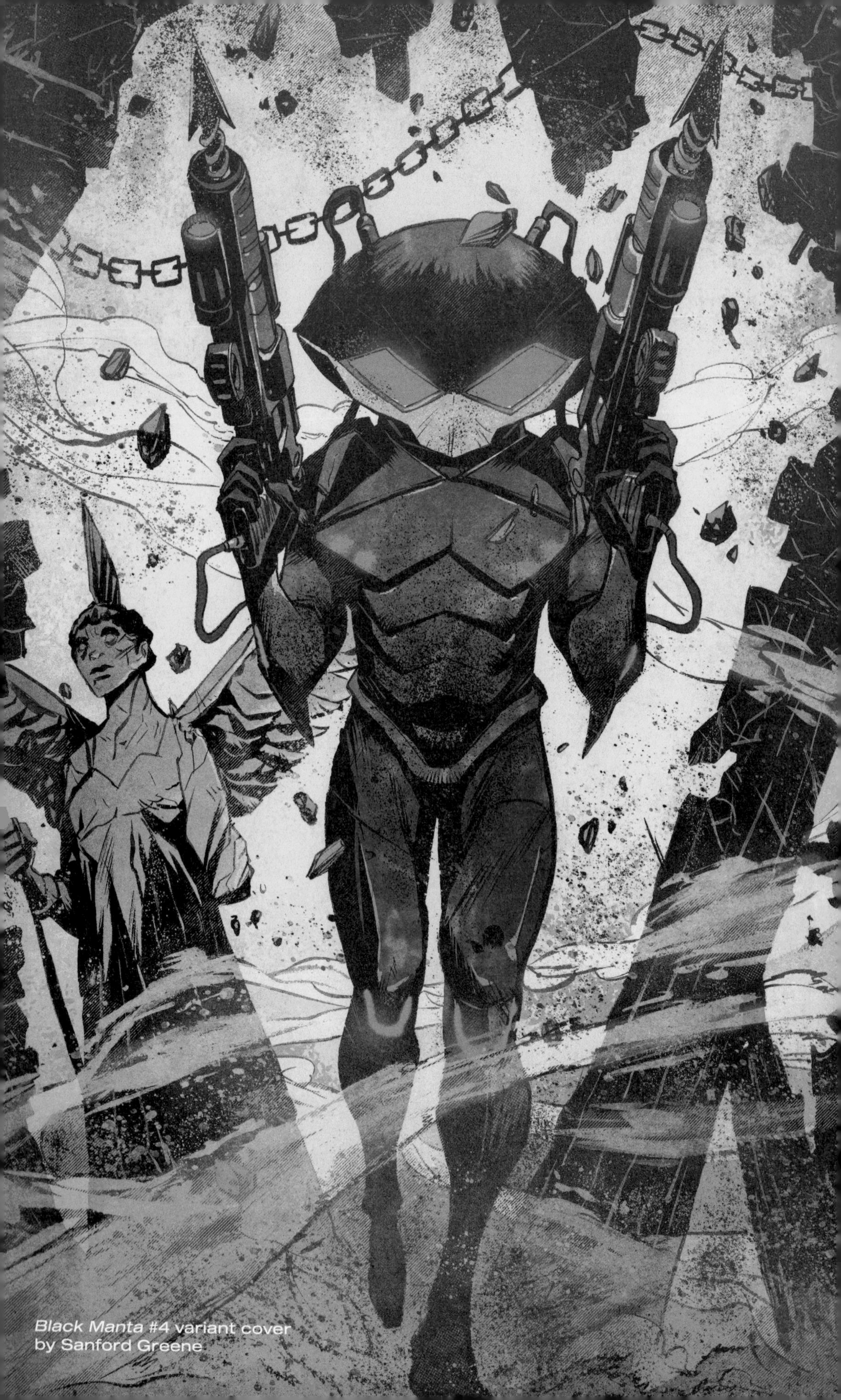

Black Manta #4 variant cover
by Sanford Greene

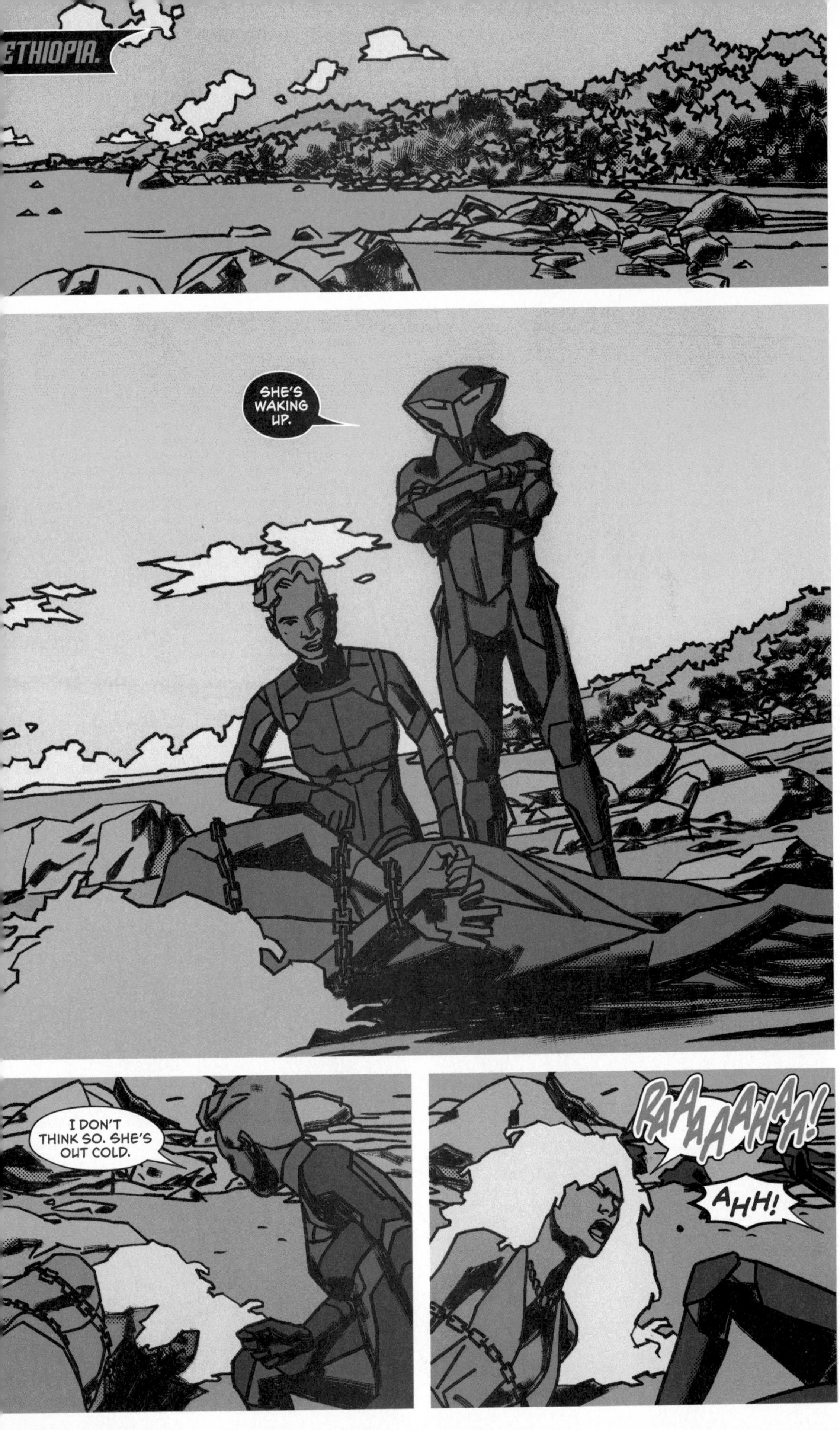

ETHIOPIA.
SHE'S WAKING UP.
I DON'T THINK SO. SHE'S OUT COLD.
RAAAAAAHAAA!
AHH!

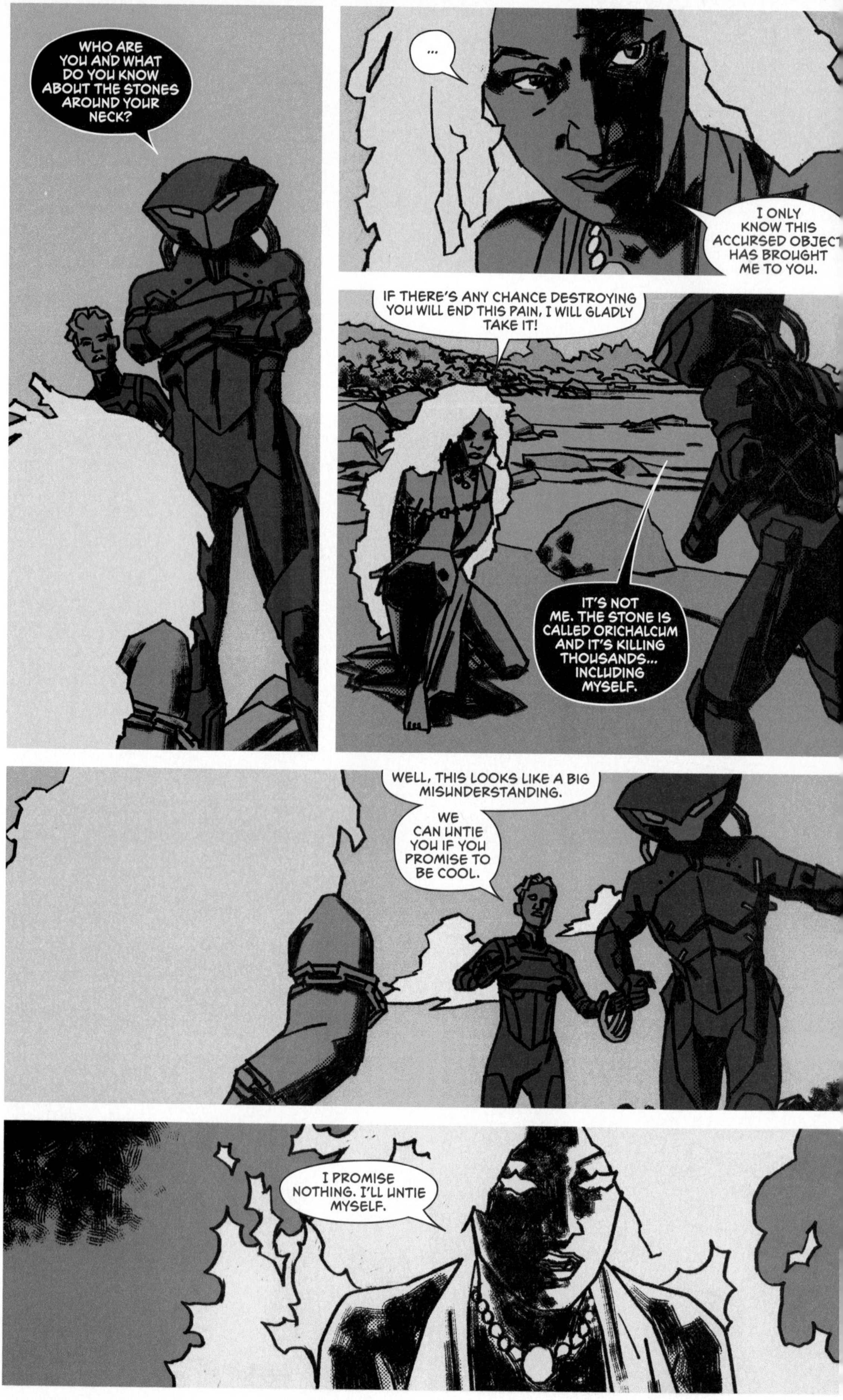
WHO ARE YOU AND WHAT DO YOU KNOW ABOUT THE STONES AROUND YOUR NECK?
...
I ONLY KNOW THIS ACCURSED OBJECT HAS BROUGHT ME TO YOU.
IF THERE'S ANY CHANCE DESTROYING YOU WILL END THIS PAIN, I WILL GLADLY TAKE IT!
IT'S NOT ME. THE STONE IS CALLED ORICHALCUM AND IT'S KILLING THOUSANDS... INCLUDING MYSELF.
WELL, THIS LOOKS LIKE A BIG MISUNDERSTANDING.
WE CAN UNTIE YOU IF YOU PROMISE TO BE COOL.
I PROMISE NOTHING. I'LL UNTIE MYSELF.

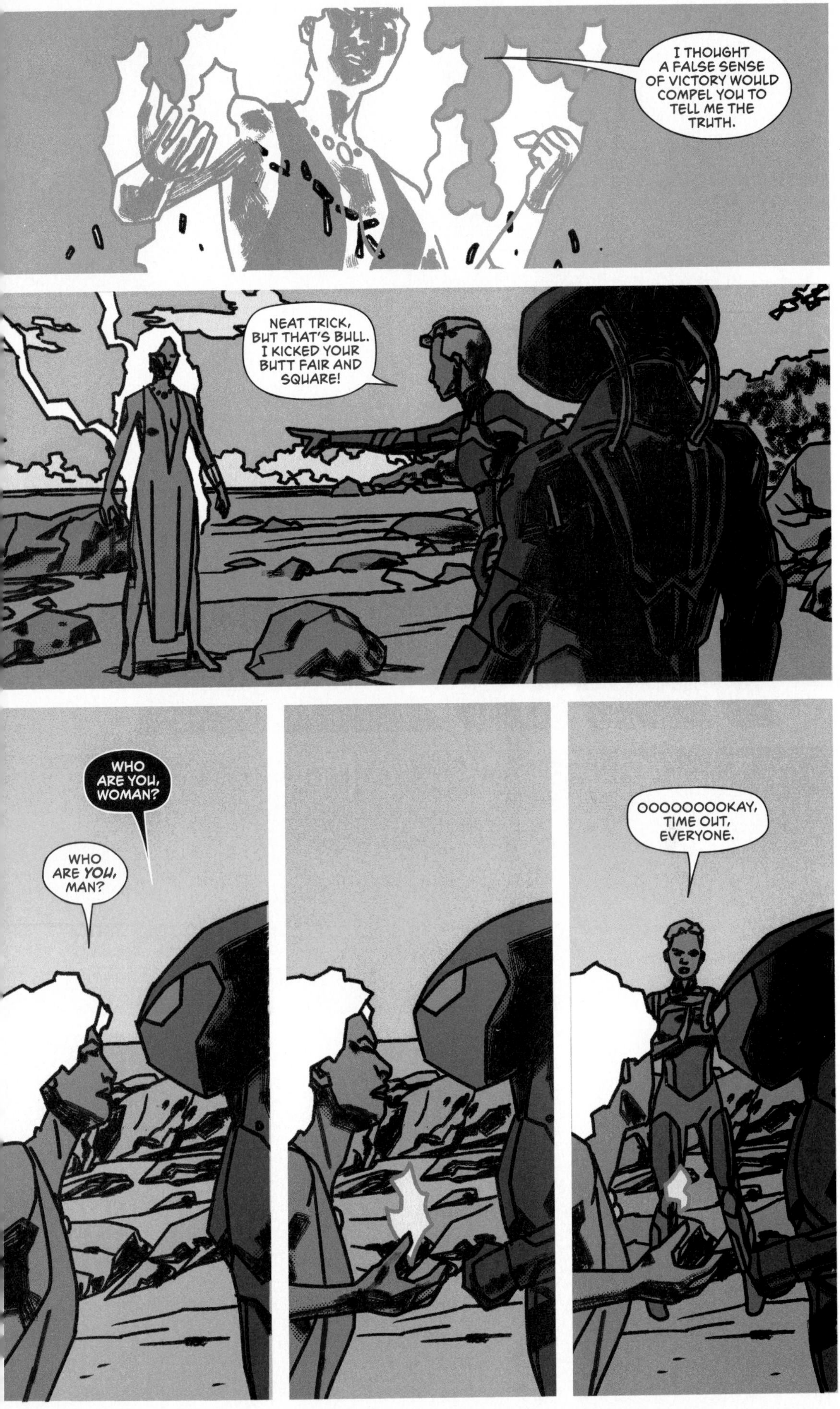
I THOUGHT A FALSE SENSE OF VICTORY WOULD COMPEL YOU TO TELL ME THE TRUTH.
NEAT TRICK, BUT THAT'S BULL. I KICKED YOUR BUTT FAIR AND SQUARE!
WHO ARE YOU, WOMAN?
WHO ARE YOU, MAN?
OOOOOOOOKAY, TIME OUT, EVERYONE.

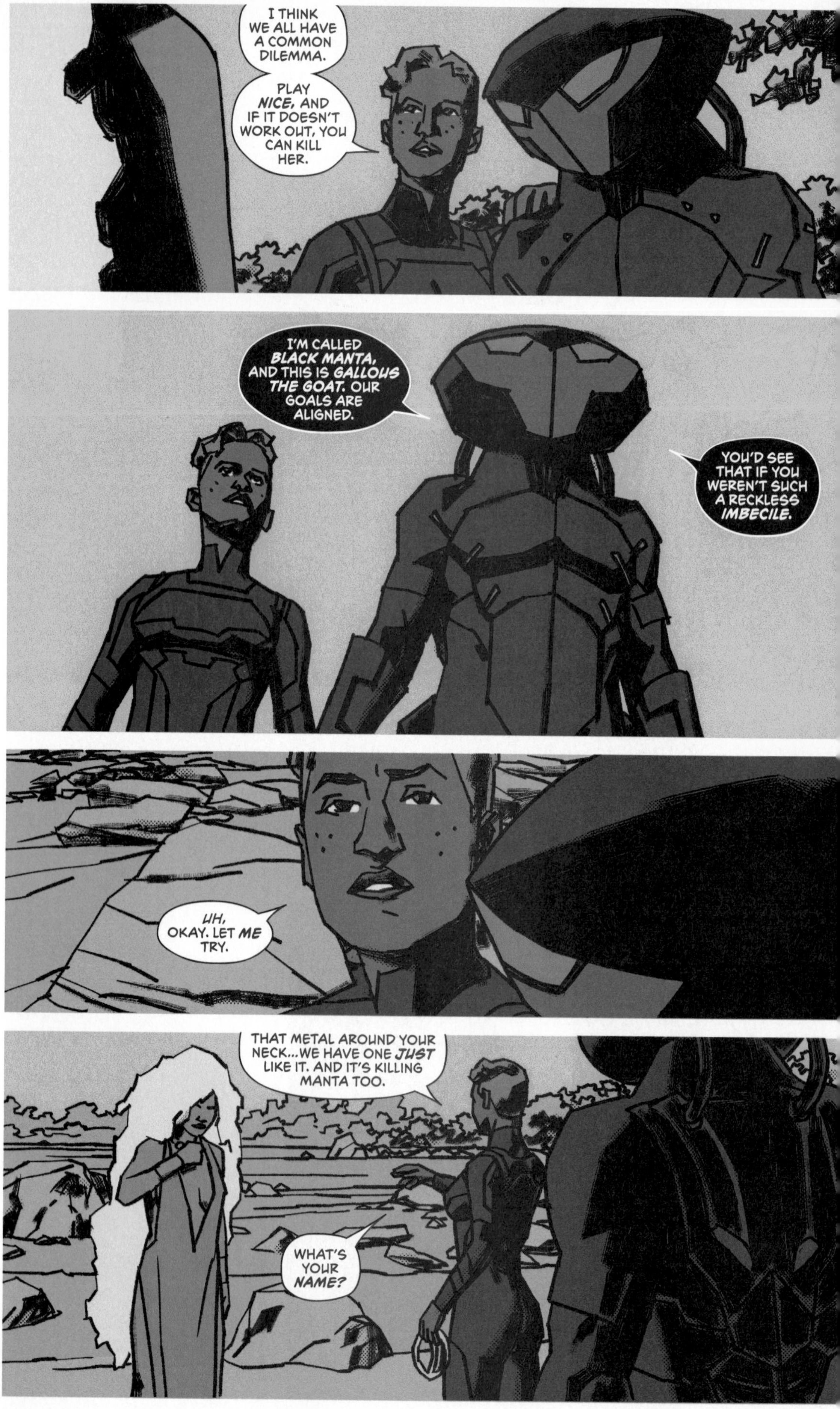
I THINK WE ALL HAVE A COMMON DILEMMA.
PLAY NICE, AND IF IT DOESN'T WORK OUT, YOU CAN KILL HER.
I'M CALLED BLACK MANTA, AND THIS IS GALLOUS THE GOAT. OUR GOALS ARE ALIGNED.
YOU'D SEE THAT IF YOU WEREN'T SUCH A RECKLESS IMBECILE.
UH, OKAY. LET ME TRY.
THAT METAL AROUND YOUR NECK...WE HAVE ONE JUST LIKE IT. AND IT'S KILLING MANTA TOO.
WHAT'S YOUR NAME?

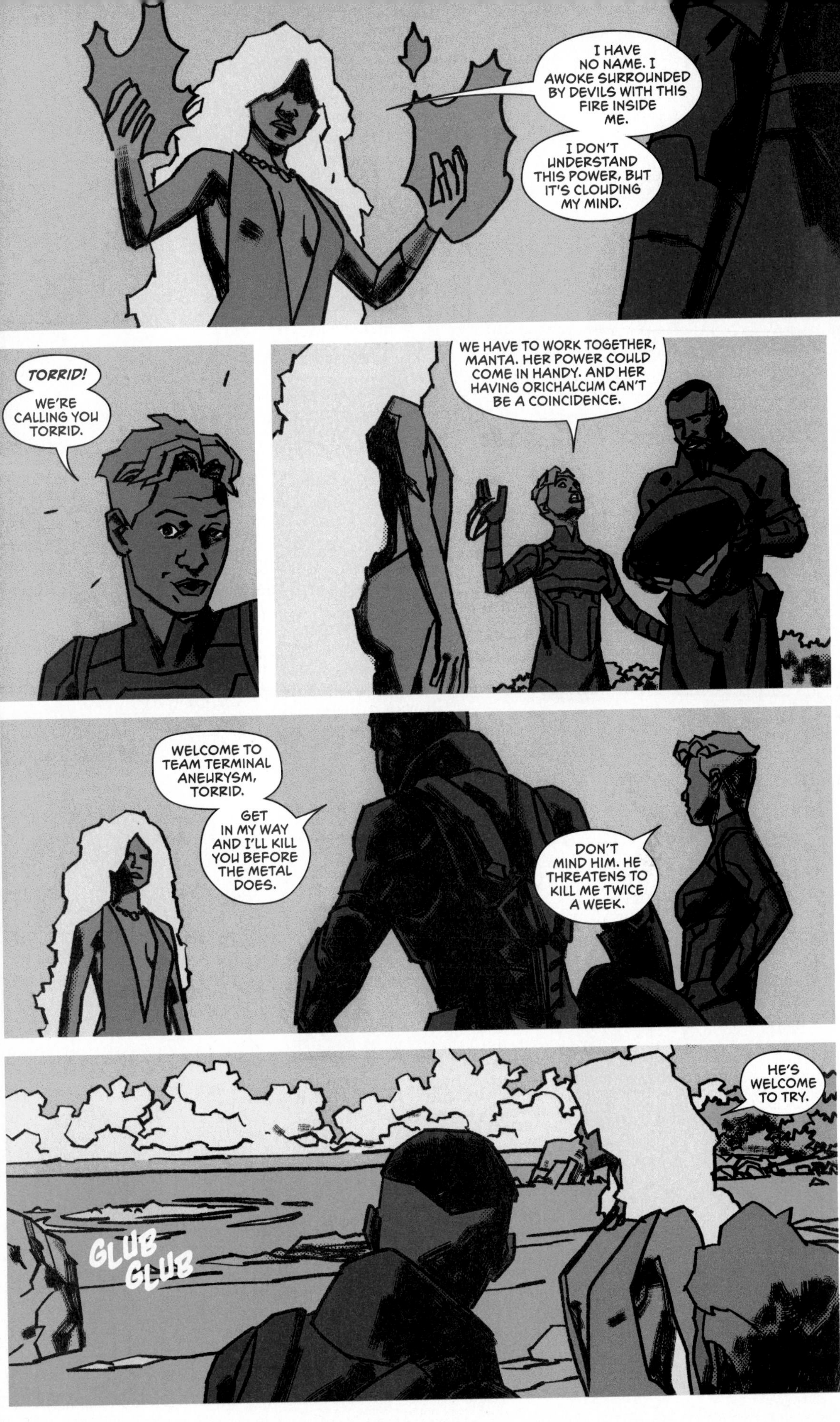
I HAVE NO NAME. I AWOKE SURROUNDED BY DEVILS WITH THIS FIRE INSIDE ME.
I DON'T UNDERSTAND THIS POWER, BUT IT'S CLOUDING MY MIND.
TORRID!
WE'RE CALLING YOU TORRID.
WE HAVE TO WORK TOGETHER, MANTA. HER POWER COULD COME IN HANDY. AND HER HAVING ORICHALCUM CAN'T BE A COINCIDENCE.
WELCOME TO TEAM TERMINAL ANEURYSM, TORRID.
GET IN MY WAY AND I'LL KILL YOU BEFORE THE METAL DOES.
DON'T MIND HIM. HE THREATENS TO KILL ME TWICE A WEEK.
HE'S WELCOME TO TRY.
GLUB GLUB

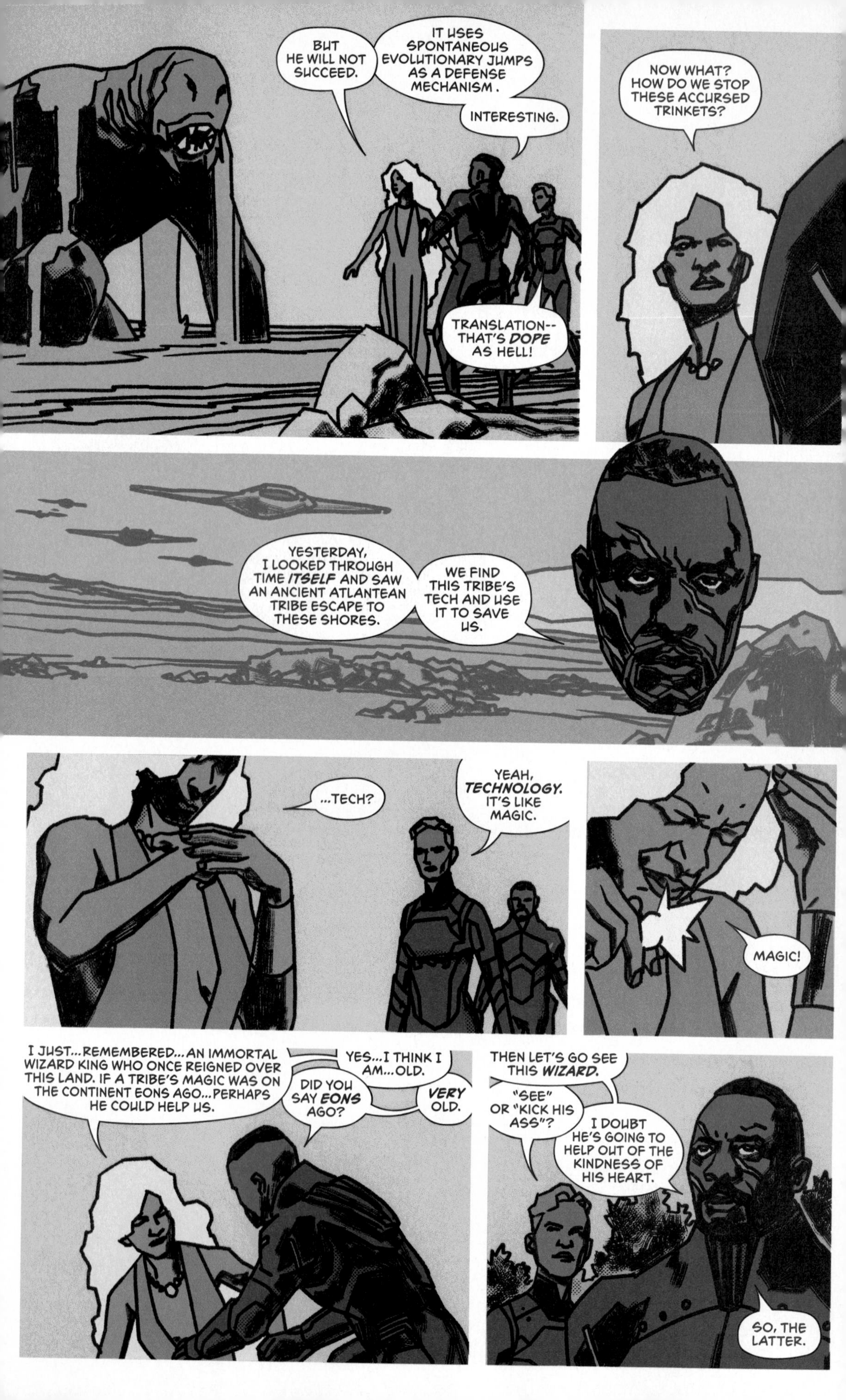
BUT HE WILL NOT SUCCEED.
IT USES SPONTANEOUS EVOLUTIONARY JUMPS AS A DEFENSE MECHANISM.
INTERESTING.
TRANSLATION--THAT'S *DOPE* AS HELL!
NOW WHAT? HOW DO WE STOP THESE ACCURSED TRINKETS?
YESTERDAY, I LOOKED THROUGH TIME *ITSELF* AND SAW AN ANCIENT ATLANTEAN TRIBE ESCAPE TO THESE SHORES.
WE FIND THIS TRIBE'S TECH AND USE IT TO SAVE US.
...TECH?
YEAH, ***TECHNOLOGY.*** IT'S LIKE MAGIC.
MAGIC!
I JUST...REMEMBERED...AN IMMORTAL WIZARD KING WHO ONCE REIGNED OVER THIS LAND. IF A TRIBE'S MAGIC WAS ON THE CONTINENT EONS AGO...PERHAPS HE COULD HELP US.
DID YOU SAY *EONS* AGO?
YES...I THINK I AM...OLD.
VERY OLD.
THEN LET'S GO SEE THIS *WIZARD.*
"SEE" OR "KICK HIS ASS"?
I DOUBT HE'S GOING TO HELP OUT OF THE KINDNESS OF HIS HEART.
SO, THE LATTER.

DOCTOR THNITA! WHAT'S THE STATUS OF THE COUNCIL MEMBERS?

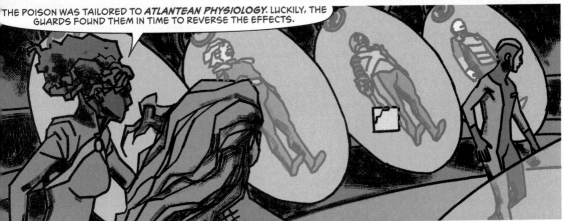

THE POISON WAS TAILORED TO *ATLANTEAN PHYSIOLOGY*. LUCKILY, THE GUARDS FOUND THEM IN TIME TO REVERSE THE EFFECTS.

THEIR LIVERS EXPELLED THE TOXINS BEFORE ANY PERMANENT DAMAGE WAS DONE.

LUCKY INDEED.

NO!

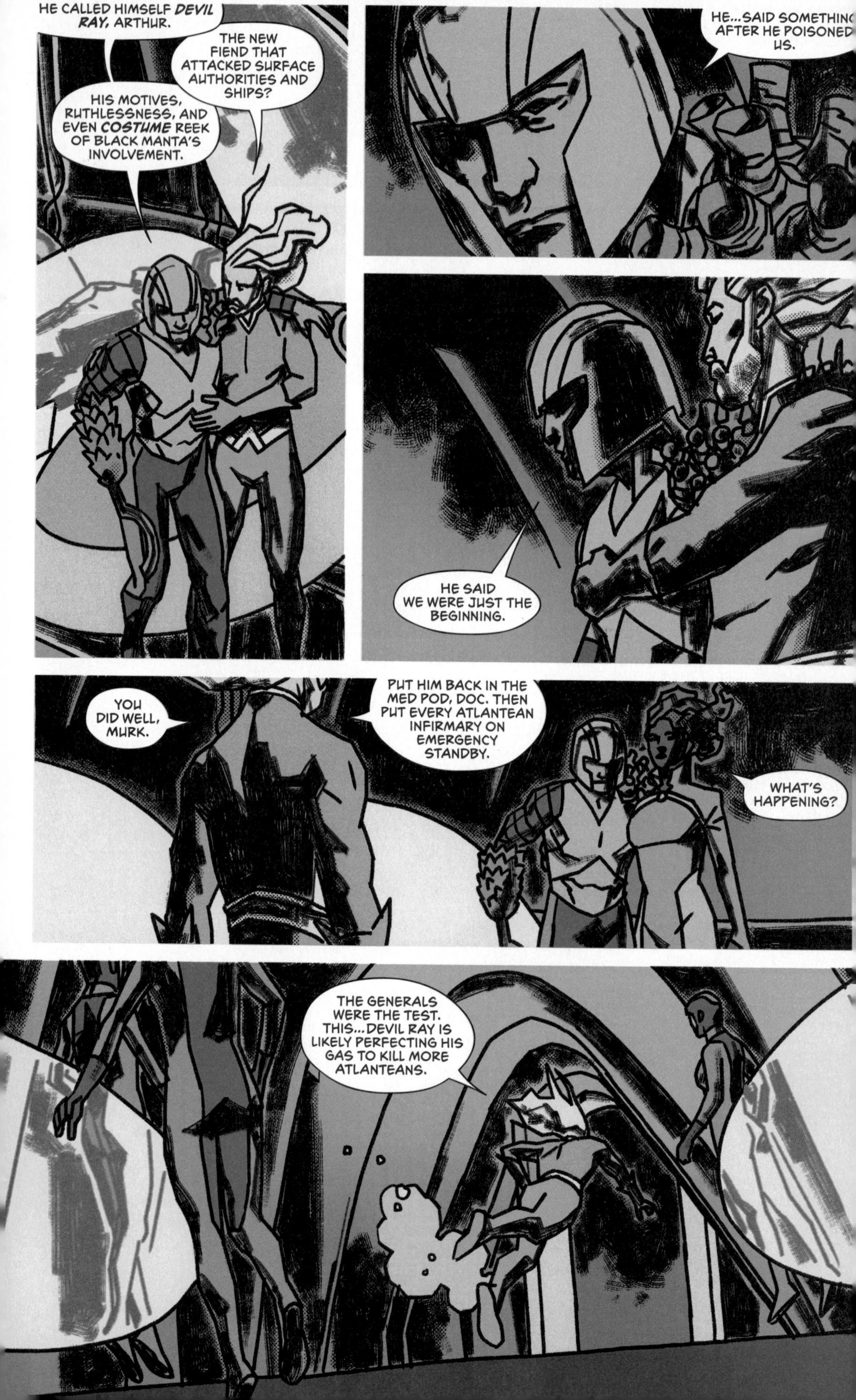
HE CALLED HIMSELF DEVIL RAY, ARTHUR.
HIS MOTIVES, RUTHLESSNESS, AND EVEN COSTUME REEK OF BLACK MANTA'S INVOLVEMENT.
THE NEW FIEND THAT ATTACKED SURFACE AUTHORITIES AND SHIPS?
HE...SAID SOMETHING AFTER HE POISONED US.
HE SAID WE WERE JUST THE BEGINNING.
YOU DID WELL, MURK.
PUT HIM BACK IN THE MED POD, DOC. THEN PUT EVERY ATLANTEAN INFIRMARY ON EMERGENCY STANDBY.
WHAT'S HAPPENING?
THE GENERALS WERE THE TEST. THIS...DEVIL RAY IS LIKELY PERFECTING HIS GAS TO KILL MORE ATLANTEANS.

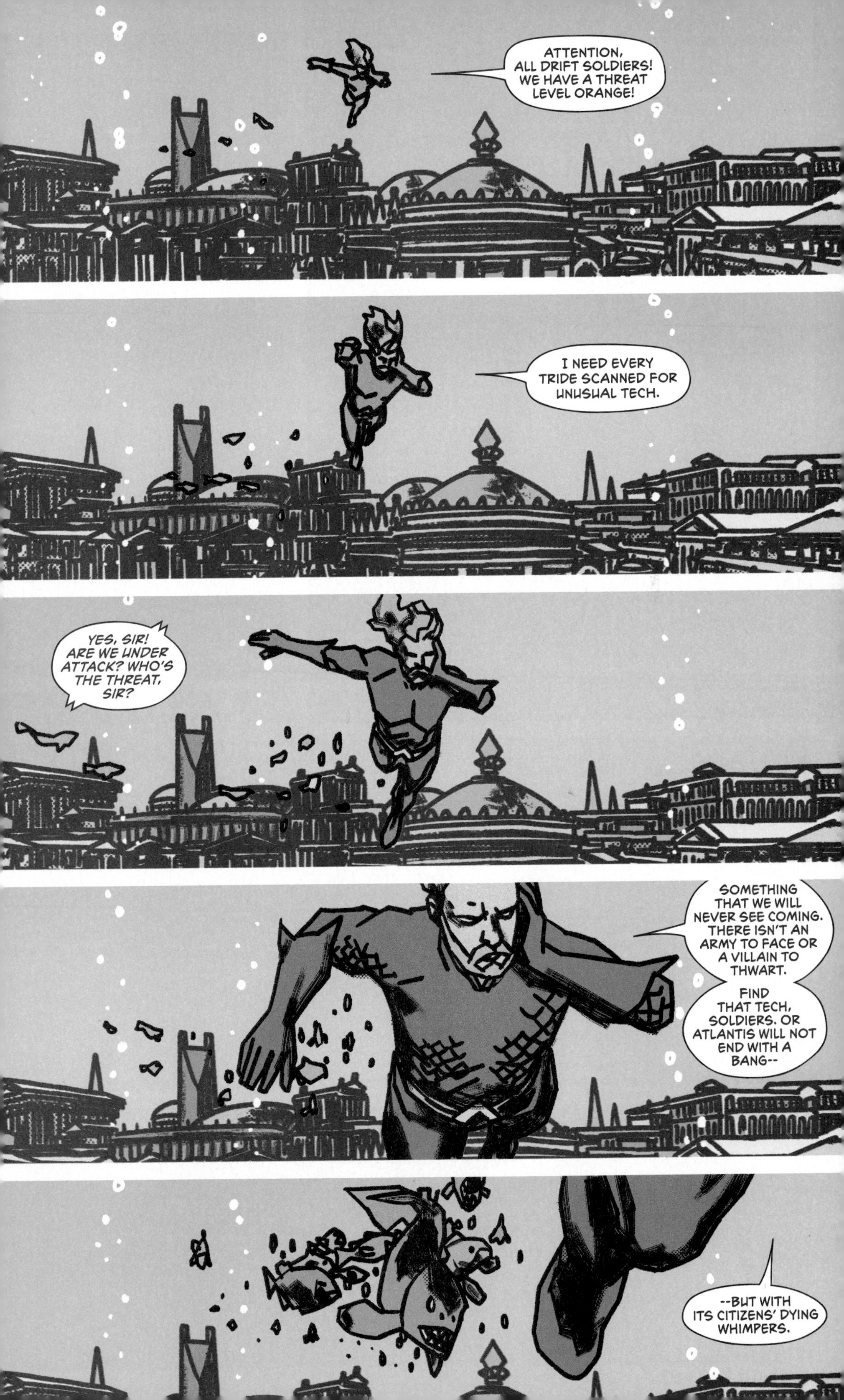
ATTENTION, ALL DRIFT SOLDIERS! WE HAVE A THREAT LEVEL ORANGE!
I NEED EVERY TRIDE SCANNED FOR UNUSUAL TECH.
YES, SIR! ARE WE UNDER ATTACK? WHO'S THE THREAT, SIR?
SOMETHING THAT WE WILL NEVER SEE COMING. THERE ISN'T AN ARMY TO FACE OR A VILLAIN TO THWART.
FIND THAT TECH, SOLDIERS. OR ATLANTIS WILL NOT END WITH A BANG--
--BUT WITH ITS CITIZENS' DYING WHIMPERS.

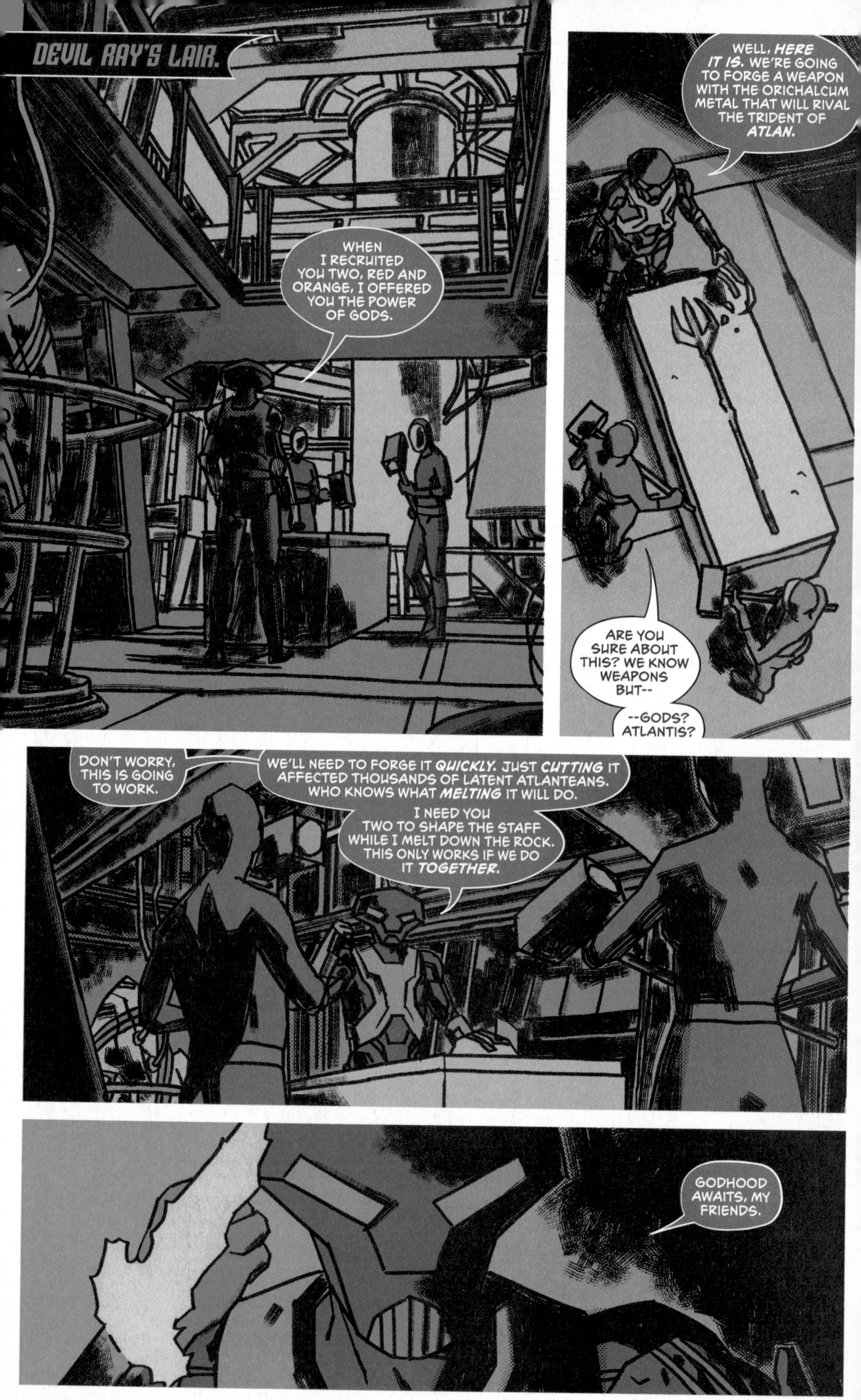
DEVIL RAY'S LAIR.
WHEN I RECRUITED YOU TWO, RED AND ORANGE, I OFFERED YOU THE POWER OF GODS.
WELL, HERE IT IS. WE'RE GOING TO FORGE A WEAPON WITH THE ORICHALCUM METAL THAT WILL RIVAL THE TRIDENT OF ATLAN.
ARE YOU SURE ABOUT THIS? WE KNOW WEAPONS BUT--
--GODS? ATLANTIS?
DON'T WORRY, THIS IS GOING TO WORK.
WE'LL NEED TO FORGE IT QUICKLY. JUST CUTTING IT AFFECTED THOUSANDS OF LATENT ATLANTEANS. WHO KNOWS WHAT MELTING IT WILL DO.
I NEED YOU TWO TO SHAPE THE STAFF WHILE I MELT DOWN THE ROCK. THIS ONLY WORKS IF WE DO IT TOGETHER.
GODHOOD AWAITS, MY FRIENDS.

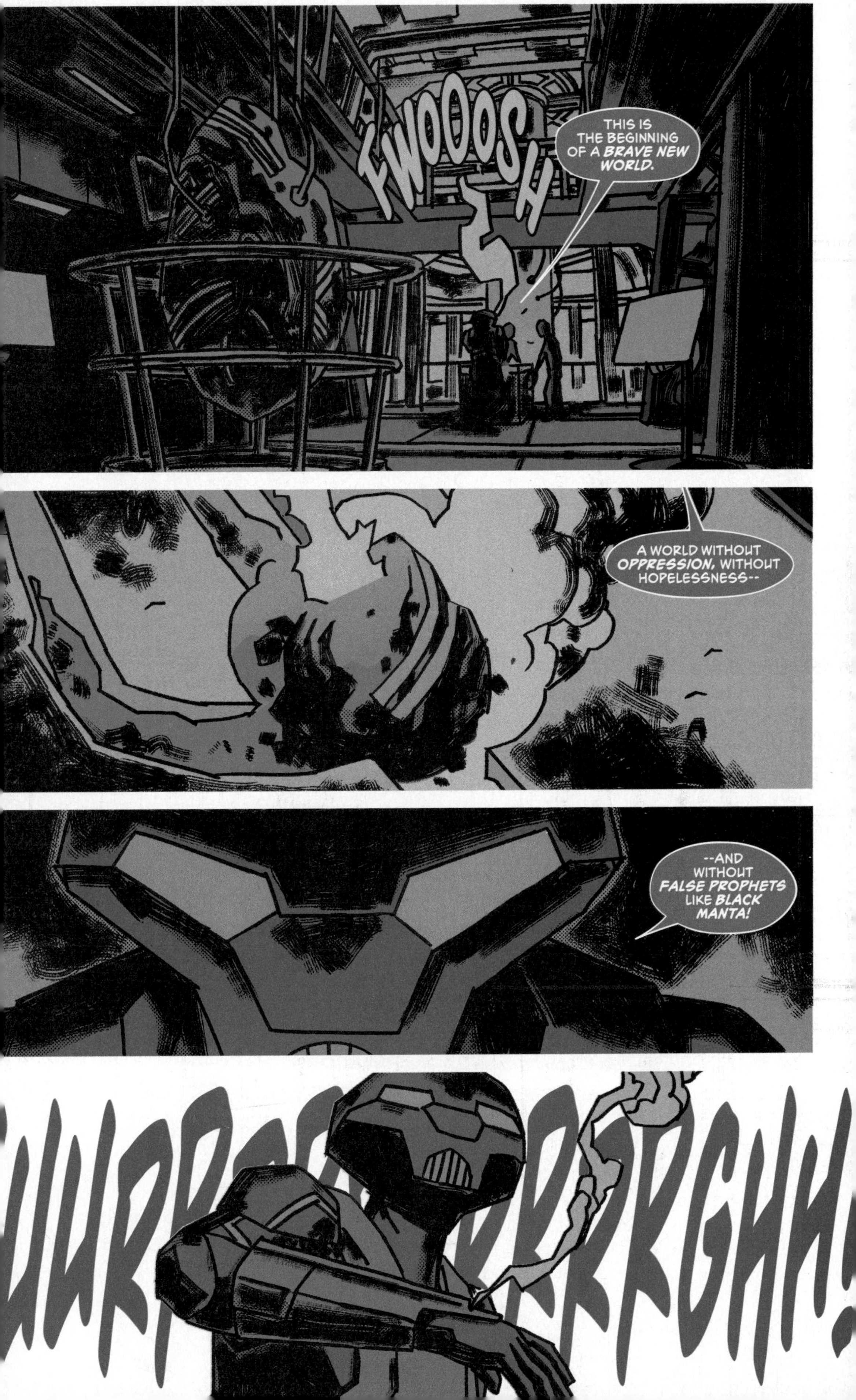

FWOOOSH
THIS IS THE BEGINNING OF A BRAVE NEW WORLD.
A WORLD WITHOUT OPPRESSION, WITHOUT HOPELESSNESS--
--AND WITHOUT FALSE PROPHETS LIKE BLACK MANTA!

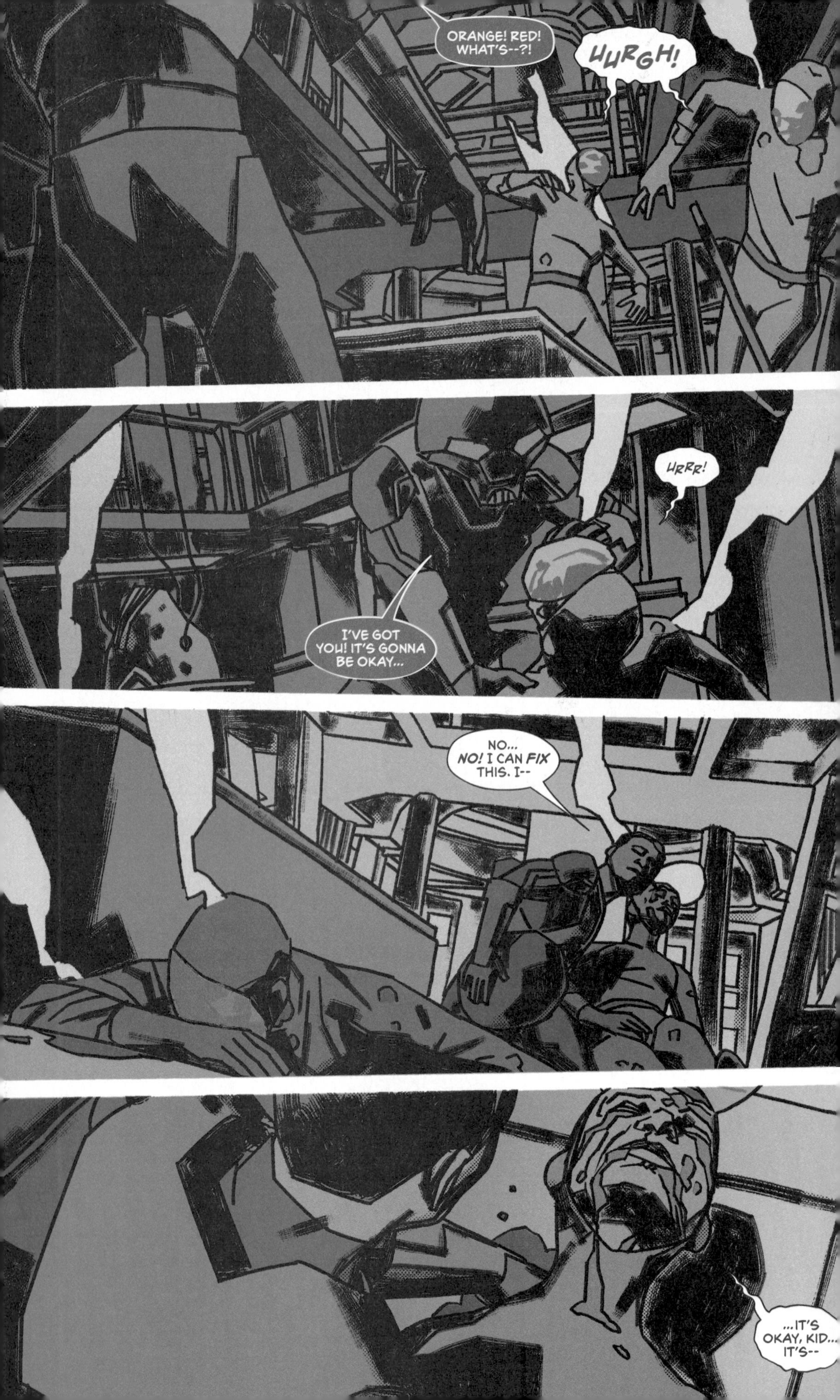
ORANGE! RED! WHAT'S--?!
UURGH!
URRR!
I'VE GOT YOU! IT'S GONNA BE OKAY...
NO... NO! I CAN FIX THIS. I--
...IT'S OKAY, KID... IT'S--

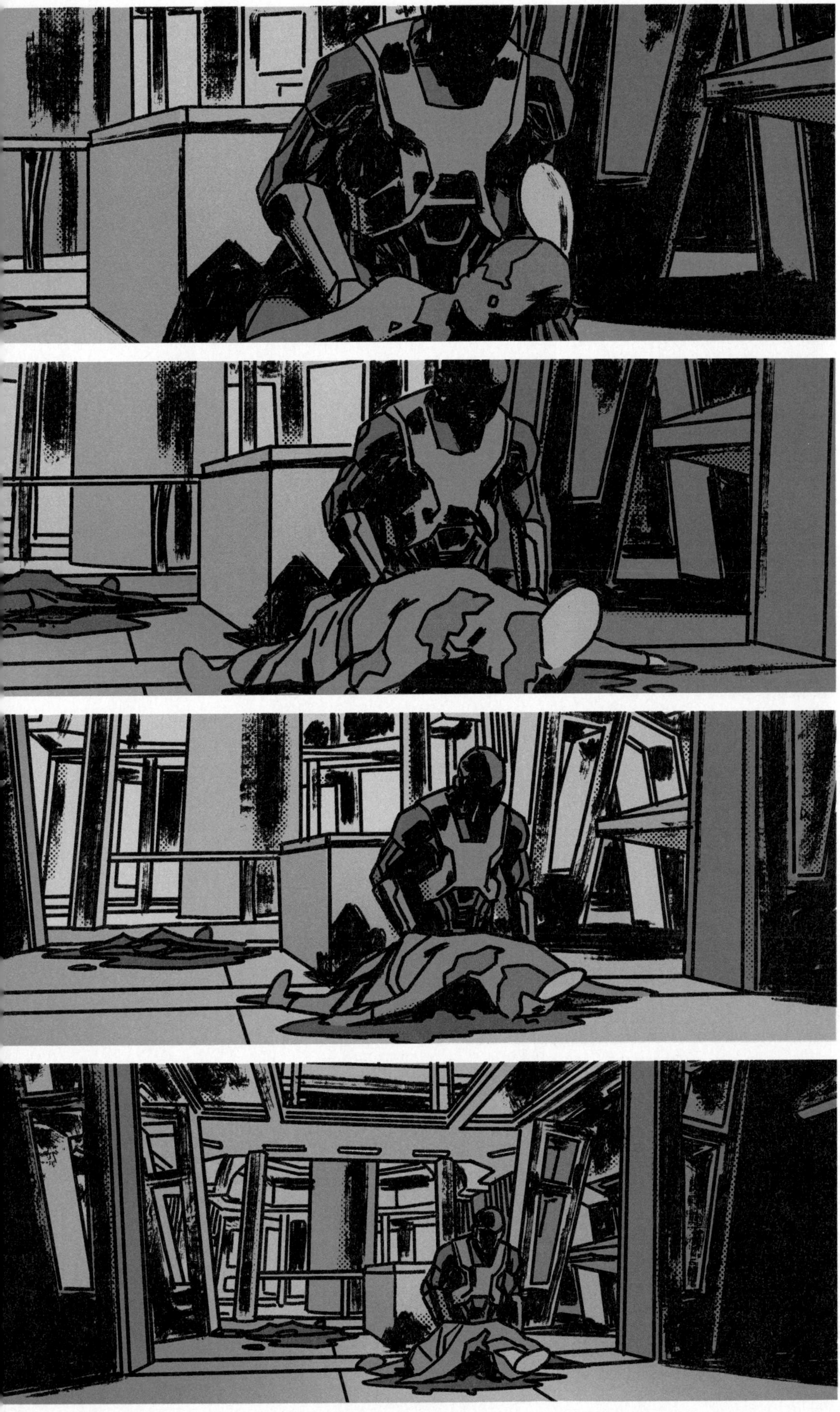

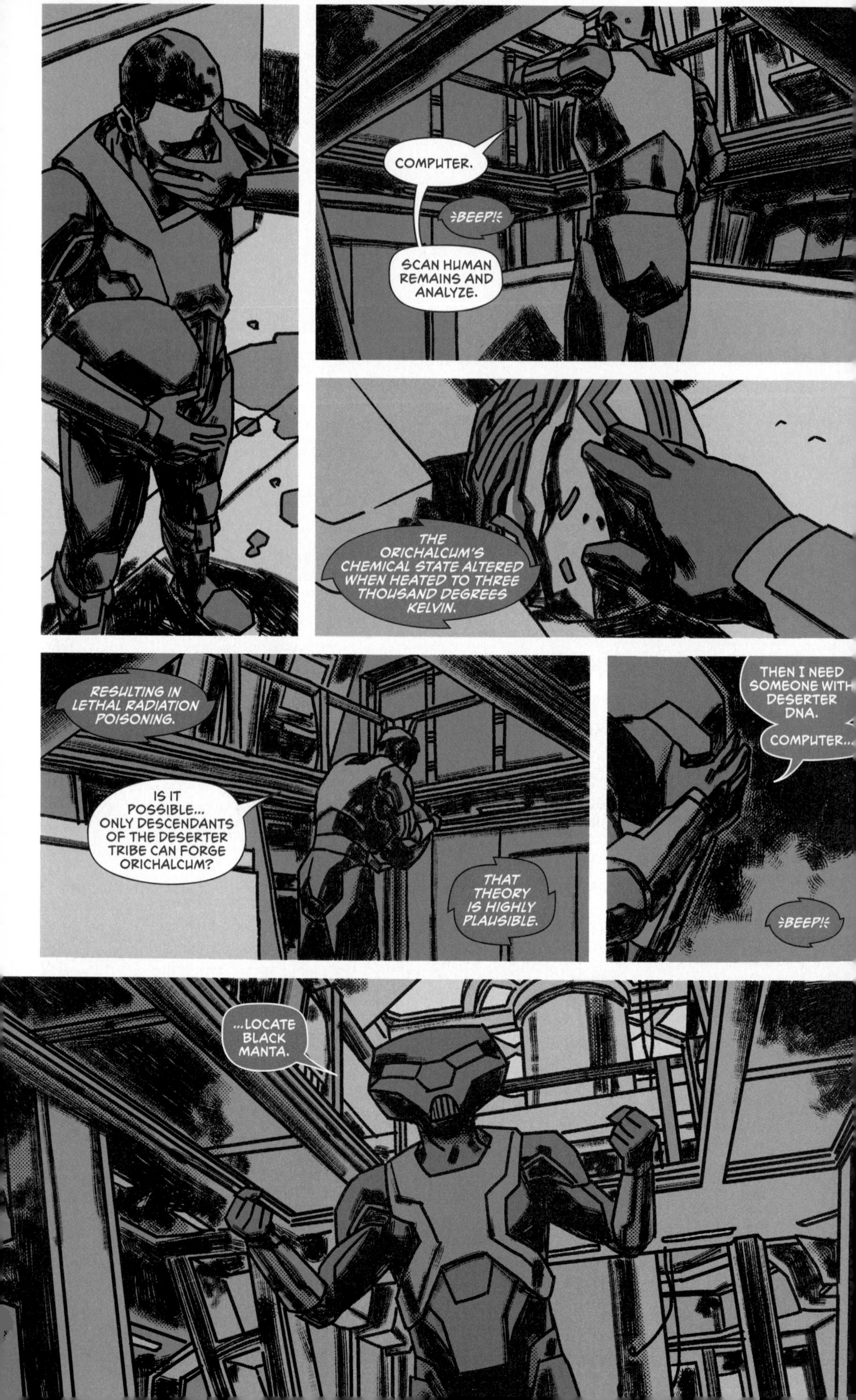
COMPUTER.
⇉BEEP!⇇
SCAN HUMAN REMAINS AND ANALYZE.
THE ORICHALCUM'S CHEMICAL STATE ALTERED WHEN HEATED TO THREE THOUSAND DEGREES KELVIN.
RESULTING IN LETHAL RADIATION POISONING.
IS IT POSSIBLE... ONLY DESCENDANTS OF THE DESERTER TRIBE CAN FORGE ORICHALCUM?
THAT THEORY IS HIGHLY PLAUSIBLE.
THEN I NEED SOMEONE WITH DESERTER DNA.
COMPUTER...
⇉BEEP!⇇
...LOCATE BLACK MANTA.

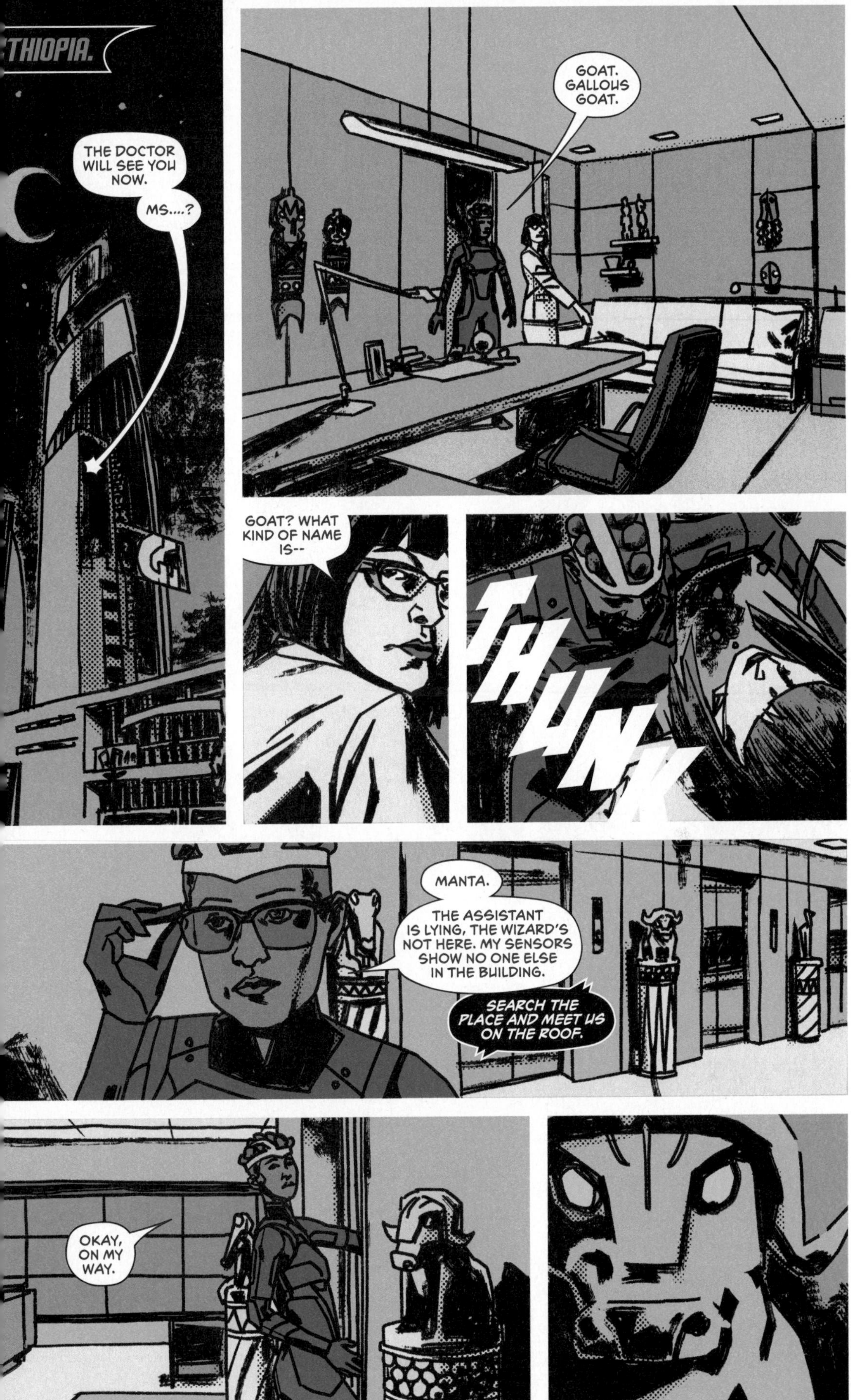
THIOPIA.
THE DOCTOR WILL SEE YOU NOW.
MS....?
GOAT. GALLOWS GOAT.
GOAT? WHAT KIND OF NAME IS--
THUNK
MANTA.
THE ASSISTANT IS LYING, THE WIZARD'S NOT HERE. MY SENSORS SHOW NO ONE ELSE IN THE BUILDING.
SEARCH THE PLACE AND MEET US ON THE ROOF.
OKAY, ON MY WAY.

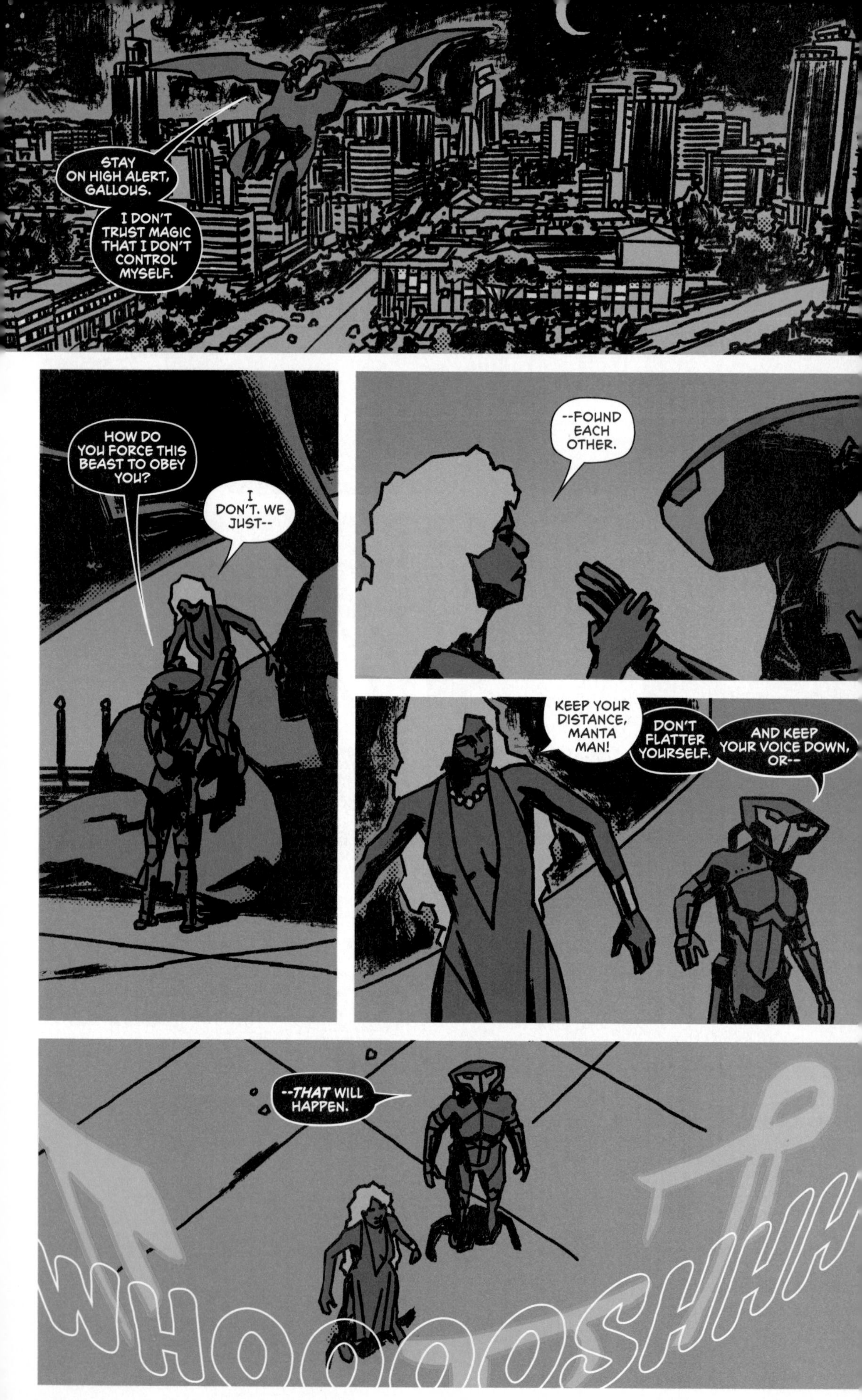
STAY ON HIGH ALERT, GALLOUS.
I DON'T TRUST MAGIC THAT I DON'T CONTROL MYSELF.
HOW DO YOU FORCE THIS BEAST TO OBEY YOU?
I DON'T. WE JUST--
--FOUND EACH OTHER.
KEEP YOUR DISTANCE, MANTA MAN!
DON'T FLATTER YOURSELF.
AND KEEP YOUR VOICE DOWN, OR--
--THAT WILL HAPPEN.
WHOOOOSHHH

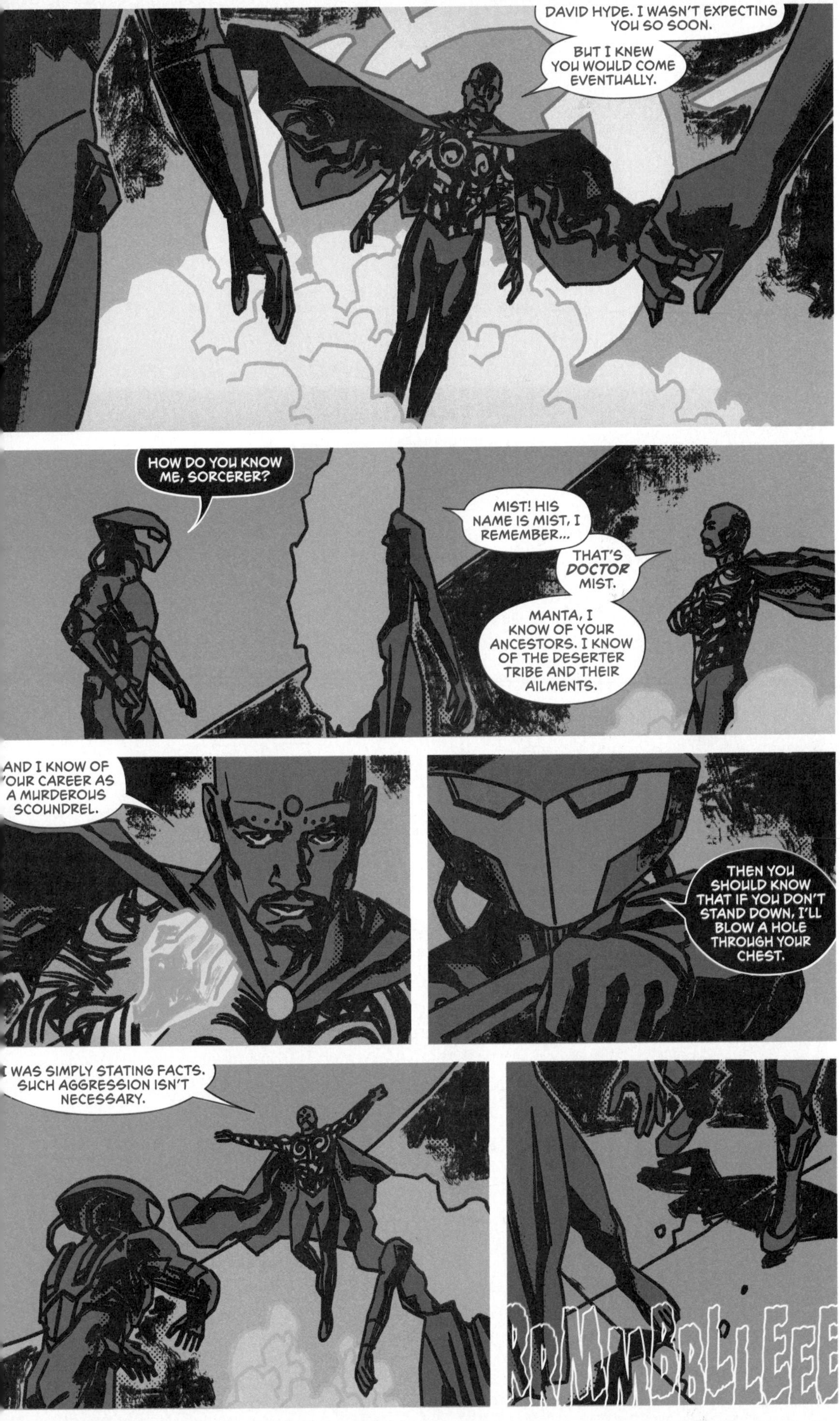
DAVID HYDE. I WASN'T EXPECTING YOU SO SOON.
BUT I KNEW YOU WOULD COME EVENTUALLY.
HOW DO YOU KNOW ME, SORCERER?
MIST! HIS NAME IS MIST, I REMEMBER...
THAT'S *DOCTOR* MIST.
MANTA, I KNOW OF YOUR ANCESTORS. I KNOW OF THE DESERTER TRIBE AND THEIR AILMENTS.
AND I KNOW OF YOUR CAREER AS A MURDEROUS SCOUNDREL.
THEN YOU SHOULD KNOW THAT IF YOU DON'T STAND DOWN, I'LL BLOW A HOLE THROUGH YOUR CHEST.
I WAS SIMPLY STATING FACTS. SUCH AGGRESSION ISN'T NECESSARY.
RRMMMBBLLEEE

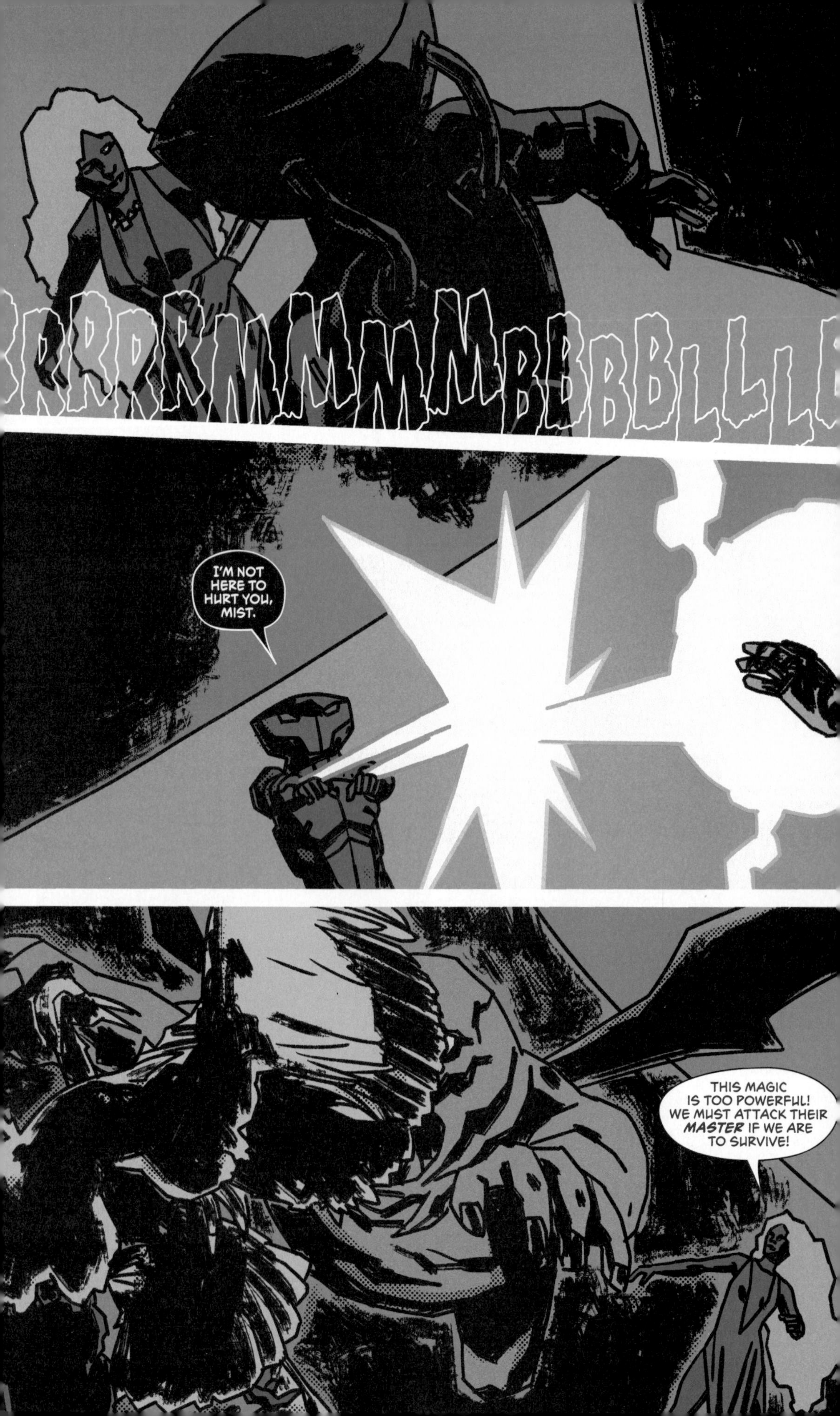
RRRRMMMMBBBLLL
I'M NOT HERE TO HURT YOU, MIST.
THIS MAGIC IS TOO POWERFUL! WE MUST ATTACK THEIR MASTER IF WE ARE TO SURVIVE!

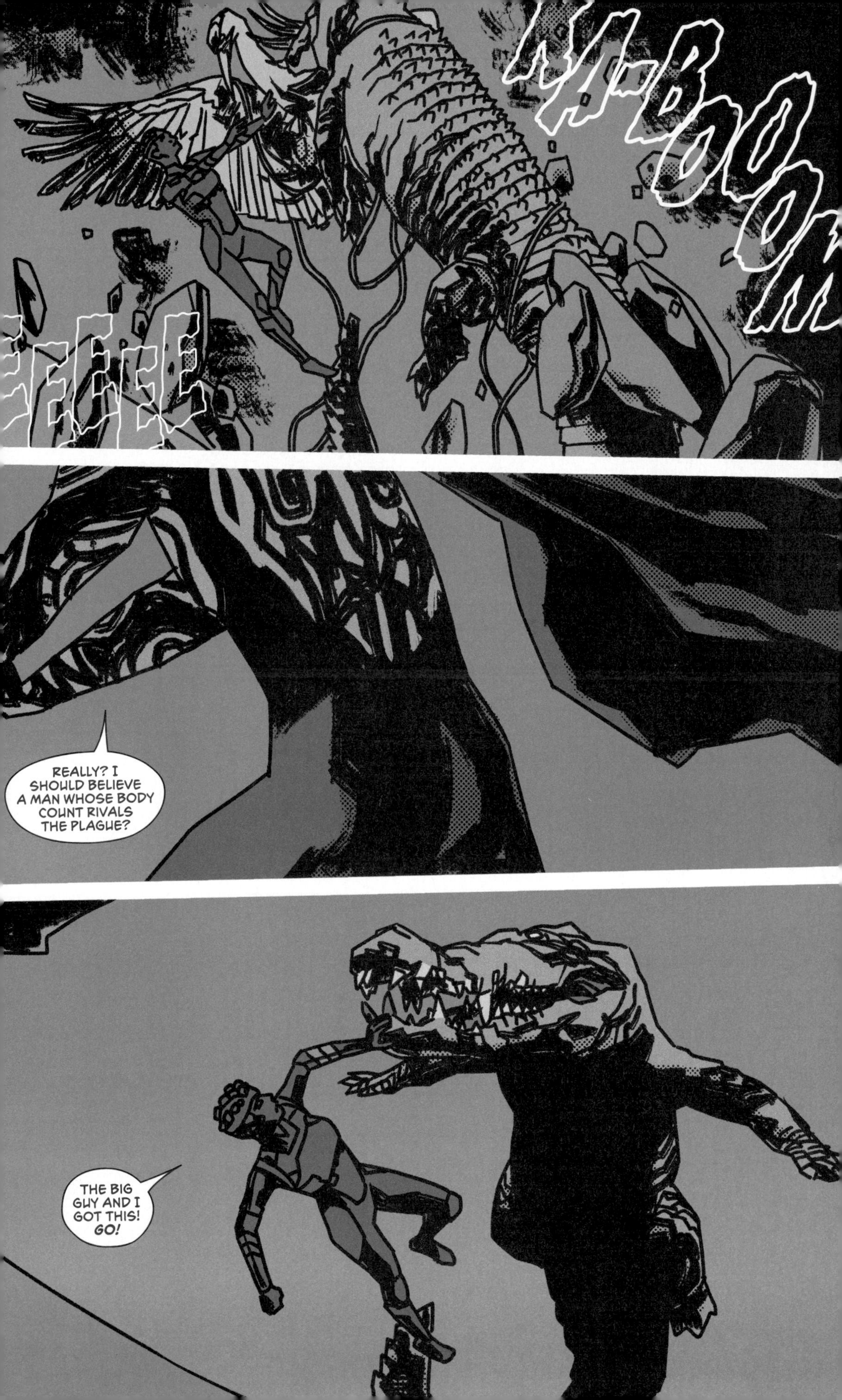
KA-BOOM
EEEEE
REALLY? I SHOULD BELIEVE A MAN WHOSE BODY COUNT RIVALS THE PLAGUE?
THE BIG GUY AND I GOT THIS! GO!

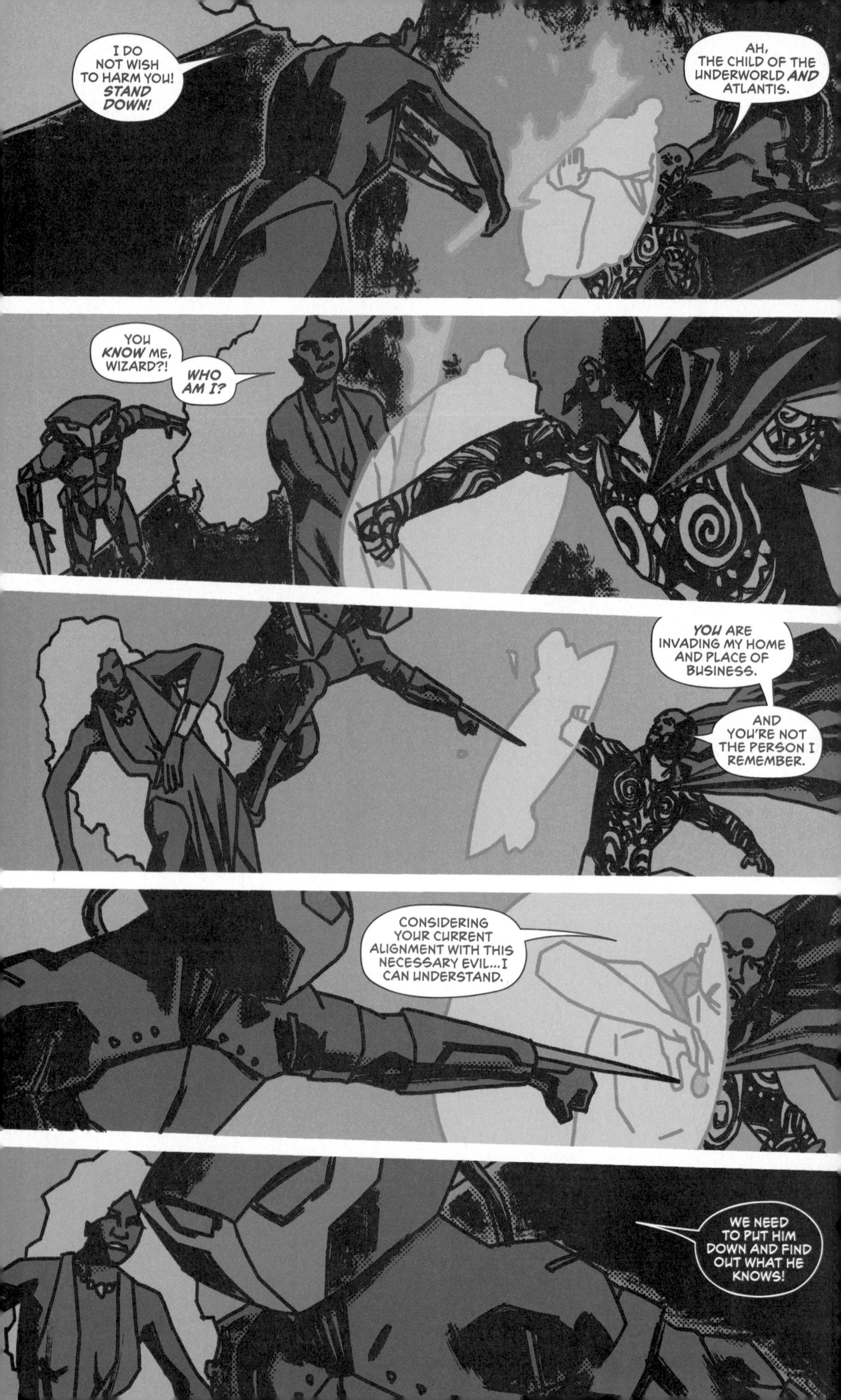
I DO NOT WISH TO HARM YOU! STAND DOWN!
AH, THE CHILD OF THE UNDERWORLD AND ATLANTIS.
YOU KNOW ME, WIZARD?!
WHO AM I?
YOU ARE INVADING MY HOME AND PLACE OF BUSINESS.
AND YOU'RE NOT THE PERSON I REMEMBER.
CONSIDERING YOUR CURRENT ALIGNMENT WITH THIS NECESSARY EVIL...I CAN UNDERSTAND.
WE NEED TO PUT HIM DOWN AND FIND OUT WHAT HE KNOWS!

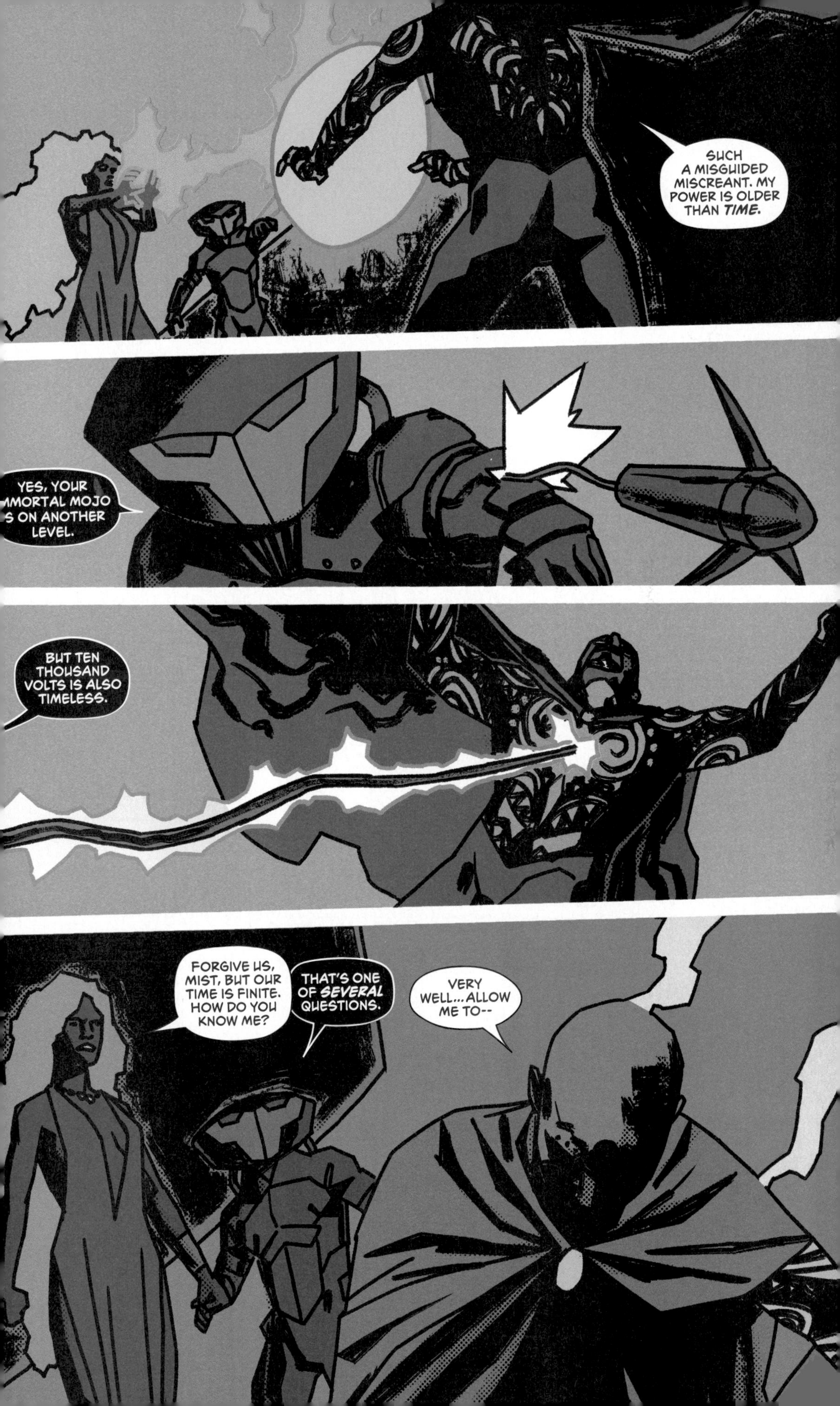
SUCH A MISGUIDED MISCREANT. MY POWER IS OLDER THAN *TIME.*
YES, YOUR
MMORTAL MOJO
S ON ANOTHER
LEVEL.
BUT TEN THOUSAND VOLTS IS ALSO TIMELESS.
FORGIVE US, MIST, BUT OUR TIME IS FINITE. HOW DO YOU KNOW ME?
THAT'S ONE OF *SEVERAL* QUESTIONS.
VERY WELL... ALLOW ME TO--

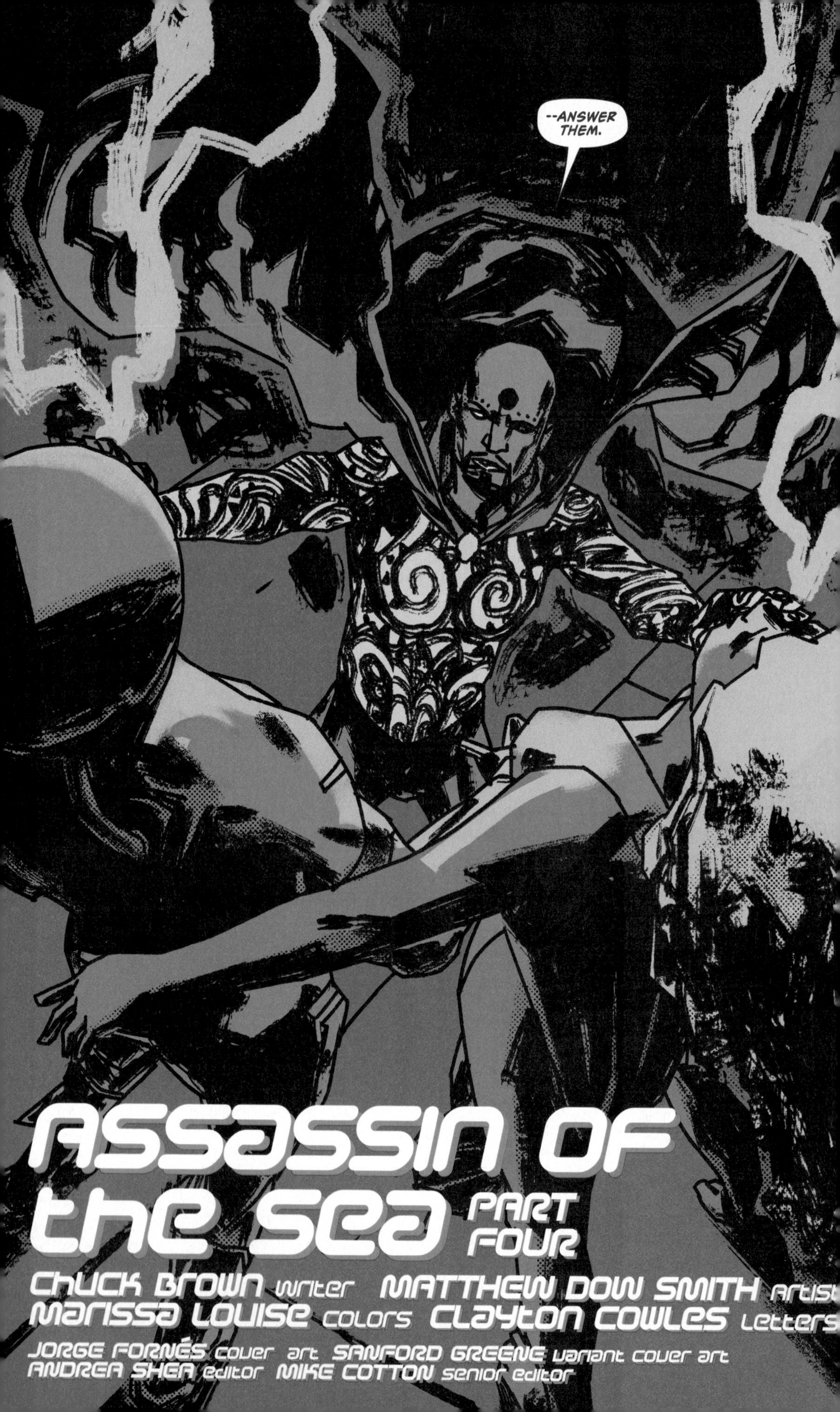

--ANSWER THEM.
ASSASSIN OF THE SEA PART FOUR
CHUCK BROWN writer MATTHEW DOW SMITH artist
MARISSA LOUISE colors CLAYTON COWLES letters
JORGE FORNÉS cover art SANFORD GREENE variant cover art
ANDREA SHEA editor MIKE COTTON senior editor

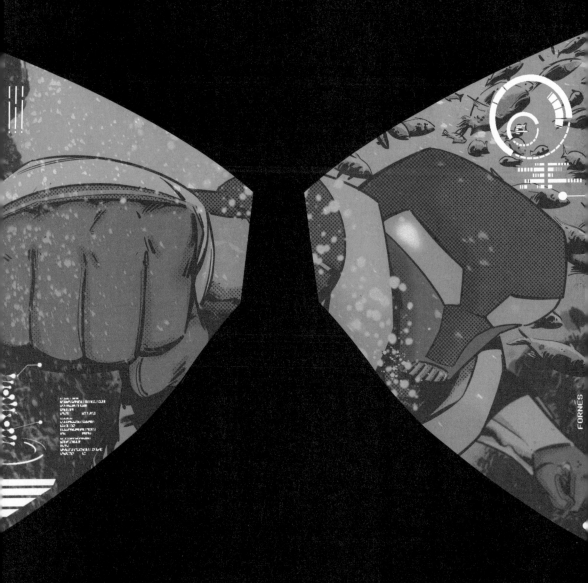

Black Manta #5 cover by Jorge Fornés

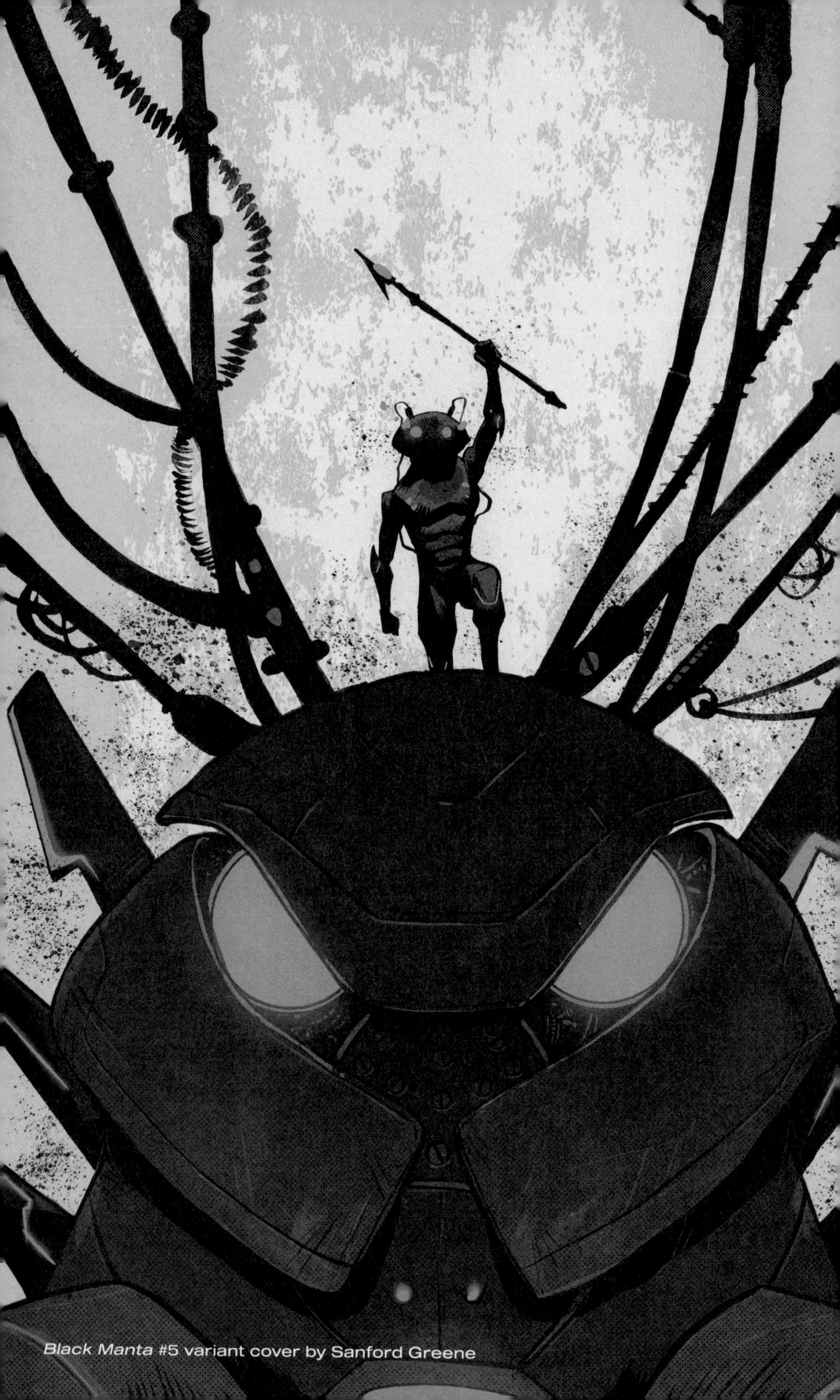

Black Manta #5 variant cover by Sanford Greene

Dear Black Manta,

I've patterned my life after yours.

But I did one thing wrong.

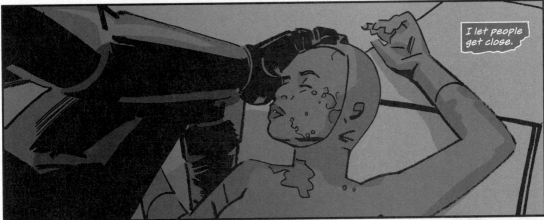

I let people get close.

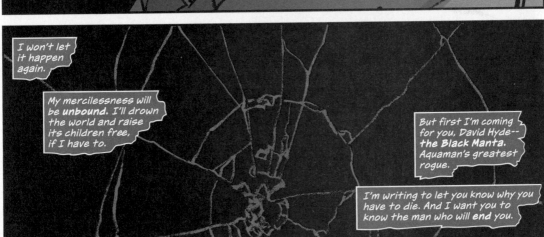

I won't let it happen again.

My mercilessness will be **unbound.** I'll drown the world and raise its children free, if I have to.

But first I'm coming for you, David Hyde-- **the Black Manta.** Aquaman's greatest rogue.

I'm writing to let you know why you have to die. And I want you to know the man who will **end** you.

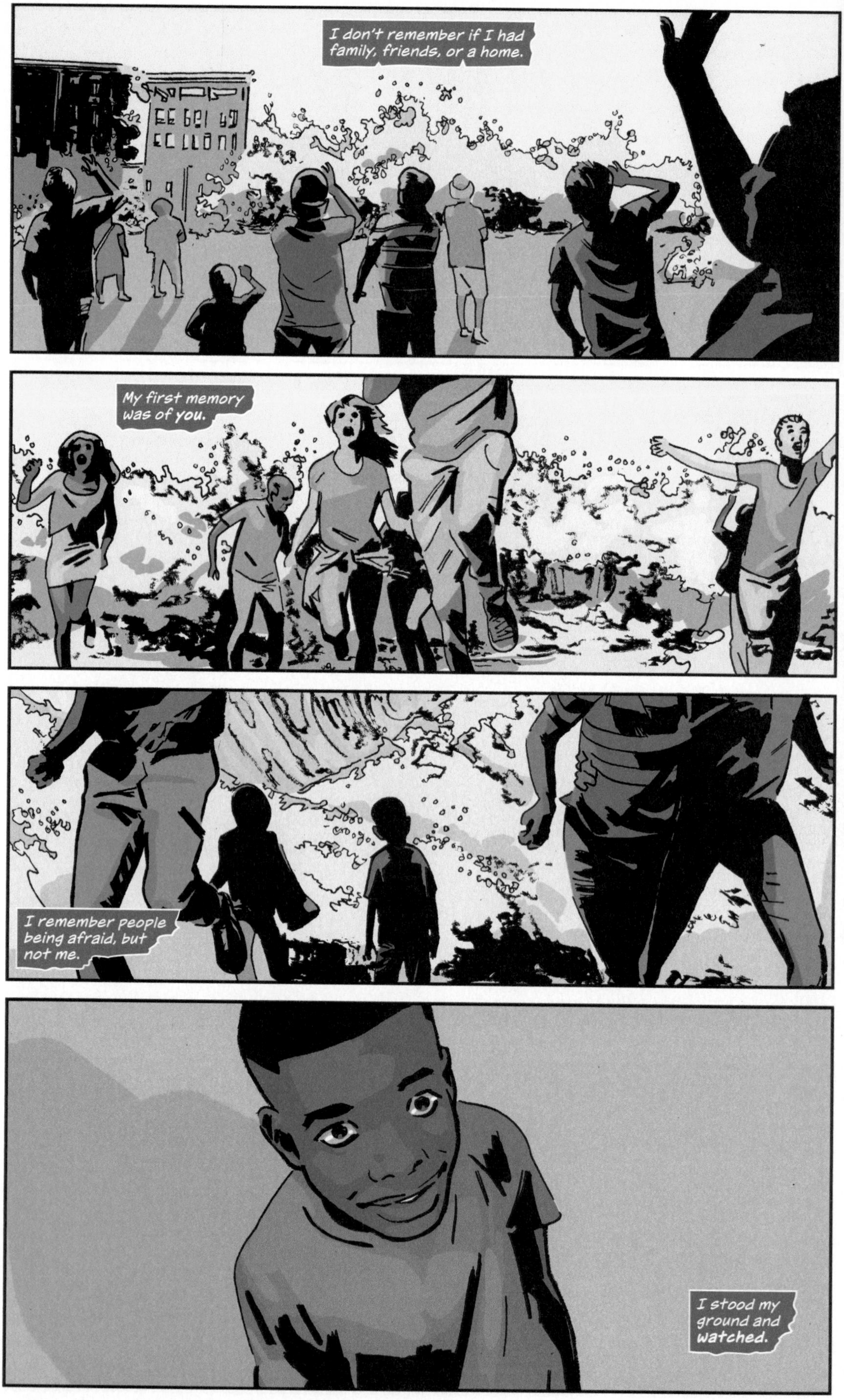
I don't remember if I had family, friends, or a home.
My first memory was of you.
I remember people being afraid, but not me.
I stood my ground and watched.

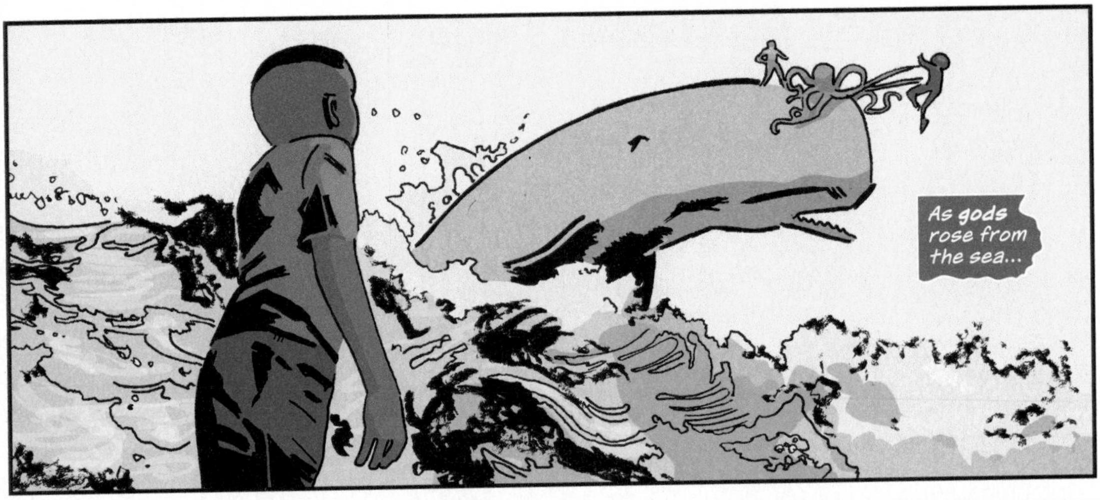
As gods rose from the sea...
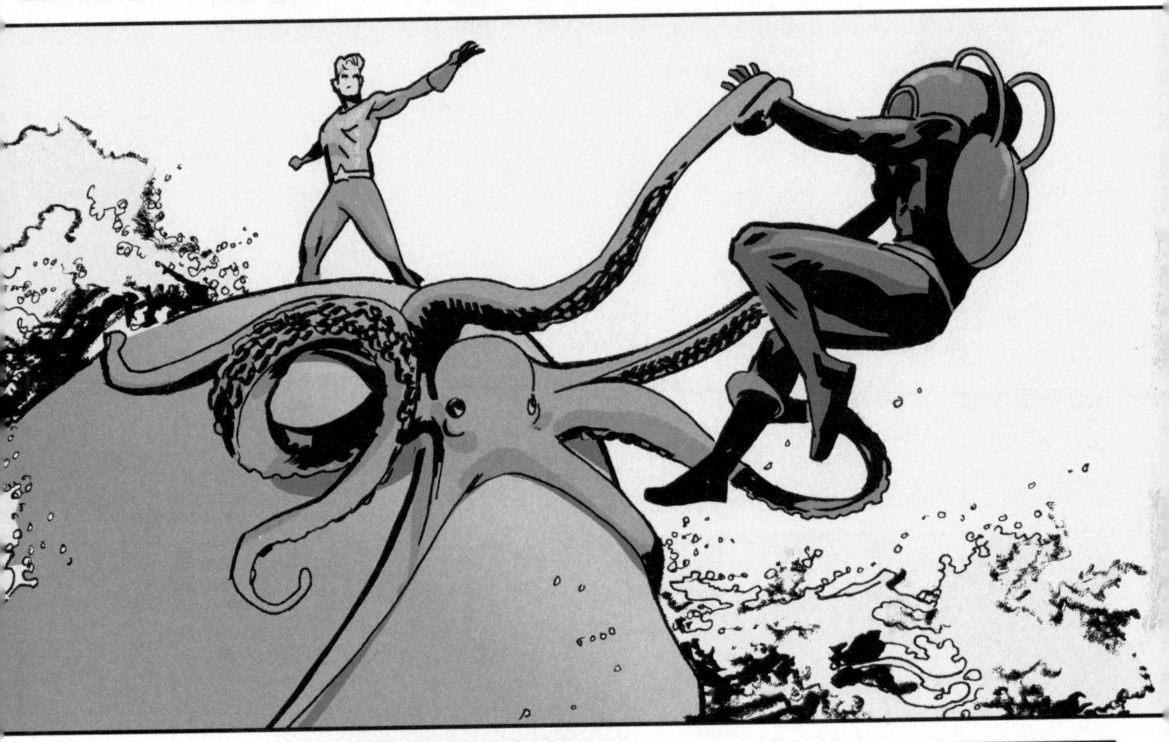
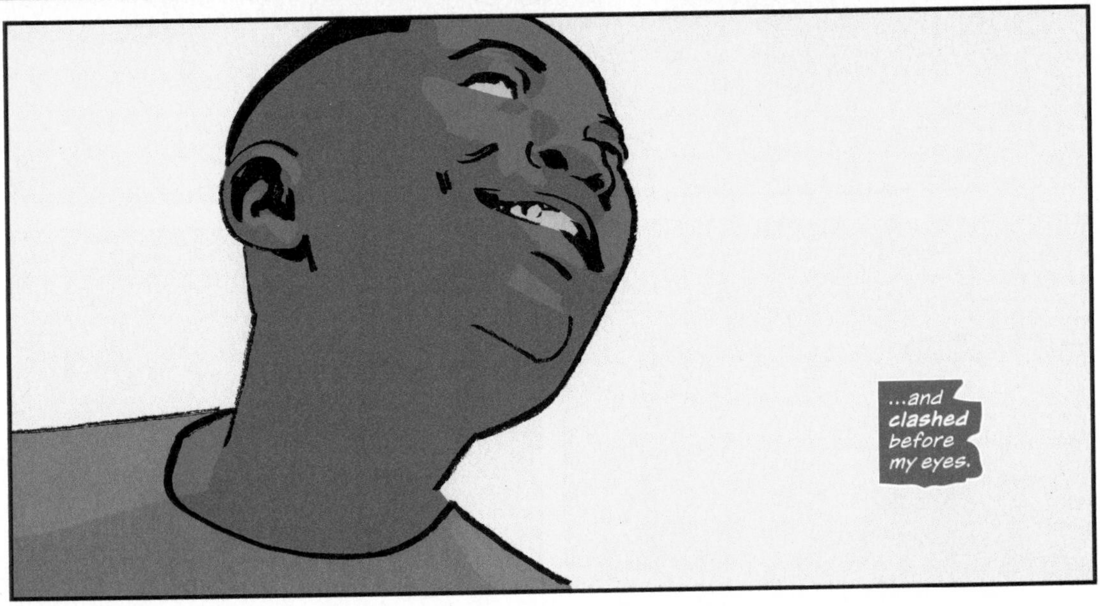
...and clashed before my eyes.

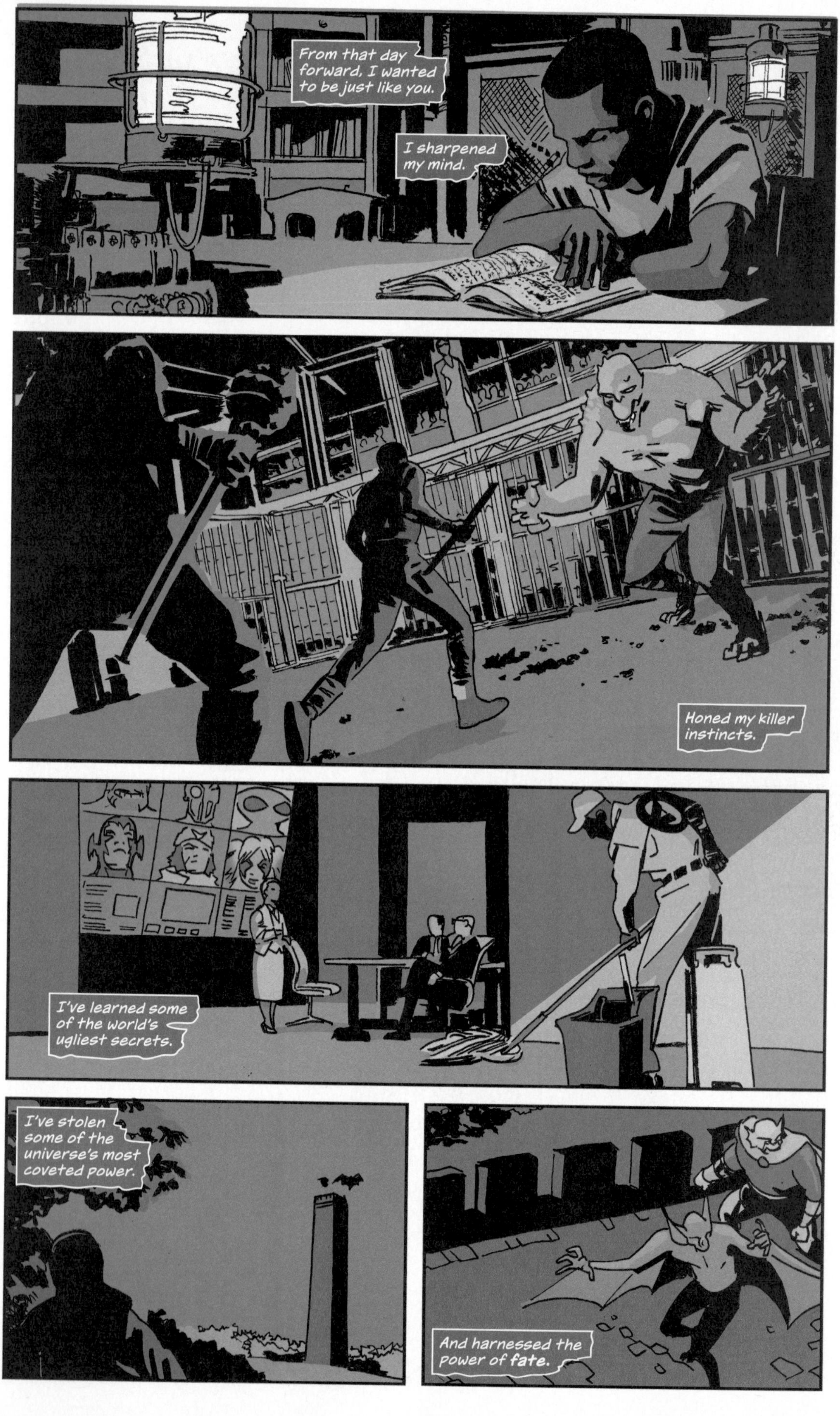
From that day forward, I wanted to be just like you.
I sharpened my mind.
Honed my killer instincts.
I've learned some of the world's ugliest secrets.
I've stolen some of the universe's most coveted power.
And harnessed the power of fate.

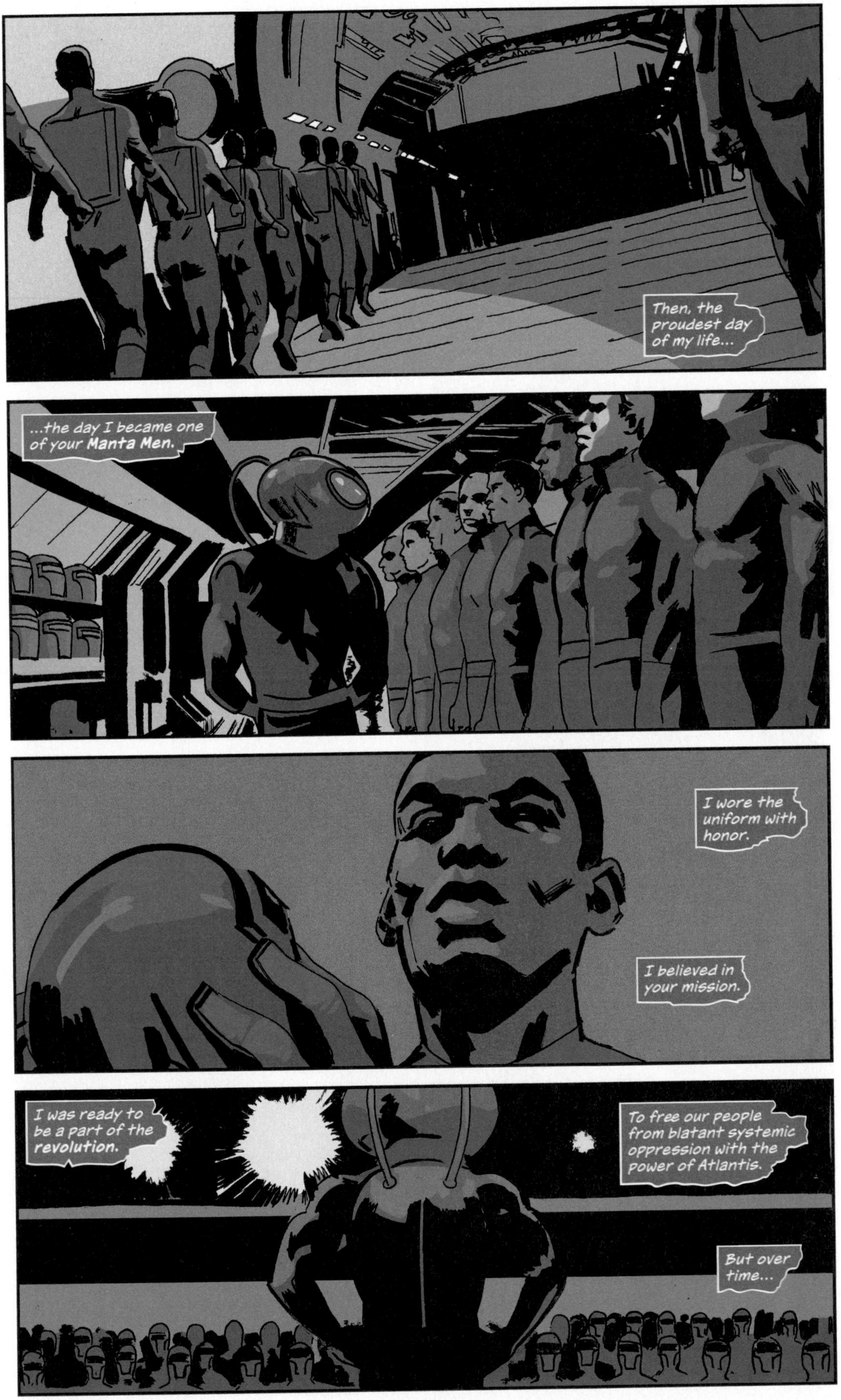

Then, the proudest day of my life...
...the day I became one of your **Manta Men.**
I wore the uniform with honor.
I believed in your mission.
I was ready to be a part of the **revolution.**
To free our people from blatant systemic oppression with the power of Atlantis.
But over time...

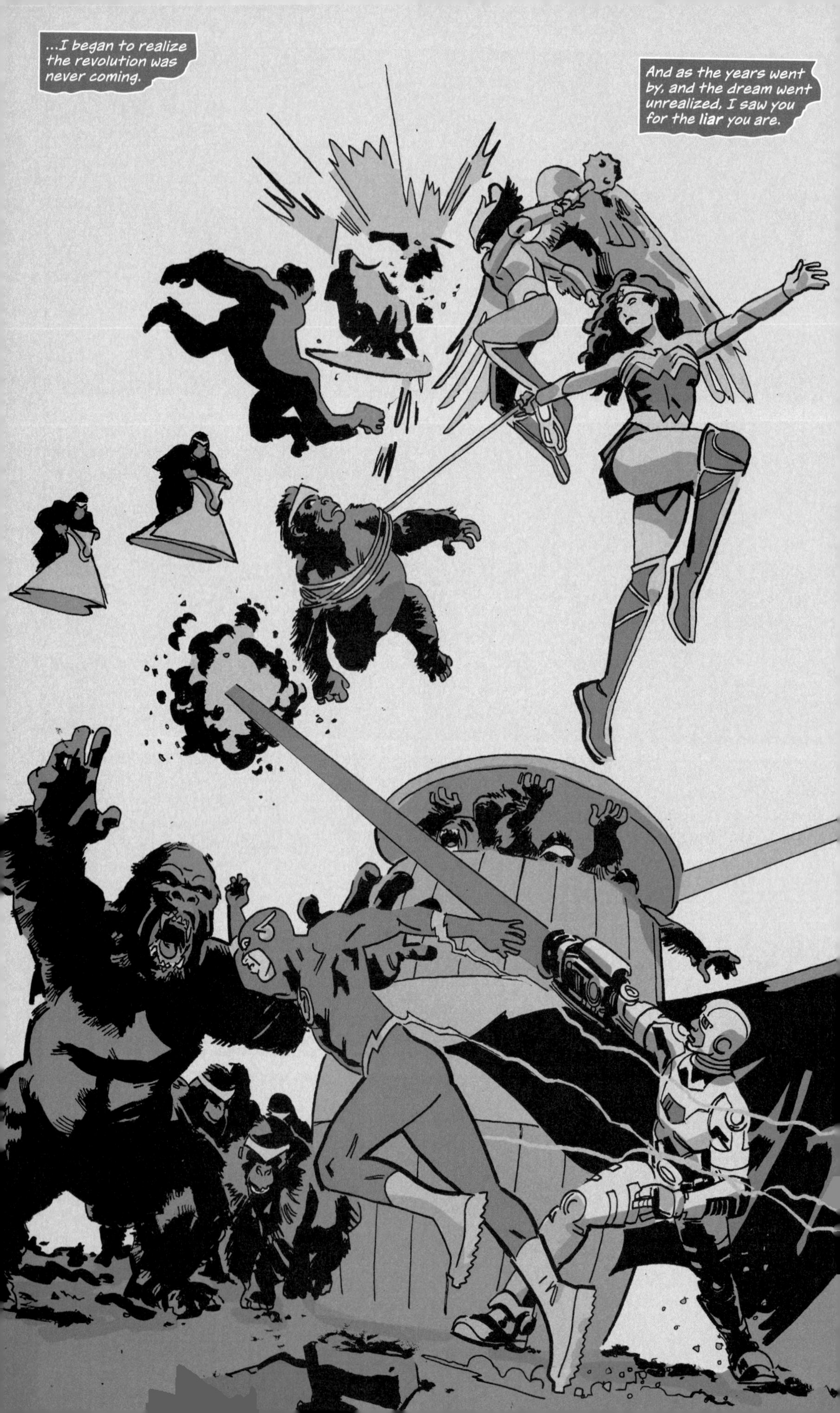
...I began to realize the revolution was never coming.
And as the years went by, and the dream went unrealized, I saw you for the **liar** you are.

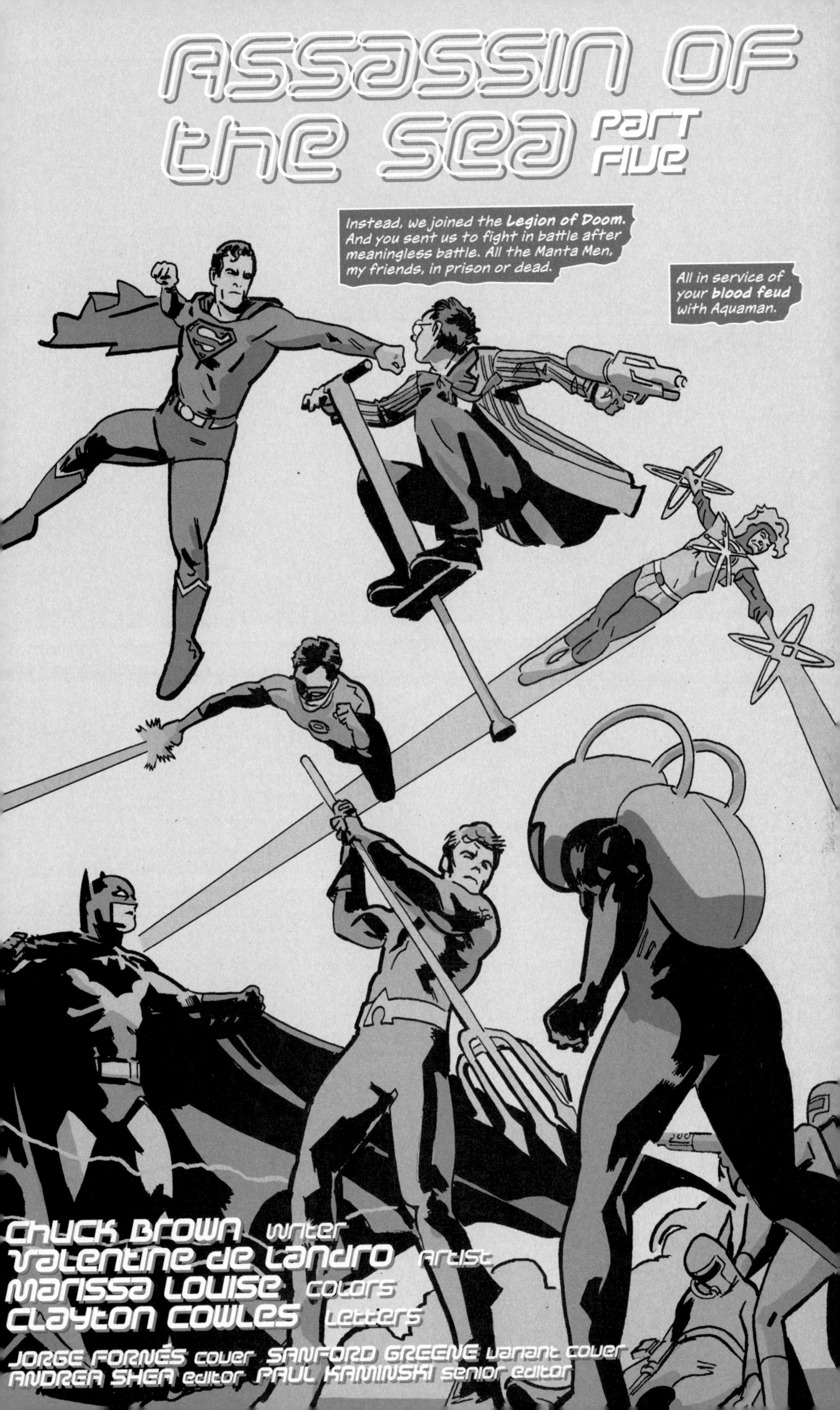
ASSASSIN OF THE SEA PART FIVE
Instead, we joined the Legion of Doom. And you sent us to fight in battle after meaningless battle. All the Manta Men, my friends, in prison or dead.
All in service of your blood feud with Aquaman.
CHUCK BROWN writer
VALENTINE DE LANDRO artist
MARISSA LOUISE colors
CLAYTON COWLES letters
JORGE FORNÉS cover SANFORD GREENE variant cover
ANDREA SHEA editor PAUL KAMINSKI senior editor

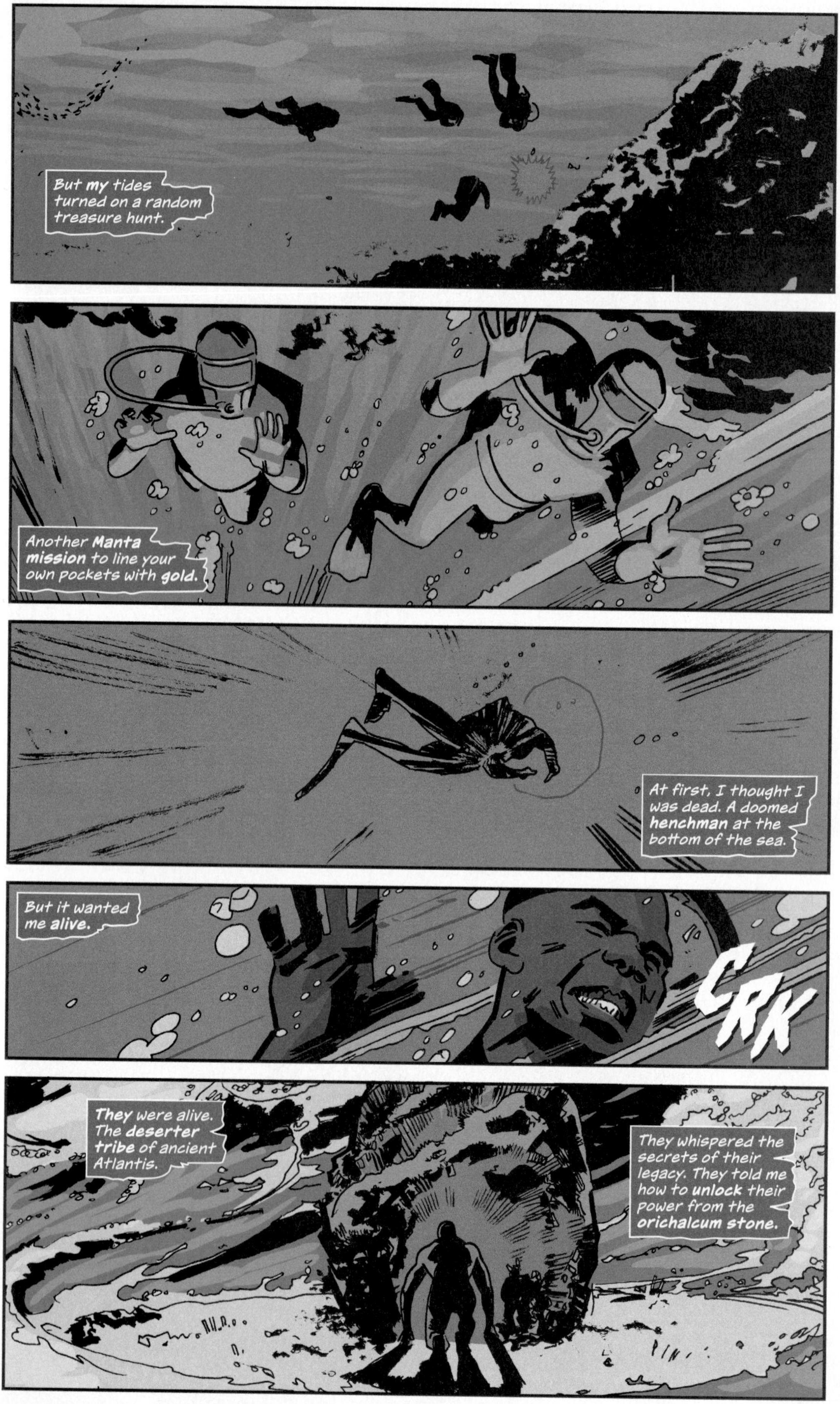
But my tides turned on a random treasure hunt.
Another Manta mission to line your own pockets with gold.
At first, I thought I was dead. A doomed henchman at the bottom of the sea.
But it wanted me alive.
CRK
They were alive. The deserter tribe of ancient Atlantis.
They whispered the secrets of their legacy. They told me how to unlock their power from the orichalcum stone.

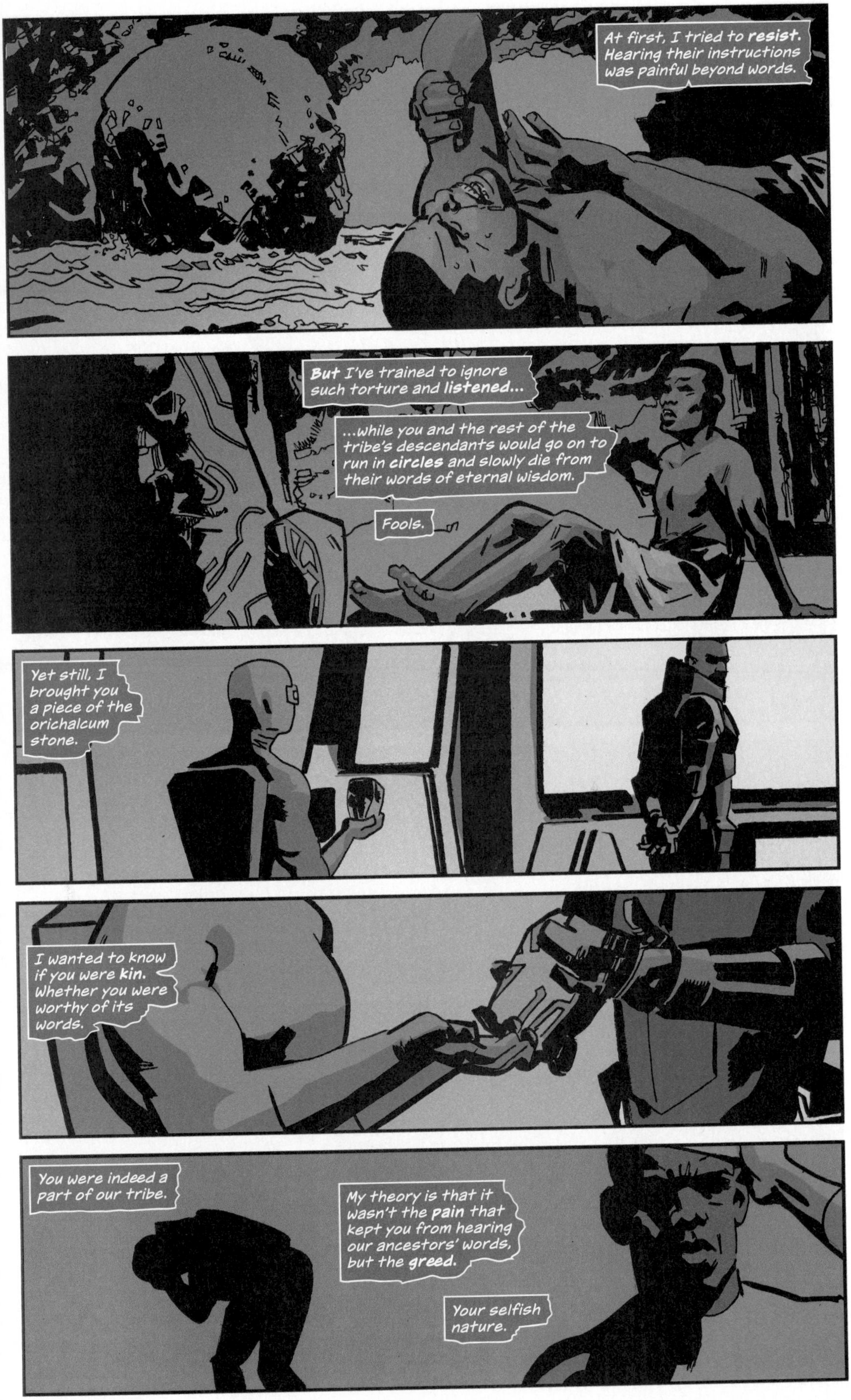
At first, I tried to resist. Hearing their instructions was painful beyond words.
But I've trained to ignore such torture and listened...
...while you and the rest of the tribe's descendants would go on to run in circles and slowly die from their words of eternal wisdom.
Fools.
Yet still, I brought you a piece of the orichalcum stone.
I wanted to know if you were kin. Whether you were worthy of its words.
You were indeed a part of our tribe.
My theory is that it wasn't the pain that kept you from hearing our ancestors' words, but the greed.
Your selfish nature.

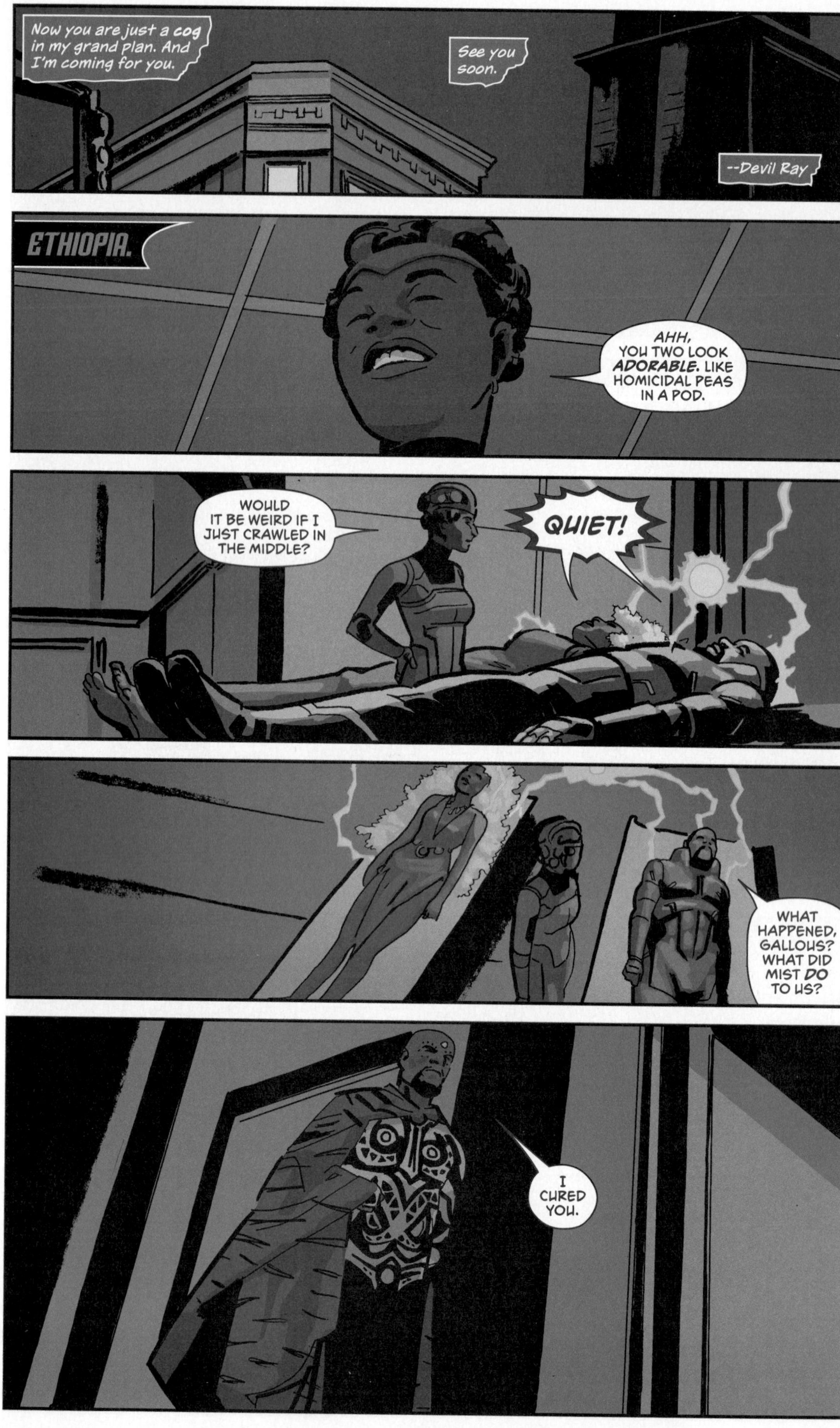

Now you are just a cog in my grand plan. And I'm coming for you.
See you soon.
--Devil Ray
ETHIOPIA.
AHH, YOU TWO LOOK ADORABLE. LIKE HOMICIDAL PEAS IN A POD.
WOULD IT BE WEIRD IF I JUST CRAWLED IN THE MIDDLE?
QUIET!
WHAT HAPPENED, GALLOUS? WHAT DID MIST DO TO US?
I CURED YOU.

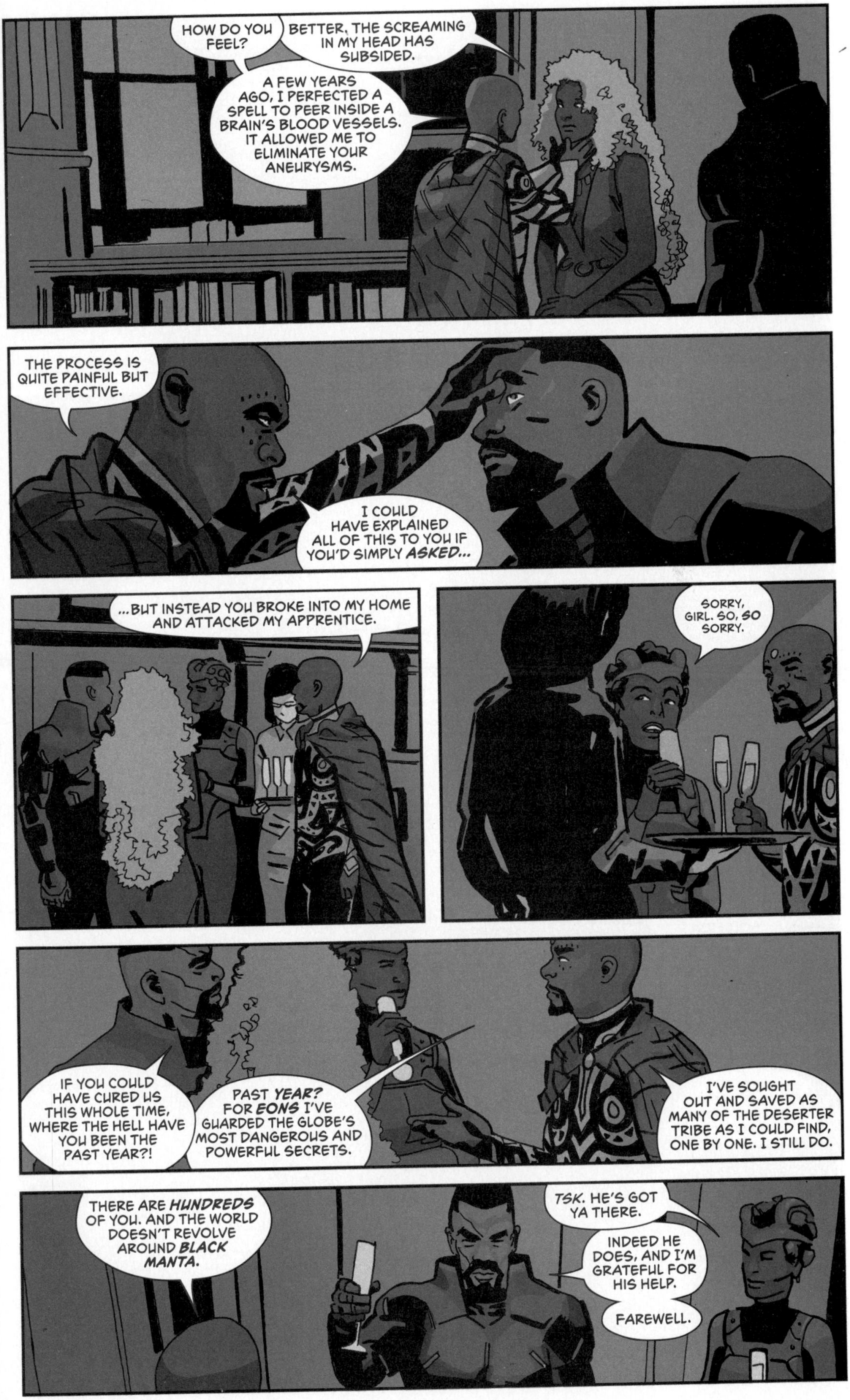
HOW DO YOU FEEL?
BETTER. THE SCREAMING IN MY HEAD HAS SUBSIDED.
A FEW YEARS AGO, I PERFECTED A SPELL TO PEER INSIDE A BRAIN'S BLOOD VESSELS. IT ALLOWED ME TO ELIMINATE YOUR ANEURYSMS.
THE PROCESS IS QUITE PAINFUL BUT EFFECTIVE.
I COULD HAVE EXPLAINED ALL OF THIS TO YOU IF YOU'D SIMPLY *ASKED*...
...BUT INSTEAD YOU BROKE INTO MY HOME AND ATTACKED MY APPRENTICE.
SORRY, GIRL. SO, *SO* SORRY.
IF YOU COULD HAVE CURED US THIS WHOLE TIME, WHERE THE HELL HAVE YOU BEEN THE PAST YEAR?!
PAST *YEAR?* FOR *EONS* I'VE GUARDED THE GLOBE'S MOST DANGEROUS AND POWERFUL SECRETS.
I'VE SOUGHT OUT AND SAVED AS MANY OF THE DESERTER TRIBE AS I COULD FIND, ONE BY ONE. I STILL DO.
THERE ARE *HUNDREDS* OF YOU. AND THE WORLD DOESN'T REVOLVE AROUND *BLACK MANTA.*
TSK. HE'S GOT YA THERE.
INDEED HE DOES, AND I'M GRATEFUL FOR HIS HELP.
FAREWELL.

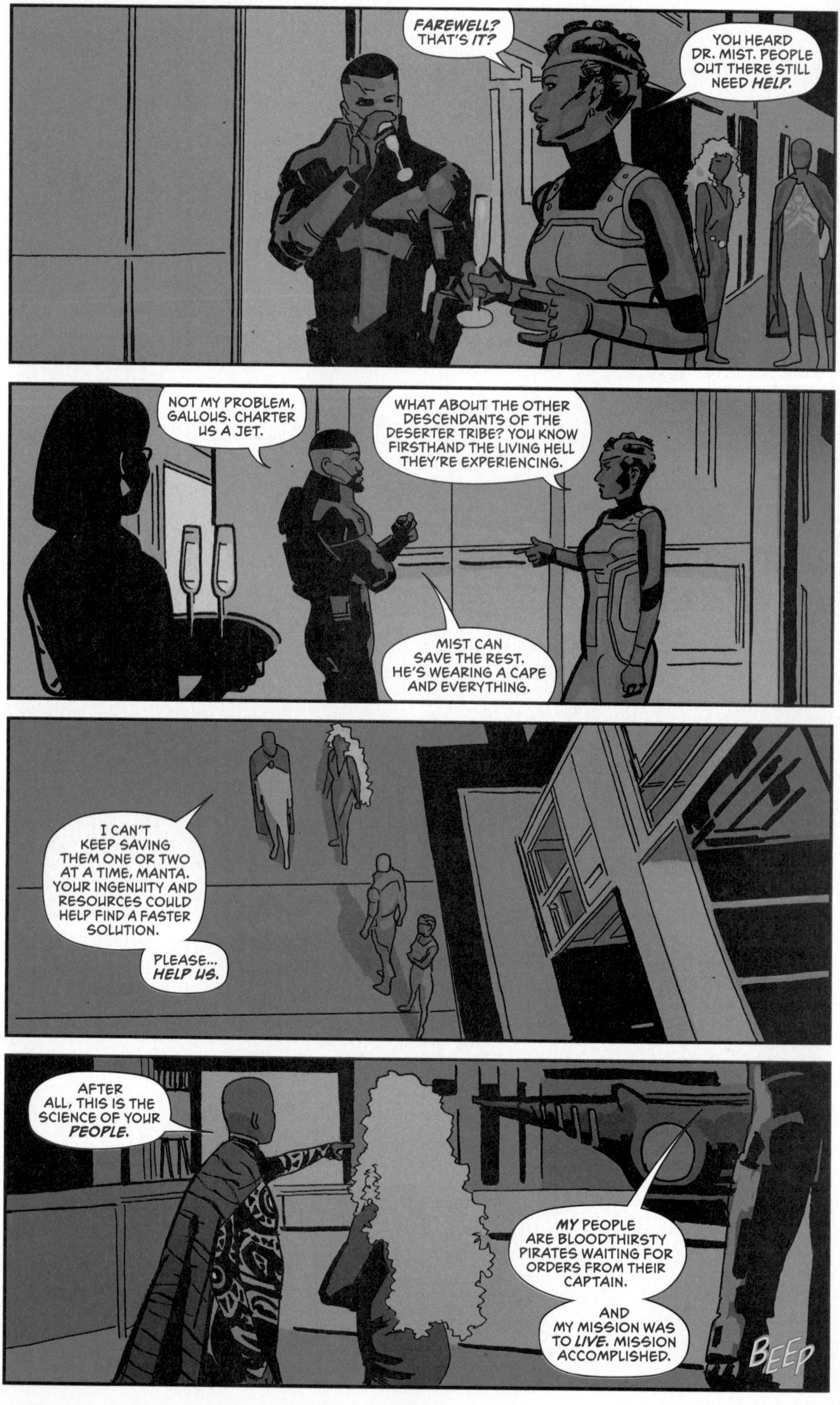

FAREWELL? THAT'S IT?
YOU HEARD DR. MIST. PEOPLE OUT THERE STILL NEED HELP.
NOT MY PROBLEM, GALLOUS. CHARTER US A JET.
WHAT ABOUT THE OTHER DESCENDANTS OF THE DESERTER TRIBE? YOU KNOW FIRSTHAND THE LIVING HELL THEY'RE EXPERIENCING.
MIST CAN SAVE THE REST. HE'S WEARING A CAPE AND EVERYTHING.
I CAN'T KEEP SAVING THEM ONE OR TWO AT A TIME, MANTA. YOUR INGENUITY AND RESOURCES COULD HELP FIND A FASTER SOLUTION.
PLEASE... HELP US.
AFTER ALL, THIS IS THE SCIENCE OF YOUR PEOPLE.
MY PEOPLE ARE BLOODTHIRSTY PIRATES WAITING FOR ORDERS FROM THEIR CAPTAIN.
AND MY MISSION WAS TO LIVE. MISSION ACCOMPLISHED.
BEEP

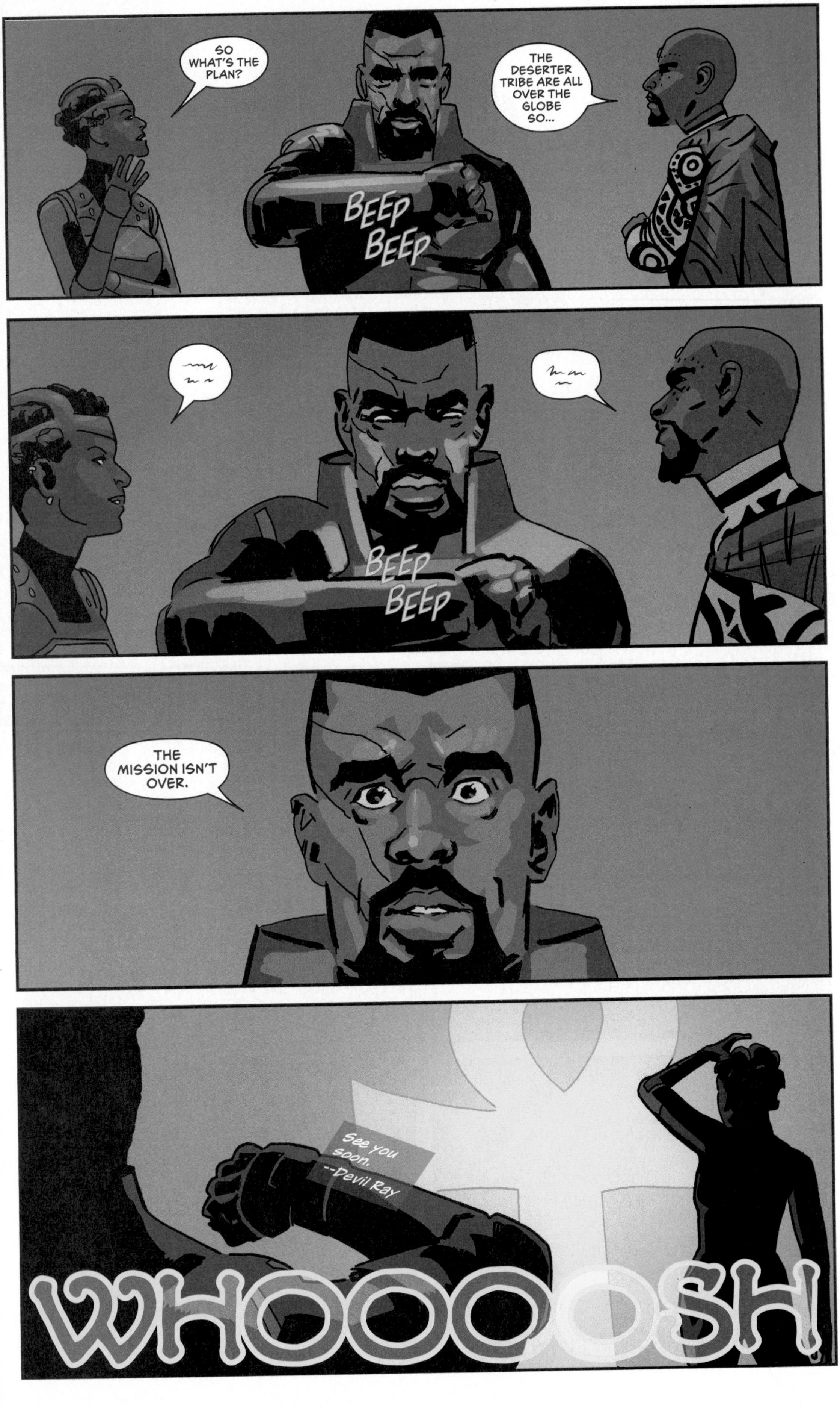
SO WHAT'S THE PLAN?
THE DESERTER TRIBE ARE ALL OVER THE GLOBE SO...
BEEP BEEP
BEEP BEEP
THE MISSION ISN'T OVER.
See you soon.
--Devil Ray
WHOOOOSH

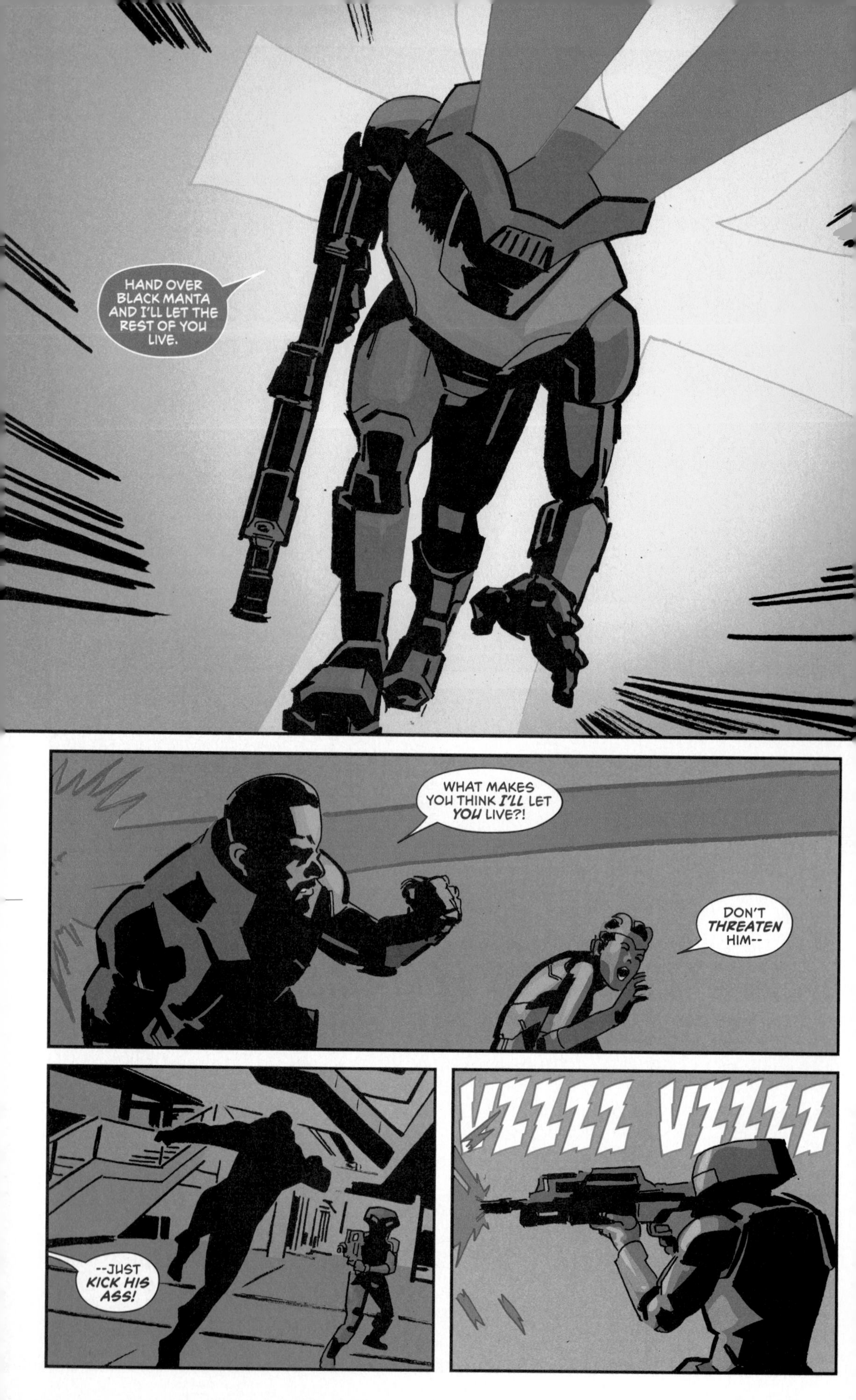
HAND OVER BLACK MANTA AND I'LL LET THE REST OF YOU LIVE.
WHAT MAKES YOU THINK I'LL LET YOU LIVE?!
DON'T THREATEN HIM--
--JUST KICK HIS ASS!
VZZZZ VZZZZ

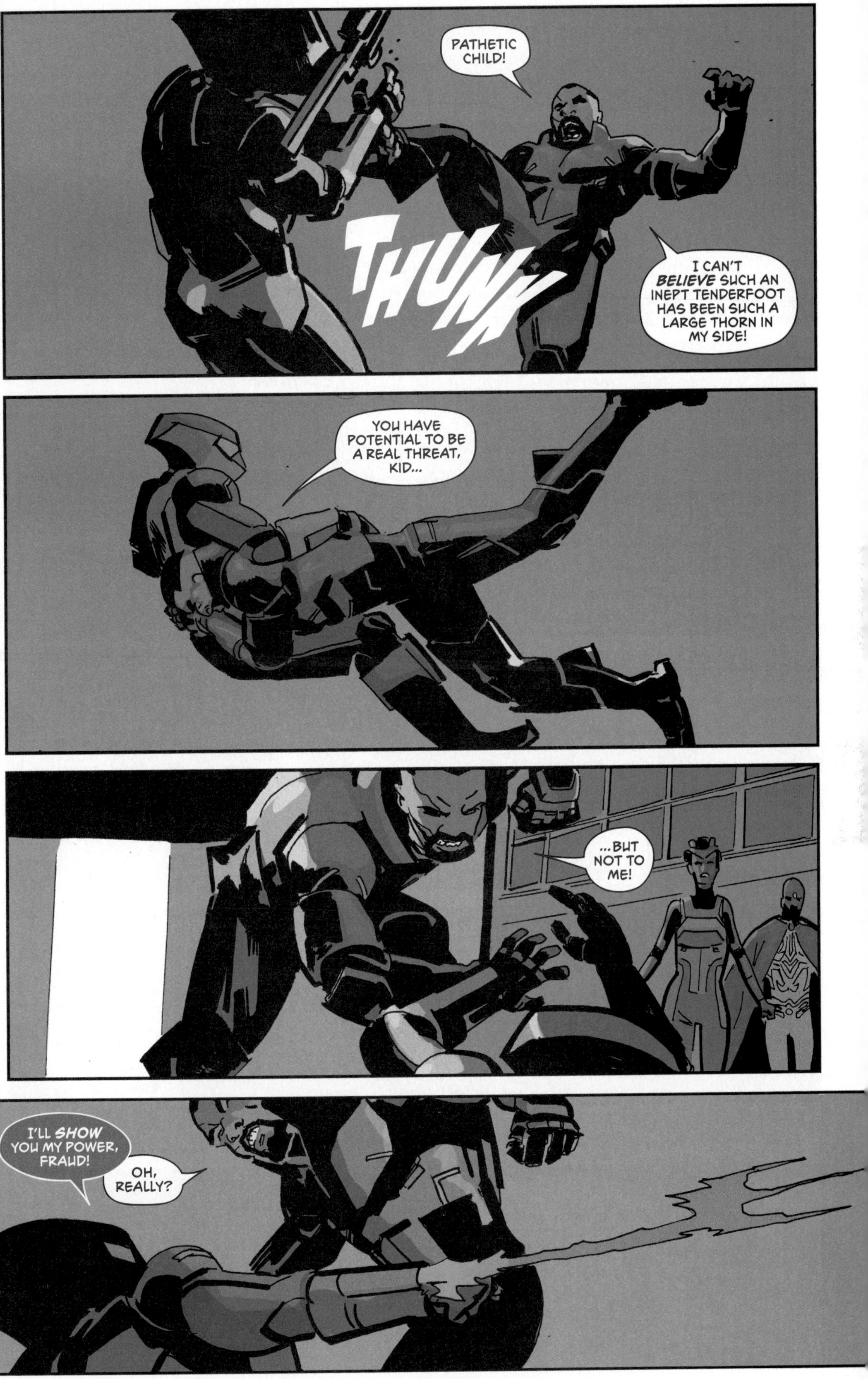

PATHETIC CHILD!
THUNK
I CAN'T BELIEVE SUCH AN INEPT TENDERFOOT HAS BEEN SUCH A LARGE THORN IN MY SIDE!
YOU HAVE POTENTIAL TO BE A REAL THREAT, KID...
...BUT NOT TO ME!
I'LL SHOW YOU MY POWER, FRAUD!
OH, REALLY?

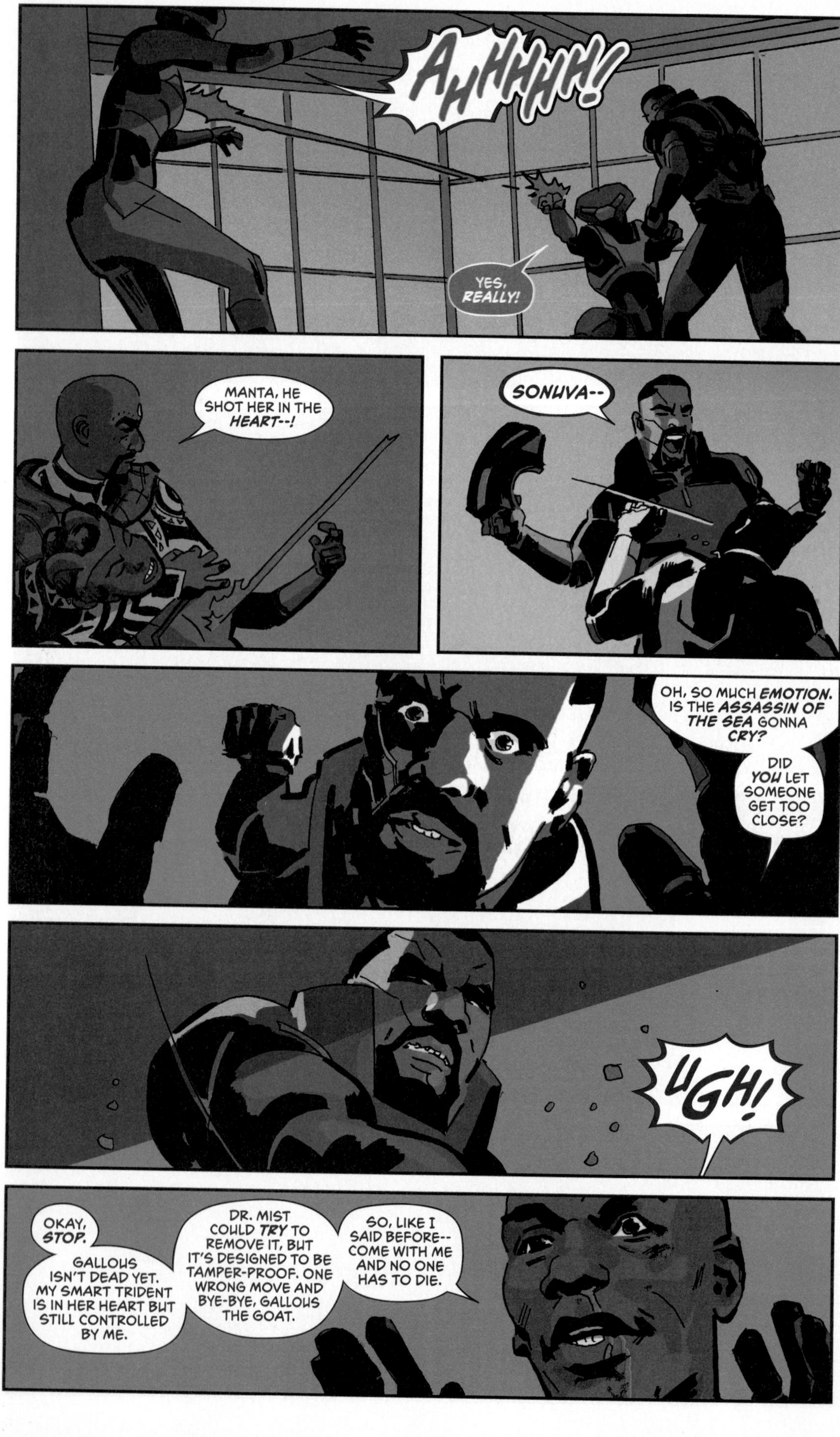
AHHHHHH!
YES, REALLY!
MANTA, HE SHOT HER IN THE HEART--!
SONUVA--
OH, SO MUCH EMOTION. IS THE ASSASSIN OF THE SEA GONNA CRY?
DID YOU LET SOMEONE GET TOO CLOSE?
UGH!
OKAY, STOP.
GALLOUS ISN'T DEAD YET. MY SMART TRIDENT IS IN HER HEART BUT STILL CONTROLLED BY ME.
DR. MIST COULD TRY TO REMOVE IT, BUT IT'S DESIGNED TO BE TAMPER-PROOF. ONE WRONG MOVE AND BYE-BYE, GALLOUS THE GOAT.
SO, LIKE I SAID BEFORE-- COME WITH ME AND NO ONE HAS TO DIE.

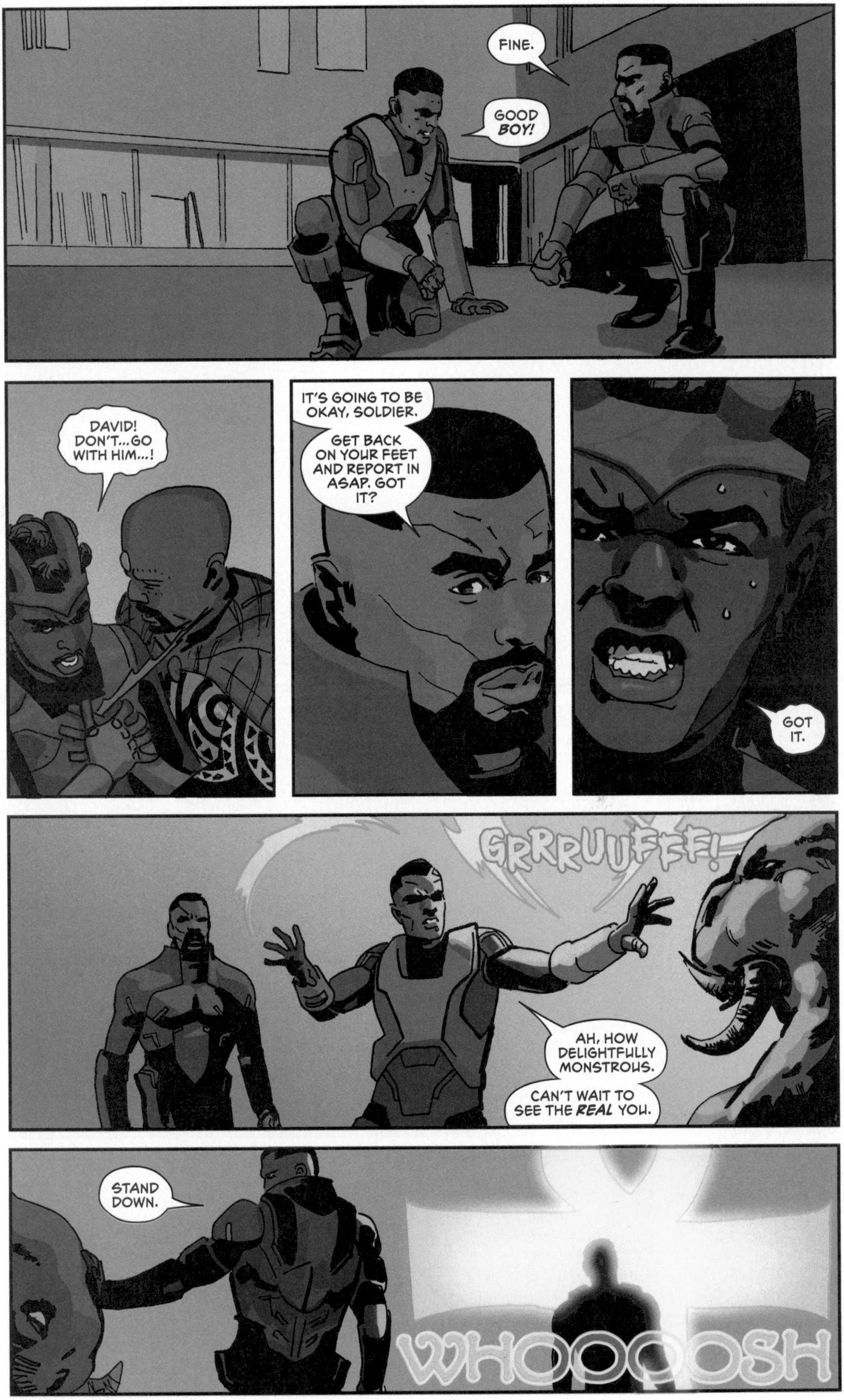

FINE.
GOOD BOY!
DAVID! DON'T...GO WITH HIM...!
IT'S GOING TO BE OKAY, SOLDIER.
GET BACK ON YOUR FEET AND REPORT IN ASAP. GOT IT?
GOT IT.
GRRRUUFFF!
AH, HOW DELIGHTFULLY MONSTROUS.
CAN'T WAIT TO SEE THE *REAL* YOU.
STAND DOWN.
WHOOOOOSH

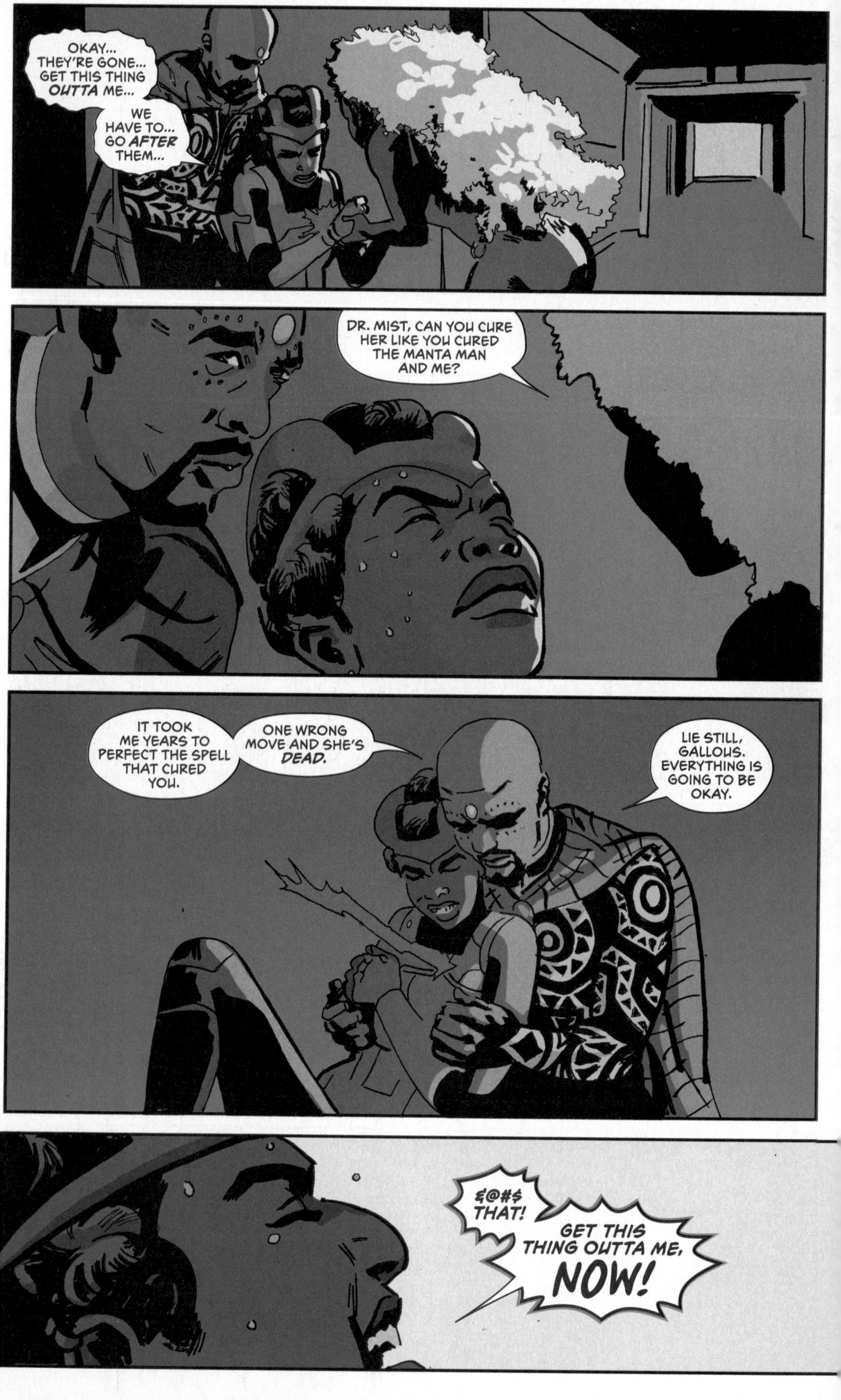

OKAY... THEY'RE GONE... GET THIS THING OUTTA ME...
WE HAVE TO... GO AFTER THEM...
DR. MIST, CAN YOU CURE HER LIKE YOU CURED THE MANTA MAN AND ME?
IT TOOK ME YEARS TO PERFECT THE SPELL THAT CURED YOU.
ONE WRONG MOVE AND SHE'S DEAD.
LIE STILL, GALLOUS. EVERYTHING IS GOING TO BE OKAY.
&@#$ THAT!
GET THIS THING OUTTA ME, NOW!

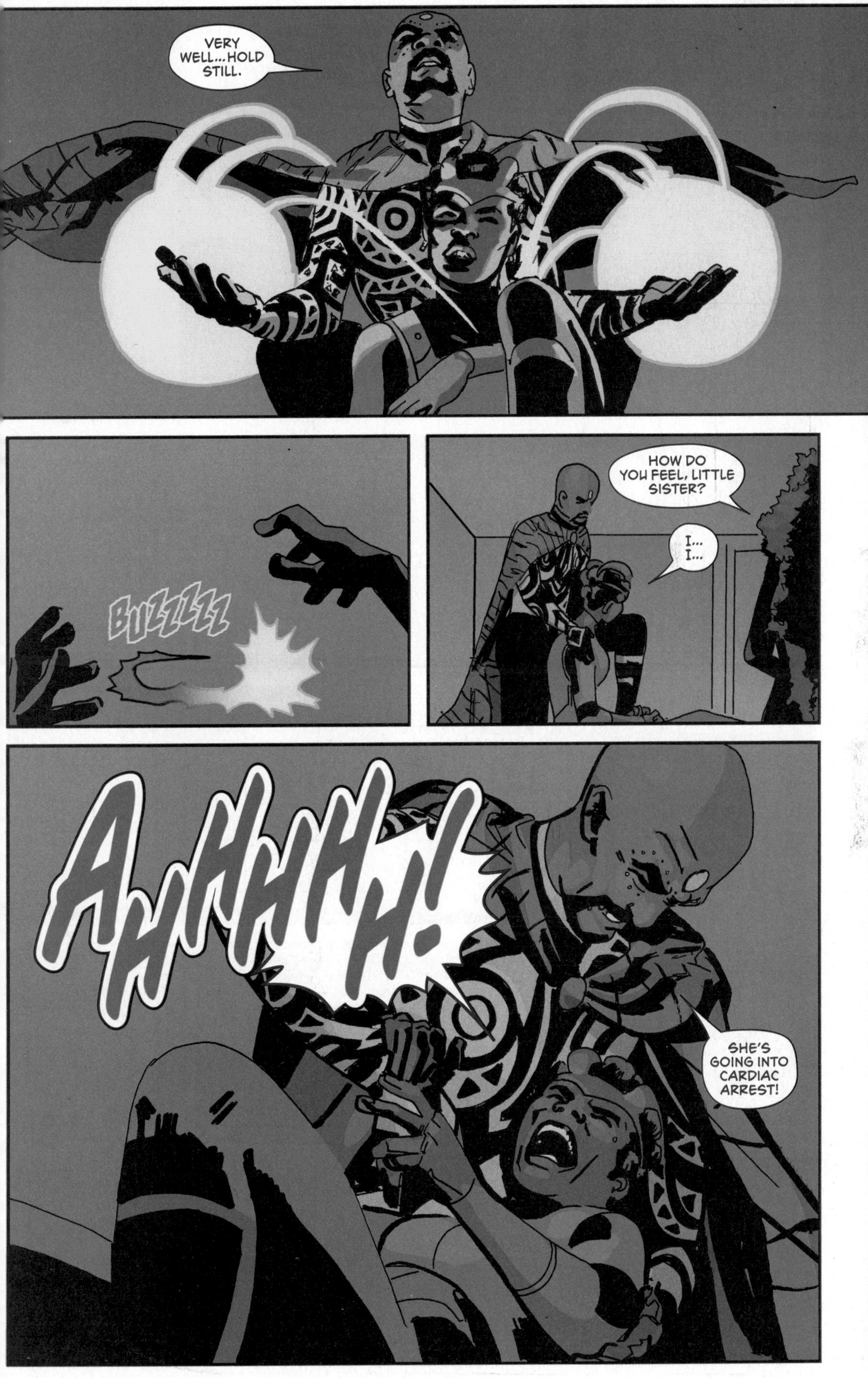
VERY WELL...HOLD STILL.
BUZZZZZ
HOW DO YOU FEEL, LITTLE SISTER?
I... I...
AAHHHHH!
SHE'S GOING INTO CARDIAC ARREST!

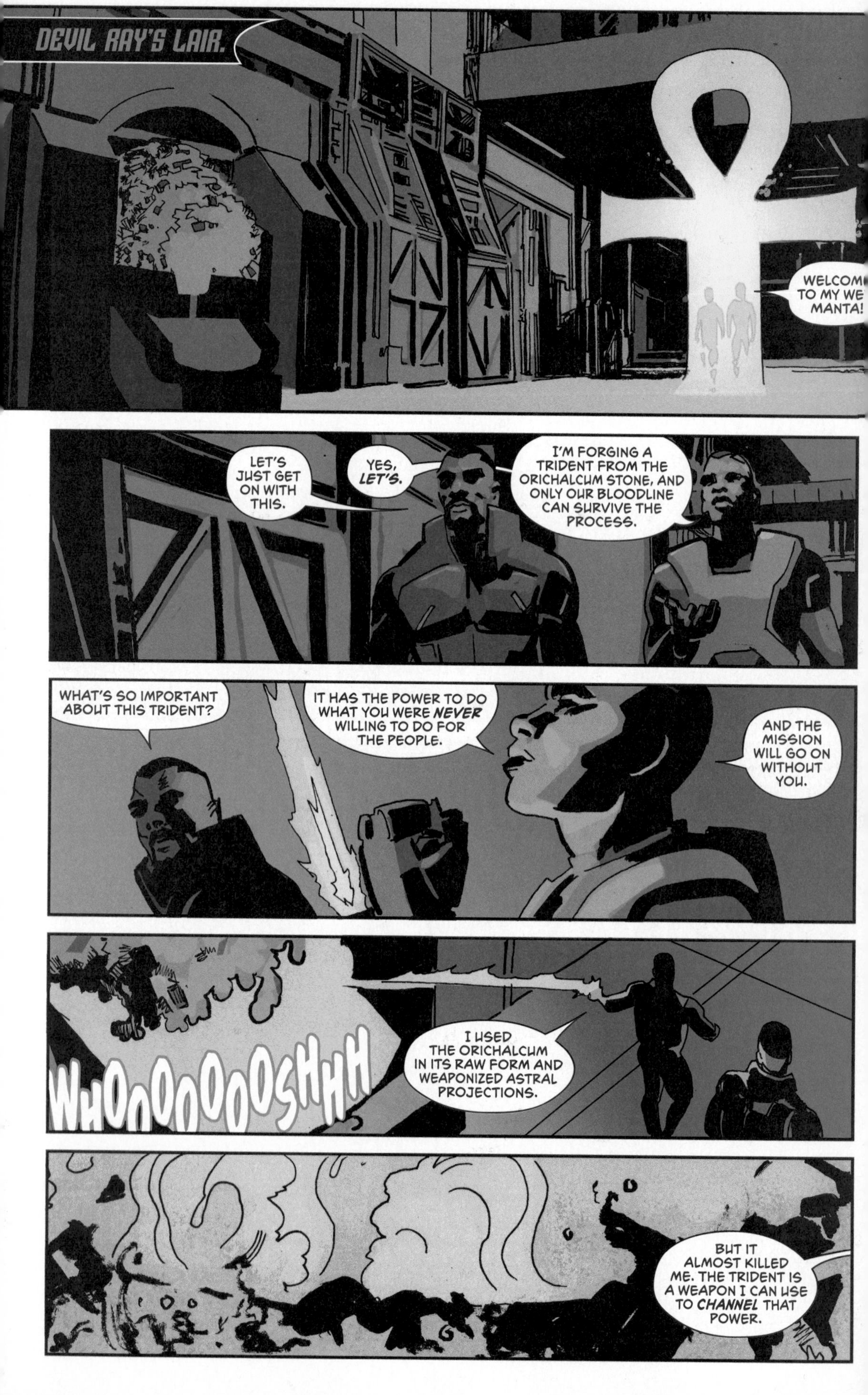
DEVIL RAY'S LAIR.
WELCOM TO MY WE MANTA!
LET'S JUST GET ON WITH THIS.
YES, *LET'S*.
I'M FORGING A TRIDENT FROM THE ORICHALCUM STONE, AND ONLY OUR BLOODLINE CAN SURVIVE THE PROCESS.
WHAT'S SO IMPORTANT ABOUT THIS TRIDENT?
IT HAS THE POWER TO DO WHAT YOU WERE *NEVER* WILLING TO DO FOR THE PEOPLE.
AND THE MISSION WILL GO ON WITHOUT YOU.
WHOOOOOOOOSHHH
I USED THE ORICHALCUM IN ITS RAW FORM AND WEAPONIZED ASTRAL PROJECTIONS.
BUT IT ALMOST KILLED ME. THE TRIDENT IS A WEAPON I CAN USE TO *CHANNEL* THAT POWER.

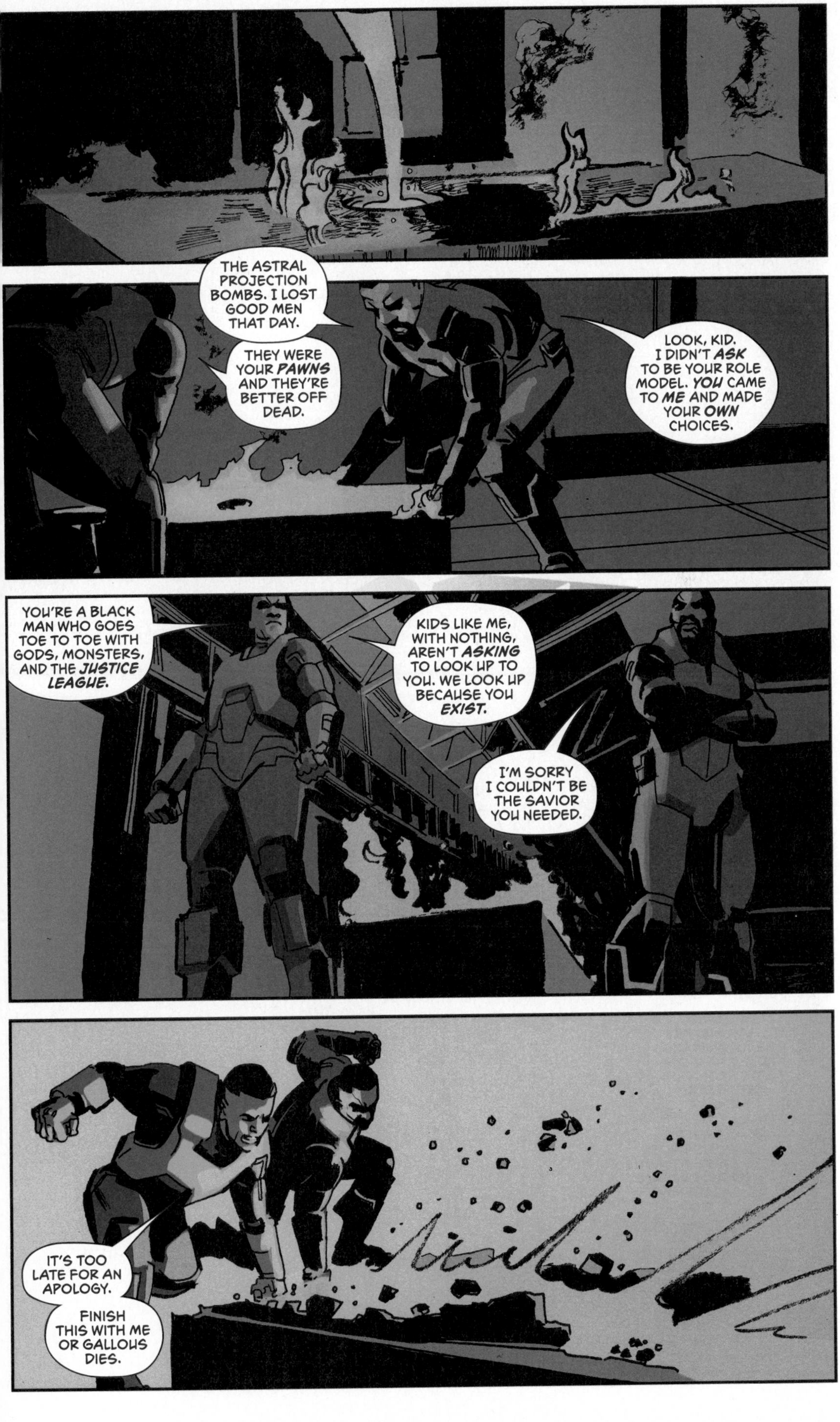
THE ASTRAL PROJECTION BOMBS. I LOST GOOD MEN THAT DAY.
THEY WERE YOUR PAWNS AND THEY'RE BETTER OFF DEAD.
LOOK, KID. I DIDN'T ASK TO BE YOUR ROLE MODEL. YOU CAME TO ME AND MADE YOUR OWN CHOICES.
YOU'RE A BLACK MAN WHO GOES TOE TO TOE WITH GODS, MONSTERS, AND THE JUSTICE LEAGUE.
KIDS LIKE ME, WITH NOTHING, AREN'T ASKING TO LOOK UP TO YOU. WE LOOK UP BECAUSE YOU EXIST.
I'M SORRY I COULDN'T BE THE SAVIOR YOU NEEDED.
IT'S TOO LATE FOR AN APOLOGY.
FINISH THIS WITH ME OR GALLOUS DIES.

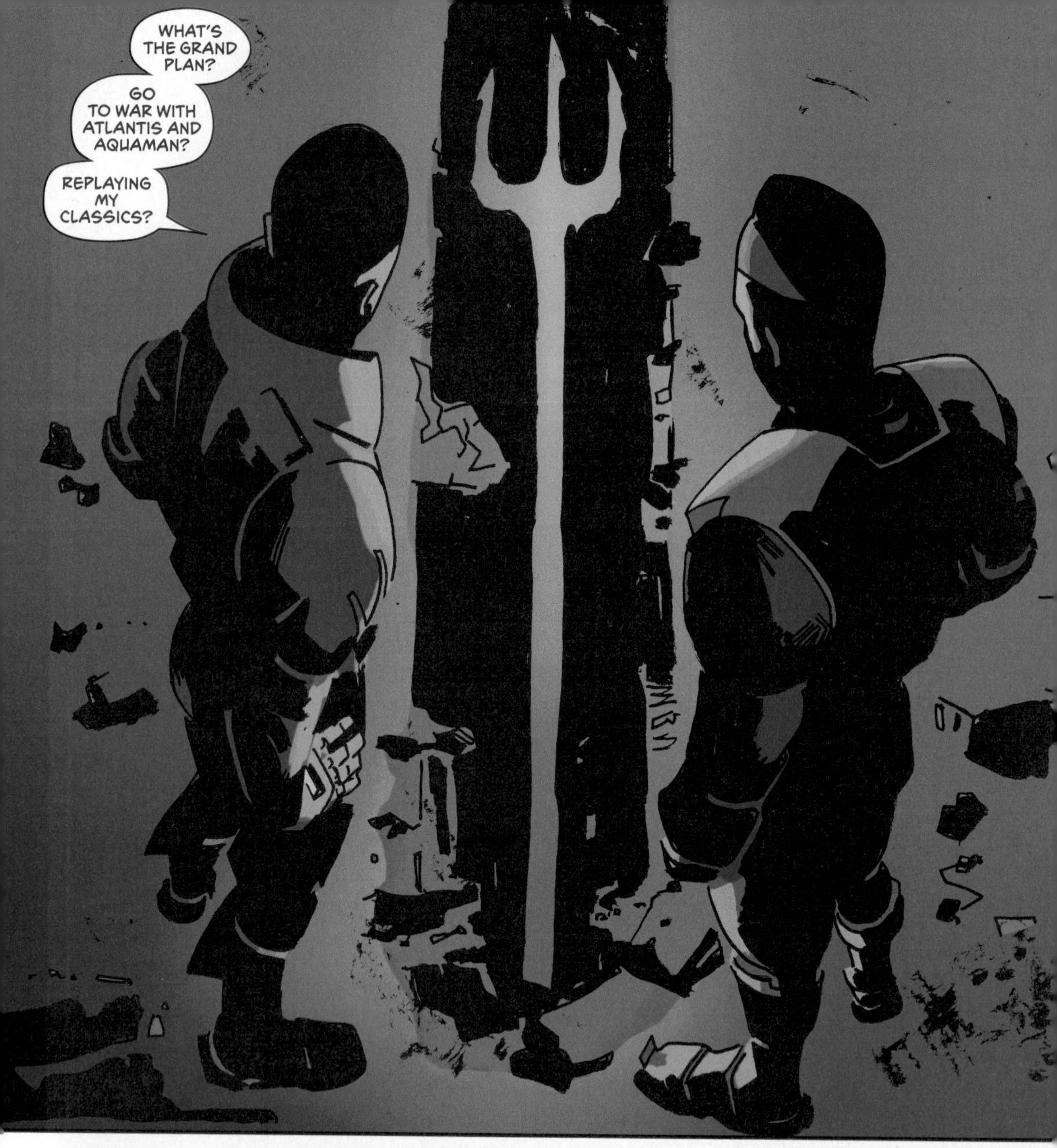
WHAT'S THE GRAND PLAN?
GO TO WAR WITH ATLANTIS AND AQUAMAN?
REPLAYING MY CLASSICS?

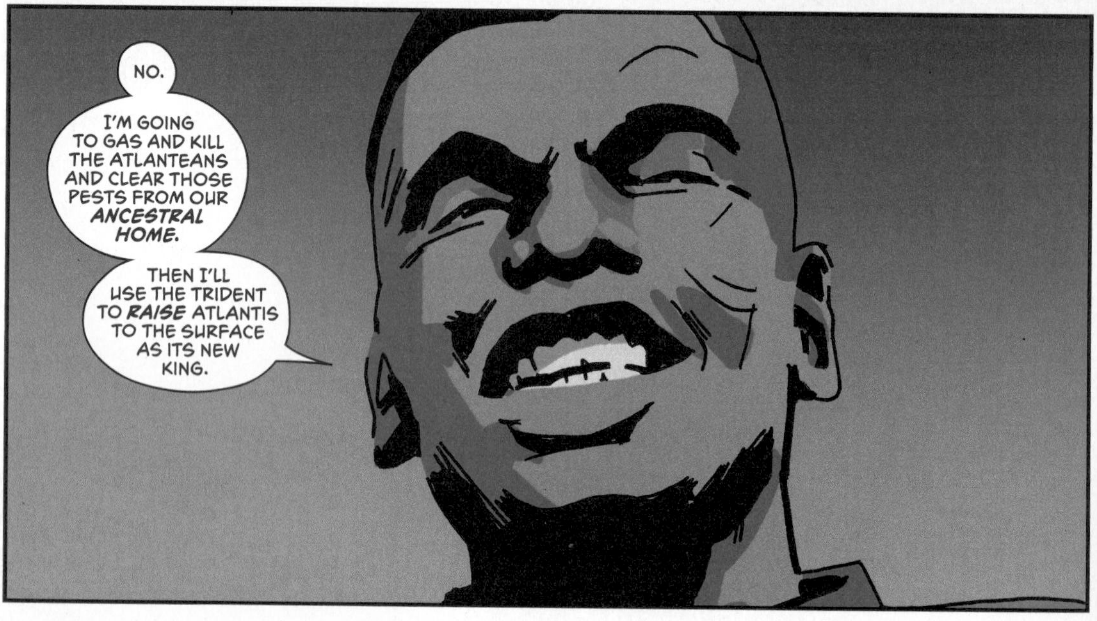
NO.
I'M GOING TO GAS AND KILL THE ATLANTEANS AND CLEAR THOSE PESTS FROM OUR *ANCESTRAL HOME.*
THEN I'LL USE THE TRIDENT TO *RAISE* ATLANTIS TO THE SURFACE AS ITS NEW KING.

Black Manta #6 cover
by Valentine De Landro
and Marissa Louise

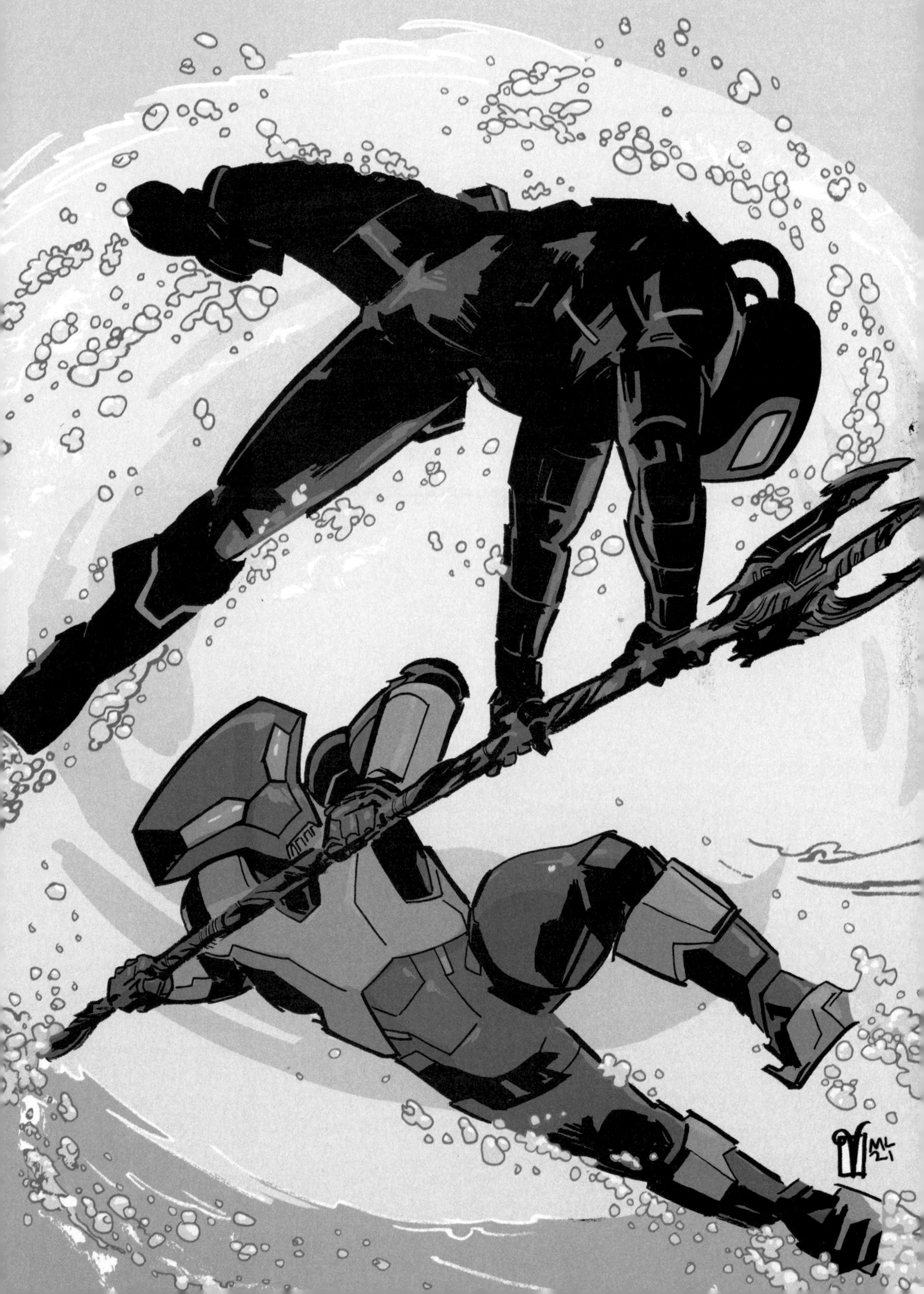

Black Manta #6 variant cover by Sanford Greene

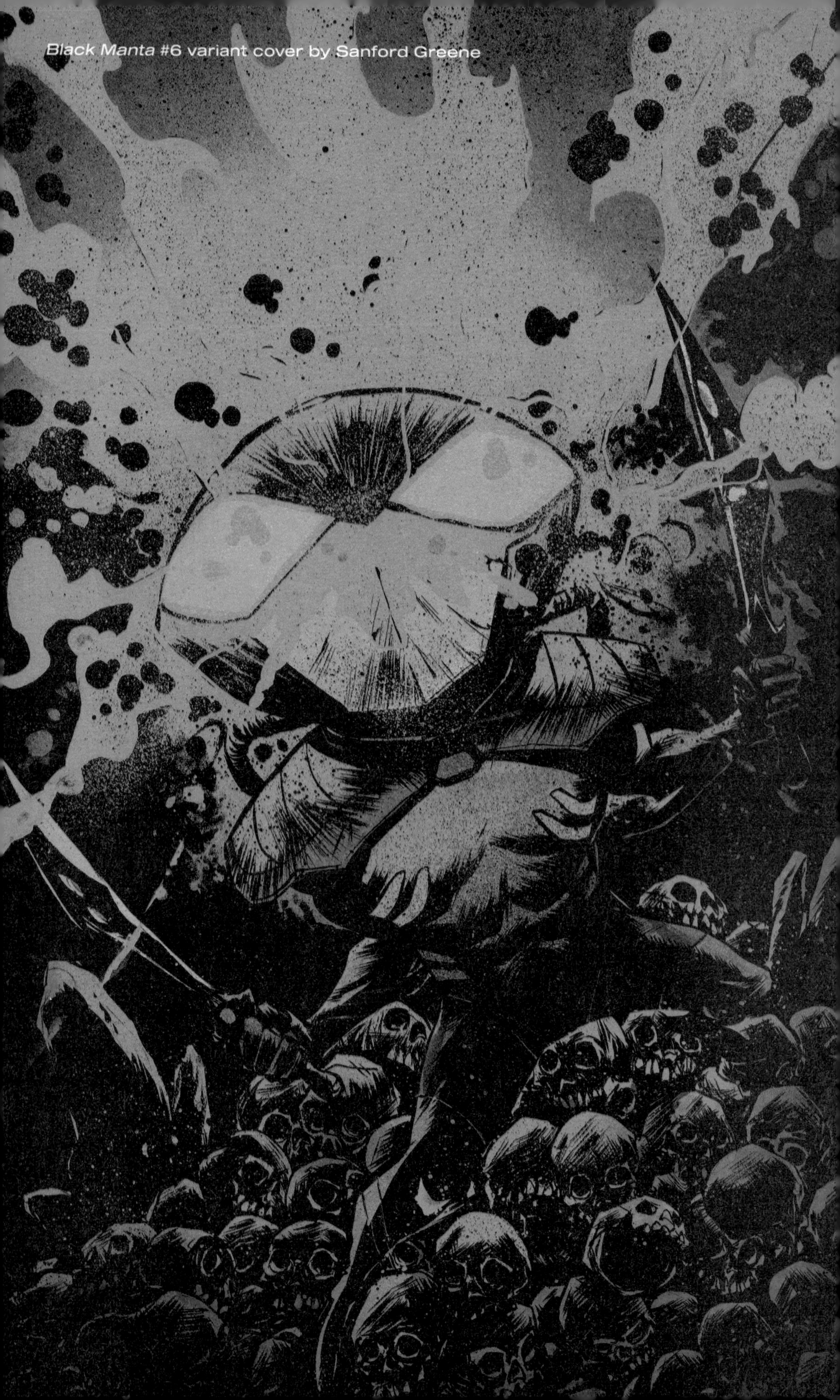

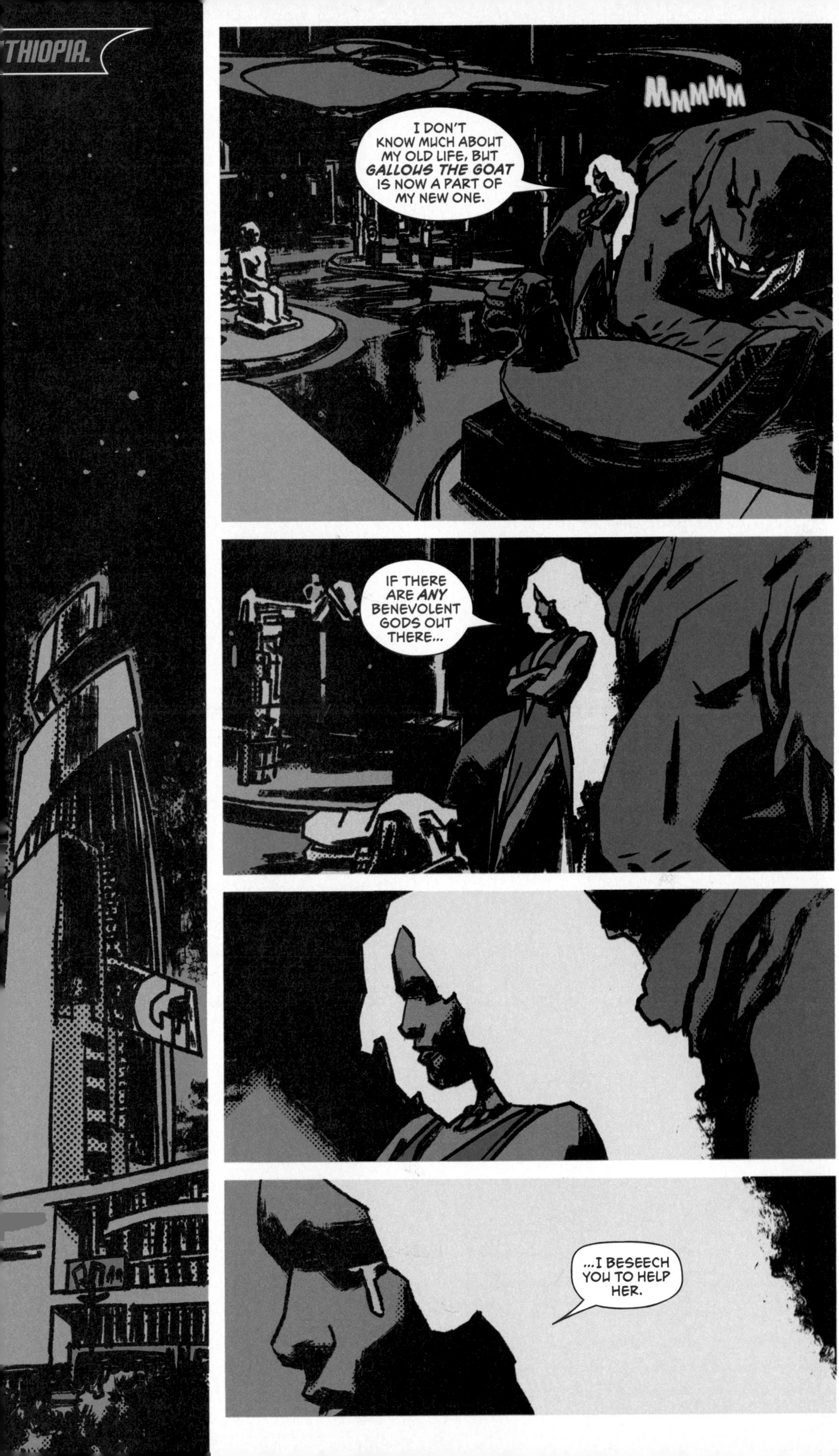

THIOPIA.
MMMMM
I DON'T KNOW MUCH ABOUT MY OLD LIFE, BUT GALLOUS THE GOAT IS NOW A PART OF MY NEW ONE.
IF THERE ARE ANY BENEVOLENT GODS OUT THERE...
...I BESEECH YOU TO HELP HER.

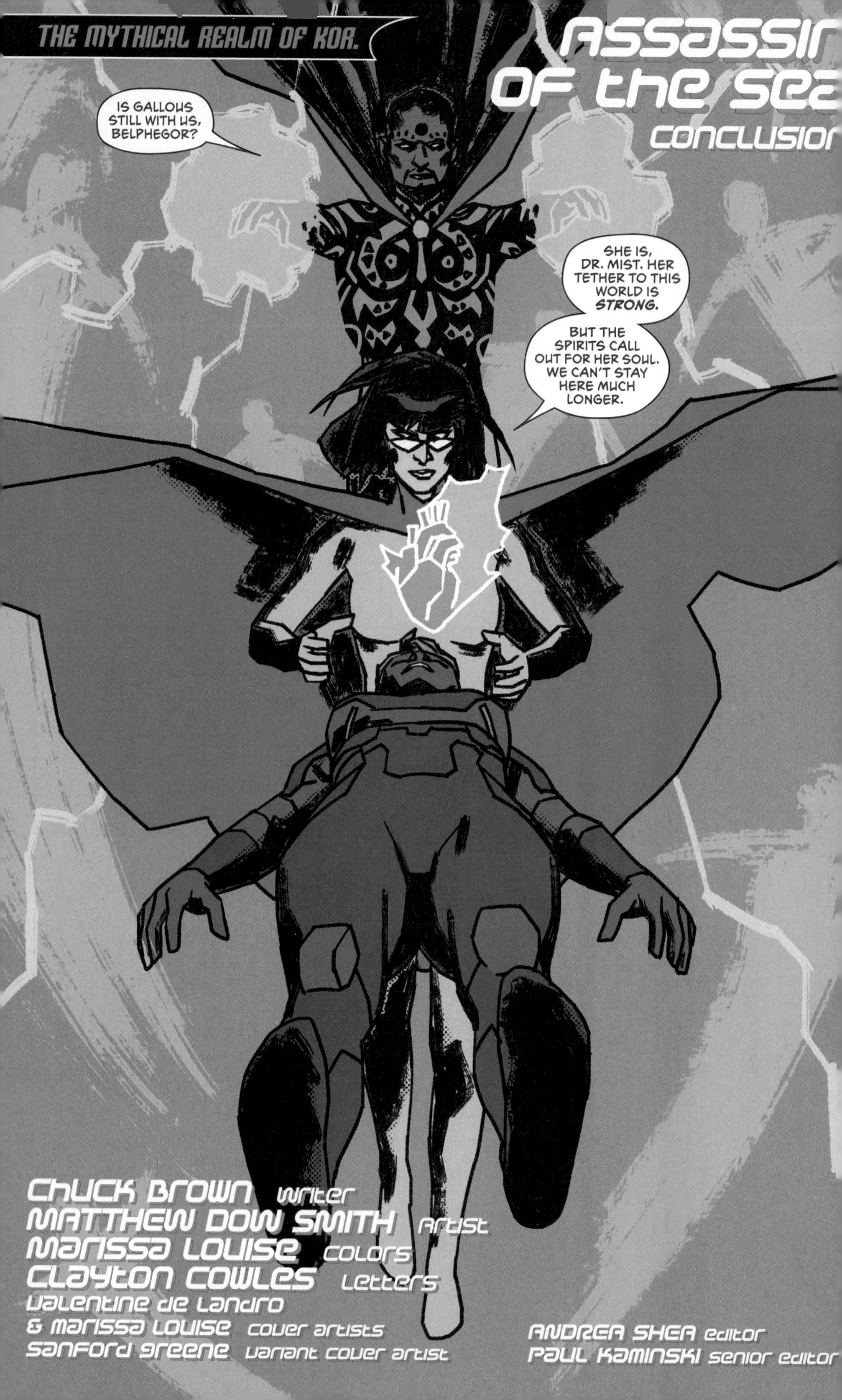
THE MYTHICAL REALM OF KOR.
ASSASSIN OF THE SEA
CONCLUSION
IS GALLOWS STILL WITH US, BELPHEGOR?
SHE IS, DR. MIST. HER TETHER TO THIS WORLD IS STRONG.
BUT THE SPIRITS CALL OUT FOR HER SOUL. WE CAN'T STAY HERE MUCH LONGER.
CHUCK BROWN writer
MATTHEW DOW SMITH artist
MARISSA LOUISE colors
CLAYTON COWLES letters
VALENTINE DE LANDRO
& MARISSA LOUISE cover artists
SANFORD GREENE variant cover artist
ANDREA SHEA editor
PAUL KAMINSKI senior editor

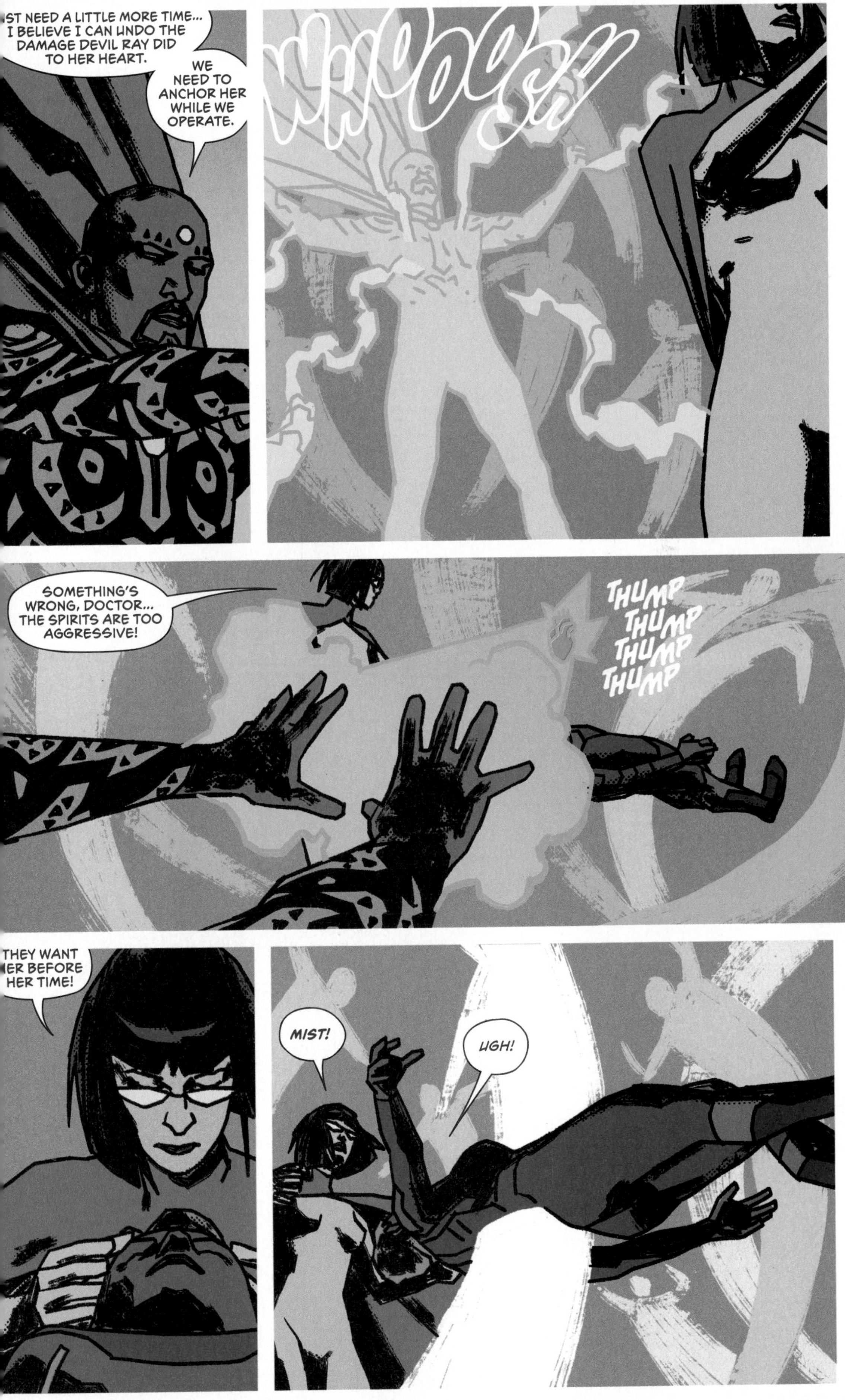

ST NEED A LITTLE MORE TIME... I BELIEVE I CAN UNDO THE DAMAGE DEVIL RAY DID TO HER HEART.
WE NEED TO ANCHOR HER WHILE WE OPERATE.
WHOOOSH!
SOMETHING'S WRONG, DOCTOR... THE SPIRITS ARE TOO AGGRESSIVE!
THUMP THUMP THUMP THUMP
THEY WANT ER BEFORE HER TIME!
MIST!
UGH!

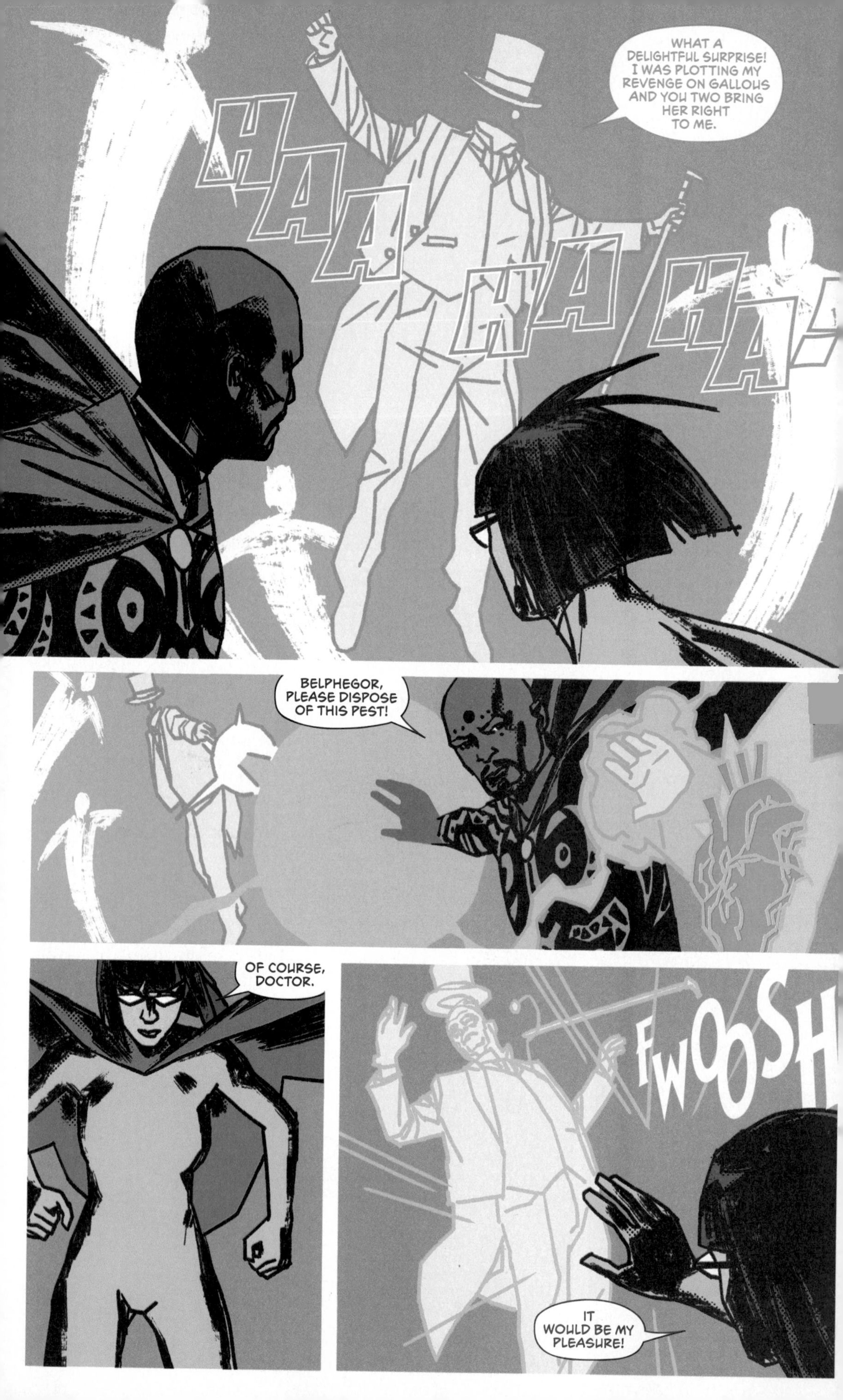
HAA-HA-HA-HA!
WHAT A DELIGHTFUL SURPRISE! I WAS PLOTTING MY REVENGE ON GALLOWS AND YOU TWO BRING HER RIGHT TO ME.
BELPHEGOR, PLEASE DISPOSE OF THIS PEST!
OF COURSE, DOCTOR.
FWOOSH
IT WOULD BE MY PLEASURE!

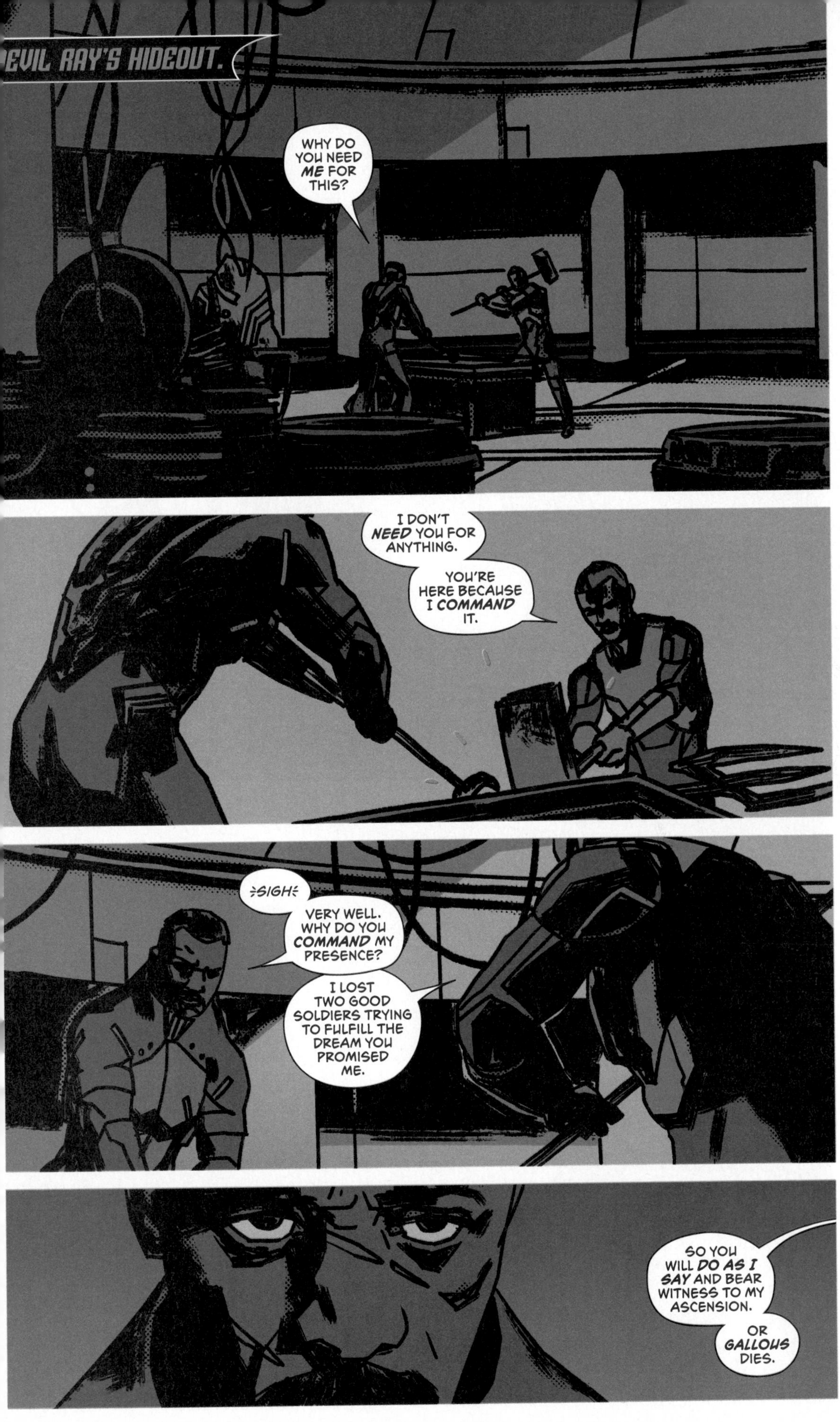
EVIL RAY'S HIDEOUT.
WHY DO YOU NEED ME FOR THIS?
I DON'T NEED YOU FOR ANYTHING.
YOU'RE HERE BECAUSE I COMMAND IT.
SIGH
VERY WELL. WHY DO YOU COMMAND MY PRESENCE?
I LOST TWO GOOD SOLDIERS TRYING TO FULFILL THE DREAM YOU PROMISED ME.
SO YOU WILL DO AS I SAY AND BEAR WITNESS TO MY ASCENSION.
OR GALLOWS DIES.

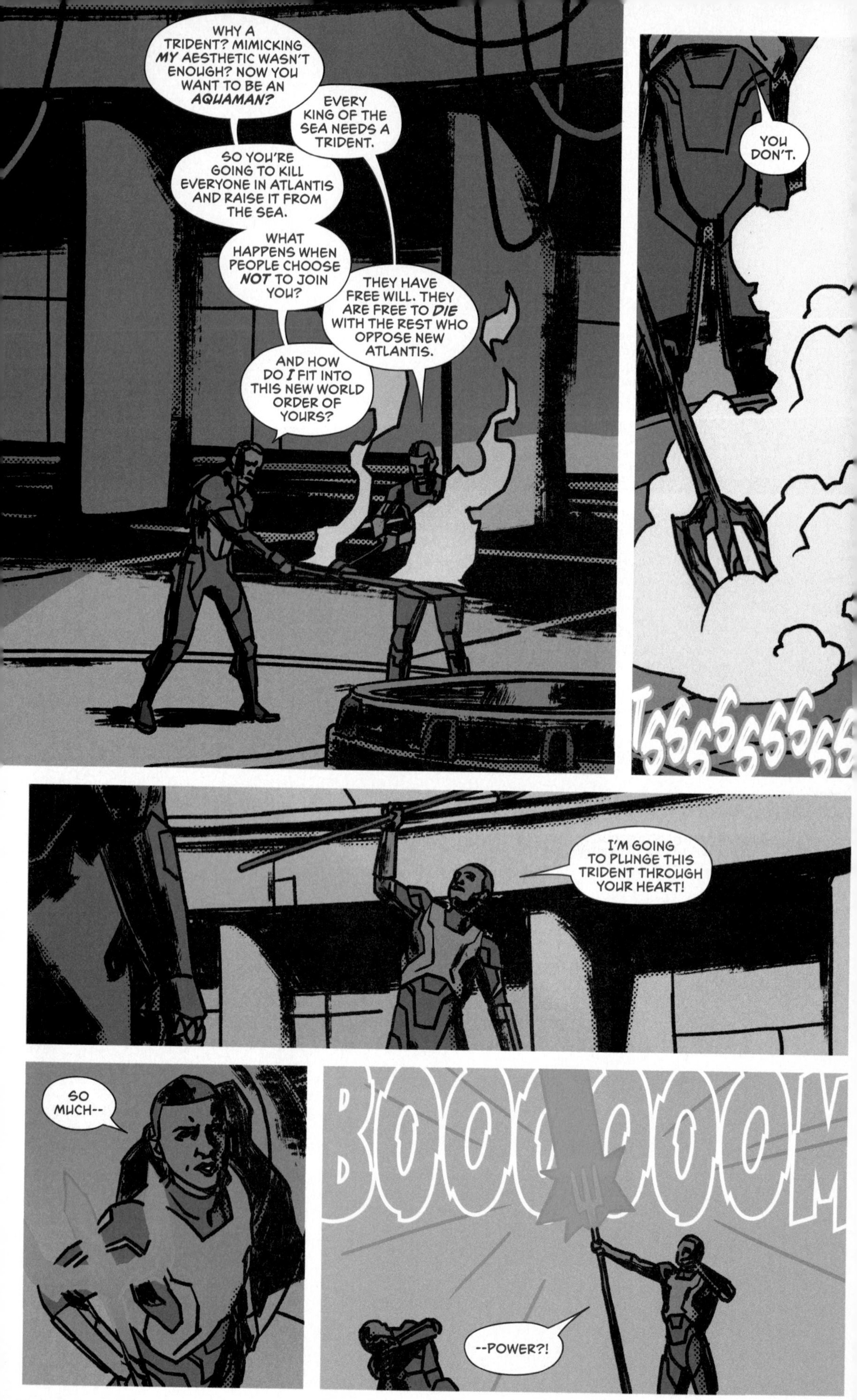
WHY A TRIDENT? MIMICKING MY AESTHETIC WASN'T ENOUGH? NOW YOU WANT TO BE AN AQUAMAN?
EVERY KING OF THE SEA NEEDS A TRIDENT.
SO YOU'RE GOING TO KILL EVERYONE IN ATLANTIS AND RAISE IT FROM THE SEA.
WHAT HAPPENS WHEN PEOPLE CHOOSE NOT TO JOIN YOU?
THEY HAVE FREE WILL. THEY ARE FREE TO DIE WITH THE REST WHO OPPOSE NEW ATLANTIS.
AND HOW DO I FIT INTO THIS NEW WORLD ORDER OF YOURS?
YOU DON'T.
TSSSSSSSSSS
I'M GOING TO PLUNGE THIS TRIDENT THROUGH YOUR HEART!
SO MUCH--
BOOOOOOOM
--POWER?!

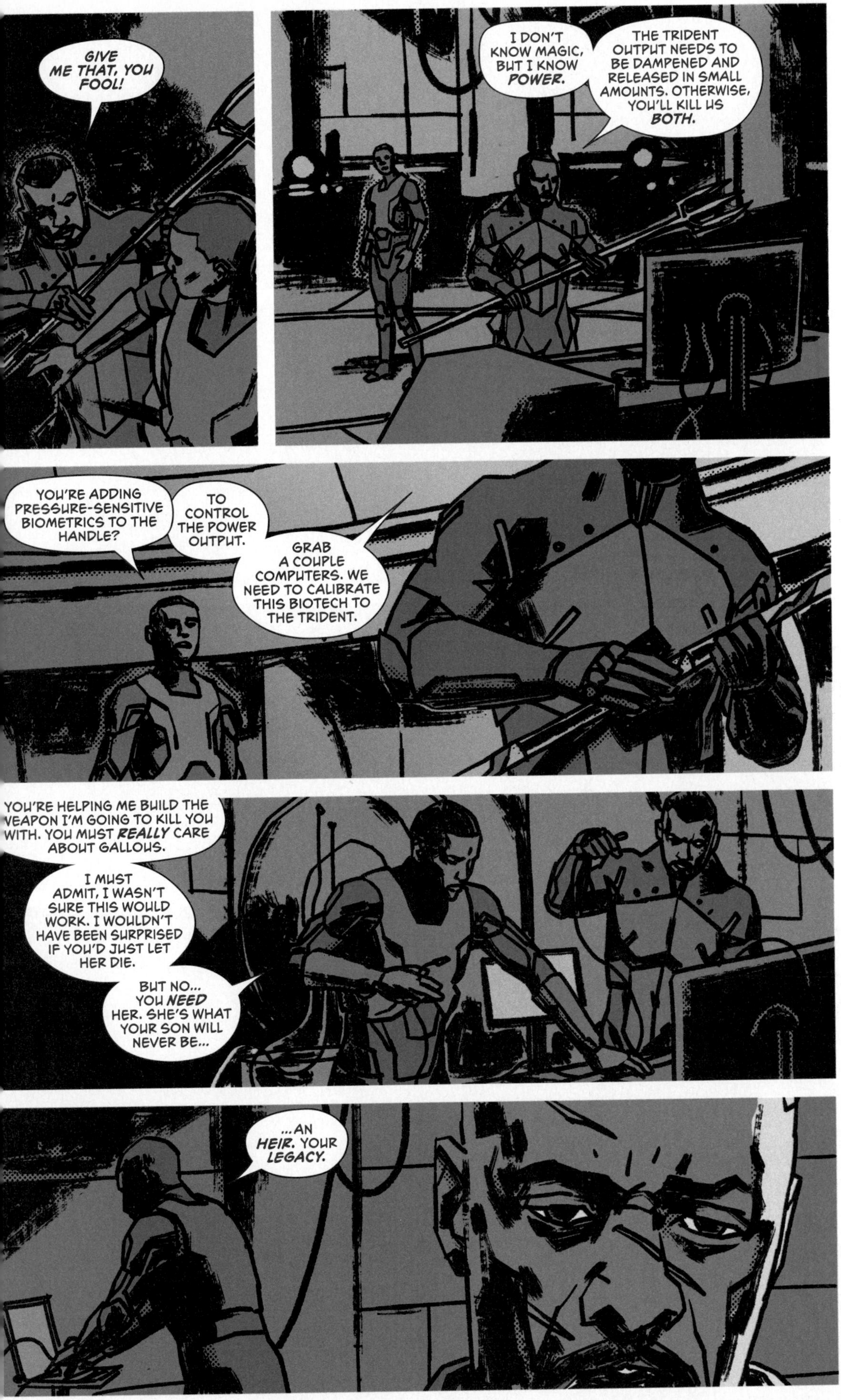
GIVE ME THAT, YOU FOOL!
I DON'T KNOW MAGIC, BUT I KNOW POWER.
THE TRIDENT OUTPUT NEEDS TO BE DAMPENED AND RELEASED IN SMALL AMOUNTS. OTHERWISE, YOU'LL KILL US BOTH.
YOU'RE ADDING PRESSURE-SENSITIVE BIOMETRICS TO THE HANDLE?
TO CONTROL THE POWER OUTPUT.
GRAB A COUPLE COMPUTERS. WE NEED TO CALIBRATE THIS BIOTECH TO THE TRIDENT.
YOU'RE HELPING ME BUILD THE WEAPON I'M GOING TO KILL YOU WITH. YOU MUST REALLY CARE ABOUT GALLOUS.
I MUST ADMIT, I WASN'T SURE THIS WOULD WORK. I WOULDN'T HAVE BEEN SURPRISED IF YOU'D JUST LET HER DIE.
BUT NO... YOU NEED HER. SHE'S WHAT YOUR SON WILL NEVER BE...
...AN HEIR. YOUR LEGACY.

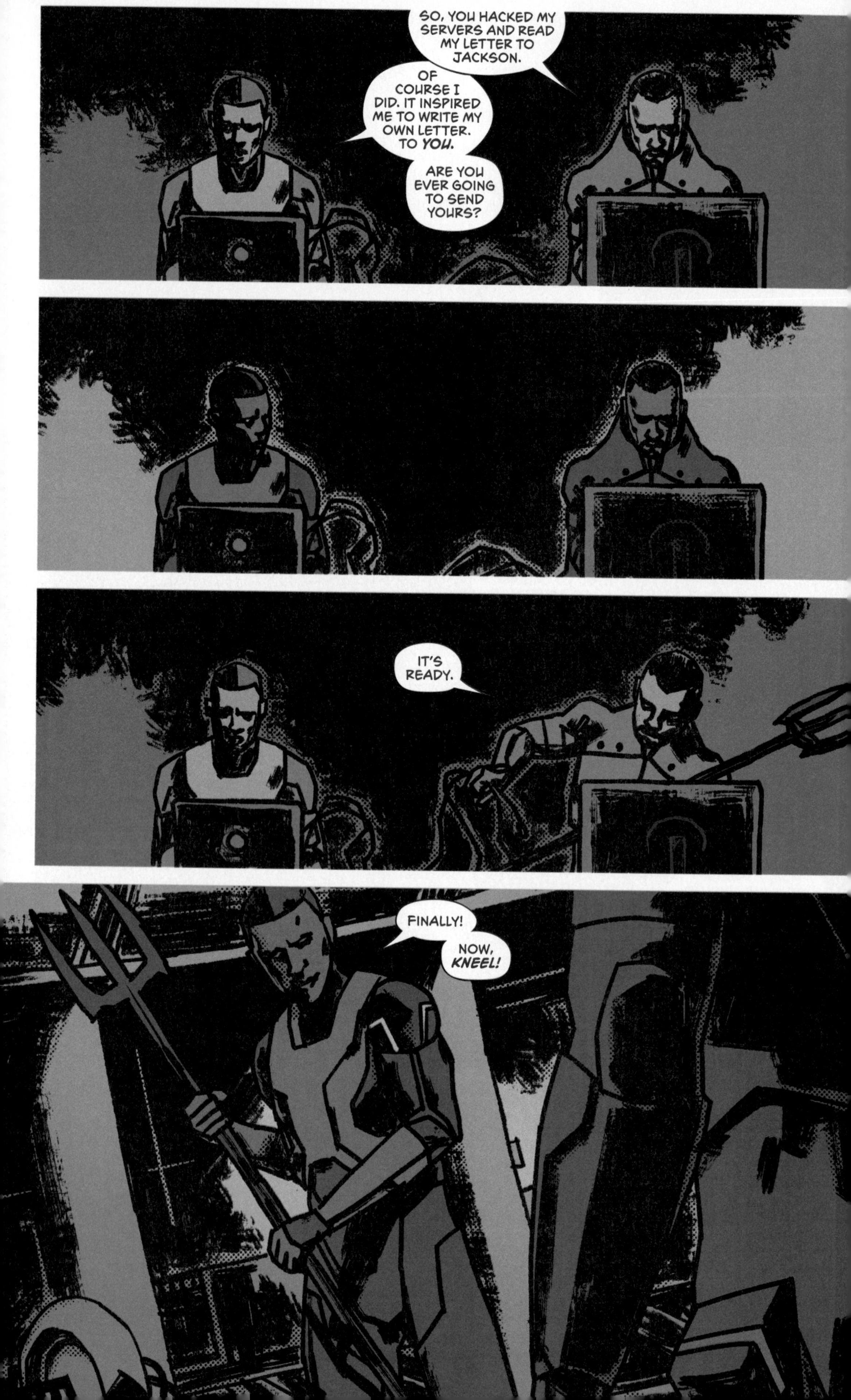
SO, YOU HACKED MY SERVERS AND READ MY LETTER TO JACKSON.
OF COURSE I DID. IT INSPIRED ME TO WRITE MY OWN LETTER. TO *YOU.*
ARE YOU EVER GOING TO SEND YOURS?
IT'S READY.
FINALLY!
NOW, ***KNEEL!***

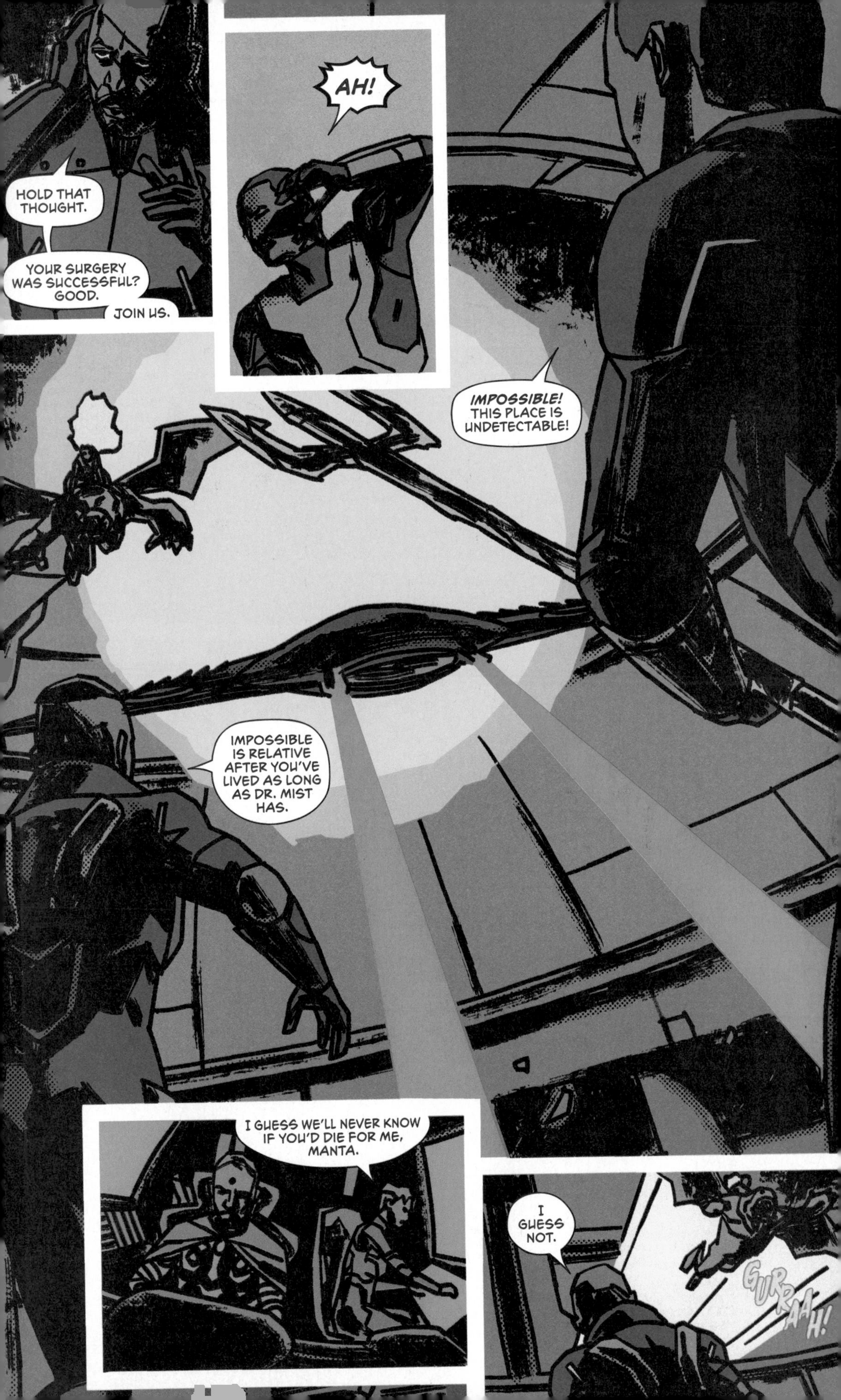
HOLD THAT THOUGHT.
YOUR SURGERY WAS SUCCESSFUL? GOOD.
JOIN US.
AH!
IMPOSSIBLE! THIS PLACE IS UNDETECTABLE!
IMPOSSIBLE IS RELATIVE AFTER YOU'VE LIVED AS LONG AS DR. MIST HAS.
I GUESS WE'LL NEVER KNOW IF YOU'D DIE FOR ME, MANTA.
I GUESS NOT.
GURRAAH!

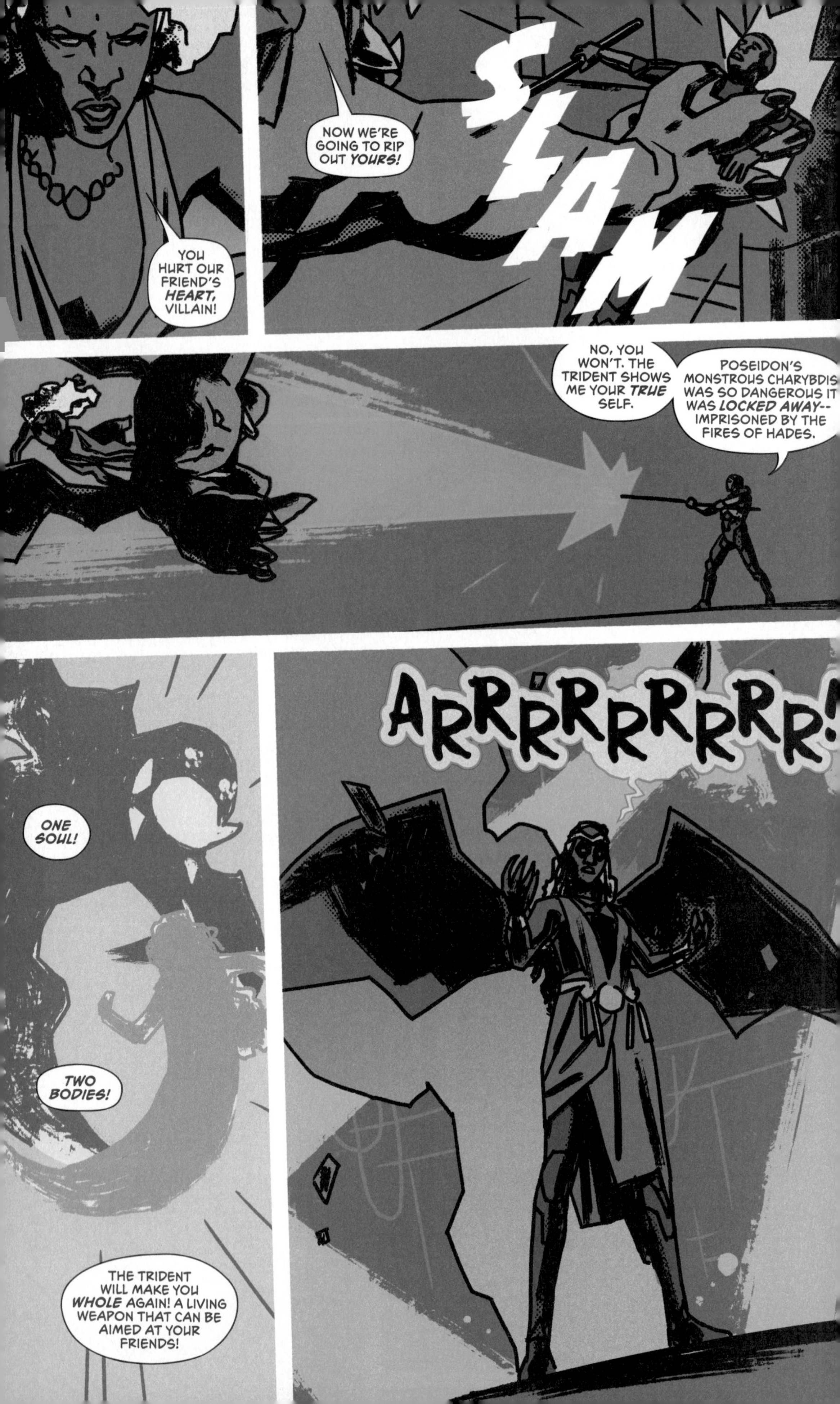
YOU HURT OUR FRIEND'S HEART, VILLAIN!
NOW WE'RE GOING TO RIP OUT YOURS!
SLAM
NO, YOU WON'T. THE TRIDENT SHOWS ME YOUR TRUE SELF.
POSEIDON'S MONSTROUS CHARYBDIS WAS SO DANGEROUS IT WAS LOCKED AWAY-- IMPRISONED BY THE FIRES OF HADES.
ONE SOUL!
TWO BODIES!
THE TRIDENT WILL MAKE YOU WHOLE AGAIN! A LIVING WEAPON THAT CAN BE AIMED AT YOUR FRIENDS!
ARRRRRRRRR!

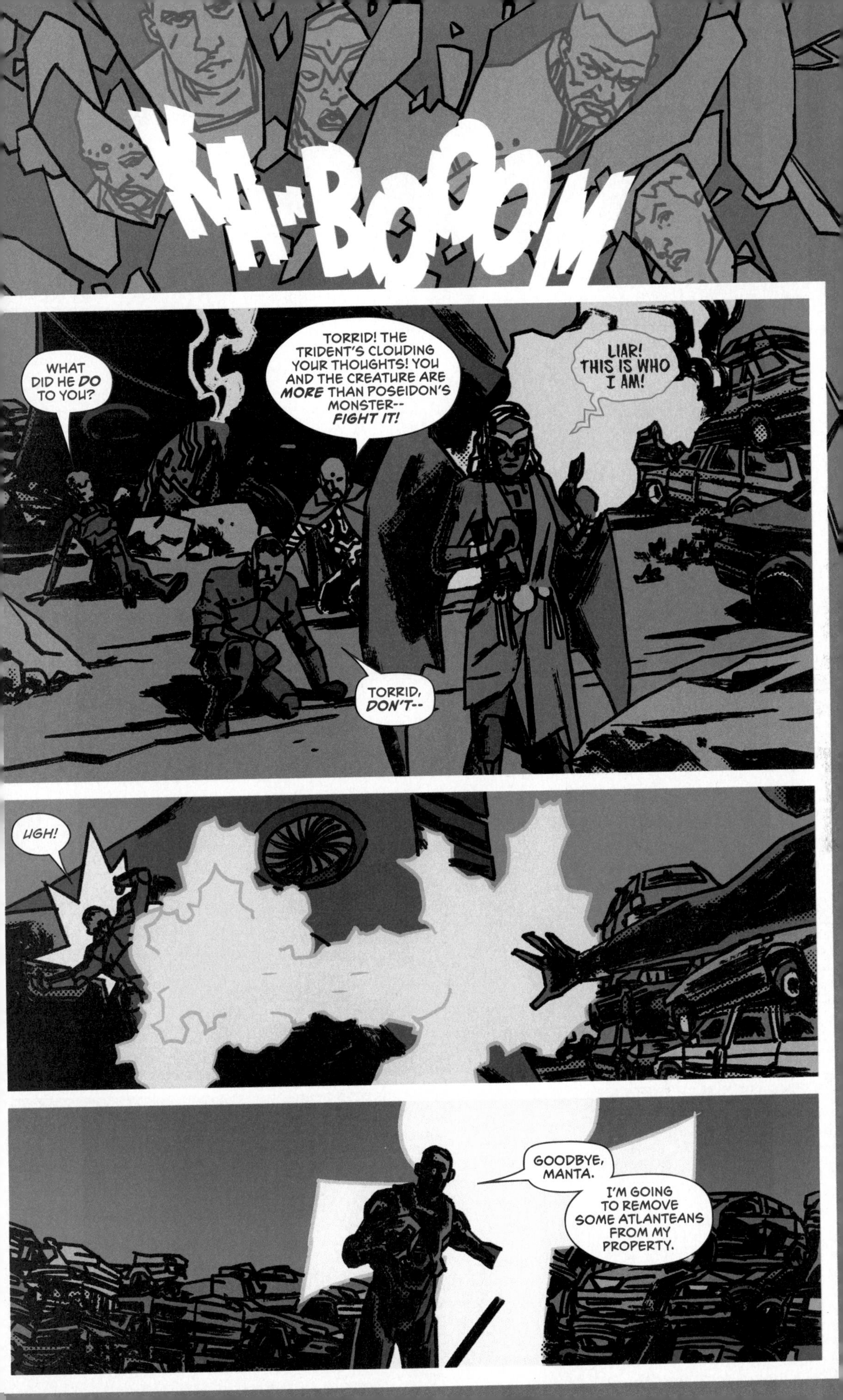
KA-BOOOOM
WHAT DID HE DO TO YOU?
TORRID! THE TRIDENT'S CLOUDING YOUR THOUGHTS! YOU AND THE CREATURE ARE MORE THAN POSEIDON'S MONSTER-- FIGHT IT!
LIAR! THIS IS WHO I AM!
TORRID, DON'T--
UGH!
GOODBYE, MANTA.
I'M GOING TO REMOVE SOME ATLANTEANS FROM MY PROPERTY.

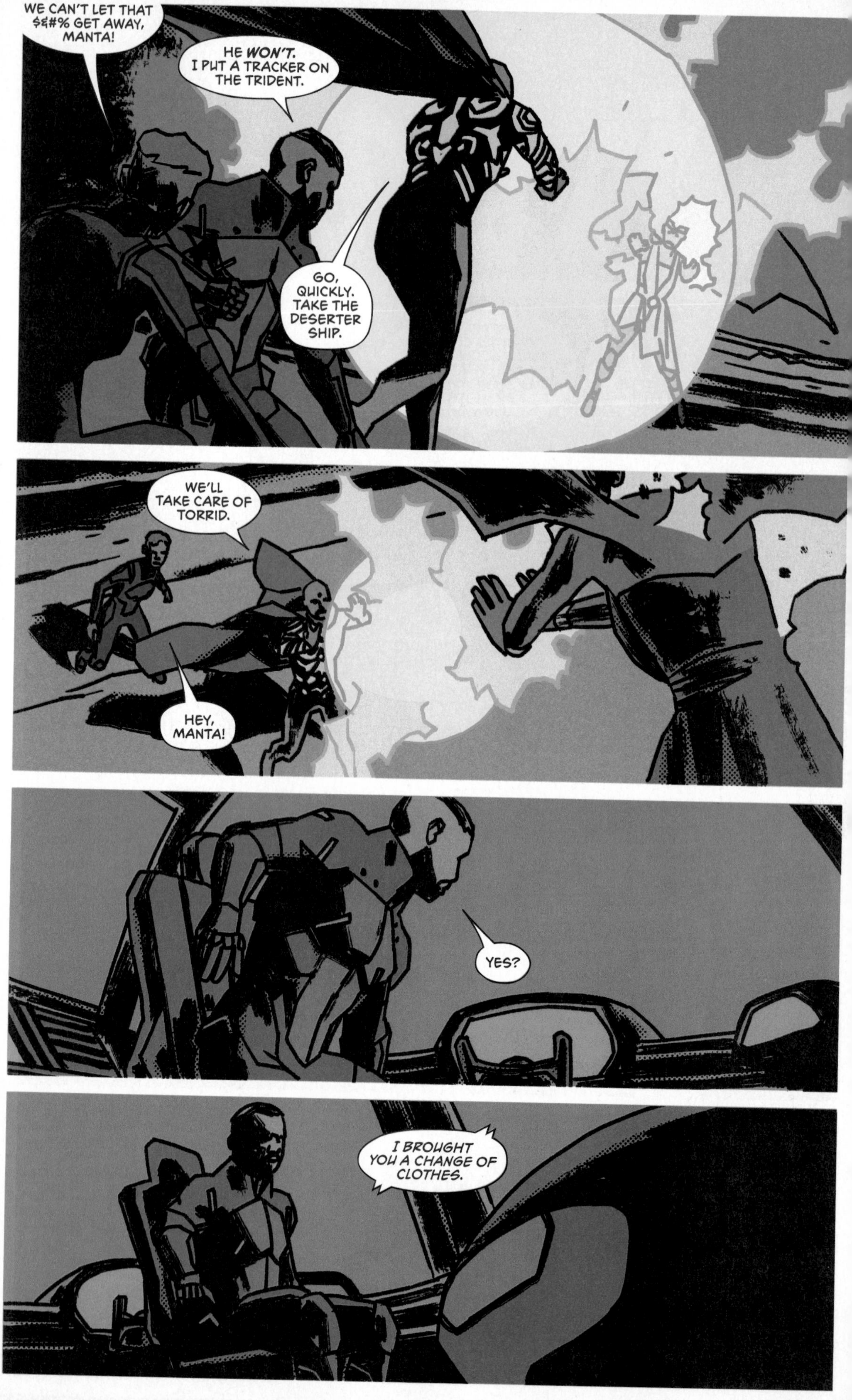

WE CAN'T LET THAT $&#% GET AWAY, MANTA!
HE *WON'T.* I PUT A TRACKER ON THE TRIDENT.
GO, QUICKLY. TAKE THE DESERTER SHIP.
WE'LL TAKE CARE OF TORRID.
HEY, MANTA!
YES?
I BROUGHT YOU A CHANGE OF CLOTHES.

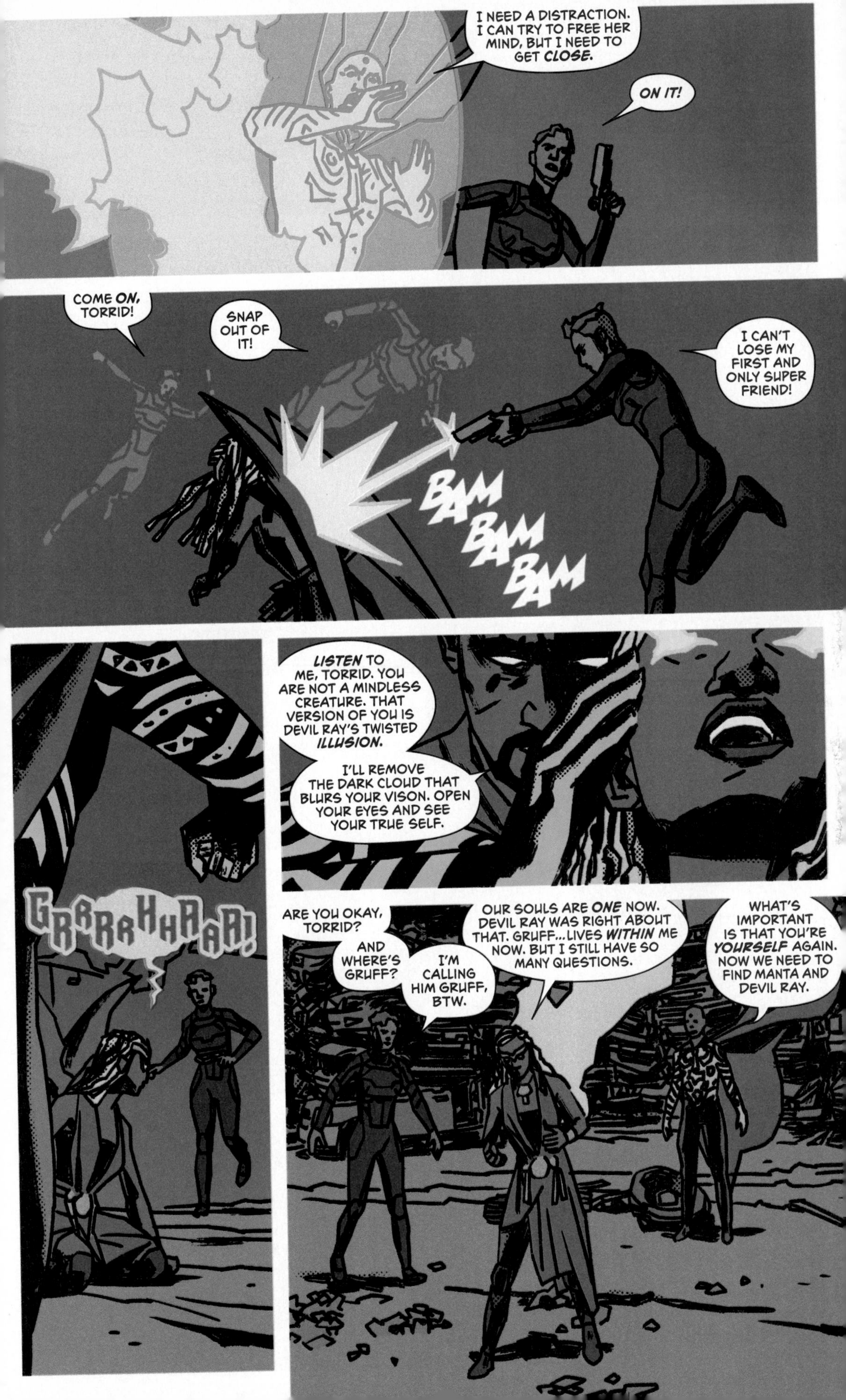
I NEED A DISTRACTION. I CAN TRY TO FREE HER MIND, BUT I NEED TO GET CLOSE.
ON IT!
COME ON, TORRID!
SNAP OUT OF IT!
I CAN'T LOSE MY FIRST AND ONLY SUPER FRIEND!
BAM BAM BAM
GRRRRHHAAR!
LISTEN TO ME, TORRID. YOU ARE NOT A MINDLESS CREATURE. THAT VERSION OF YOU IS DEVIL RAY'S TWISTED ILLUSION.
I'LL REMOVE THE DARK CLOUD THAT BLURS YOUR VISON. OPEN YOUR EYES AND SEE YOUR TRUE SELF.
ARE YOU OKAY, TORRID?
AND WHERE'S GRUFF?
I'M CALLING HIM GRUFF, BTW.
OUR SOULS ARE ONE NOW. DEVIL RAY WAS RIGHT ABOUT THAT. GRUFF...LIVES WITHIN ME NOW. BUT I STILL HAVE SO MANY QUESTIONS.
WHAT'S IMPORTANT IS THAT YOU'RE YOURSELF AGAIN. NOW WE NEED TO FIND MANTA AND DEVIL RAY.

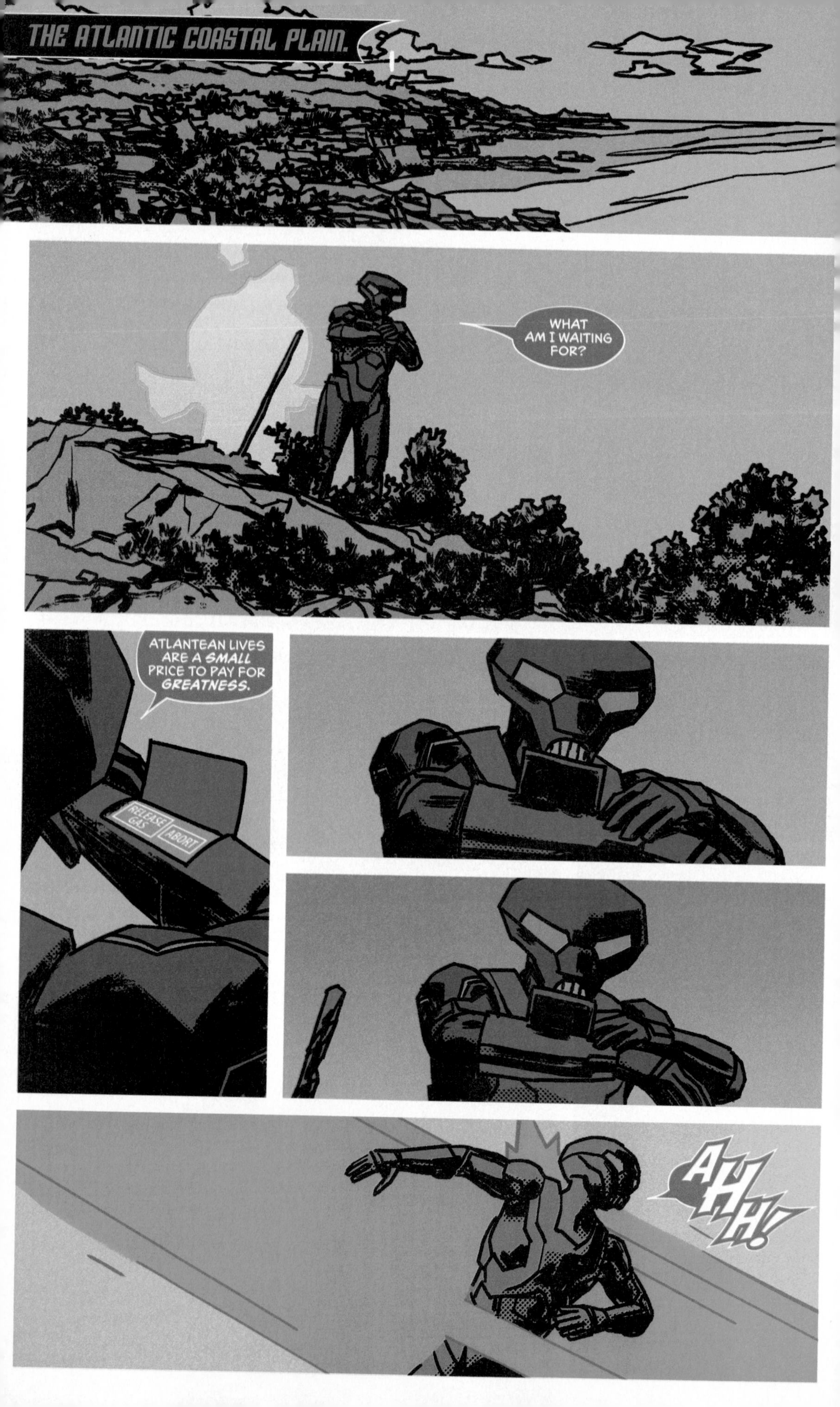
THE ATLANTIC COASTAL PLAIN.
WHAT AM I WAITING FOR?
ATLANTEAN LIVES ARE A *SMALL* PRICE TO PAY FOR *GREATNESS.*
RELEASE GAS
ABORT
AHH!

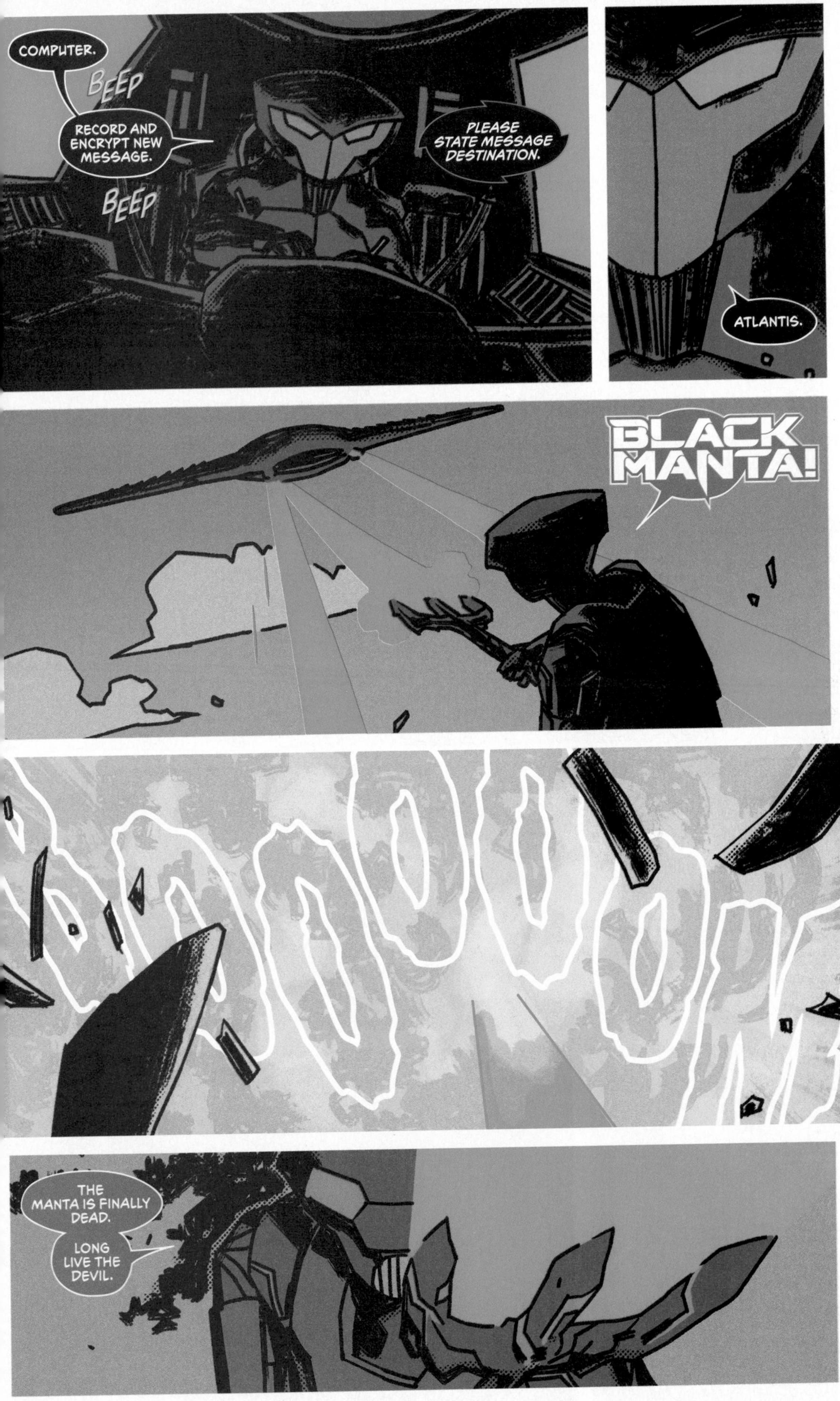
COMPUTER.
BEEP
RECORD AND ENCRYPT NEW MESSAGE.
BEEP
PLEASE STATE MESSAGE DESTINATION.
ATLANTIS.
BLACK MANTA!
THE MANTA IS FINALLY DEAD.
LONG LIVE THE DEVIL.

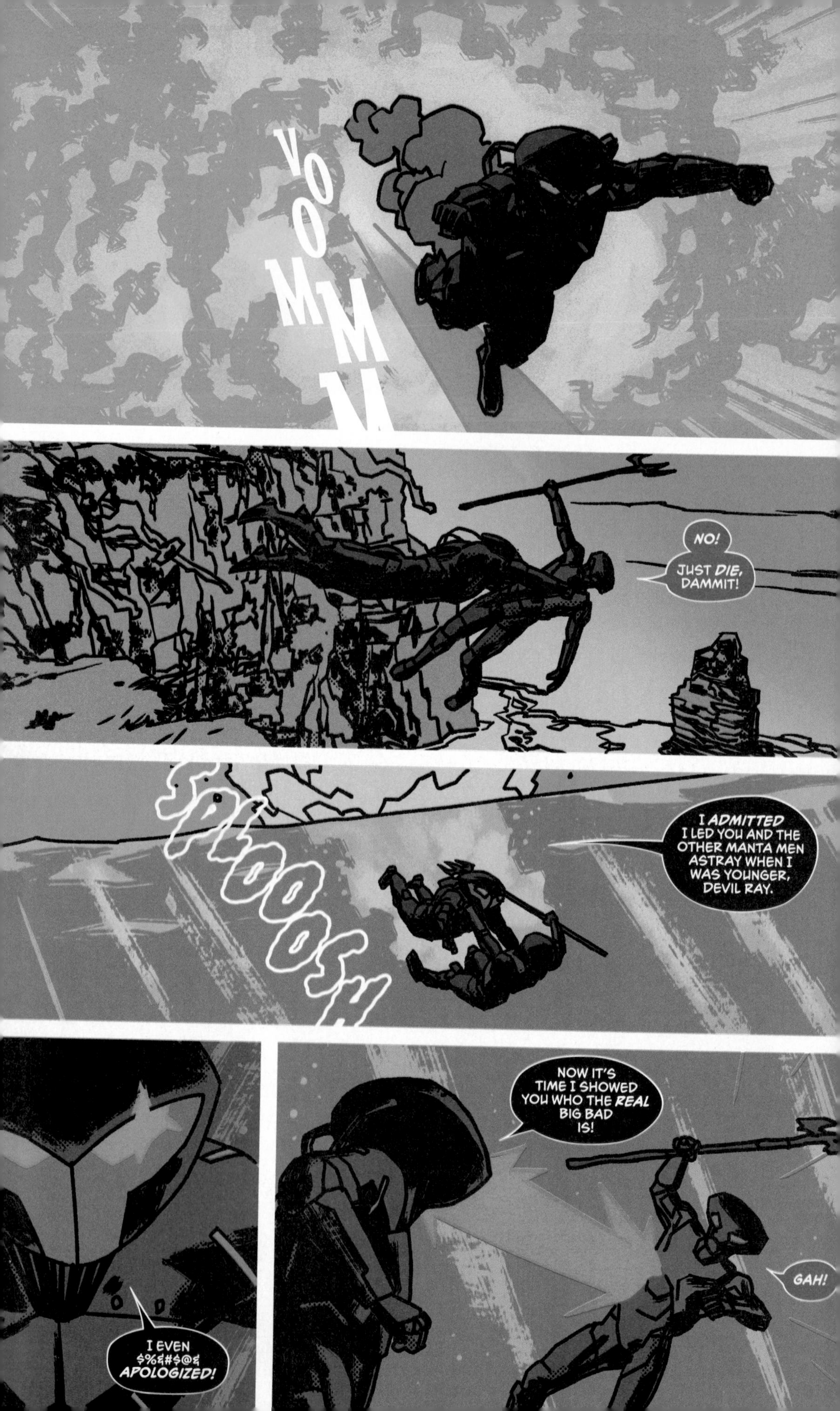
VOOMMM
NO!
JUST DIE, DAMMIT!
SPLOOSH
I ADMITTED I LED YOU AND THE OTHER MANTA MEN ASTRAY WHEN I WAS YOUNGER, DEVIL RAY.
I EVEN $%&#$@& APOLOGIZED!
NOW IT'S TIME I SHOWED YOU WHO THE REAL BIG BAD IS!
GAH!

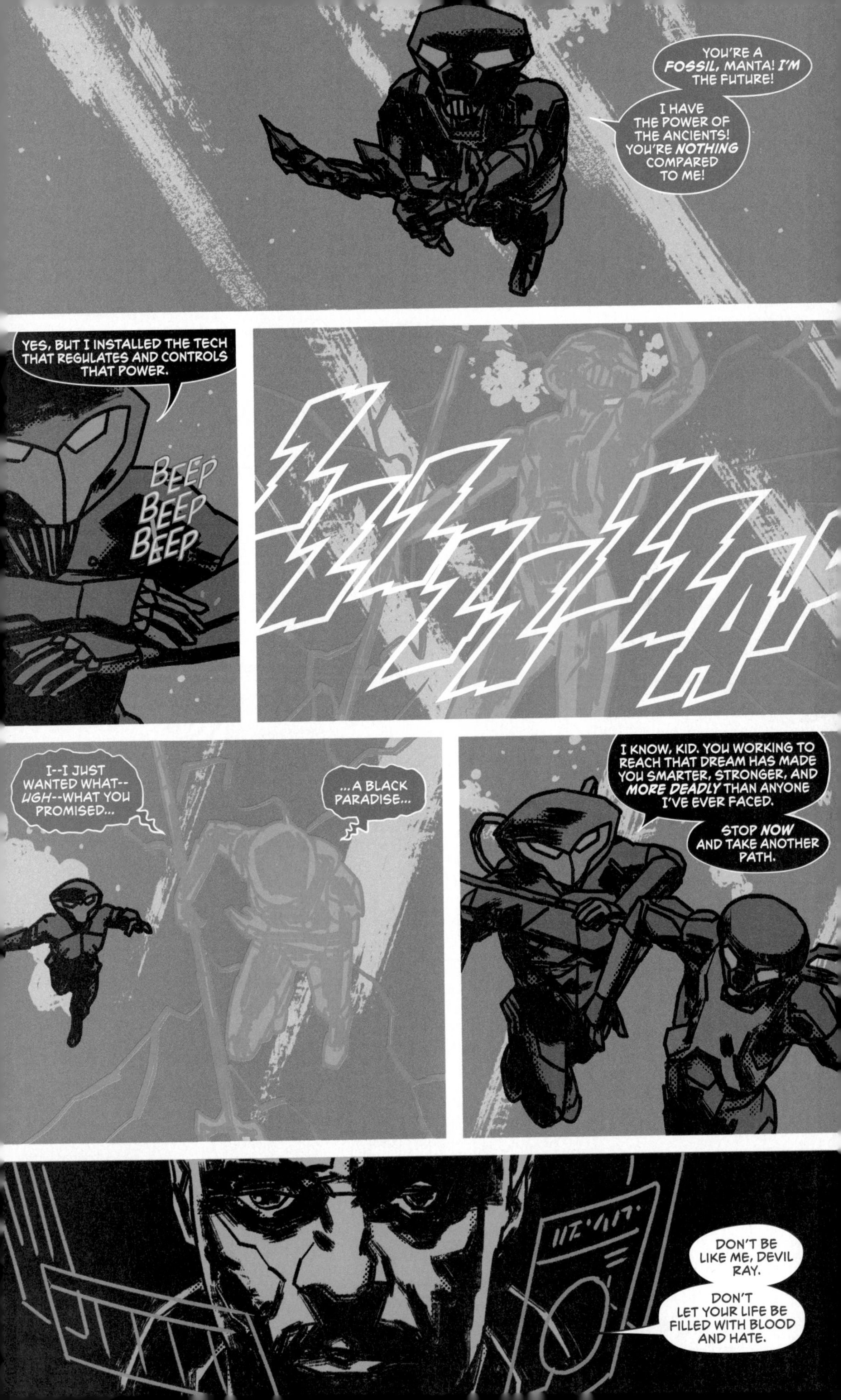

YOU'RE A *FOSSIL*, MANTA! *I'M* THE FUTURE!
I HAVE THE POWER OF THE ANCIENTS! YOU'RE *NOTHING* COMPARED TO ME!
YES, BUT I INSTALLED THE TECH THAT REGULATES AND CONTROLS THAT POWER.
BEEP BEEP BEEP
I--I JUST WANTED WHAT-- *UGH*--WHAT YOU PROMISED...
...A BLACK PARADISE...
I KNOW, KID. YOU WORKING TO REACH THAT DREAM HAS MADE YOU SMARTER, STRONGER, AND *MORE DEADLY* THAN ANYONE I'VE EVER FACED.
STOP *NOW* AND TAKE ANOTHER PATH.
DON'T BE LIKE ME, DEVIL RAY.
DON'T LET YOUR LIFE BE FILLED WITH BLOOD AND HATE.

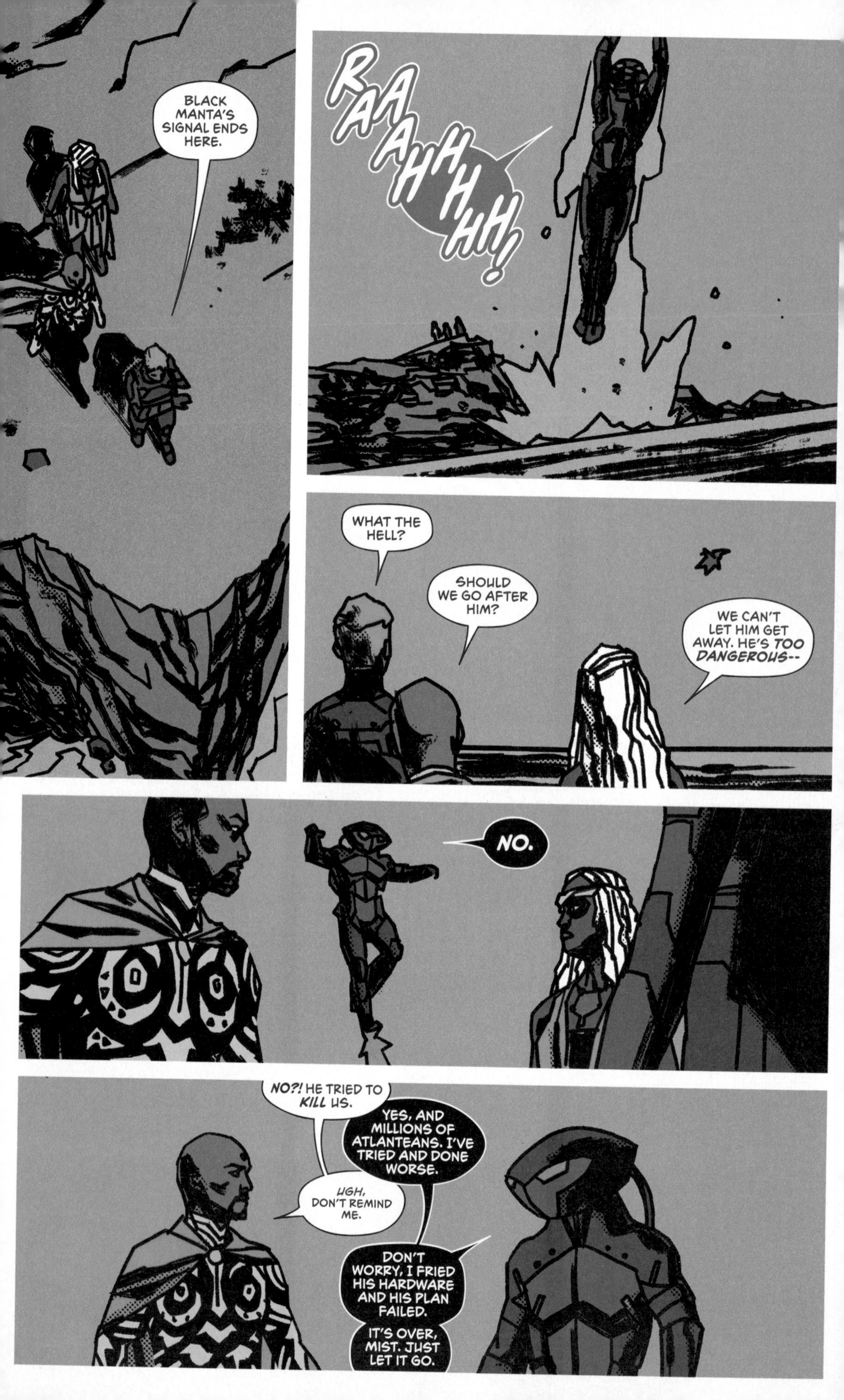
BLACK MANTA'S SIGNAL ENDS HERE.
RAAAHHHHH!
WHAT THE HELL?
SHOULD WE GO AFTER HIM?
WE CAN'T LET HIM GET AWAY. HE'S TOO DANGEROUS--
NO.
NO?! HE TRIED TO KILL US.
YES, AND MILLIONS OF ATLANTEANS. I'VE TRIED AND DONE WORSE.
UGH, DON'T REMIND ME.
DON'T WORRY, I FRIED HIS HARDWARE AND HIS PLAN FAILED.
IT'S OVER, MIST. JUST LET IT GO.

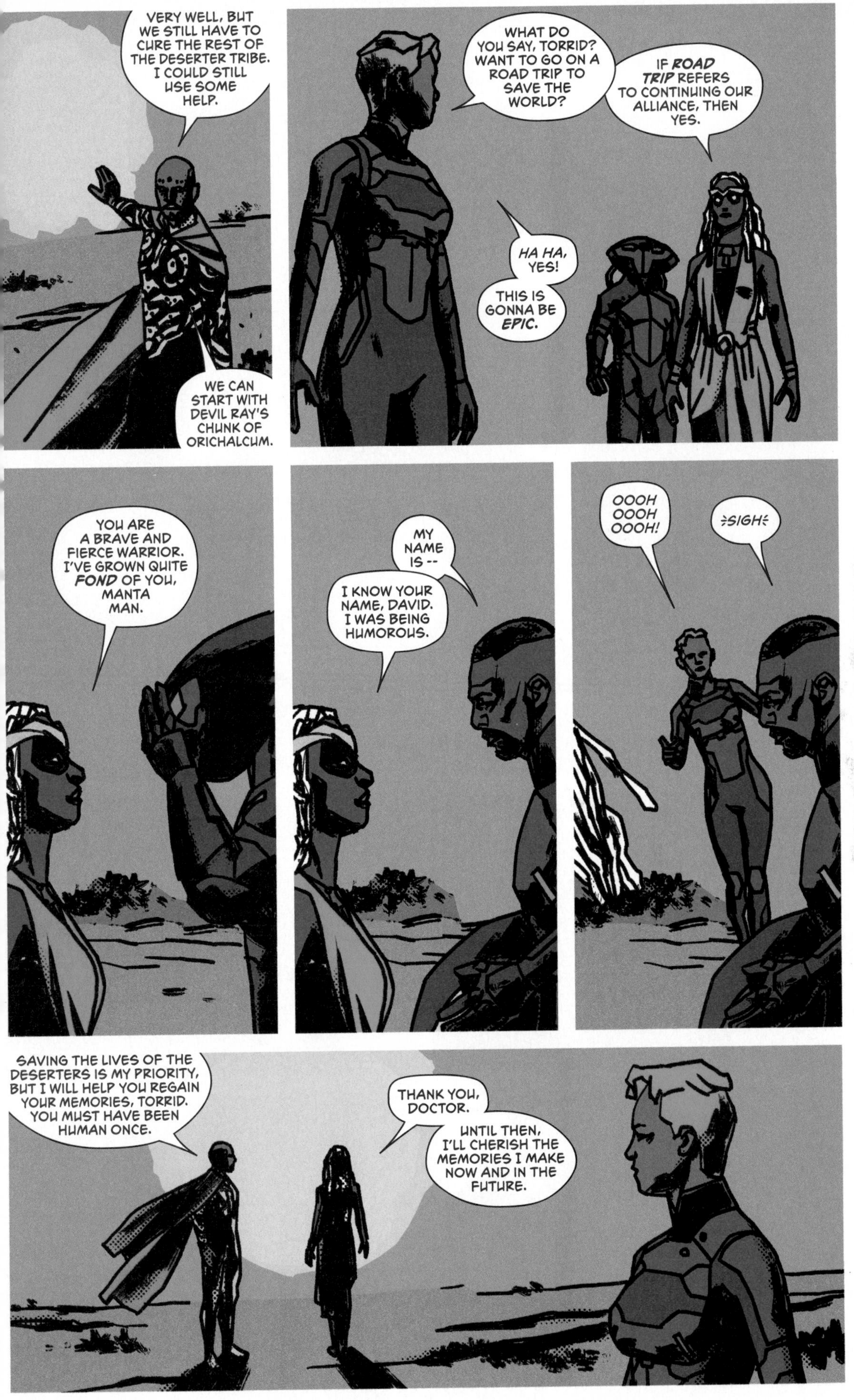
VERY WELL, BUT WE STILL HAVE TO CURE THE REST OF THE DESERTER TRIBE. I COULD STILL USE SOME HELP.
WE CAN START WITH DEVIL RAY'S CHUNK OF ORICHALCUM.
WHAT DO YOU SAY, TORRID? WANT TO GO ON A ROAD TRIP TO SAVE THE WORLD?
IF ROAD TRIP REFERS TO CONTINUING OUR ALLIANCE, THEN YES.
HA HA, YES!
THIS IS GONNA BE EPIC.
YOU ARE A BRAVE AND FIERCE WARRIOR. I'VE GROWN QUITE FOND OF YOU, MANTA MAN.
MY NAME IS --
I KNOW YOUR NAME, DAVID. I WAS BEING HUMOROUS.
OOOH OOOH OOOH!
SIGH
SAVING THE LIVES OF THE DESERTERS IS MY PRIORITY, BUT I WILL HELP YOU REGAIN YOUR MEMORIES, TORRID. YOU MUST HAVE BEEN HUMAN ONCE.
THANK YOU, DOCTOR.
UNTIL THEN, I'LL CHERISH THE MEMORIES I MAKE NOW AND IN THE FUTURE.

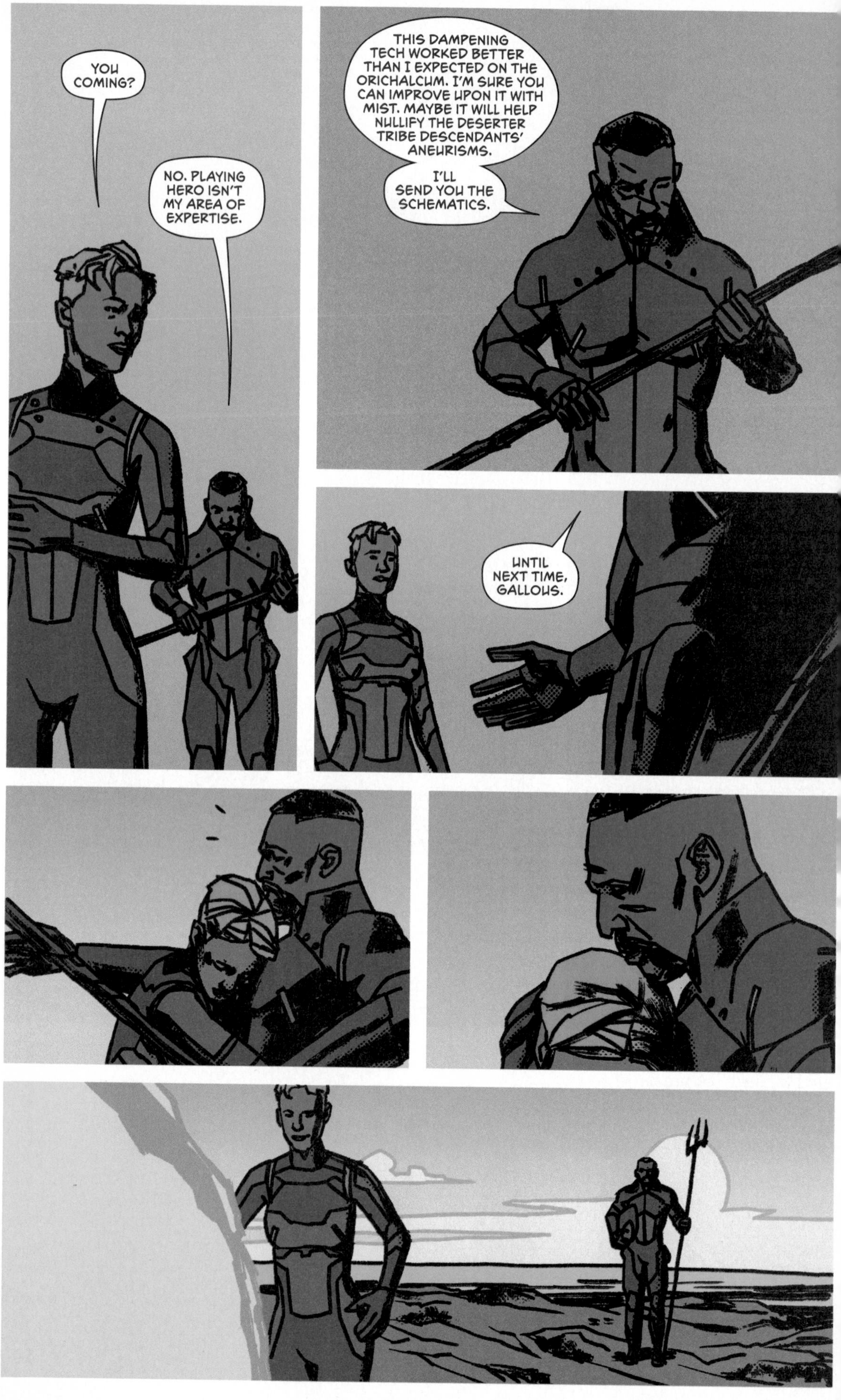
YOU COMING?
NO. PLAYING HERO ISN'T MY AREA OF EXPERTISE.
THIS DAMPENING TECH WORKED BETTER THAN I EXPECTED ON THE ORICHALCUM. I'M SURE YOU CAN IMPROVE UPON IT WITH MIST. MAYBE IT WILL HELP NULLIFY THE DESERTER TRIBE DESCENDANTS' ANEURISMS.
I'LL SEND YOU THE SCHEMATICS.
UNTIL NEXT TIME, GALLOUS.

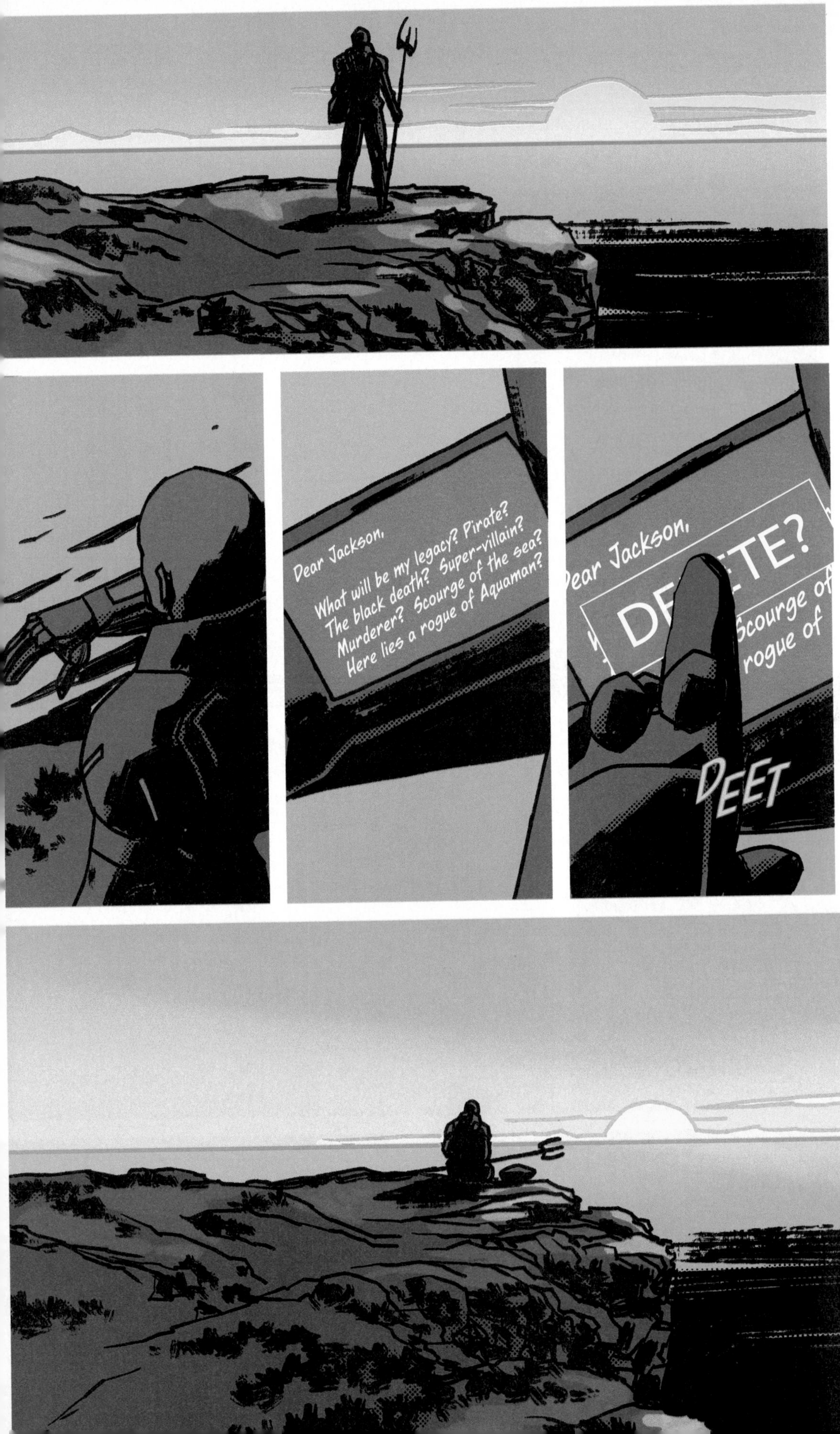

Dear Jackson,
What will be my legacy? Pirate? The black death? Super-villain? Murderer? Scourge of the sea? Here lies a rogue of Aquaman?
Dear Jackson,
DE ETE?
Scourge of
rogue of
DEET

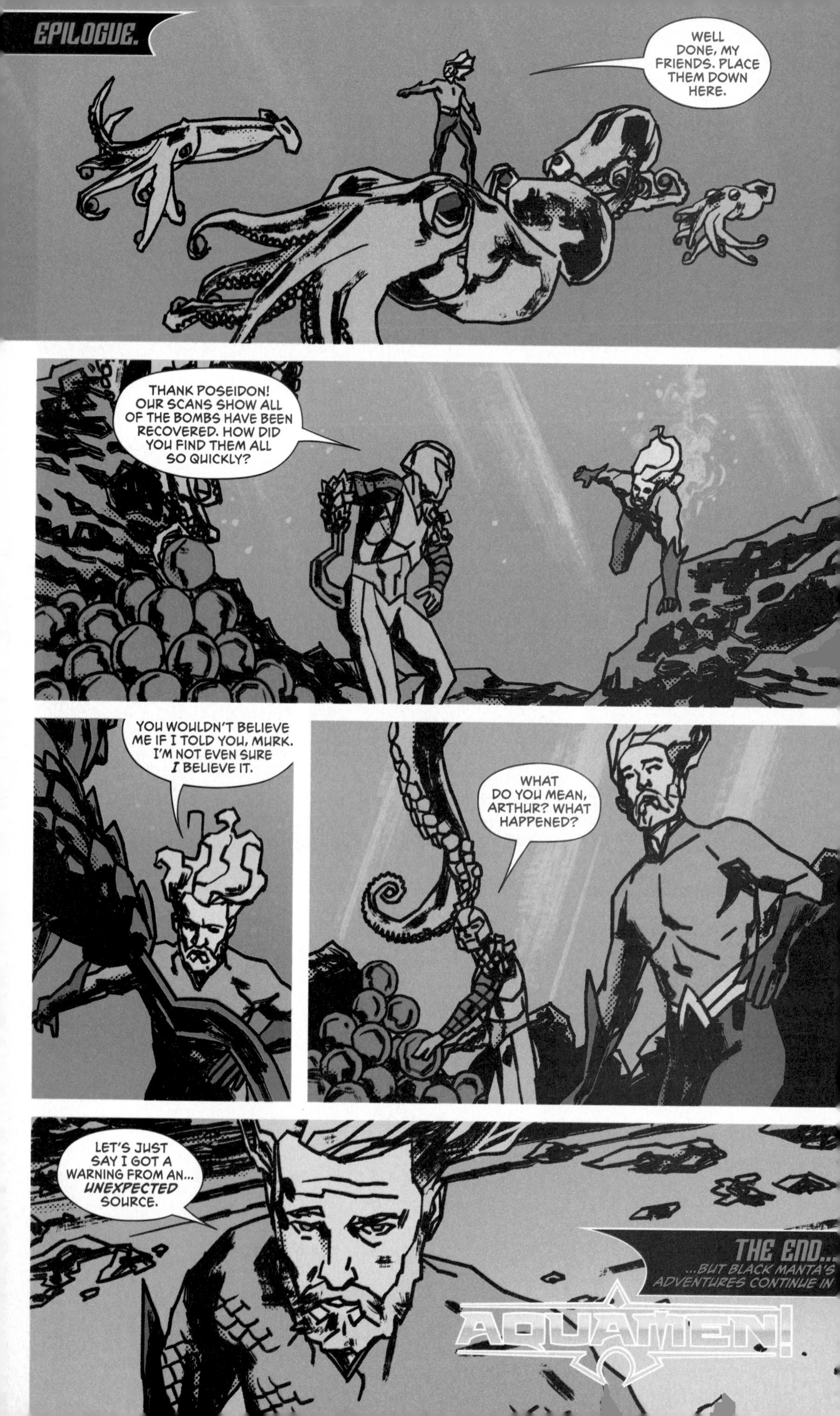
EPILOGUE.
WELL DONE, MY FRIENDS. PLACE THEM DOWN HERE.
THANK POSEIDON! OUR SCANS SHOW ALL OF THE BOMBS HAVE BEEN RECOVERED. HOW DID YOU FIND THEM ALL SO QUICKLY?
YOU WOULDN'T BELIEVE ME IF I TOLD YOU, MURK. I'M NOT EVEN SURE *I* BELIEVE IT.
WHAT DO YOU MEAN, ARTHUR? WHAT HAPPENED?
LET'S JUST SAY I GOT A WARNING FROM AN... *UNEXPECTED* SOURCE.
THE END...
...BUT BLACK MANTA'S ADVENTURES CONTINUE IN
AQUAMEN!

SCOURGE OF THE SEVEN SEAS

The Designs of
Black Manta by
Valentine De Landro

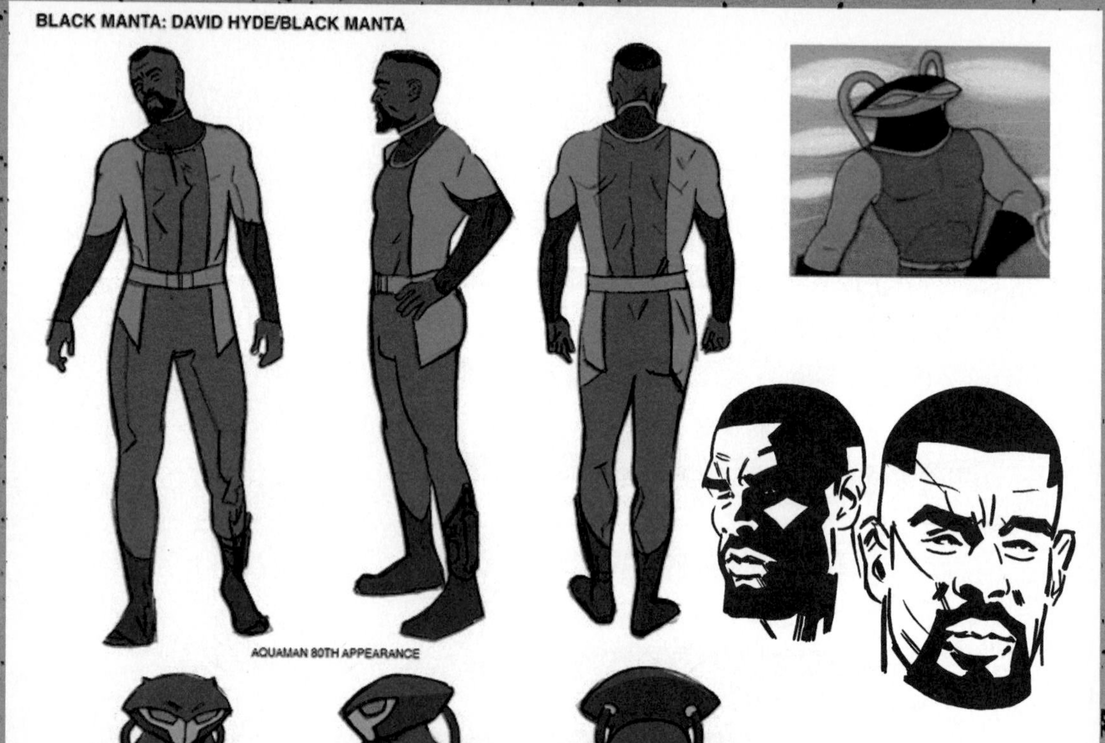

BLACK MANTA: DAVID HYDE/BLACK MANTA

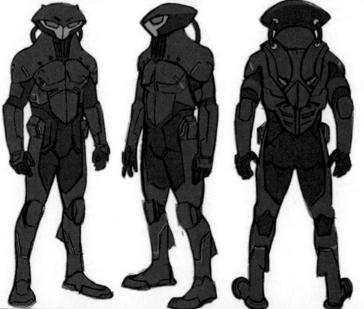

AQUAMAN 80TH APPEARANCE

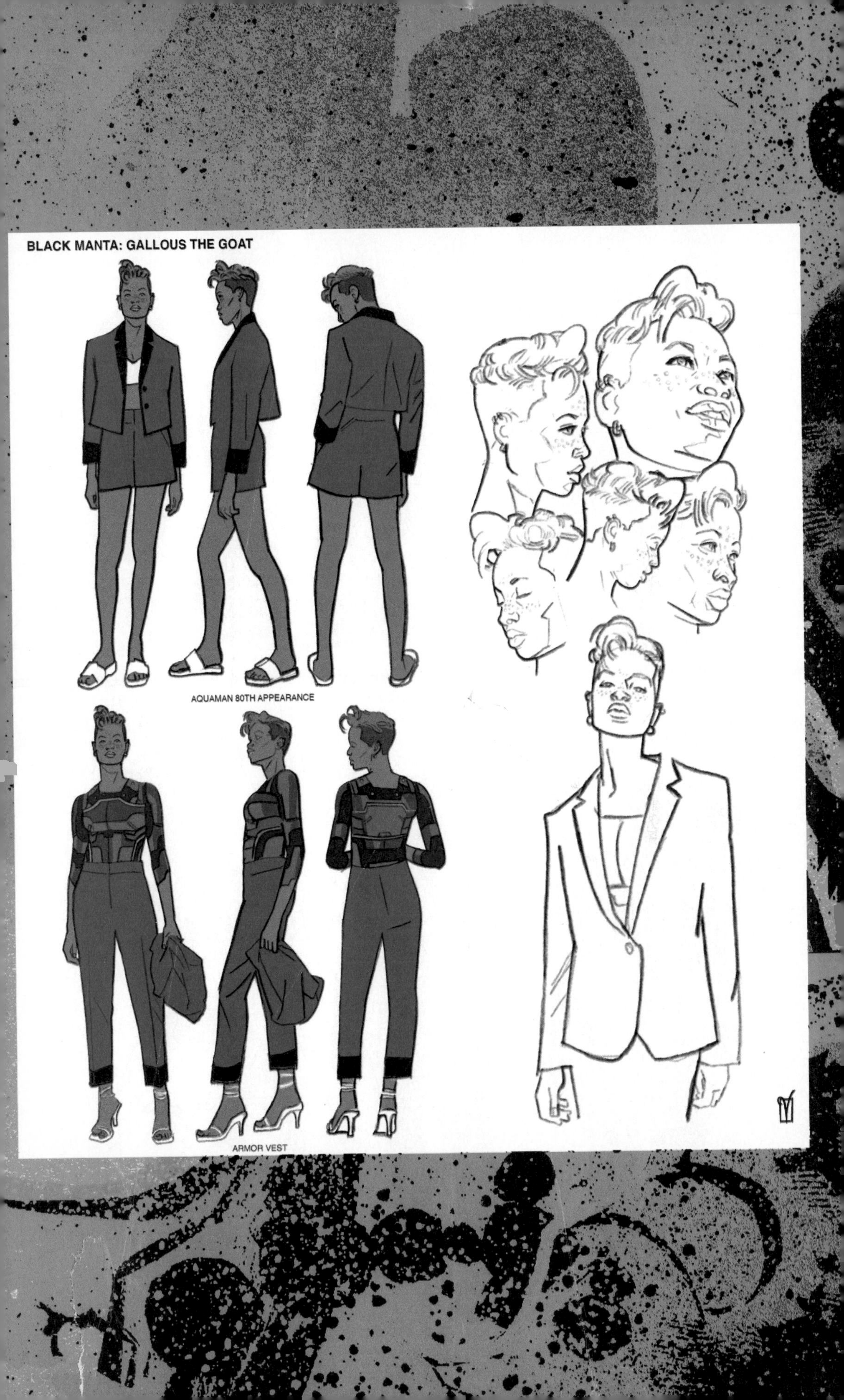
BLACK MANTA: GALLOUS THE GOAT
AQUAMAN 80TH APPEARANCE
ARMOR VEST

BLACK MANTA: TORRID

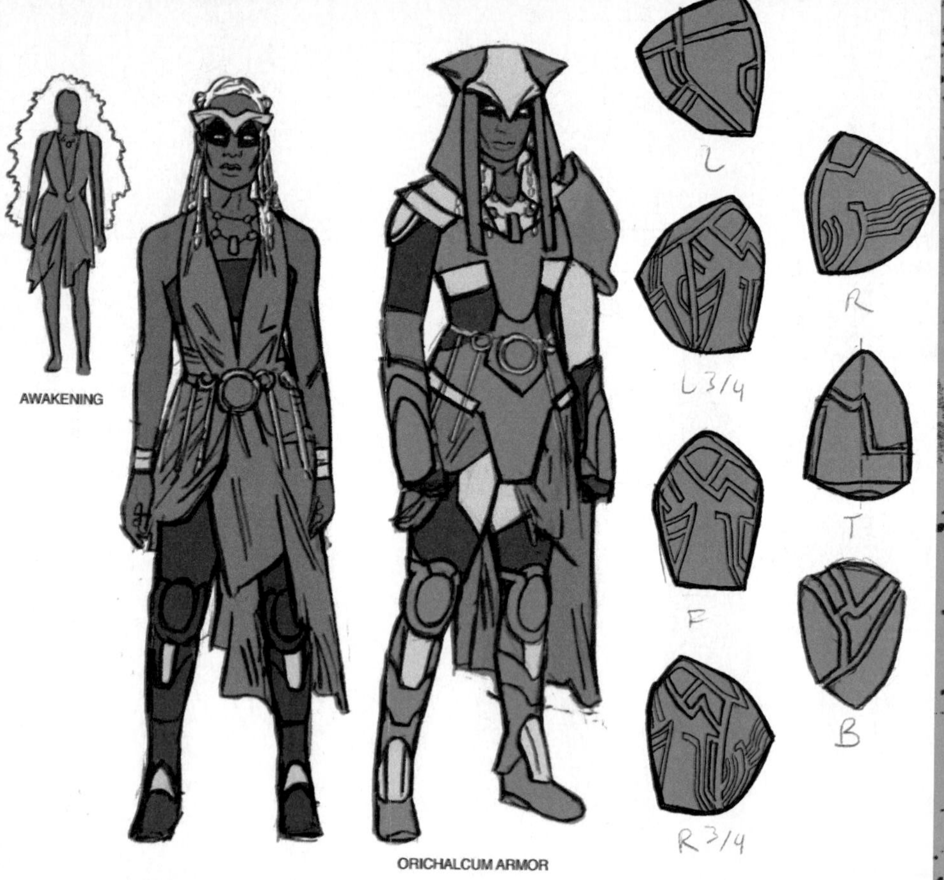
AWAKENING
L
R
L3/4
T
F
B
R3/4
ORICHALCUM ARMOR

BLACK MANTA: DEVIL RAY

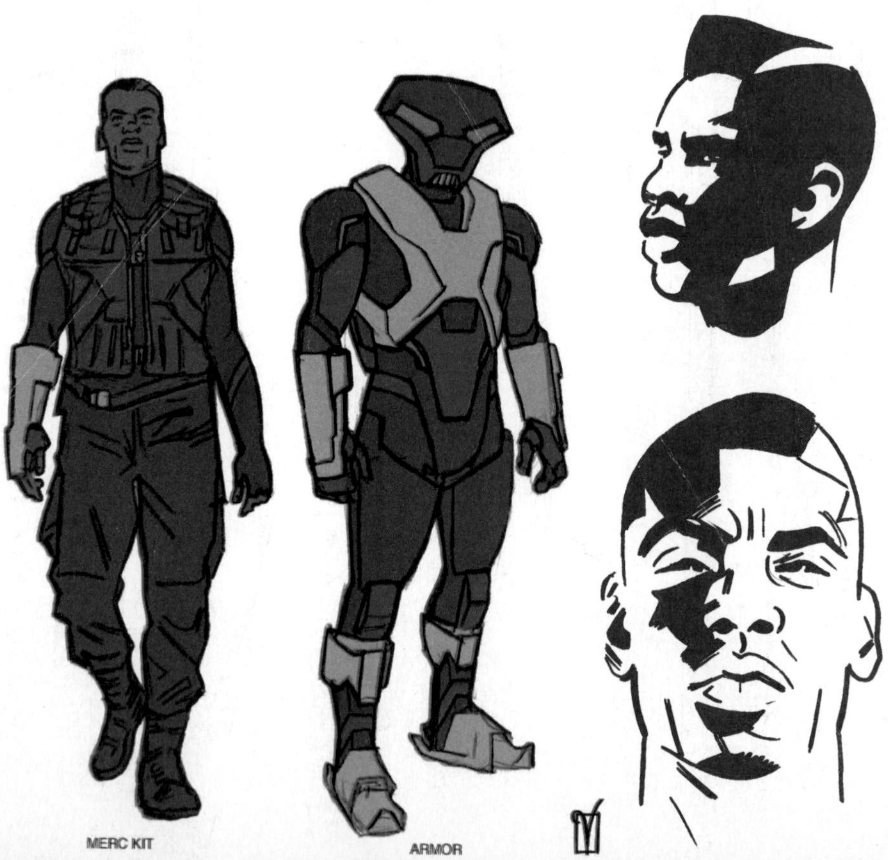
MERC KIT
ARMOR